# The Experimental Society

# The Experimental Society

Marshall S. Shapo

Routledge
Taylor & Francis Group
NEW YORK AND LONDON

First published in paperback 2024

First published 2016 by Transaction Publishers

Published 2017 by Routledge
605 Third Avenue, New York, NY 10158

and by Routledge
4 Park Square, Milton Park, Abingdon, Oxon OX14 4RN

*Routledge is an imprint of the Taylor & Francis Group, an informa business*



Publisher's Note
The publisher has gone to great lengths to ensure the quality of this reprint but points out that some imperfections in the original copies may be apparent.

Library of Congress Catalog Number: 2015015313

Library of Congress Cataloging-in-Publication Data

Shapo, Marshall S., 1936-
The experimental society / Marshall S. Shapo.
pages cm
Includes bibliographical references and index.
ISBN 978-1-4128-5703-1
1. Product safety--United States. 2. Consumer protection--United States. I. Title.
TS175.S53 2015
363.190973--dc23

2015015313

ISBN 13: 978-1-41-285703-1 (hbk)
ISBN 13: 978-1-03-292045-0 (pbk)
ISBN 13: 978-1-31-513195-5 (ebk)

DOI: 10.4324/9781315131955

For Helene
Always the nonpareil

And for

Ben and Jackie
Nat and Robin
Aaron, Gabrielle, Jonathan, Joshua, Michaela, Noah

To the memory of my parents
Norma Shapo and Mitchell Shapo

# Contents

# Preface

We are all experimenters, and we are all subjects of experiments, some conducted by us on ourselves and some conducted by others. This book seeks to capture several dimensions of that reality—including scientific, legal, and political dimensions—in the environment, the workplace, and the household.

I have reviewed thousands of sources on the risks and benefits of many kinds of innovation, in an effort to advance our ability to criticize this experimental process and to conceive and implement solutions to the problems it generates. The notes record only a fraction of those sources.

There are many people who have contributed to my work in this area over the span of a half-century. I can mention only a few. I have benefited in various ways from the colleagueship of faculty members at my law schools, at Texas, Virginia, and Northwestern. Many teachers at the University of Miami, both in college and in law school, were instrumental in my education; I want to name, specially, Minnette Massey and Richard Hausler at the law school. I think with particular gratitude of Page Keeton, my first dean when I began law teaching, and my colleague Leon Green at Texas, for apparently seeing some imagination as well as dedication in a very young scholar. Most recently, I appreciate various kinds of encouragement from Dan Rodriguez at Northwestern.

Over the years, I have learned much about this subject from people in diverse lines of work. Faculty workshops at my schools—for more than thirty-five years at Northwestern—have contributed to my knowledge of the law and related areas.

I have learned much from the writings of legal scholars, practicing lawyers, and journalists.

The law library at Northwestern has consistently provided fuel for my research in many areas. I have received indispensable support from a splendid crew of reference librarians: Marcia Lehr, Pegeen Bassett,

Irene Berkey, Heidi Kuehl, Jamie Sommer, Maribel Nash, and Tom Gaylord, and their chieftains Jim McMasters and George Pike.

Student research assistants have given substantial help to me on a variety of projects. Those who aided most in gathering material for this work include Alyssa Markenson, Jody Platt, Chris Dyess, John Adams, and Mara Alioto. For prior research leading up to this book, I also acknowledge James Larry, Kelly Hollingsworth, Jonathan Shaub, and Leighton Leib.

I am especially indebted to my faculty assistant Shona Bonds for her work in the production of the manuscript.

I have been fortunate beyond words in my family. Early, my parents, Mitchell Shapo and Norma Shapo, taught me to think, and to have respect both for evidence and for ideas and the words that attempt to capture them. I am always learning from my sons, Benjamin and Nathaniel. I continue to learn from Nat's wife, Robin, and Ben's wife, Jackie, and, as they grow up, my grandchildren: Noah, Gabrielle, Aaron, Joshua, Jonathan, and Michaela.

Finally, I thank Helene S. Shapo, who has fascinated and inspired me for fifty-six years. I am ever grateful to her for an endless number of blessings, just a few of which are her affection, her critical facility, and her good sense.

# Introduction

Human beings have always searched for better ways to do things. They have innovated since the history-shrouded dawn of the race—from the mortar and pestle through cuneiform writing and on through the time of the printing press. The entire process has been one of experiment, of individuals and groups trying new approaches to solving problems and trying to make their lives better.

Along the way the process has claimed victims—some who directly and willingly accepted the risks that came with experimentation and some who were experimental subjects in the hands of others who did not tell them of their status as subjects. The experimenters, it should be said, often do not even think if themselves as testing, on their fellows, hypotheses involving risk.

Focusing on risk, this book analyzes society's responses to many kinds of experimentation, broadly defined as the testing of ideas for new physical and chemical ways of doing things. It also includes, less tangibly, the testing of ways of thinking, including those related to social organization, and even ways of controlling the process itself. Typically, the aim of these tryout processes is the assessment of their practical utility. For those who conduct experiments, there are varied benefits. People derive a sense of adventure and discovery from experimentation. Often, they get great material benefits—for example, professional advancement in the case of people who directly do research, and corporate profit in the case of firms that market the fruits of successful research.

The process of experimentation that elides into invention is a mysterious and complicated one. First there is the idea, which today more often than not springs from a substantial base of scientific knowledge and represents one stage in a quest for more knowledge. For its developers, part of the attraction of the idea may reside in its elegance. In an area an order of magnitude much greater than the experiments that typically affect our lives, J. Robert Oppenheimer was able, for a time, to stifle his concerns about the development of the hydrogen bomb. He reportedly said that the program to develop the H-bomb became "technically so sweet that you could not argue about that"—a case where "you go ahead and do it and you argue what to do about it only after you have had your technical success."[1]

Eventually a developer's idea becomes converted into a blueprint, which might be literally one on paper or a metaphorical one. Just one example of a suddenly breathless pace of an experiment long in progress is the chemical BPA, which has been used in consumer products ranging from baby bottles to liners of canned foods and from dental resins to eyeglass lenses. BPA was first synthesized in 1891 and first mentioned in a scientific paper in 1905.[2] It did not find commercial application until the 1950s. When it did come into the consumer marketplace, it appears that this occurred without full forethought as to its potential consequences to health; perhaps some of those consequences could not have been discerned at the time. In any event, the people who brought the chemical into everyday life did so meaning no harm. For them, it was useful and a source of profit.

Progress, or what we are willing to call progress, has come in fits and starts—surges of successful experiment occurring after periods of quiescence. The history of technology over many centuries features some occasions of surge. Leonardo da Vinci, operating on his own with a genius not found in most large companies that pursue industrial innovation, generated new concepts of machines—even flying machines—painstakingly drafted his designs, and used trial and error to see what worked.

In the last century and half, the surge has been pronounced and increasingly explosive. The story of the Industrial Revolution, with its eighteenth-century beginnings, has been often told. A landmark piece of poetry in prose was Henry Adams's description, in the first limited publication of *The Education of Henry Adams* in 1907, of the rocketing pace of technological change—a rendering that uncannily captures today's environment of constant experiment. Entranced by the cathedral at Chartres, he wrote that "all the steam in the world couldn't, like the Virginia, build Chartres" and that "symbol or energy, the Virgin had acted as the greatest force the western world ever felt, and had drawn man's activities to herself more strongly than any other power, natural or supernatural, had ever done." But now, as a historian, he found it his business "to follow the track of the energy; to find where it came from and where it went to; its complex source and shifting channels; its values, equivalents, conversions."[3] By the first decade of the twentieth century, Adams wrote of the "stupendous acceleration" of "new forces, chemical and mechanical" after 1800 that "ended in 1900 with the appearance of the new class of supersensual forces, before which the man of science stood, at first, as bewildered and helpless as, in the fourth century, a priest of Isis before the Cross of Christ."[4] He concluded by remarking, "In the earlier stages of progress, the forces to be assimilated were simple and easy to absorb, but, as the mind of man enlarged its range, it enlarged the field of complexity, and must continue to do so, even unto chaos, until the reservoirs of sensuous or supersensuous energies are exhausted, or cease to affect [man], or until he succumbs to their excess."[5]

The manuscript for this book itself is symbolic of the developments described in Adams's sometimes dizzying prose. Many of the basic drafts were produced on hardware (a computer), using software (a word processor). A predecessor volume[6] utilized the ancient hardware known as a typewriter.

When I grew up, a popular form of home entertainment, at first regarded as something of a novelty, was television, watched with intense interest in purplish "black and white" images on a small screen, and decorously filtered to screen out sex and violence. Today, television is just a part of a "home entertainment center" on which motion pictures of sex and violence are a staple—and on which "news" itself can feature bleeding human bodies. The incredible reach of the Internet has changed the terms of many discourses, to the point that, as a recent review summarized a book, "the ability to 'be online' (already an antiquated phrase) anywhere and anytime may ultimately be seen as the twenty-first century's version of DDT: a technological innovation blithely presumed to be a good until its unintended consequences became impossible to ignore."[7] One thread running through this fabric is the fact that pornography, once a furtive feature of fraternity rush parties, is now widely available and includes the most vulgar images of exploited children.

Many studies focus on the effects of this expanded visual fare on the behavior of both adults and children. Modern screens of various sizes generate dozens of parallel experiments, embodying risk, that entrepreneurs of many kinds run on the public at large or segments of it. Holmes, who had survived three wounds in a bloody internal conflict and who was at the vortex of the pace of change described by Henry Adams, borrowed from Emerson, without attribution, an aphorism for the phenomenon: "All life is an experiment."[8]

This book seeks to capture the breadth of the great experiment that goes on all around us, utilizing both individuals who have been told that they are serving as contributors to a database and many members of the general public who are unaware of their function as experimental subjects. It analyzes several large, uncontrolled national experiments that have cost hundreds of thousands, even millions, of lives. Heading the list are the marketing of cigarettes and the sale of products containing asbestos. The principal context I use is that of the law, broadly viewed as including decisions by courts and choices made by elected representatives of the people. And I note that the law itself is a constant experiment. Courts, for example, invent new ideas of what justice is in particular cases, sometimes elaborating on those ideas and sometimes paring them back.[9]

As all these experiments progress—in the marketplace and even in the body of the law itself—lives hang in the balance. The experiment with a drug or device, in which the subjects are randomly divided into those who receive the product and those who do not, will sometimes produce significant advantages in longevity and health for those who receive the product. I emphasize those benefits. The most casual survey of the material aspects of our lives yields dozens of examples of how experimenters have made those lives more comfortable and convenient. A catalog over the last century and more includes such varied tangible items as typewriters, computers, and voice-recognition software, fans and home air conditioners, ice cream cones, detergents, cell phones and smartphones, automobiles with seatbelts, push-button locks, keyless starters, GPS systems and Bluetooth devices, television and streaming video, heart valve replacements and heart transplants, drugs that include uses in chemotherapy and contraception, artificial insemination, power saws, and DNA testing. More conceptually, we have seen in medicine new methods of diagnosis; and in the wider society, the desegregation of public schools and the admission of women to elite colleges and universities. All of these things and events have come into our lives because initially, someone had an idea and began to test it. All of them owe their genesis to what I would call the experimental imperative—that mysterious mental process that seizes people's minds and urges them to create new things.

On other occasions experiments will cause net harm to their subjects, with the collateral effect that the "control group"—those who do not receive the product—is better off than those harmed by the experimental product. I note in this connection that in the realm of medicine, each visit to the doctor has experimental features. Different doses of a drug are experiments, as indeed are decisions not to prescribe a drug when orthodox medical practice indicates that one should be prescribed.

The range of experiments with injurious consequences is broad. In some cases—few but unfortunately not unique—the experimenters behave in an unquestionably irresponsible manner. One case that recently came to light centered on the deliberate infection of several hundred Guatemalans with syphilis in the 1940s. The aim of the experiments, conducted by American doctors funded by the National Institutes of Health, was to find out how effective penicillin was in treating the disease.[10] Perhaps the most extraordinary outcropping of damage in the last decade—one primarily involving environmental harm—arose from the ongoing experiment that is offshore drilling for oil. This was the widespread spill from BP's Deepwater Horizon drilling rig in 2010, which spread oil across areas of the Gulf of Mexico that adjoined several states. Unlike clinical medical experiments that select particular individuals as subjects—although those enterprises may include thousands of people—large oil spills are the externalities of experiments that can affect hundreds of thousands of people in various ways. (Beyond oil spills is the literally global experiment with hydrocarbons and global warning, which I do not discuss here.)

In both the foreground and background of these events are the continuing experiments on members of the public, both in broad environmental settings and in the spaces of individual households, with various kinds of chemicals. The EPA inventory has listed eighty-four thousand of these substances in its Chemical Substance Inventory.[11]

In the broader sphere of what I have called "market experimentation," we may only be able to measure the effects of products and new activities over long periods of time with data on many thousands or even millions of people. This has been a matter of concern for many years. Illustrating the paucity of information about the effects of chemical toxicities on humans was a 1991 report by a committee of the National Research Council that said that "[m]any compounds have not been investigated for toxicity at all" and that "[d]espite the major resources that have been devoted to chemical toxicity testing by government agencies and by corporations, there is a serious need to develop faster and more effective methods of predicting long-term chemical toxicity."[12] A report on a scientific workshop on research needs held in 1989 lamented that "[t]he absence of relevant scientific knowledge and understanding makes it difficult to generate rational environmental policy to deal with problems as they arise." This report said there were "reasons to believe that many of the current estimates of risk, and hence of the urgency of the requirement for particular actions, may be in error by factors *as great as a million* and, therefore, that the funds spent for alleviating environmental risk may be grossly misallocated."[13] In language that might well be taken to refer to the situation of environmental impacts in the present day, the report said that the emphasis on "health and injury effects, direct economic impacts, and effects on a small number of specific, measurable environmental indicators," omitted "many issues relevant to public values and concerns and thus contributes to the seemingly perplexing divergence between the evaluation of the importance of problems by public agencies and the public's responses."[14]

A contemporaneous report referred to the "range of neurologic and psychiatric disorders" caused by toxic chemicals in the environment. It listed several kinds of chemicals to which "many thousands of Americans are regularly exposed at work and to which even more are exposed in smaller doses in the general environment" as being "associated with subclinical neurotoxicity." It pointed out that several hundred of the seventy thousand chemicals used in commerce were known neurotoxicants but that "less than 10% of the chemicals in commerce have been tested at all for neurotoxicity, and only a handful have been evaluated thoroughly."[15] It noted that a 1986 review of secondary literature found that more than one-third of 197 chemicals "to which American workers were exposed in the occupational setting for all or part of each working day" had the potential, "if the doses were large enough, to produce adverse effects on the nervous system."[16]

When a new technology proves to cause harm to people, they may go to court to seek compensation for their injuries. If harm becomes widespread, members of Congress may act to constrain, or even ban, the products or activities that caused the harm. Decisions made by courts and legislatures on how to deal with the consequences of experimentation, both that done in closed scientific settings and that done on the open market, are manifestations of national culture. When courts use defenses like "assumption of risk" in cases involving suits for various kinds of injuries, they are enforcing a cultural preference for people taking responsibility for their own safety in situations where they are cognizant of a risk. By contrast, when Congress passes a law like the Occupational Safety and Health Act, it overrides a preference for allowing people to take particular kinds of risk at work, and it effectively enacts the idea that certain "bargains" for risky employment are not "fair" bargains. Typically that kind of law responds to statistics on injuries and data on the consequences of injury to victims as well as on the impact of injuries on society more generally.

Other statutes respond to experiments on workers and consumers who may not, in even a metaphorical sense, have made "bargains" about risk, for they may not know of the existence of a risk. Just one example is the case of agricultural chemicals. It may take some time for what are literally field experiments to show harmful effects on those who plant and harvest crops. As the experiment spills over into the consumer market, data about risk may appear only over longer periods of time, when it becomes evident—sometimes requiring sophisticated statistical analysis—that a chemical residue in food is producing cancers.

A striking recent example of this phenomenon in the medical area is the case of hormone products, including estrogens and progestin, prescribed for women to relieve the symptoms of menopause. The use of estrogen for those purposes provided the ingredients for a long-running drama extending over two generations. Here I summarize briefly some of the essentials of that story, which I have previously analyzed in detail. The use of estrogens for postmenopausal symptoms, first approved in 1942, became the subject of the worshipful book *Feminine Forever* in 1966, which asserted that "[m]enopause is curable" and that it was "now possible to restore full femininity even to women long past menopause."[17]

Beginning in the 1970s, however, there appeared some scientific studies that suggested that estrogen use correlated strongly with some malignancies, particularly endometrial cancer. Then, in the 1980s, about the same time as what I have described as the slowing of "a roller coaster of controversy" about the drugs, fresh controversy arose about the effects of estrogen therapy on the heart. Complicating the issue were questions about the health effects of products that combined estrogens and progestin, a substance that had begun to be used to "oppose" some of the harmful effects of estrogen.[18]

In 1991 an important study began, conducted by the Women's Health Initiative (WHI) of the National Institutes of Health. The purpose was ambitious—"to assess the overlapping effects of hormone replacement therapy, low dietary fat, and calcium/Vitamin D supplements on cardiovascular disease, osteoporosis, and cancer in post-menopausal women." And the time frame was long, symbolic of the tedious process of gathering data among large populations on such questions. Another element in the complex process of data collection was the Heart and Estrogen/Progestin Replacement Study (HERS), focusing only on women with existing heart disease, which reported in 1998 that the combination therapy did not reduce the "overall risk of nonfatal" heart attacks or deaths from coronary heart disease "or other cardiovascular outcomes" in women under eighty.[19]

Twin thunderclaps came in 2002. An extension of the HERS study produced findings of "no cardiovascular benefit of randomized treatment with hormone therapy" and of increases in the rates of blood clots in the veins. One investigator capsuled the conclusion: "For women with heart disease, there were harms, and zero benefit."[20] Dr. Brian Walsh, the director of the menopause center at Brigham and Women's Hospital, commented that "HRT should not be continued with the expectation that it is cardioprotective," and Stacie Geller, director of the Center for Excellence in Women's Health at the University of Illinois-Chicago, said that women "taking HRT for long-term [problems] associated with aging" should think again: "If it is secondary protection [of the heart], the data is clear: it does not work." At the same time, it was noted that women had to consider the well-established benefits of hormone therapy in treating menopausal symptoms and preventing bone loss.[21]

Within a week, the WHI reported that it was stopping the part of its study that used the combination drug, because "health risks exceeded health benefits over an average follow-up of 3.2 years."[22] Just two years later, the WHI investigators told study participants who were taking only estrogen that they should "stop taking their study pills": estrogen alone was found to increase the risk of stroke. At the same time, the NIH told women that if they were thinking about hormone therapy—either estrogen alone or the combination—they should "discuss the benefits and risk with their physicians." And Dr. Barbara Alving, the director of the WHI, said that "[w]omen should not feel that this is some grand emergency for them."[23] This essentially confirmed the existence of an experiment that was still in progress.

Underlining the length of such experiments and the difficulty of collection of meaningful data was a research report almost a decade after the appearance of the data on the HERS extension and the WHI combination study. In 2011, the WHI presented new data that might have confused even women who had kept up with the statistics. This time, data on women with a prior hysterectomy who had used estrogen-only products, although they had stopped them when the WHI discontinued the estrogen-only study, had a "statistically significant reduction in breast cancer incidence."[24] Andrea Z. LaCroix, the lead investigator, said this was "something we totally didn't expect," and was a result that "differentiates estrogen alone from estrogen and progestin in a very big way," given prior data on the combination products that had shown a higher risk of breast cancer.[25] Just to cloud the picture further, writers of an accompanying editorial said that an important question was "whether the WHI population is appropriate for reaching definitive conclusions regarding younger women and the risk of breast cancer associated with" hormone therapy. Besides this "potential age effect," they pointed out that "the WHI results do not address the balance of risks and benefits associated with longer-term estrogen use," citing studies on the possibility that "[l]onger unopposed estrogen use may increase the risk of breast cancer."[26]

Paralleling these well-publicized studies on medical products taken by thousands of women, and the arguments that arose around them, were recurrent patterns of injury in everyday activities. To take one example, for some time, concern has been expressed about the heightened fatality rates associated with large trucks as compared with passenger vehicles.[27] Just one other example, in the setting of sports and games, is the number of concussions suffered by high school athletes, estimated at around three hundred thousand annually in the past decade, with girls having "higher concussion rates than boys in gender-comparable sports,"[28]—truly an experiment in progress on the playing fields.

Always in the background of uncontrolled, big-scale experiments are the controlled experiments that are grist for the mill of medical progress. The studies on hormones, which were set up and controlled by scientists, approach the boundary between the two categories. As we pursue the subject of large, uncontrolled experiments, we can keep in mind the metaphor of the controlled experiment: We can ask, for example, how we would judge tobacco companies if they were running clinical trials with millions of smokers. We can ask whether, at whatever level of consciousness, experimenters at all levels were saying to each other, "Let's try it out," creating, either explicitly or implicitly, protocols that measured risks and benefits of products and activities.

What aligns these disparate cases is this: Across a large spectrum of human activity, from the medicine cabinet to the open road to the school athletic field, people are subjected to experiments that are out of their hands, more or less—and often more. If we examine this spectrum through the prism of experiment, we may formulate a guide for analysis of intuitions and of understandings of safety and levels of acceptable risk. How has society responded to the many components of what is an enormous process of data collection on the public? I seek in this book to describe major factors that seem to have counted for decision makers in matters related to experimentation on various publics. I identify not only those things that decision makers articulate in matters related to experimentation on the public but also those features of decision that must be inferred. Presenting a critical analysis of social decision making, I suggest some ways that we can better approach the regulation of our nationwide Great Experiment.

## Notes

1. Philip M. Stern, *The Oppenheimer Case* (Harper & Row, 1969), p. 175.
2. See Heather Caliendo, "History of BPA," *Packaging Digest,* June 29, 2012, taken from the Internet, Aug. 6, 2013.
3. Edward Chalfant and Conrad Edick Wright (eds.), *The Education of Henry Adams: A Centennial Version* (Univ. of Virginia Press, 2007), pp. 304–05.
4. Ibid., pp. 381–82.
5. Ibid., p. 383.
6. Marshall Shapo, *A Nation of Guinea Pigs* (Free Press, 1979).
7. Ruth Franklin, "Dechronification" (review of Gary Shteyngapt, *Super Sad True Love Story*), *New Republic,* Sept. 23, 2010, p. 43.
8. *Abrams v. United States,* 250 Wis. 616, 630 (1919) (Holmes, J., dissenting).
9. One example of a paring back is *Boyles v. Kerr,* 855 S.W. 2d 593 (Tex. 1993), partly overruling *St. Elizabeth Hosp. v. Garrard,* 730 S.W. 2d 649 (Tex. 1987), to the extent that the earlier case "recognize[d] an independent right to recover for negligently inflicted emotional distress."
10. See Donald G. McNeil Jr., "U.S. Infected Guatemalans With Syphilis in 40s," *New York Times,* Oct. 2, 2010, pp. Al and A6.
11. http://www.epa.gov/oppt/newchems/pubs/inventory.html.
12. Committee on Opportunities in Applied Environmental Research and Development, *Opportunities in Applied Environmental Research and Development* (Nat'l Acad. Press, 1991), p. 6 (emphasis added).
13. Ibid., Appendix D, p. 159.
14. Ibid., p. 162.
15. Committee on Neurotoxicology & Models for Assessing Risk, Board on Environmental Studies and Toxicology, Nat'l Research Council, *Environmental Neurotoxicology* (Nat'l Academics Press, 1992), p. 1–2.
16. See ibid., p. 17, referring to W. K. Anger, "Workplace Exposures," in Z. Annau (ed.), *Neurobehavioral Toxicology* (John Hopkins Univ. Press, 1986), pp. 331–47.
17. Summarized in Marshall S. Shapo, *Experimenting With the Consumer* (Praeger Publishers, 2009), pp. 128–29.
18. See ibid., pp. 134 and 140–142.
19. See ibid., 146–53.

20. See ibid., p. 159.
21. See "HERS II: HRT Provides No Heart Benefits," *ABC News*, July 3, 2002.
22. See *Experimenting With the Consumer*, supra note 17, p. 160.
23. See ibid., pp. 170–71.
24. Andrea Z. LaCroix et al., "Health Outcomes After Stopping Conjugated Equine Estrogens Among Postmenopausal Women," 305 *JAMA* 1305, 1312 (2011).
25. Tara Parker-Pope, "Heart and Cancer Risks Drop For Some in an Estrogen Study," *New York Times*, April 6, 2011, pp. A1 and A15.
26. Emily S. Jungheim and Graham A. Colditz, "Short-Term Use of Unopposed Estrogen: A Balance of Inferred Risks and Benefits," 305 *JAMA* 1354, 1354–55 (2011).
27. "Ins. Inst. for Highway Safety, Q&As: Large Trucks" (June 2010) (printed from the Internet April 27, 2011, latest version, http://www.iihs.org/iihs/topics/t/large-trucks/fatalityfacts/large-trucks.
28. See Mallika Marar, "Epidemiology of Concussions Among United States High School Athletes," 40 *Am. J. Sports Med.* 747, 753 (2012).

# 1

# Varieties of Experimentation

The process of human experimentation takes place against a background of assumptions concerning individual choice—choices by consumers and workers to engage in activities or purchase goods they perceive to carry various types of risks and benefits. In a free society, a principal assumption is that the individual is sovereign and should be able to choose among a smorgasbord of risks and benefits. A corollary premise is that individuals possess a certain degree of information about the potential hazards and advantages that will be associated with a particular choice. We know that in practice, information is never "perfect," but on many occasions it will be adequate. Often there exist substitutes that people may choose for one kind of activity or another. It is important to the performance of free markets that people are able to distinguish among competitors who offer substitutes.

## I. Science As a Search, Science As Combat

The existence of adequate consumer information and competition among those who conduct activities or sell products—or the lack of information and competition—is important to an understanding of how experimentation runs through the bloodstream of our economic and cultural lives.

I shall identify several different types of experimentation. But first I will mention some basic elements of science—how they are ideally visualized and how they work in practice. An important aspect of science is that it proceeds by formulating hypotheses and testing them, a process that, as one writer has said, "is ambiguous and convoluted with lots of dead ends,"[1] and which a Nobel Prize winner said of biology in particular is "complex, messy, and richly various."[2] On occasion, surprises lead to innovation: research for an anti-angina medication stumbled on penile erections in human volunteers, which led to Viagra.[3] The process is always in flux, with even the "calling" of the scientific community being "tentative."[4] An important distinction with law is that, by contrast with trials in court, "there is never an end to trial by science," where "credibility . . . inevitably remains open," subject to "additional experimental work to assimilate, validate, corroborate, and verify matters of substance and methodology."[5]

It should be noted in this connection that although ideally science is an entirely dispassionate pursuit, often it involves combat about methodology and data. The question has been raised as to whether "advocacy by different researchers promote[s] objectivity." One writer has said that the idea that "heated, intense, and biased confrontation" of ideas does this is "not intuitively obvious."[6] He cites a survey of scientists that concluded that "the vast majority preferred experiments that confirmed their hypotheses."[7] A relevant observation about the intellectual commitments of scientists is that they "usually conduct their research under quite different philosophies from one another—each has a unique background, certain values and set notions of procedure."[8]

In this connection, we also note the role of ego and ambition in scientific research. One observer has said that "given science as it has been structured since its inception and the sorts of human beings who becomes scientists, individual credit has served as a powerful spur to effort."[9] He remarks, "For those who have never come under the sway of a compulsion, it is difficult to understand the intensity with which scientists pursue their investigations."[10] Although saying that "in a sufficiently high percentage of cases," scientists can overcome careerist tendencies and recognize that the best way "to further their careers is to fulfill the loftier goals of their profession," he also observes that "scientists compete in a quite literal sense as they race to solve an easily identifiable, conspicuous problem."[11]

These commitments, however sincerely they are held, provide background for the puzzles about the reliability of data that abound in the field of human experimentation. One set of controversies arises from economic limitations on experiments with people—it is not feasible to do nearly all the large-scale randomized, controlled studies on effects of medical products that one would wish. The result is that one basis for decisions on clinical choices of products is "meta-analysis," a technique that combines the results of several relatively small trials. Analysts of a set of the two kinds of trials concluded that "the outcomes of . . . 12 large randomized, controlled trials . . . were not predicted accurately 35 percent of the time by the meta-analyses published previously on the same topics."[12] The negative payoff was that "if there had been no subsequent randomized, controlled trials, the meta-analysis would have led to the adoption of an ineffective treatment in 32 percent of cases . . . and to the rejection of a useful treatment in 33 percent of cases."[13] One possible explanation the authors advanced for this discrepancy was "publication bias," discussed in some detail below, which "refers to the tendency of investigators to preferentially submit studies with positive results for publication, and the tendency of editors to accept them." Another potential explanation referred to "[t]he heterogeneity of . . . trials included in [a] meta-analysis, "since meta-analysis assumes that such variation is mostly caused by random error, rather than by differences in the characteristics of the selected studies."[14]

A rather different view appeared in a study that challenged the idea of a "design hierarchy" that tended to low-rate "observational studies," which accumulate data on outcomes in people with particular kinds of exposures, as contrasted with studies involving controls imposed by the experimenter. The authors of this study concluded that "the 'average results' from well-designed observational studies (with a cohort or case-controlled design) did not systematically overestimate the magnitude of the associations between exposure and outcome as compared with the results of randomized, controlled trials of the same topic."[15] They also noted some limitations of both types of studies: "The result of a single randomized, controlled trial, or of only one observational study, should be interpreted cautiously." They loosed a concluding arrow with the declaration that "the popular belief that only randomized, controlled trials produce trustworthy results and that all observational studies are misleading does a disservice to patient care, clinical investigation, and the education of health care professionals."[16] Support for this position appeared in a simultaneously published article concluding that "observational studies and randomized, controlled trials usually produce similar results." Noting that the observational studies from the 1980s on which those authors relied "may be methodologically superior to earlier studies," they declared that "observational studies usually do provide valid information."[17]

The idea of publication bias, which first surfaced in a published study in 1959,[18] drew a substantial amount of discussion beginning in the 1990s, and the effect extended not only to publication but also to the inclination to submit results for publication. A British study in 1991 reported that "studies with a statistically significant result for the main outcome of interest were more likely to be submitted for publication and more likely to be published than studies with null results."[19] These authors said that "the presence of a null result was the most frequent reason for failing to write up the study."[20] By contrast, they said that one factor that was "significantly predictive of publication was a high rating on the importance of the study findings by the investigator, underscoring the contribution of an investigator's enthusiasm for a study in determining its publication fate." A portentous practical result of this phenomenon was that "publication bias may . . . enhance the impact of . . . potentially flawed studies." The authors concluded that "the main implication of publication bias is that the conclusions of literature reviews or meta-analyses based only on published work may be misleading."[21]

A strong numerical indicator of publication bias was a study indicating that twenty-eight out of forty-nine abstracts on the effects on fetuses carried by mothers who used cocaine were accepted, but only one of nine abstracts showing no effect was accepted.[22] The evidence for publication bias resided in several sources, including "acceptance of abstracts for presentation at meetings" and "subsequent full publication of initiated studies" and also including "reporting of published results by the lay press."[23] Indeed, the media did run in the same track. Newspaper reports "focused 10 out of 19 times" on two studies published in the same issue of the *Journal of the American Medical Association*, which had positive and negative results respectively, with those reports focusing "9 out of 19 times on the study with positive findings" but no report focusing "solely on the study with negative results."[24]

Later, other writers, confirming the "evidence of publication bias," added the existence of "a delay in publication of studies with negative results." They expressed a concern about the increasingly common "use of meta-analysis in medical research," with results that "seem to be precise and convincing," and noted that meta-analysis was "beginning to have an impact on clinical practice and on the planning of future research."[25]

## II. Scientific and Industrial Experiments with Potential Large-Scale Risk

There are certain kinds of experimental activity that may have low probabilities of risk but that could harm many people if their risks come to fruition. The story of recombinant DNA technology is an interesting case study of an experiment that involved concerns about widespread injury but turned out to be beneficent with the adoption of proper controls.

DNA, deoxyribonucleic acid, is the building block of heredity in our cells. The idea that one could manipulate genes by constructing "biologically active recombinant DNA molecules in vitro" had begun to capture the imagination of scientists as early as the 1960s.[26] By 1972, a group of authors had described a recombinant technique in a scientific publication.[27] The same year, under the title "A Two-Edged Sword,"[28] a critical essay in the British journal *Nature* expressed concern about the potential hazards of the technology. At the same time, scientists envisioned benefits in medical therapies including the production of various kinds of drugs, and agricultural advances including products that might substitute for chemical fertilizers.

Yet even those who foresaw such benefits were concerned about the possibility that recombinant labs might unleash monstrosities like new forms of bacteria. Thoughtful scientists found themselves torn between potential risks and benefits. One, Richard Roblin of the Harvard Medical School, worried about the "widespread dissemination" of new strains of bacteria but also declared that to constrain research on the technology "could doom future cancer patients and the undernourished."[29]

A notable event in self-regulation of experimentation occurred at a conference in Asilomar, California, in February 1975. There, high priests and priestesses of the recombinant temple proposed a set of containment levels for "moderate" or "high" risk recombinant experiments.[30] Over the next year, the National Institutes of Health entered the picture. Its director noted questions that had arisen over whether the ability of harmful recombinant products to survive in the environment was "sharply limited" or the alteration of "host" biologic materials could be altered in "unpredictable and undesirable" ways. He declared simply, that "[t]he fact is that we do not know which of the above-stated propositions is correct."[31]

In this rather compressed time period, NIH issued a series of guidelines for the control of recombinant research. These included physical containment guidelines that paralleled those that came out of Asilomar and guidelines for "biological" containment, which specified certain plasmids and bacteriophages for use in experiments.[32] The Environmental Defense Fund and the National Resources Defense Council petitioned to have guidelines adopted to govern all recombinant research in the country. Robert Sinsheimer, chairman of biology at the California Institute of Technology (Caltech), who had been an early enthusiast of the technology, supported the petition with a letter expressing concern that, as a press report summarized it, "no one [could] predict how the new organisms will act or possibly evolve into yet different forms." A focal point of his concern was the possibility of threats to health from the bacterium *E. coli*, which was used as the host for recombinant experiments and is involved in many kinds of human infections.[33]

As time went on, safeguards like those in the recombinant guidelines became part of the landscape. There were no reports of rogue viruses infecting entire communities. Recombinant DNA technology is now part of the national landscape, yielding benefits in cancer research, diabetes treatments, and—not without controversy—the development of genetically modified crops.

A large experiment, which continues as I write, delves into the micro- crevices of nanotechnology, in which scientists manipulate particles at the atomic level to create new products. As with recombinant DNA technology, the process of experiment carries large doses of uncertainty, both as to risks and benefits. And the experimental process takes places at three or four levels. First, there is experimentation as we generally think about it—the process of formulating a hypothesis about the behavior of materials, followed by an increasingly refined process of testing through trial and error to develop useful things. In an intermediate stage, those who work with nanomaterials themselves become subjects of risk experiments, with uncertainty existing about the effects of those materials on their bodies, for example by aspiration. In 2005, a document co-issued by the Centers for Disease Control and the National Institute for Occupational Safety and Health (NIOSH) spoke of an "information gap" that was "critical because of the unknown risk that nanomaterials pose to workers." It noted that "[v]ery few studies" had "measured exposure to nanoparticles that are purposely produced and not incidental to an industrial process."[34] Part of the difficulty of determining risk levels—for example with respect to clouds of particles that might waft through workplaces—lay in the lack of standardization of measurement. The report boldfaced the statement that "**there is not one sampling method that can be used to characterize exposure to nanosized aerosols.**"[35]

The uncertainty extended to risks to consumers, and here nanotechnology shares problems with many other innovations: as a new process yields marketable items, a vast set of tryouts occur on people across the country. With many uncertainties yet unresolved, by 2013 one inventory catalogued 1,317 consumer products that used nanomaterials,[36] and the number of patent applications for nano-products grew from 14,250 in 2007 to almost 18,900 in 2012.[37]

Concern about the effects of these engineered materials on human health continued as more nanotech products poured onto the market.[38] Across the industrialized world, governments and supranational institutions struggled to reduce the margin of uncertainty and to provide rules for the use of these products.[39]

## III. Unregulated Clinical Experimentation

Scientists have been using human beings as experimental subjects for many years, and unfortunately not always in good faith. A notorious set of cases was the dreadful experiments that Nazi doctors conducted on Jews and other captive peoples.[40] But even the United States has harbored some infamous experiments. We noted in the introduction the deliberate infection of hundreds of Guatemalans with syphilis. Another experiment, often mentioned, began several years before World War II. This was the Tuskegee Syphilis Study, in which four hundred poor African American men with syphilis were enrolled, receiving medication for the disease, with investigators seeking to determine its effects on the body but giving no information about "the goals of the study, its potential effects on their health, or the health of their potential partners."[41] Allegations of another shockingly unconsented experiment involved prestigious institutions, including Vanderbilt University and the Rockefeller Foundation. They, among others, were defendants in a case brought for the use of radioactive isotopes to track the absorption of iron in pregnant women. The plaintiffs asserted that they had never been told that they had been exposed to radiation and that the defendants knew of the dangers to health from such exposures; moreover, they claimed that a follow-up study revealed a "disproportionately high incidence of cancer among experimental subjects."[42]

A single case of pioneering heart surgery provides a dramatic example of experimentation on individuals within a reputable hospital setting. This case, which eventuated in a tort suit, arose from an encounter between a very sick heart patient and a famous surgeon. The patient, Haskell Karp, with a history of four heart attacks and thirteen hospitalizations, had had a pacemaker implanted. The surgeon was the renowned Dr. Denton Cooley of Houston, who was truly operating on the frontier of heart surgery. After Mr. Karp rejected his suggestion of a heart transplant, Dr. Cooley recommended a procedure that involved a surgical resection of the heart muscle, but he said that if that did not work, he would turn to a mechanical heart as a "stopgap to a transplant." Mr. Karp signed a consent form that authorized Dr. Cooley to "remove my diseased heart and insert a mechanical substitute," and said that he understood "that this mechanical device will not be permanent and will require replacement by a heart transplant." The form also indicated that the patient "realize[d] that his device has been tested in the laboratory but has not been used to sustain a human being and . . . no assurance of success can be made."

One must picture the charged scene in Mr. Karp's hospital room when Dr. Cooley explained to Haskell Karp's wife, Shirley, that her husband had "taken a sudden turn for the worse" and said that there was "a donor heart that will be available and . . . we will use if there's that need for it." After Haskell Karp said he would sign the agreement, his wife testified that she said, "I got to read it first." When she came across a reference to what she termed "some sort of a mechanical device," she said, "Dr. Cooley, what's this thing you have here? . . . what's mechanical device?" Mrs. Karp said that in Dr. Cooley's explanation of the procedure, he said that "this here one was a new model and it was proven in the laboratory but . . . hasn't been used on a human being yet." She claimed, as the court summarized it, that Cooley had not said "that the device was any different from the heart-lung device ordinarily used for open heart surgery, stating that it was a 'newer model' that had not been used before."[43]

After Dr. Cooley and his team performed the resection, they concluded that Mr. Karp's heart was so scarred that it did not have enough muscle to sustain life. They then inserted a mechanical device, which was the first totally mechanical heart to be implanted in a human being. Mr. Karp lived with the device for sixty-four hours, when a donor heart was found and implanted. He died thirty-two hours later, and there was some testimony that could be taken to indicate that the machine was possibly a contributing cause of his death.[44] In her tort action, Mrs. Karp contended that her husband had not given an "informed consent" to the operation, pointing out that he had not been given specific information about the results of animal tests on the device, that he was not told that the device might cause permanent injury to his body, and that he was not told "that the device was 'completely experimental.'"[45] The appellate court rejected this claim, saying that "whether there was informed consent is necessarily linked to the charge of experimentation" and that "Mr. Karp's consent was expressly to all three stages of the operation actually performed—each an alternative in the event of a preceding failure."[46] In this context, the court viewed consent to an experimental procedure as being governed by Texas state law for "traditional malpractice actions," which required "expert medical testimony to determine how a reasonably careful and prudent physician would have acted under the same or similar circumstances."[47]

*Karp v. Cooley* is an unusual episode in this body of law, because it is entirely focused on one patient and one procedure. The court's technical resolution of the problem subordinates the experimental feature of the procedure to the general law of medical malpractice. This, however, does not obscure the fact that if the device used on Haskell Karp did in fact contribute to his death, the operation was one step along the road to the improvement of cardiac surgery generally. In the background is the question of who should pay for such experiments, which over time presumably will often redound to the benefit of many patients.

Perhaps the starkest example of individual consent to experimental medicine is a case in which Cecelia Zyjewski, a sixty-five-year-old woman with cancer, refused her doctors' advice to have surgery and sought a noninvasive alternative. Her choice was a ninety-six-year-old physician, Emanuel Revici, who treated cancer patients with a combination of "urine monitoring, urinalyses and the ingestion of various mineral compounds." Although he told her that "he thought she would respond to his treatment and that he thought he could cure her," he allegedly also told her that "his medications were not FDA approved and that he could offer no guarantees." The parties stipulated that Dr. Revici's treatment plan was "legally negligent" because "it did not conform to accepted medical standards." The trial judge refused a request from Revici to instruct the jury about the doctrine of "express assumption of risk," and the jury found for Zyjewski's administrator with a verdict for more than a million dollars. The appellate court overturned the trial court's judgment for the administrator, saying that "a jury should decide whether a plaintiff has accepted all the risks of the defendant's negligence."[48] Here, with experimentation fully in the spotlight, personal choice of an avowedly experimental medical adventure trumps the general standard of care.

Another decision makes it clear that a doctor must inform a patient of the experimental character of a procedure. A North Carolina appellate court took that position in a case in which surgeons used a procedure that involved the insertion of a small steel coil into an artery, presumably weakened by a bullet, in an effort to cut off the flow of blood and prevent a rupture. Interpreting a state statute that required physicians to provide "a general understanding . . . of the usual and most frequent risks and hazards inherent in the proposed procedures or treatments which are recognized and followed by other health care providers," the court said that while the statutory language was "not entirely clear, it appears to require that informed consent be obtained to *established* procedure or treatments." It reasoned from this that "obviously, experimental procedures, by their very untested nature, do not fall within the category of practices described." Since "just as obviously . . . medical innovation must go forward, and there will also be some cases in which no recognized procedure will offer any prospect of success," the court said it did not think "the legislature intended to preclude any valid consent to experimental procedures." Given this premise, the court declared that "where the health care provider offers an experimental procedure or treatment to a patient, the health care provider has a duty, in exercising reasonable care under the circumstances, to inform the patient of the experimental nature of the proposed procedure," noting that "with experimental procedures the 'most frequent risks and hazards' will remain unknown until the procedure becomes established."[49]

The court further reasoned that "if the health care provider has a duty to inform of *known* risks for *established* procedures, common sense and the purposes of the statute equally require that the health care provider inform the patient of any *uncertainty* regarding the risks associated with *experimental* procedures," including "the experimental nature of the procedure and the *known or projected most likely risks*." Although in the case at issue, "the surgeons presented a full picture of the risks of the surgical procedure and simply advised" the plaintiff that it "might not work," they did not "comport with the reasonable disclosure standards" of the statute when they did not inform him of "its experimental nature and their consequent lack of knowledge of the risks of whether it would fail or not."[50]

Aligning its decisions with "the majority of courts and commentators," the court said that "[t]he underlying tort principles of rationality that require informing before operating clearly demand more information when the proposed procedure is new and untested."[51] It thus reversed a summary judgment in favor of the surgeons. Thus, in one-on-one medical practice, consent requires full information about experimentation. The premise is one of "rationality." You have to know about a risk, in the round, before you can make a reasonable decision.

There are practical limitations on the principle, of course. In a sense, every visit to the doctor involves a little experiment: because of the biochemical individuality of each patient, there is always a little bit of uncertainty in every diagnosis and every prescription. The law draws common-sense boundaries around the concept of experimentation here. But as new methods of diagnosis and treatment flood the medical marketplace, the concept of experiment edges into the realm of physician judgment about what risks to identify.

*Autism: Faded Hopes*

The search for a cure for autism has generated much attention from parents of autistic children and in the media. It has drawn many suggestions for solutions that have not made their way through established scientific channels, and it has also produced a major alleged scientific fraud.

The term "snake oil" has been applied through the centuries to many remedies that had no scientific support. Parents of autistic children have been willing to seize upon a variety of treatments. One quite unproved theory that attracted parents is that a cause of autism is exposure to certain metals, especially a form of mercury used in vaccines. This theory led to the use of chelating drugs, which "convert lead, mercury, and other metals into chemically insert compounds" that can be excreted in urine and that in fact have been used to treat lead poisoning. The NIH planned a controlled study of chelation for autism but then decided not to proceed with it, because there was "no clear evidence of direct benefit," and because of a concern that the treatment would put children at "more than a minimal risk."[52] A physical attack on autism was the use of a hyperbaric oxygen chamber, which had been used to combat decompression sickness and was recommended for one or two hourly sessions a day at a price tag of at least $100 an hour.[53]

Parents also sought a solution in diet. A writer summarized the efforts of an Oregon couple, the Laidlers, to give their two sons "vitamin B6 and magnesium [and] the nutritional supplements dimethylglycine and trimethylglycine," as well as "vitamin A-, gluten- and casein-free diets" and the digestive hormone secretin, in addition to chelation. The parents kept feeding "dozen of supplements" to their children, "calibrating doses up and down with every change in behavior." Nothing worked. A particularly poignant aspect of this case was that the father of the children was an anesthesiologist, who "at first . . . tried to resist," but, as the writer put it, "hope won out over skepticism."[54]

Some clinical trials bridging the turn of the century turned up no benefit from casein- and gluten-free diets and secretin. One physician who aided in the secretin trials explained the time delay for getting results: "Research is very labor-intensive, and progress may be slow."[55] Meanwhile, the marketing of various remedies continued, although they were described by a retired psychiatrist as "a combination of pseudoscience and fraud."[56]

A striking example of alleged outright fraud in published autism research was a British paper published in 1998 that implied that the measles, mumps, and rubella (MMR) vaccine might be linked to autism. An article in the *British Medical Journal* condemned the paper, which was said to have significantly reduced the vaccination rate in the United Kingdom, saying that "no case" of the twelve cases reported in the study was "free of misreporting or alteration."[57] Editorials in the journal described the case as involving "deliberate fraud" and a "deeply shocking" "breach of trust,"[58] savagely asserting that "a great deal of thought and effort must have gone into drafting the paper to achieve the results [the author] wanted."[59] Various skeins of medical history thus wound together in the decline in British vaccination rates: generally, a willingness of consumers to believe things labeled as science; specifically, parents' desperation about their children's fate; and, by allegation at least, reprehensibly bad science.

In recording how an important scientific establishment angrily discredited the argument associating MMR vaccine with autism, we should note a startling conclusion about the fragility of many findings that come out of the research establishment generally—specifically a finding that many published research studies on medical topics were later contradicted. John Ioannidis, analyzing 115 articles that had each received more than a thousand citations, found that "five of 6 highly cited nonrandomized studies had been contradicted or had initially stronger effects while this was seen in only 9 of 39 highly cited randomized trials." The studies he surveyed included topics of life-and-death interest; for example, the relationship of hormone therapy and ingestion of vitamin E to coronary artery disease, and the effects of angioplasty on the rate of heart attacks. Ioannidis wrote, "Trials with contradicted or initially stronger effects had significantly smaller sample sizes or tended to be older than those with replicated or unchallenged findings."[60] In presenting this "fascinating look at the process of science," he noted that four of the highly cited articles he examined "were refuting investigations with 'negative' results," and that "even the other highly cited articles with 'positive' results refuted prior knowledge and practice by introducing new concepts and proposing new interventions."[61]

An important practical aspect of Ioannidis's study lay in his observation that "most research publications have little impact while a small minority receives most attention and dominates scientific thinking and clinical practice."[62] This was particularly significant because of a reality, which we have mentioned earlier, of the economics of research: that "for most clinical questions of interest, no large trials are ever conducted and evidence is based only on small trials or nonrandomized studies."[63]

Ioannidis encapsulated the vastness of the uncharted landscape of medical research with his remark that "large-scale evidence is impossible to obtain for all of the millions and trillions of research questions posed in current research."[64] Under the provocative title "Why Most Published Research Findings Are False," he pointed to what might be called the glitz factor in medical research: "The hotter a scientific field (with more scientific teams involved), the less likely research findings are to be true."[65] Identifying what he viewed as factors that bore on the question of truth in research findings, he gave as one example that "investigators working in fields where true effect sizes are perceived to be small may be more likely to perform large studies than investigators working in fields where true effect sizes are perceived to be large." He also observed that "prejudice may prevail in a hot scientific field, further undermining the predictive value of its research findings," saying that "highly prejudiced stakeholders may even create a barrier that aborts effort at obtaining and disseminating opposing results." An example of techniques representative of the dark side of research was a hypothetical case of research on the association of a gene with susceptibility to schizophrenia. Ioannidis cited the "manipulation" of a research design with, among other things, "serendipitous inclusion or exclusion of certain patients or controls," "investigation of genetic contrasts that were not originally specified," and "various combinations of selective or distorted reporting of the results."[66]

At the same time, he identified more hopeful converse effects: "The fact that a field is hot or has strong invested interests may sometimes promote larger studies and improve standards of research, enhancing the predictive value of its research findings." He also mentioned the possibility that "massive discovery-oriented testing may result in such a large yield of significant relationships that investigators have enough to report and search further and thus refrain from data dredging and manipulation."[67] But he concluded by mentioning a problem for efforts at critical analysis of research findings: "Usually it is impossible to decipher how much data dredging by the reporting authors or other research teams has preceded a reported research finding."[68]

### IV. Regulation of Clinical Experimentation on Drugs and Devices

The halcyon days of the cowboy investigator using human subjects officially ended in 1974, when federal regulations for the protection of research subjects, originally issued in 1966, first became effective. One method of protection is the institutional review board (IRB), now a standard element of all institutions doing research on human subjects.[69] The membership of IRBs includes physicians, scientists, and lay members. I served on IRBs at two universities for several years, and at many meetings there were serious disagreements about the propriety of research projects, including the consent forms proposed for signature by subjects. On at least a couple of these occasions, when investigators appeared before the board to argue for their projects, it was clear that they were old-style cowboys who had very little understanding of the reason for the board's scrutiny. I note that as IRBs became part of the landscape of clinical trials, consent forms had evolved to a point where they included catalogs of side effects and hazards. Some of these lists were literally as long as my arm and were positively frightening, although the risks they identified would be acceptable to many persons with serious illnesses. For example, one might be willing to undergo much pain and nausea in an effort to stave off, even for a time, death from a late-stage cancer.

The research enterprises for which IRBs exercise oversight are big business. In 2001, funds linked to clinical trials at Johns Hopkins alone were in the $300 million range.[70] There are continual skirmishes about the role of IRBs, featuring issues that include questions concerning their effectiveness. One example, which symbolizes the cross-country complexity of medical research, is the situation where a study is being conducted at several institutions, each of which must get approval for the research from its local IRB. Institutions can designate IRBs at other places to do a review, but as a commentator has pointed out, many institutions are averse to doing that. One reason is that if "it is later determined that the study was not in compliance with regulations, the institution will be tarnished—and possibly sued—even though its employees were not responsible for any misdeeds." What can occur, he said, is a great waste of resources "devoted to the ethics review of multisite studies," with "nearly identical processes" being "repeated at many locations." Additionally, "in many instances," a particular IRB's "concerns are not even conveyed to IRBs at other study sites." Moreover, administrators may have to spend time on reconciling "relatively minor preferences as to word choice and grammar," and more substantively, if "an IRB correctly identifies serious problems with a consent form and asks for changes to be made in the version used at its site, these concerns are frequently not communicated to other IRBs, and inadequate consent forms may still be used at many or most sites." The commentator said there was "little evidence that having multiple IRBs review a single study has led to the ethical improvement of protocols or consent forms," and that indeed the practice "seems to pose a significant risk of diminishing studies' ethical integrity." One possible solution was "to have sponsors require the use of a central IRB as a condition for participating in a study."[71] A lesson that appears is that the very nature of big science, as it is practiced across the country, increases the expense of research on human subjects, sometimes even contributing to deficiencies in communication to patients. Playing in the competitive environment of clinical research incurs those costs.

The IRB model is applicable only where investigators, no matter how many human subjects they use, must have at least some direct personal contact with those persons. By contrast, there are two very different kinds of experimentation where patients, consumers, and citizens have no forewarning about potential risks, or benefits, of an experiment. One category of these cases embraces what amount to large-scale environmental experiments, the harmful effects of which sometimes do not turn up in individuals in ways like side effects linked to a particular drug, and do not present themselves as pins in the map across the nation. We discuss these cases in Chapter Two. The other group of cases, unregulated at least at the outset of the experiment, consists of products and activities that enter the general marketplace with or without prior screening in clinical settings. We focus on one case study of this sort of product in Chapter 3.

## Notes

1. Frederick Grinnell, *Everyday Practice of Science* (Oxford Univ. Press, 2009), p. 4.
2. Ibid., quoting Peter Medawar, *Plato's Republic* (Oxford Univ. Press, 1982). Grinnell, supra at 31, describes the results of an early experiment: "Everything looks messy."
3. See ibid., p. 23.

4. See ibid, p. 16 ("with discovery oriented toward completion and correction, the scientific attitude defers Truth to the future and aims for credibility in the present").
5. Ibid., p. 82.
6. J. Scott Armstrong, "Advocacy and Objectivity in Science," 25 *Management Science* 423, 424 (1979).
7. Ibid., p. 425, referring to Michael J. Mahoney and T. P. Kimper, "Publication Prejudices: A Experimental Study of Confirmatory Bias in the Peer Review System," 1 *Cognitive Therapy & Res.* 161 (1977).
8. Adrian M. Wenner, "Science As a Process: The Question of Bee 'Language,'" 64 *Bios* 78, 80 (1993).
9. David Hull, *Science As a Process: An Evolutionary Account of the Social and Conceptual Development of Science* (U. of Chicago Press, 1988), p. 352.
10. Ibid.
11. Ibid., p. 514.
12. Jacques LeLorier et al., "Discrepancies Between Meta-Analyses and Subsequent Large Randomized, Controlled Trials," 337 *N. Eng. J. Med.* 536, 535 (1997).
13. Ibid., p. 593.
14. Ibid., p. 540.
15. John Concato et al., "Randomized, Controlled Trials, Observational Studies, and the Hierarchy of Research Designs," 342 *N. Eng. J. Med.* 1887, 1890. (2000).
16. Ibid., p. 1892.
17. See Kjell Benson and Arthur J. Hartz, "A Comparison of Observational Studies and Randomized, Controlled Trials," 342 *N. Eng. J. Med.* 1878, 1884 (2000).
18. See Kay Dickersin and Yuan-I Min, "Publication Bias: The Problem That Won't Go Away," *Annals N.Y. Acad. Scis.* 703 (1993): 135, 135, citing T. D. Sterling, "Publication Decisions and Their Possible Effects on Inferences Drawn From Tests of Significance—Or Vice Versa," 54 *J. Am. Stat. Ass'n* 30 (1959).
19. P. J. Easterbrook and J. A. Berlin, "Publication Bias in Clinical Research," 337 *Lancet* 867 (1991); printout at 7.
20. Ibid., printout at 5. See also Dickersin and Min, supra, p. 139: "Most of the time, investigators stated that they did not publish their findings because the results were 'not interesting' (61%) or because they 'did not have the time' (7%)."
21. Ibid., printout at 8.
22. Dickersin and Min, supra note 15, pp. 141–42, citing G. Koren et al., "Bias Against the Null Hypothesis: The Reproductive Hazards of Cocaine," *Lancet* 2: 1440 (1989).
23. Ibid., p. 141.
24. Ibid., p. 143.
25. See Jerome M. Stern and R. John Simes, "Publication Bias: Evidence of Delayed Publication in a Cohort Study of Clinical Research," 315 *Br. Med. J.* 640, 640, 644 (1997).
26. The description appears in Paul Berg et al., "Potential Hazards of Recombinant DNA Molecules," 185 *Science* 303 (1974).

27. See ibid.
28. "Genetics: A Two-Edged Sword," 240 *Nature* 73 (1972).
29. See Marshall S. Shapo, *A Nation of Guinea Pigs* (The Free Press, 1979), p. 222.
30. See ibid., pp. 224–25.
31. See ibid., p. 227.
32. See ibid., pp. 228–32.
33. Associated Press, "Stiffer Controls on Gene Research Urged," *Washington Post*, Nov. 12, 1976, p. A8.
34. Nat'l Inst. for Occupational Safety and Health Centers for Disease Control and Prevention, *Approaches to Safe Nanotechnology: An Information Exchange with NIOSH 7–8* (2005), pp. 3, 13–14.
35. See ibid., p. 20.
36. http://www.nanotechproject.org/inventories/consumer, accessed Aug. 9, 2013.
37. See Erin Geiger Smith, "U.S.-Based Investors Lead World in Nanotechnology Patents: Study," *Chicago Tribune Business*, Feb. 4, 2013, printed from the Internet, Aug. 9, 2013.
38. See for example Evica Kica and Diana M. Bowman, "Regulation of Means of Standardization: Key Legitimacy Issues of Health and Safety Nanotechnology Standards," 53 *Jurimetrics* 11, 12–13 (2012).
39. See for example "NIOSH Recommends Workplace Exposure Limit for Carbon Nanotubes, Nanofibers," 43 OSH Rep. 383 (April 25, 2013); "European Chemical Group Advises Members to Update Dossiers for Nanoscale Compounds," Prod. Safety & Liab. Rep. 1150 (Oct. 8, 2012); "Germany Backs Stricter Reporting Rules for Nanomaterials Under REACH," Prod. Safety & Liab. Rep. 529 (April 29, 2013).
40. See for example Tessa Chelouche, "Medicine and the Holocaust: Lessons for Present and Future Physicians," 27 *Med. L.* 787, 800–02 (citing sources).
41. See for example 20120265 AHLA-Sem 17, text accompanying notes 65–103; NPR, "Remembering Tuskegee," July 20, 2002, printed from the Internet, May 5, 2011.
42. See *Craft v. Vanderbilt University*, 18 F. Supp.2d 786 (M.D. Tenn. 1998) (denying summary judgment sought on the grounds that the defendants were not "state actors").
43. *Karp v. Cooley*, 493 F.2d 408, 413 (5th Cir. 1974).
44. See for example ibid., pp. 418 and 422.
45. Ibid., p. 420.
46. Ibid., p. 424.
47. Ibid., p. 423.
48. *Boyle v. Revici*, 961 F.2d 1062, 1063 (2d Cir. 1992).
49. *Estrada v. Jaques*, 321 S.E.2d 240, 253-54 (N.C. Ct. App.1984).
50. Ibid., p. 254.
51. Ibid., p. 255.
52. Nancy Shute, "Desperate for an Autism Cure," *Scientific American*, Oct. 2010, pp. 82–83.
53. Ibid.
54. Ibid., pp. 81–82.
55. Ibid., p. 84.

56. Ibid., p. 82.
57. Brian Deer, "How the Case Against the MMR Vaccine Was Fixed," 342 *Br. Med. J.* 80, 81 (2011), criticizing Andrew Wakefield et al., "Ileal Lymphoid Nodular Hyperplasia, Non-Specific Colitis, and Pervasive Developmental Disorder in Children," 351 *Lancet* 637 (1998), retracted in 375 *Lancet* 445 (2010).
58. See Fiona Goodlee, "Editor's Choice: The Fraud Behind the MMR Scare," 342 *Br. Med. J.* d.22 (2011).
59. Editorial, "Wakefield's Article Linking MMR Vaccine and Autism Was Fraudulent," 342 *Br. Med. J.* e7452 (2011).
60. See John P.A. Ioannidis, "Contradicted and Initially Stronger Effects in Highly Cited Clinical Research," 294 *JAMA* 218, 220, 223, 224 (2005).
61. Ibid., p. 224.
62. Ibid., p. 218.
63. Ibid., p. 224.
64. John P. A. Ioannidis, "Why Most Published Research Findings Are False," 2 *PLoS Medicine* 0696, 0700 (2005).
65. Ibid., p. 0698.
66. See ibid., p. 0699 (box).
67. See Ibid., p. 0699.
68. Ibid., p. 0701.
69. See generally *Institutional Review Board Guidebook*, http://www.hhs.gov/ohrp/archive/irb/irb_guidebook.htm.,last consulted July 4, 2015.
70. See Susan Levine, "FDA Faults Clinical Research at Hopkins," *Washington Post*, Sept. 8, 2001.
71. Jerry Menikoff, "The Paradoxical Problem With Multiple-IRB Review," 363 *N. Eng. J. Med.* 1591, 1592–93 (2010).

# 2

# Major Environmental Experiments

## I. The Atomic Weapons Tests

A very large continuing outdoor experiment, one of the biggest in American history and one of the riskiest to human health, took place at a test site for atomic weapons in Nevada over more than a decade beginning in 1951. The story of this group of tests, the way in which they were conducted, and the consequences of lawsuits for injuries attributed to them provides a fascinating lesson in how society reacts to vast trials of very dangerous products.

A group of 1,192 named plaintiffs sued the government for injuries and deaths from radioactive fallout over a plot of countryside extending from southeastern Nevada to southern Utah and northern Arizona. The case divided two federal courts over the technical question of whether the government's conduct of the tests constituted a "discretionary function." That language in the Federal Tort Claims Act bars suits that could otherwise be brought against the United States for injury or death "caused by the negligent or wrongful act or omission of any employees of the Government . . . under circumstances where the United States, if a private person, would be liable" under the law of the state where an "act or omission" alleged to have caused harm occurred.

The federal trial judge was Bruce Jenkins, a gravel-voiced bear of a man from Utah, who produced a 225-page opinion in part favoring the plaintiffs. With respect to the design of the weapons that were tested and the decision to test them in the atmosphere, he concluded that these were "discretionary" activities. By contrast, he opined, "When each explosion was actually detonated, and *what* was to be done as a consequence, were decisions made at the *operational* level"—that "they were choices and judgments made by those charged with particular duties not discretionary in nature."[1] Undergirding this mighty judicial effort were more than sixty pages on the science of the subject, including data-laden sections on "Basic Principles of Radiation and Nuclear Physics" and "Basic Principles of Health Physics."[2]

Judge Jenkins summarized "the essence" of the plaintiffs' complaint as not "what defendant did do," but rather "what defendant didn't do—namely that it did not adequately warn, did not adequately and contemporaneously measure, and did not adequately educate the population at hazard in simple and inexpensive preventative and mitigating measures."[3] Lending emphasis to his decision that many choices at issue were not discretionary was his salty declaration that "[n]owhere were there to be human guinea pigs as a matter of policy." He referred to actions "at the operational level" that "were negligently insufficient—not as a matter of discretion at all—a matter of deliberate choice making—but as a matter of negligently failing to warn, to measure, and to inform, at a level sufficient to meet the stated goals of the Congress, the Executive Branch and the Atomic Energy Commission."[4]

The standard he set for the government was that of "a legal duty to act with *the highest degree of care in light of the best of available scientific knowledge*."[5] He critically applied this standard, for example, to the "astounding fact" that "at no time during the period 1951 through 1962 did the off-site radiation safety program make any concrete effort to directly monitor and record internal contamination or dosage in off-site residents on a comprehensive person-specific basis."[6] This language is particularly interesting in the way that, as applied in a vast geographical environment, it parallels the particularized consents required in clinical medical experimentation. With respect to the element of public information, Judge Jenkins concluded that while "off-site residents were not—at least, not *routinely*—exposed to radiation in tens or hundreds of rads at a time, they were not fully and accurately informed of what it was they *were* exposed to, to what it might entail in terms of long-term consequences, or how to keep the additional risk as low as was possible at that time."[7] He detailed that conclusion with a long paragraph summarizing the deficiencies of the program, including not only failure to give information about risk—information that he said was "essentially non-existent"—and failure to give instructions on "how to avoid or how to minimize such risk." His list also included failure to warn of radiation risks "to children, infants and pregnant mothers" and of "the dangers of fallout entering into the food chain and the potential long-term biological risks involved in the eating of such foods—particularly to children," and also the failure to "adequately, intensively, and periodically advise persons at risk" about simple precautions, including staying indoors, showering and scrubbing, and cleaning food.[8]

This reasoning did not, however, persuade the Tenth Circuit Court of Appeals. In a fairly brief opinion, Judge James Logan tied the activities of on-site personnel to the policy choices made higher up. He said there was no evidence of "a single instance in which test-site personnel ignored or failed to implement specific procedures mandated by the AEC for monitoring and informing the public." He declared that "government liability cannot logically be predicated on the failure of test-site personnel to go beyond what the operational plans specifically required them to do."[9] Additionally, he said there was no proof that "the AEC or its employees . . . clearly contravened a specific statutory or regulatory duty, or . . . exceeded statutory or regulatory authority." He gave as specific examples that there was no evidence "that the Test Information Officer failed to release information he was required to give out, or that the Radsafe Officer failed to take a specific radiation measurement that had been decided upon."[10] A melancholy concurring opinion by Judge Monroe McKay acknowledged that the trial judge had found "ample evidence" of deviations from "optimum practices based on the best available knowledge" that "would clearly support liability for injury under standard tort analysis as applied by the trial court." However, he said that the "translation" of "the broad safety language of the Atomic Energy Acts" into "concrete plans" had "involved the very essence of social, economic, and political decision making—the precise policy choices protected by the discretionary function exception." Although he professed "great sympathy for the individual cancer victims who have borne alone the costs of the AEC's choices," he said "their plight is a matter for Congress"—for example, through passage of "a specific relief bill for individual victims."[11]

There are several lessons to be drawn from the various opinions on this episode of experimentation. One, although it did not ultimately prevail, is that the model of individual communication of risk information can in fact be applied in at least some cases of large-scale experimentation. Another, however, is that such bigness of scale can be an obstacle to righting the wrongs of injuries inflicted on people who do not know about risks that are known to those who create them. Finally, there is a belief that when some governmental choices are crucially vital on behalf of society as a whole, with the result that public guinea pigs become sacrificial lambs, the lambs must bear the burden of the sacrifice. This was the Procrustean bed constructed by the court of appeals, which found itself bound by precedents that Judge McKay summed up as saying that "the rule that 'the king can do no wrong' still prevails at the federal level in all but the most trivial matters"[12]—meaning that the scope of "operational activities" is squeezed down by the broad scope of the category of "discretionary" ones.

## II. Three Mile Island

A presidential commission described the events in March 1979 at the nuclear power facility at Three Mile Island (TMI) near Harrisburg, Pennsylvania, as "the worst accident in the history of commercial nuclear power generation."[13] Although the results of the Japanese nuclear disaster in 2011, to be discussed shortly, dwarfed the external consequences of the accident at Three Mile Island, at the time a U.S. senator described those events as "the most serious such accident that we know of anywhere in the world."[14]

I have distilled from several sources an account of the TMI accident. Darrell Eisenhut, director of licensing for the Nuclear Regulatory Commission at the time, described a malfunction in the non-nuclear cooling system at the facility that "caused the feed-water pumps to turn off (trip), which in turn caused the turbine generator to turn off and stop generating electricity." A series of events in the "first 30 seconds following the accident"—at about 4:00 AM on Wednesday, March 28—resulted in a stoppage of the nuclear chain reaction, "leaving behind principally residual, or decay, heat." After a "plant response" that was "expected" came an unexpected series of events, the result of which—within a dozen minutes—was that "an indication of a rapidly rising pressurizer level apparently misled the plant operators to terminate" a flow of cold water from the emergency core cooling system of the reactor.[15] As a Senate report summarized it, "for the first 1¾ hours, control room personnel struggled to understand what was happening in the plant." With "hundreds of alarms" sounding, "the conditions that developed were beyond those that control room personnel had experienced in the training or in their operation of the plant," and "the symptoms described in . . . emergency procedures did not exactly fit the situation and proved of little help."[16] Within the first couple of hours, "the operators turned off the four large pumps which circulate the reactor coolant through the reactor," after which experts later inferred that "severe damage to the nuclear fuel began." As that fuel damage occurred, coolant was "discharged to the reactor containment floor," and some of that coolant, which contained radioactivity, was automatically pumped from the reactor containment building to tanks in the unsealed auxiliary building. At the tanks overflowed, radioactivity was "vented from the auxiliary building," a discharge that "was secured in about 40 minutes."[17] A site emergency was declared at 6:45, "based on radiation levels inside the plant," and a general emergency was declared at 7:24, "based on the potential for offsite radioactive releases." As the Senate committee summarized it, "for the rest of the day, control room personnel struggled to regain stability in the plant." Various uncertainties led the operators to depressurize the primary system. After halting the depressurization at 1:10 PM, they began it again forty minutes later, but as a block valve was opened, "there was an extremely sharp increase in pressure and temperature in the containment, accompanied by activation of the containment sprays," which occurred "when hydrogen in the containment ignited," although the hydrogen "burned only a few seconds." With depressurization "again . . . unsuccessful," "utility executives off-site ordered the emergency command team to repressurize the system again." By 7:50 PM, "relatively stable conditions were achieved." But "all the damage to the core" had occurred on that day,[18] and there was more to come.

Two mornings later, "confusion and consternation" arose because of a "significant release of radiation from the plant's auxiliary building," which was done "to relieve pressure on the primary system and avoid curtailing the flow of coolant to the core." In what a report of the NRC described as "an atmosphere of growing uncertainty about the condition of the plant," Governor Thornburgh of Pennsylvania and NRC chairman Joseph Hendrie "agreed that it would be prudent" for people "most vulnerable to radiation to evacuate the area." Specifically, the governor advised "pregnant women and pre-school-age children within a 5-mile radius of the plant to leave the area."[19]

Then came what a Senate committee referred to as "the now-famous hydrogen bubble,"[20] which appeared on Friday, March 30, "in the dome of the pressure vessel, the container that holds the reactor core."[21] There was fear that the bubble "might burn or even explode and rupture the pressure vessel," causing the core to "fall into the containment building and perhaps cause a breach of containment." Anxiety about these risks continued through Saturday, but the crisis ended on Sunday when experts judged that "the bubble could not burn or explode because of the absence of oxygen in the pressure vessel," and that the utility had greatly "reduce[d] the size of the bubble."[22]

The President's Commission ladled out several helpings of blame for the accident. Noting that "popular discussions of nuclear power plants tend to concentrate on questions of equipment safety," it said that "the fundamental problems are people-related problems and not equipment problems." It said that it did "not mean to limit this term to shortcomings of individual human beings," but that it meant "more generally . . . problems with the 'system' that manufactures, operates, and regulates nuclear power plants." These problems occupied a large spectrum of problems created by people: "structural problems in the various organizations . . . deficiencies in various processes, and . . . a lack of communication among key individuals and groups." The Commission noted that "one word occurred over and over again" among the witnesses it heard: the word "mindset." This attitude posited that if those who created the system "concentrated on equipment, assuming that the presence of operators could only improve the situation—they would not be part of the problem." This, the Commission concluded, was "the tragedy of Three Mile Island, where the equipment failures . . . were significantly less dramatic than those that had been thoroughly analyzed, but where the results confused those who managed the accident."[23]

The Commission identified as "some of the factors that significantly contributed to operator confusion" the "greatly deficient" training of operators," the fact that "the specific operating procedures" were "at least very confusing and could be read in such a way as to lead the operators to take the incorrect actions they did," and the problem that "the lessons from previous accidents did not result in new, clear instructions being passed on to the operators."[24] Fortunately, the Commission concluded, the radiation release would have only "negligible effects on the physical health of individuals." And although there was mental distress to residents in the area that was "quite severe," it was "short-lived."[25]

The Commission also found that the "public's right to information during the emergency" was not "well-served." It referred to "an attempt by the utility" on the first day "to minimize [the] significance" of the accident, and to the NRC later being "the source of exaggerated stories." It also noted that "some of those who briefed the press lacked the technical expertise to explain the events and seemed to be cut off from those could have provided this expertise."[26]

Training its fire on the NRC, the Commission found "serious inadequacies" in both the agency's "licensing function and its inspection and enforcement . . . activities." Among other things, it noted that the agency was only "required to analyze single-failure accidents" and not "what happens when two systems fail independently of each other," as happened at TMI. It also said the agency did not pay "enough attention . . . to the training of operating personnel and operator procedures in the licensing process."[27] It cited "operating personnel" for "some improper decisions . . . improper actions," and failure "to take some correct actions," which in combination "caused what should have been a minor incident to develop into the TMI-2 accident."[28]

The Commission also aimed a blunderbuss of criticisms at the government. Quite generally, it said that "at all levels of government, planning for the offsite consequences of radiological emergencies at nuclear power plants has been characterized by a lack of coordination and urgency." It found "insufficient" "interaction among NRC, Met Ed [the utility], and state and local emergency organizations in the development, review, and drill of emergency plans." It also taxed NRC personnel who were "on-site within hours of the declaration of a site emergency" as not being "able to determine and to understand the true seriousness and source of the accident for about 2 days, when the fact of extensive core damage and the existence of the hydrogen bubble were generally recognized within NRC."[29]

In an extensive set of recommendations, the Commission declared that "to the extent that the industrial institutions we have examined are representative of the nuclear industry, the nuclear industry must dramatically change its attitudes toward safety and regulations." Among its particular recommendations was the establishment of "a program that specifies appropriate safety standards including those for management, quality assurance, and operating procedures and practices, and that conducts independent evaluations." It also recommended "systematic gathering, review, and analysis of operating experience at all nuclear power plants coupled with an industry-wide international communications network" to disseminate this information. Moreover, it declared that "[s]ubstantially more attention and care must be devoted to the writing, revising, and monitoring of plant procedures."[30]

There is a certain sameness about events of this kind. A repetitive feature is the publication of recommendations that might have prevented problems that arose when the barn door could still be closed. Another is the wish-list tone of such recommendations. One senses that in a world of limited resources and vaulting technologies, the recommenders are not only fighting past wars but are also desperately trying to generate an attack on safety problems that continually push beyond them, out of reach.

It should be noted that Three Mile Island also contributed a lesson on long-term harms to a growing catalog of such injuries. As we noted, the President's Commission had been optimistic about radiation effects on health, speaking of "a negligible effect on the physical health of individuals." Although the Commission acknowledged that "even low levels of radiation" could have serious health effects and that there was "no direct way of measuring the danger of low-level radiation to health," it found that "the radiation doses were so low that we concluded that the overall health effects will be minimal." It said, "There either will be no case of cancer or the number of cases will be so small that it will never be possible to detect them."[31]

Almost two decades later, though, researchers at the University of North Carolina presented some rather forbidding statistics, drawn from a study of "incident cancers from 1975 to 1985," "ascertained from hospital records and assigned to study tracts."[32] Their striking conclusion was that "the cancer incidence, specifically lung cancer and leukemia, increased more following the TMI accident in areas estimated to have been in the pathway of radioactive plumes than in other areas." They commented, "The observation of a change in association is analytically powerful because it shows that the effect is temporally associated with the hypothesized causal event." Contrasting their study with other epidemiological research was their observation that "causal interpretation is further strengthened by the observation that the dose pattern resulting from plume travel is unlike many behavioral, occupational, and environmental exposures which are related in a complex biosocial process that makes them interdependent and potentially influenced by medical care and detection."[33] They noted that other researchers have "found some positive associations in their analyses of these data, but reasoned that the evidence did not suggest that the TMI accident affected cancer rates in the surrounding population."[34] Dryly, they commented that it was "therefore interesting to note that situations in which positive results have been interpreted as negative due to a collision of evidence and assumptions have been reported previously."[35]

## III. A Tsunami and a Tidal Wave of Criticism

The radiation birds of prey that hovered over Three Mile Island came to roost at Tokyo Electric's Fukushima Daiichi nuclear facility on the east coast of Japan on March 11, 2011, with the principal culprits being two extraordinary natural events in the vicinity of the plant and alleged planning failures on the part of the Japanese nuclear industry. The natural events were an earthquake measuring 9.0 on the Richter scale, the most powerful quake in Japanese history, and a tsunami that towered up to forty-six feet. The human failures included the adoption of inadequate safety rules against a history that suggested portents of disaster. There had been an earthquake, although not one accompanied by a tsunami, at Tokyo Electric's Kashiwazaki plant on the west coast of the country in 2007 that, as one report summarized it, shook the ground "as much as two and a half times the maximum intensity envisioned in the plant's design."[36] Although upgrades were made at Kashiwazaki, a California expert said that "they had years to prepare at that point, after Kashiwazaki, and I am seeing the same thing at Fukushima."[37]

One account of the disaster summarized a "knockout of the cooling systems" that "resulted in partial to total meltdowns of the reactor cores," the explosion of one reactor building, and severe damage to others. It described the "radiation that escaped into the atmosphere" as "twenty to thirty times that released by the atomic bomb over Hiroshima." The event caused as many as 20,000 deaths—at least 15,854 confirmed dead—and led to the government's creation of a group of concentric evacuation zones that required 10,500 people to leave their homes and put almost 60,000 on notice to prepare for evacuation.[38]

The catastrophic added element at Fukushima was the tsunami, but here again there was some forewarning. A quake that registered 7.8 on the west coast had generated tsunamis about 30 feet high at the island of Okushiri, which had tsunami walls up to 15 feet. The Fukushima facility sat on a bluff 13 feet high. But although Tokyo Electric had raised its calculation of the highest tsunami to as high at 18.7 feet, its principal response was to raise "an electric pump near the coast by 8 inches."

Critics assailed the Japanese for ignoring new science on "seismology and risk assessment." Greg Hardy, an American structural engineer, said that the Japanese "fell behind"—that having "made the proclamation" that the Kashiwazaki quake "was the maximum earthquake, they had a hard time evaluating that as new data came in." Kenji Sumita, who had served as deputy chairman of Japan's Nuclear Safety Commission, reportedly said that the utilities, "focusing on completing the construction of a dozen reactors," had "resisted adopting tougher standards." "Engaged in foot-dragging," he said, they had not sent representatives to Commission meetings.[39]

The Fukushima disaster appears to have been the main trigger for a flurry of U.S. reports reflecting regulatory and legislative concern that arose twenty-two years after Three Mile Island. Indeed, the days immediately following the Fukushima disaster generated uncertainty among U.S. regulators that replicated their reaction during the Pennsylvania crisis. These officials of the NRC, initially concerned about the possible impact that tsunamis set off by earthquakes could have on plants like the Diablo Canyon plant in California, became especially worried about language in a cable from the International Atomic Energy Agency about the failure of the backup and cooling systems at Fukushima. The regulators' uncertainty was apparent in redacted transcripts of conversations among officials over more than two weeks following the Fukushima events. One official, responding to "meager" information, said, "We're dying in a sea of silence," a remark echoed by NRC chairman Gregory Jaczko, who said that the early days at Fukushima "reflect the fog of war, so to speak."[40]

On May 12, 2011, the NRC released a first set of findings from a safety review, which according to a press report "overall gave the 104 U.S. nuclear reactors a clean bill of health on safety and emergency planning." However, commission spokesmen noted that fuel for cooling pumps "wasn't always readily available" and, according to the press report, that "equipment was sometimes stored in areas where it could be affected by an earthquake or flood."[41]

On the same day, Congressman Ed Markey of Massachusetts released a report that was summarized as observing that NRC regulations "did not require emergency diesel generators to be operational when there is no fuel in a reactor core—even though it could leave spent-fuel pools without any backup cooling system in case power is lost"—a problem associated with the escape of radioactive materials from a spent-fuel pool at the Fukushima facility. The Markey report declared that "an examination of NRC regulations demonstrates that flawed assumptions and under-estimation of safety risks are currently a part of the NRC regulatory program, due to a long history of decisions made by prior Commissions or by the NRC staff that have all too often acquiesced to industry requests for a weakening of safety standards."[42]

Just two months later, a report by an NRC task force criticized the agency itself for using a "'patchwork' of requirements and voluntary measures" to achieve reactor safety. One recommendation of the report was to require plants to have "backup electricity for spent-fuel pools and better monitoring and cooling." Another was to order plants like the Fukushima one "to have better ways to prevent dangerous hydrogen gas and prevent explosions." Gregory Jaczko, the NRC chairman, was summarized as saying in a press interview that he wanted the agency to decide within sixty days "how to proceed with far-reaching safety changes." An industry spokesman counseled delay until more was known about the Fukushima accident. However, although Jaczko said he would "seek input" from the industry, he declared that he did not want the industry to "get bogged down" in rule-making that might take two to five years.[43]

Only two weeks after the report of that interview came a report of a draft of a Commission study that was characterized as having "conclude[d] that a meltdown at a typical American reactor would lead to far fewer deaths than previously assumed." The conclusions of the draft, and criticisms of it, present a typical pattern of disagreement about the scope and danger of hazards from environmental experiments. The draft report focused on two common types of reactors, boiling water reactors at the Peach Bottom station in Pennsylvania and pressurized-water reactors at the Surry Power Station in Virginia. An assumption of the draft was that "big releases of radioactive materials would not be immediate," providing enough time for evacuations that "the chance of a death from acute radiation exposure within 10 miles" would be "near zero," "although some people would receive doses high enough to cause fatal cancers in decades to come." A critic from the Union of Concerned Scientists pointed out that the study assumed a successful evacuation of 99.5 percent of people within ten miles, emphasized the many variables involved in the estimate, and asserted that the proper focus was on populations within fifty miles, which would expand the average number of persons exposed from sixty-two thousand to five million. He noted that there were "more than 100 reactors of different designs and vintage, in areas with disparate population densities."[44]

Perhaps portentously in the very same time period, a medical journal article summarized the consequences of human exposure to radiation from reactor accidents. It identified as the "primary mechanism" for exposure the ingestion or inhalation of radiation or its entrance into the body through open wounds. It noted as methods of contamination the inhalation or consumption of iodine-131 through the food chain, including seafood contaminated by seawater. Pointing out that "radiation exposure can potentially result in short-term and long-term effects in every organ system in the body," the authors mentioned "strong evidence of an increased rate of secondary thyroid cancers among" children living near the site of the 1986 nuclear disaster at Chernobyl, Ukraine. At the same time, though, they noted that apart from people who suffered acute radiation sickness at Chernobyl, "long-term follow-up" in the region had "shown no increases in cancer mortality."[45] As to Fukushima, the authors said it appeared that the consequences of that event were "still unclear"[46]—a hallmark of such large-scale experiments.

As concerns mounted about the possible danger from American reactors, a series of criticisms about Fukushima became public in Japan, bringing some transparency to what some said was a secretive culture that promoted atomic energy at the expense of safety. The Japanese parliament established a bipartisan panel to investigate the disaster.[47] A former inspector for the Japan Nuclear Energy Safety Organization claimed that after he "refused to approve a routine test" at a reactor on the island of Hokkaido, he was told that his "job was just to approve reactors, not to raise doubts about them" and that his employment contract was not renewed. Reports appeared that in 2008, Tepco engineers had "made three separate sets of calculations" indicating that tsunamis as high as fifty feet could hit Fukushima Daiichi, and that the company had not told agency regulators this for almost a year—as it turned out, just four days before the Fukushima tsunami.[48]

An interim report of the investigative panel sounded echoes of Three Mile Island—and worse. It was said that regulators left the plant quickly after the quake and that the workers who were left "had not been trained to handle multiple failures and lacked a clear manual to follow."[49] The final report, released in July 2012, was scathing. The chairman called the event "a profoundly man-made disaster . . . that could and should have been foreseen and prevented" and said that the effects of the events "could have been mitigated by a more effective human response." Among other features of the 641-page report was the suggestion that the "more foreseeable" earthquake, and not the tsunami, might have been responsible for a significant amount of the damage to one reactor—a suggestion that was at odds with Tepco's contention that the plant had withstood the quake and that all the blame should be put on what it said was a "once in a millennium" tsunami.[50]

Indeed, in the summer of 2013, there was a report that three hundred tons of "highly contaminated water [had] leaked from a storage tank" at Fukushima. The water, with "levels of radioactive cesium and strontium many hundreds of times as high as legal safety limits," had been in a tank that contained one thousand tons of liquid, one of almost one thousand tanks on the premises near the shoreline. Although it had been assumed that the tanks would last at least five years, the tank that leaked had been in place for no more than two years.

If there was any good news, it was that the release was at Level 1 on a scale that at its highest was Level 7, which had occurred in the 2011 tsunami and at Chernobyl.[51] Yet—just so one would not indulge in even faint optimism—within three days of the report on the leak, the operator of the plant said that as many as 220,000 tons of water were stored in the almost 1,000 tanks—they were 36 feet tall and described as "makeshift"—that were "similar to the one" that was leaking. The operator, Tepco, said that the tanks, which had been "meant as a temporary repository" for radioactive water, "used vulnerable rubber sealing" and that "their ability to withstand radiation was not tested." A spokesman said that "[o]nly two workers were assigned" to check the tanks "on two-hour patrols twice a day." Although the Japanese regulatory authority had told Tepco to starting moving water from the "makeshift" tanks to "better-built" ones, an authority commissioner said that the vast amount of water made it "unrealistic" to think about doing that quickly.[52] Within in a few days came a discovery of "high radioactivity at other spots near the tanks,"[53] which reportedly were "spread across at least 150 miles of the ocean bottom offshore from the plant." Although this did not seem to present worries about human health to "[e]ven the most alarmed of scientists" interviewed on the problem, findings of cesium-137 in fish caught off Fukushima were still a cause for concern, because the number of fish affected had not "dropped as quickly as expected." A researcher who was monitoring cesium said that was "no precedent for what is happening, so we are on untrodden ground."[54] There was, of course, a beneficial side to the international nuclear risk experiment. Nuclear power, putting aside the hazards that might emanate from the necessity of containing spent fuel over the long run, is a lifesaver when compared with coal. It does not generate the coal mine accidents that occasionally kill American miners and are estimated to kill six thousand Chinese miners a year. In that connection, one may note a technological irony associated with mining accidents in this country: for some time, innovative techniques—"coal cutting machines, electricity and mechanized hauling methods"—actually increased the dangers of mining.[55]

Nuclear power generation also does not cause premature deaths from illnesses in people who live in mining communities, or those who live in areas laden with pollution caused by the burning of coal. However, one of the many ways that the great nuclear experiment differs from the kind of clinical experiment overseen by IRBs is how information is dispensed to the vast numbers of people who are unwitting subjects. Michael Levi of the Council on Foreign Relations said, "[w]hen you read these arguments that pollution from coal plants costs so many thousands of lives compared to minimal or no deaths from nuclear accidents, that may be technically true, but it leaves a lot of people cold." "Experts should not say, 'Here's how you should feel about risk,'" he declared. "They should be saying, 'Here are the facts. You decide what matters to you.'"[56] That, position, at least, has some philosophical consistency. Whether ordinary people can make those determinations is another question, akin to questions about how well they can assess the risks of drugs and devices or medical procedures. With Fukushima, it was as if a widely reported series of experiments with medicines in the United States that had yielded unacceptable numbers of injuries, and had been terminated for that reason, had been repeated in Japan with even direr consequences.

Three developments bridging the years 2012 to 2014—in court, in a legislative hearing, and overseas—symbolized the difficulty of containing the continuing national, and indeed worldwide, experiment with nuclear power. On the judicial front, the Court of Appeals for the Second Circuit affirmed a decision of the district court that barred the state of Vermont from effectively shutting down the Vermont Yankee nuclear power plant. This court drew on language in a Supreme Court decision that held that the Atomic Energy Act preempted states from imposing a "state moratorium on nuclear construction grounded in safety concerns."[57] This preemption decision underlined the fact that—as we note in the concluding chapters—the law of the United States itself is a continuing experiment in the effort to minimize safety hazards. In the legislative arena, the impending retirement of five American reactors created concern about storage of spent fuel from those reactors. Senator Boxer curtly asked an NRC official, "If [moving the fuel] concerns you, then why aren't you moving now?" As a reporter noted, "a part of the problem" lay in the lack of a national repository for spent fuel.[58] The international dimensions of the subject were apparent in Russia's determination to sell reactors to other nations. An official of the state-owned nuclear company told a press conference in 2012, "[t]here is no country in which we will not be interested to build a plant." Although a spokesman for the Russian agency said that its reactor technology was the most modern available, it was reported that "some Western experts" were "dubious" about that claim.[59] A special dimension of the problem inhered in Russia's training of personnel from other countries—projected to be a "flood of foreigners" over a period of years—to run reactors.[60]

## IV. Hydrofracking: A Balance of Environmental Poisons

A very large environmental experiment in progress has featured not only factual uncertainties and arguments but also a program of balancing acts among alternative sets of costs and benefits. The experiment, at this writing most focally centered in Western Pennsylvania but proceeding nationwide, involves "hydrofracking," the industry shorthand for the drilling process of high-volume horizontal hydraulic fracturing, used to pull natural gas from sites often more than a mile below the surface of the earth. One author describes the process of "inject[ing] a fluid solvent into [a] target formation at sufficient pressure to crack the rocks," using material—usually sand ("the proppant")—to "prop the fractures open and [keep] them open." Technical innovations that "differentiated contemporary fracking from its predecessors" used "millions of gallons of fluid and thousands of tons of proppant . . . requir[ing] larger pumps on the surface."[61] The dimensions of the process are large nationwide. One estimate was that fracking was used in "90 percent of 3,400 wells drilled each year on public lands and Indian lands" and that 13,000 wells were drilled by fracking on private lands annually.[62]

The catalog of hazards from fracking is lengthy. A major concern is contamination of fresh water sources by chemicals used in the process. Reportedly, most companies drilling in Pennsylvania had "stopped sending their wastewater through treatment plants that were unable to remove many of the contaminants" before the water went into rivers.[63] As the *Times* reporter Ian Urbina described it, hydrofracking at a single well could "produce over a million gallons of wastewater that is often laced with highly corrosive salts, carcinogens like benzene and radioactive elements like radium."[64] At a hearing, Senator Benjamin Cardin asserted that the industry had "failed to meet minimal acceptable performance levels for protecting human health and the environment."[65]

By 2013, two industry groups had announced a study of radioactive material emanating from shale oil and gas sites—both those where fracking was and was not used—at the same time that the Pennsylvania Department of Environmental Protection was doing a study of its own. Symbolic of the importance of an immense deposit of natural gas that ran into Pennsylvania was the eponymous name of one of the organizations: the Marcellus Shale Coalition; the other was the Pennsylvania

Independent Oil and Gas Association. Contemporaneously, a spokesman for the Marcellus Shale Coalition criticized a report by a Duke University research team that reported on findings of radium in sediments at a discharge point of a wastewater treatment plant in the state. The Coalition spokesman was summarized as saying that the report "was based on outdated information that did not reflect current industry practices."[66]

One nuance was wrapped up in the question of just where in the process the problem lay. It was clear that gas had bubbled into water wells. And the industry had "acknowledged that fracking liquids can end up in aquifers because of failures in wells" and spills above ground, among other things. But "most drilling experts" agreed that "contamination of drinking water with fracking liquids is highly improbable," and the industry "emphasize[d] that no . . . cases exist in which the fracking process itself caused drilling liquids to contaminate drinking water." For water users, this may have been a distinction without a difference, since "both types of contamination can render . . . water unusable," although "contamination from fracking fluids is widely considered more worrisome because the fluids can contain carcinogens like benzene."[67] Moreover, there was some evidence that the improbable had come to pass in Wyoming. An EPA draft report was summarized as indicating that chemicals used in fracking in the Pavilion oil field in the state "were the likely cause of contaminated water supplies." The agency conducted the study after complaints from residents "about the smell and taste of their water." Although noting in something of an extenuation that gas wells in the Pavilion field were much shallower than was typical for fracked wells around the country, the draft report said that "the suite of chemicals found in two test wells . . . could not be explained entirely by natural processes." The "suite" included "glycols and alcohols consistent with gas production and hydraulic fracturing fluids, benzene concentrations well above Federal Safe Drinking Water Act standards, and high methane levels."[68]

Methane was of particular concern. A study by the Environmental Defense Fund concluded that "[m]ethane is 28 times more powerful than $CO_2$ as a greenhouse gas over the longer term and 84 times more potent in the short term."[69] One study found "methane in shallow water wells in the vicinity of deep shale gas wells." One writer noted that "the explicit pathway for this contamination is unknown, though poor well cementing practices are suspected." Saying that "[i]dentifying the causal pathway is a challenge," he declared that "the discovery itself poses a different problem for environmentalists concerned with contamination," namely that since some water wells have naturally occurring methane, "the more salient concern is that if methane appears from an unknown source, perhaps other toxic substances are also finding their way into drinking water supplies."[70]

Parallel to the problem of contamination, however caused, was the reduction of water in aquifers. Illustrative were concerns about diminishing water levels, complicated by drought, near Eagle Ford, a large oil field that was being developed by fracking in South Texas.[71] There were predictions that the number of wells drilled in South Texas, about two thousand around 2011, would increase to as many as twenty-five thousand over the next twenty years. Oil companies were buying, and seeking to buy, rights to water from rivers like the Rio Grande.[72] The state of North Dakota, concerned about the depletion of aquifers, threatened to sue the federal government to release water from behind a dam run by the Army Corps of Engineers, and Louisiana "passed a law to regulate . . . the industry's 'unprecedented use of enormous amounts of water,'" which, if unchecked, has the "potential for chaos and conflict."[73] A dozen local governments in California, operating in the shadow of a drought, had "voted to restrict or prohibit fracking," and sentiment grew for a statewide moratorium. A reporter noted that "fracking a single oil well in California . . . took 87 percent of the water consumed by a family of four." Illustrative of the impact of the drought was the fact that a lake that was the second-largest reservoir in the state held "only two-thirds of" its normal amount of water.[74] Opposition to fracking spread overseas. In 2014, two German ministers bypassed the regulatory plans of Chancellor Merkel's government by proposing plans that the minister for the environment, Barbara Hendricks, said would assure that "there will be no fracking for economic purposes in Germany in the near future."[75]

Another concern was the possibility that fracking could cause earthquakes; it was asserted that quakes were associated with fracking in Texas, Oklahoma, and Ohio.[76] A study published in 2014 reported an association of 2,547 small quakes in Oklahoma with a group of wastewater wells. The suggested cause was water pressure from injection wells "used to bury massive amounts of wastewater"; the theory was that "four of the state's most prolific wastewater wells could be responsible for creating a wave of pressure that crawled through the subsurface and triggered" that "swarm" of quakes.[77] A catalog of other problems included blowouts of wells, devaluation of neighboring properties, "damage to crops or livestock," and "improper transportation."[78] A summary of a book on the topic quoted the author as saying that the fracking of a single well required a "movable factory," with equipment including "trucks, pipelines, and all the other associated infrastructure." The process brought "demands on" water, waste, and manpower. These things, taken together, were what make "modern gas drilling such a disruptive force in communities."[79]

Like many episodes of long-term environmental experiments, the time frame for the acquisition of information was an extended one. In 2011, a subcommittee of the Department of Energy published recommendations for improvements in safety of fracking operations, including "better tracking and more careful disposal of . . . waste" and "stricter standards on air pollution and greenhouse gases associated with drilling," as well as the elimination of diesel fuel from fracking fluid.[80] But it was not until 2013 that a press article referred to a "comprehensive study" by the EPA on fracking and drinking water that would be "due in 2014."[81] Another dimension of the time frame appeared in the retreat by the Obama administration on a rule that would have required disclosure of chemicals used in fracking thirty days before a well could be started. The new proposed rule would require disclosure only after drilling had been completed.[82]

The major benefit trade-off that favors fracking involves the cleanness of natural gas when it is burned for energy; it does not produce the pollutants, including radioactive pollutants, that spew out of power plants that use coal—millions of tons of coal a year.[83] Although it was Urbina who made that point, something of a slantwise disagreement by another well-credentialed *New York Times* writer reflected major dimensions of the problem. Joe Nocera, defending himself against criticisms of a pro-hydrofracking column, called the deposits in the Marcellus Shale "an incredible gift" to the country.[84] This was no backyard industry—unless, as Nocera phrased it, you employed the popular phrase "Not in my backyard." Across the nation there were 493,000 active natural gas wells, about 90 percent of which had used hydrofracking. By 2011, the number of wells in Pennsylvania had almost doubled to 71,000 from the 36,000 figure a decade earlier. The climb in number of wells was even steeper—3,300 permits issued for Marcellus wells in Pennsylvania in 2010, compared with 117 in 2007.[85]

The "benefits-side economics" of fracking intensified the controversy. With respect to global oil economics, Daniel Yergin, the chair of an energy research firm, said that the shale oil production of U.S. wells would be "like adding another Venezuela or Kuwait."[86] More locally, the population of Carrizo Springs, near the Eagle Ford field in South Texas, had doubled in two years, with an increase in sales tax revenue to the country expected to exceed the total over the five previous years. One study predicted that the boom would support sixty-eight thousand jobs.[87]

Fracking activity also brought definite gifts to the Pennsylvania economy, including "thousands of jobs" and "five-figure windfalls for residents who lease[d] their land to drillers" as well as revenue for the hard-pressed state treasury. But hydrofracking has caused at least one episode that bordered on a public health emergency—pollution of Pittsburgh-area drinking water by a combination of "drilling and coal-mine waste" that "overwhelmed" the Monongahela River, prompting an alert to citizens to drink bottled water. An internal EPA memorandum called the episode "one of the largest failures in U.S. history to supply clean drinking water to the public." There was a special irony in the combination of drilling waste and waste from the alternative energy source of coal mining.[88]

One disturbing statistic uncovered was radium levels in wastewater that "were hundred of times" the drinking water standard set by the EPA. To be sure, radioactivity in wastewater could "be blocked by thin barriers, including skin," so, as Urbina summarized it, direct "exposure is generally harmless." The dangerous path of entry was through the food chain: Studies indicated that "once radium enters a person's body, by eating, drinking or breathing," it could "cause cancer and other health problems."[89]

There were two stumbling blocks: insufficient resources for officials to do the regulatory job and, in at least one segment of the problem, the fact that the only regulation was self-regulation by drillers. Urbina quoted an inspector with the Pennsylvania EPA as saying, "We simply can't keep up . . . There's just too much of the waste." Identifying a related problem was his lament that more stringent regulation might cause drillers to "just stop reporting their mistakes." Specifically with respect to spills, the practice was self-policing—producers "report their own spills, write their own spill response plans and lead their own cleanup efforts." Urbina's report of a review of response plans at four drilling sites in Pennsylvania indicated that the plans "often appear to be in violation of the law."[90]

Lax regulation in the real world called into question Nocera's defensive reaction to criticism of his pro-hydrofracking posture. He observed that "every problem associated with drilling for natural gas is solvable." In particular, he declared, "Strong state regulation will help ensure environmentally safe wells," quoting the hydrofracking critic Abraham Lustgarten on the idea that "while the environmental issues were real, they 'can be readily addressed by the employment of best drilling practices, technological investment, and rigorous regulatory oversight.'"[91]

Complaints about Urbina's reporting on fracking stimulated a response from the public editor of the *New York Times*, Arthur Brisbane. He focused on controversy about an article in which Urbina reviewed "hundreds of industry e-mails and internal documents" and analyzed "data from thousands of wells," finding questions about "whether companies are intentionally, and even illegally, overstating the productivity of their wells and the size of their reserves." Urbina quoted an energy analyst as saying that "the word in the world of independents [independent gas producers] is that the shale plays are just a giant Ponzi scheme and the economics just do not work," and a "retired geologist from a major oil and gas company" as saying that "these corporate giants are having an Enron moment."[92] Urbina and a deputy national editor of the paper had stressed that the article was on "independents" rather than major oil companies, although the first words in the article were a reference to "natural gas companies" generally. Brisbane said he thought that "such a pointed article needed more convincing substantiation, more space for a reasoned explanation of the other side and more clarity about its focus." The national editor of the paper responded that the article was "deeply sourced, meticulously reported and measured, and we would not change a word."[93]

Inevitably, as arguments continued about public policy issues at the level of regulation and politics, fracking issues seeped into the courts. A reported decision by a Pennsylvania federal court refused to dismiss several counts of a complaint alleging that fracking and "other natural gas production activities" had unleashed toxics onto the plaintiffs' land and into their groundwater. One count that the court refused to dismiss alleged that the defendant's activities were "abnormally dangerous," which would impose a form of liability beyond negligence—that is, strict liability. Although there was no established state law on the doctrine, the court said it thought it "improvident to automatically" exempt such activities from strict liability "without more thorough consideration."[94] The court also refused to dismiss counts based on allegations that in addition to causing physical sickness, the defendant's activities had caused "fear of future illness and . . . emotional distress."[95] Moreover, it denied a motion to strike on claims based on violations of statutes including the Hazardous Sites Cleanup Act.[96]

Injuries to workers from fracking also entered the picture. In 2012, three unions urged OSHA to reduce risks to workers engaged in fracking operations. They particularly urged the Mine Safety and Health Administration to "evaluate mines and quarries that process silica for use" in fracking, following a report by the National Institute for Occupational Safety and Health indicating that breathing zone samples for fracking workers showed high levels of exposure to silica dust. The unions referred to "massive" amounts of sand used in various stages of the fracking process.[97]

By 2013 a worker suit had come to federal court, ascribing a range of health problems to exposure to chemicals and silica. This litigation had an interesting legal feature, because it was not a traditional tort suit. Rather, it sought to use an exception to the general rule of the West Virginia workers' compensation law, which ordinarily does not permit tort suits by workers covered by the law but does allow them when they allege that an employer's culpable conduct was intentional.[98] An opinion by the court rejected the testimony of an expert proffered by the plaintiff, in part on the ground that the methodology used by the expert did not meet the evidentiary standards for causation testimony in cases involving chemical exposure.[99] The court did conclude that there was evidence of the plaintiff's exposure to a particular chemical.[100] However, it rejected his claim, based on the idea that because he was at risk for "contracting a serious latent disease," there should be medical monitoring of his condition—a staple element of plaintiffs' complaints in fracking cases.[101] The court noted, among other things, that the plaintiff's experts had "formed their opinions without knowing any information" about the chemical allegedly involved or "the nature and intensity of plaintiff's exposure."[102]

One should note that although there have been suits for chemical exposures of workers in fracking-related activities, a rise in worker injuries appeared to have been principally the product of vehicle accidents in the industry. An insurance executive said that the root of the problem lay in the fatigue of inexperienced drivers of trucks, who worked long hours carrying water and salt used in drilling operations.[103]

The story of fracking, oil-slick- and chemical-ridden as it is, will continue indefinitely, and as it continues, it will illustrate the complexity of large-scale environmental experiments. All kinds of interests are in competition—sometimes interests that are in competition within themselves—and they compete in many forums. Those forums include naked politics, regulatory agencies, and courts. The diverse economic interests obviously include the stakes for companies that drill. But they also include indirect rivalries between consumers and property owners who suffer direct physical injuries and damage to land from fracking but who also may be indirect beneficiaries of overall economies achieved by fracking. One set of competitions that sometimes involves grim ironies arises from, on the one hand, social choices that effectively allow fracking and, on the other hand, choices for more nuclear power plants. More nuclear plants will reduce the carbon load on the atmosphere, unless or until a meltdown claims lives and property that would otherwise be subject to the hazards of fracking. Complicating all of this is the problem of access to information, illustrated by the proposed rule that would require that information be given to the public about fracking chemicals only after drilling is completed. Further overlaying this complex policy landscape is the uncertainty that afflicts even companies that have substantial amounts of information about hazards but still face various kinds of unpredictability—about benefits as well as risks.

* * *

All kinds of experimentation involve human beings trying to do things better—sometimes for personal satisfaction, sometimes for fame, sometimes for personal profit. Society is well-off in terms of utility, conventionally measured, when any one of these motives produces net gains. But optimism about the effectiveness of regulation must confront strong concerns about the political reality of hydrofracking for natural gas. Reading optimistic comments gives one the sense that he has seen this movie before. As in some other areas of large environmental experiments, the game is one of catch-up, in a political environment whose parameters are significantly defined by the existence of a technology that pushes forward with few controls. The notably idealistic model of the scientists who strived to identify and limit the potential dangers of recombinant DNA research[104] is not apparent. Moreover, the environmental context of fracking, and indeed that of nuclear power, lack—for example—the rigor of the FDA's process for reviewing drugs and devices. The experimental society needs mechanisms that enable government to get out in front of problems identified with all kinds of experimentation.

## Notes

1. *Allen v. United States*, 588 F. Supp. 247, 370 (D. Utah 1984).
2. See ibid., pp. 266–329.
3. Ibid., p. 337.
4. Ibid., p. 338.
5. Ibid., p. 356.
6. Ibid., p. 375.
7. Ibid., p. 403.
8. Ibid., p. 404.
9. *Allen v. United States*, 816 F.2d 1417, 1421 (10th Cir. 1987).
10. Ibid., p. 1423–24.
11. Ibid., p. 1427 (McKay, J., concurring).
12. Ibid., p. 1424.
13. "Report of the President's Commission on the Accident at Three Mile Island" (1979), p. 1, reprinted in "Report of the President's Commission on the Three Mile Island Accident, Joint Hearing before the Subcommittee on Nuclear Regulation of the Senate Committee on Environment and Public Works and the Subcommittee on Energy and the Environment of the House Committee on Interior and Insular Affairs," Serial No. 96-H34 (Oct. 13, 1979), beginning at p. 80 [hereafter President's Commission].
14. Hearing, supra, at 1 (Senator Gary Hart).
15. Ibid., p. 9–10 (testimony of Darrell Eisenhut).
16. Report to the United States Senate by the Subcommittee on Nuclear Regulation for the Senate Committee on Environment and Public Works, "Nuclear Accident and Recovery at Three Mile Island: A Special Investigation" (1980), p. 35.
17. Eisenhut testimony, supra note 15.
18. Senate Subcommittee Report, supra note 16, pp. 37–38.
19. U.S. NRC, "Backgrounder on the Three Mile Island Accident," printed from the Internet, May 12, 2011.
20. Senate Subcommittee Report, supra note 16, p. 38.
21. U.S. NRC, supra note 19.
22. Ibid.
23. President's Commission, supra note 13, pp. 8–9.
24. Ibid., p. 10.
25. Ibid., pp. 12–13.
26. Ibid., p. 18. For a full catalog of these shortcomings, see ibid., p. 58.
27. Ibid., pp. 19–20.
28. Ibid., p. 27.
29. Ibid., p. 39.
30. Ibid., pp. 68–69.
31. President's Commission, supra note 13, p. 12.
32. Steve Wing et al., "A Reevaluation of Cancer Incidence Near the Three Mile Island Nuclear Plant: The Collision of Evidence and Assumptions," 105 *Env'l Health Perspectives* 52, 52 (1997) (abstract).
33. Ibid., p. 56.
34. Ibid., p. 57, citing M. C. Hatch et al., "Cancer near the Three Mile Island Nuclear Plant: Radiation Emissions," 132 *Am. J. Epidemiol.* 397 (1990);

M. C. Hatch et al., "Cancer Rates after the Three Mile Island Nuclear Accident and Proximity of Residence to the Plant," 81 *Am. J. Public Health* 7199 (1991).

35. Ibid.
36. Norimitsu Onishi and James Glanz, "Nuclear Rules in Japan Relied on Old Science," *New York Times*, March 27, 2011, pp. A1 and A11.
37. Ibid., quoting Peter Yanev.
38. See Robert B. Leflar et al., "Human Flotsam, Legal Fallout: Japan's Tsunami and Nuclear Meltdown," 27 *J Env'l Law & Litig.* 107, 108–10 (2012).
39. Ibid.
40. Steven Mufson, "NRC Transcripts on Japan Crisis Offer Insights," *Washington Post*, Feb. 22, 2012, p. A6.
41. Ryan Tracy, "Disaster-Readiness Flaws Found at Nuclear Plants," *Wall Street Journal* online, May 12, 2011.
42. Beth Daley, Problems cited with nuclear power backup, Boston Globe, May 13, 2011, http://www.boston.com/news/science/articles/2011/05/13/
43. Stephen Power and Rebecca Smith, "Nuclear Plant Safety Proposals Put on Fast Track," *Wall Street Journal*, July 17, 2011.
44. Matthew L. Wald, "N.R.C. Lowers Estimate of How Many Would Die in Meltdown," *New York Times*, July 30, 2011 (some questions for reporter's text).
45. John P. Cristodouleas et al., "Short-Term and Long-Term Health Risks of Nuclear-Power-Plant Accidents," 364 *N. Eng. J. Med.* 2234, 2238 (2011).
46. Ibid., p. 2234.
47. Hiroko Tabuchi, "Independent Panel Challenges Japan's Account of Disaster at Nuclear Plant," *New York Times*, Jan. 16, 2012, p. B3.
48. Martin Fackler, "Nuclear Disaster in Japan Was Avoidable, Critics Contend," *New York Times*, March 1, 2012, p. A4.
49. Hiroko Tabuchi, "Japan Panel Cites Failure in Tsunami," *New York Times*, Dec. 27, 2011, p. A8.
50. Hiroko Tabuchi, "Inquiry Concludes That Nuclear Crisis in Japan Was a 'Man-Made Disaster,'" *New York Times*, July 8, 2012, p. A9.
51. Hiroko Tabuchi, "Tank Has Leaked Tons of Contaminated Water at Japan Nuclear Site," *New York Times*, Aug. 21, 2013, p. A8.
52. Hiroko Tabuchi, "Nuclear Operator Raises Alarm on Crisis," *New York Times*, Aug. 24, 2013, p. A4.
53. Martin Fackler, "Errors Cast Doubt on Japan's Nuclear Cleanup," *New York Times*, Sept. 4, 2013, pp. A1 and A8.
54. Martin Fackler and Hiroko Tabuchi, "With a Plant's Tainted Water Still Flowing, No End to Environmental Fears," *New York Times*, Oct. 25, 2013, p. A6.
55. See David Rosner and Gerald Markowitz (eds.), *Dying for Work: Workers' Safety and Health in Twentieth-Century America* (Indiana Univ. Press, 1968), p. 68.
56. John M. Broder et al., "When All Isn't Enough to Stop a Catastrophe," *New York Times*, March 29, 2011, pp. D1 and D4.
57. *Energy Nuclear Vermont Yankee v. Shumlin*, 733 F3d 393, 422 (2d Cir. 2013), quoting *Pacific Gas & Elec. Co. v. State Energy Resources Conservation & Development Comm'n*, 461 U.S. 190, 213 (1983).

58. Matthew Wald, "Panel Questions Experts On Closed Reactor Risks," *New York Times*, May 15, 2014, p. A19.
59. See Eve Conant, "Russia's New Empire: Nuclear Power," *Scientific American*, Oct. 2013, pp. 88 and 90.
60. See ibid., p. 93.
61. Timothy Fitzgerald, "Frackonomics: Some Economics of Hydraulic Fracturing," 63 *Case W. Res. L. Rev.* 1337, 1339–40 (2013).
62. See John Broder, "New Rule Requires Disclosure of Drilling Chemicals, But Only After Their Use," *New York Times*, May 5, 2012, p. A13.
63. See Robbie Brown and Ian Urbina, "Panel Seeks Stiff Rules For Drilling Of Gas Wells," *New York Times*, Aug. 11, 2011, p. A12.
64. See Ian Urbina, "Regulation Lax as Gas Wells' Tainted Water Hits River," *New York Times*, Feb. 27, 2011, p. A1.
65. Robbie Brown, "Senators Question Safety of Water Used in Gas Drilling," *New York Times*, April 13, 2011, p. A15.
66. Alan Kovski, "Study Announced on Radioactive Material Associated with Pennsylvania Shale Gas, Oil," 43 *O.S.H. Rep.* 1066–67 (Nov. 7, 2013).
67. Ian Urbina, "A Tainted Water Well, and Concern That There May Be More," *New York Times*, Aug. 4, 2011, pp. A13 and A17.
68. Kirk Johnson, "E.P.A. Links Tainted Water in Wyoming to Hydraulic Fracturing for Natural Gas," *New York Times*, Dec. 9, 2011, p. A19.
69. See Joe Nocera, "Fracking's Achilles Heel," *New York Times*, November 9, 2013, p. A23 (commending Colorado rules for regulation of methane leakage from fracked wells).
70. Fitzgerald, supra note 61, pp. 1357–58.
71. See Clifford Krauss, "Oil Hidden in Shale Sets Off a Boom in Texas," *New York Times*, May 28, 2011.
72. See Russell Gold and Ana Compoy, "Oil's Growing Thirst For Water," *Wall Street Journal*, Dec. 6, 2011, pp. A1 and A12.
73. See ibid.
74. Norimitsu Onishi, "California's Thirst Shapes Debate Over Fracking," *New York Times*, May 15, 2014, pp. A14 and A19.
75. Melissa Eddy, "Worries About Environment Prompt German Proposal to Sharply Curtail Fracking," *New York Times*, July 5, 2014, p. B5.
76. See Douglas McLeod, "Deep Trouble?" *Business Insider*, Feb. 25, 2013, pp. 13–14.
77. See Eric Hand, "Injection Wells Blamed in Oklahoma Earthquakes," 345 *Science* no. 6192, pp. 13–14 (2014).
78. See Huhnsik Chung and Gregory Hoffnagle, "The Risks of Hydrofracking," *Risk Management*, June 2011, pp. 32–33.
79. Scott Dodd, "Hard Facts About Fracking: Review of Russell Gold, *The Boom* (Simon & Schuster)," *Onearth*, Summer 2014, pp. 56–57.
80. See Brown and Urbina, supra note 63.
81. See McLeod, supra note 76.
82. See Broder, supra note 62.
83. See Ian Urbina, supra note 51, pp. A22–23.
84. Joe Nocera, "About My Support for Natural Gas," *New York Times*, April 16, 2011, p. A17.
85. Ibid., p. A22.

86. See Krauss, supra note 71.
87. See Gold and Campoy, supra note 72.
88. Urbina, supra note 63.
89. Ibid.
90. Ibid.
91. Nocera, supra, note 64.
92. Ian Urbina, "Insiders Sound an Alarm Amid a Natural Gas Rush," *New York Times*, June 25, 2011.
93. See Arthur Brisbane, "Clashing Views on the Future of Natural Gas," *New York Times*, July 17, 2011, Review section, p. 10.
94. *Fiorentino v. Cabot Oil & Gas Corp.*, 750 F. Supp.2d 506, 512 (M.D. Pa. 2010).
95. See ibid., pp. 514–15.
96. See ibid., pp. 515–16.
97. Greg Hellman, "Unions Urge Federal Safety, Health Agency to Protect Workers from Fracking Hazards," 42 *O.S.H. Rep.* 472 (May 24, 2012).
98. "Fracking Worker's Lawsuit Over Allegedly Unsafe Working Conditions Will Go to Trial," 43 *O.S.H. Rep.* 195 (Feb. 28, 2013).
99 See *Bombardiere v. Schlumberger Technology Corp.*, 934 F. Supp.2d 843, 846-51 (N.D.W. Va. 2013).
100. See ibid., p. 852.
101. See for example Rodd Zolkos, "Fracking Risks Keep Evolving as Regulatory, Legal Landscape Changes," *Business Insurance*, March 3, 2014, p. 14.
102. See 934 F. Supp.2d at 851–52.
103. See Stephanie Goldberg, "Fracking, Oil Boom Cause Spike in Energy Industry Workplace Deaths," *Business Insurance*, July 7, 2014, p. 14.
104. See supra, Chapter One.

# 3

# Established Products and Activities

For readers or viewers of media—casual or serious—it must seem that hovering above the landscape of products and activities is a grim-eyed Grinch, a critic who wants to deprive us of the most everyday pleasures. This grumbling person seems to have a mission to convince us that a large number of things that are good in life, even things that are designed to combat illness and pain, may not be good for you. Just the list of easily available products appears endless, from desserts to toothpastes, from diet supplements to pretty colors on foods. This chapter examines several cases in diverse product areas, and in one case a medical test, referring to such subthemes as lack of information about risk and underreporting of injuries.

A symbolic example of the self-administered substance that draws critical fire is the category of dietary supplement pills, for which particular marketing targets are older people. Herbal supplements and other "natural health products" generated $14 billion in sales in 2007.[1] Testimony at a 2010 hearing of the Senate's Special Committee on Aging underlined risks, lack of information about risks, and finger-pointing among sellers. One problem lay in the marketing of dietary supplements. Greg Kutz, an investigator for the Government Accountability Office, testified about a study in which he and his colleagues posed "as fictitious elderly consumers" who made phone calls "across the country" and in-store visits in the DC area and in Florida, as well as "evaluat[ing] claims made on Web sites and in other written materials."[2]

Reporting on "deceptive marketing practices" for products that were focused on the elderly, the GAO investigator referred to some "more alarming" news as "dangerous medical advice." Just illustrative of this advice was the assertion in marketing materials for garlic capsules that the product "prevents and cures cancer," not to mention that it "prevents the common cold, obesity, and diabetes." A ginseng product was promoted for "reduc[ing] brain damage from a stroke" and "treat[ing] Lou Gehrig's disease." A technical legal point was that the products, none of which had FDA approval, violated a prohibition on marketing "as a treatment or cure for specific disease" without that approval. Especially disturbing was advice that interfered with regular medical regimes—for example, that one could substitute garlic for prescription medicine used for high blood pressure. Moreover, those who followed advice to take ginkgo with daily aspirin opened themselves to an increased risk of the bleeding that can come with aspirin use.[3] One expert quoted at the hearing, Dr. Arthur Grollman, a professor of medicine and pharmacology at Stony Brook, declared that "interactions between herbal products and prescription or over-the-counter drugs constitutes one of the greatest risk posed by the use of botanical medicines."[4]

An industry representative himself expressed anger about late-night commercials for the products, which he said "made [his] blood boil." Steven Mister, the president and CEO of the Council for Responsible Nutrition, responded to a question by Senator Kohl about what the industry could to "to ensure that your blood doesn't boil and you don't have to take excessive dietary supplements" by describing a program for restraining irresponsible advertising claims. After a review of advertisements for "veracity" and a failure by sellers to change the ads, he said, an industry group would refer the case to the FTC, which tended to give "high priority" to such cases.[5]

It was not clear, however, what percentage of deceptive and harmful promotions would be captured by this program. The effects of these efforts might well be dwarfed by an FDA estimate of an annual total of "50,000 adverse events . . . related to dietary supplements," with Charles Bell of Consumers Union pointing out that there were only 900 reports of "serious events" to the FDA in the year preceding the hearing.[6] Mr. Bell noted that in 1995, *Consumer Reports* had published a list of "five supplements that according to the FDA can cause serious harm to consumers." It took nine years for one, ephedra, to be removed from the market, "many years after the FDA had received reports" on "deaths and serious injuries" from the product. At the time of the hearing, the other four products remained in stores.[7] A quite different concern to which Mr. Bell referred, which intersects with a mass experiment that is growing exponentially, was the report that "44 dietary supplement products that claim to contain nano-particles were on the market." He noted that "the FDA has little information about . . .such products," and there were "serious questions" about their safety.[8] Interestingly, yet another problem was insufficient content of advertised materials. One witness testified that 46 percent of herbal supplements tested "contained less than their expected amounts of key compounds."[9]

It was not just older people who were vulnerable to the risks of the supplements. Joshua Sharfstein, deputy commissioner of the FDA, said that the problem that gave the agency "the most concern" related to "the pharmaceutical spiking of dietary supplements," which carried "very serious risks and injuries." He said that "often" victims were "young people who don't really understand and they're—that they're taking what are actually prescription drugs or steroids through dietary supplements."[10] A problem in comprehension for a variety of consumers was that a "standard FDA disclaimer" might not be understood. One critic said that distinctions made in the disclaimers "can be confusing to consumers." He gave as an illustration consumers who did not have enough information "to separate body-function statements like "boosts brain function" from "specific . . . indications" that would pertain to a particular problem, like preventing Alzheimer's disease.[11]

## The Case of Caffeine

Coffee is a product that has been with us for centuries. It provides pleasure (although one this writer cannot understand) to many millions. Could it possibly be classified as a dangerous product? If it could, that would be due to caffeine, an embedded substance in the drink that many coffee lovers swallow. And caffeine is pervasive in the economy of ingestion—not only a "natural ingredient in coffees, chocolates, and teas," but also in "sports drinks," the herbal supplements we have been discussing that are labeled "high performance," and painkillers.[12]

In the case of caffeine, the population of the United States appears as a vast laboratory of experimental animals without the cages. Often the experiments turn out well; sometimes they do not. "Widely available, cheap, and fast-acting," caffeine taken in moderation "can improve intellectual and athletic performance"[13] and can have positive health effects, in various quantities possibly reducing the risk of diabetes, gallstone disease, and colorectal cancer.[14] However, it also stimulates a catalog of adverse effects, being associated with headaches, irritability, palpitations and sleep disorders, and "mimic[k]ing or contribut[ing]" to "a number of psychiatric and behavioral disorders" in children, including "anxiety neuroses, ADHD [and] eating disorders."[15] A special concern is the effect of caffeine as a "gateway drug" that "may sensitize users, especially children, to the reinforcing effects of all stimulants, increasing their risks for drug and alcohol abuse."[16] Another problem is the association of "caffeinated soft drinks and other beverages" with "increases in childhood obesity,"[17] which may be linked to the twinning for "millions of Americans" of the consumption of caffeinated drinks with the eating of fast food.[18] The list of adverse effects also includes physiological and psychological dependence—and withdrawal symptoms when people stop using caffeinated products, with the strung-out consequence that people do not want to stop using those products because of their apprehension about withdrawal symptoms.[19]

Feeding the national appetite for caffeine are national promotional campaigns, in particular for soft drinks, with eight of the top ten carbonated drinks being caffeinated.[20] It was only around 1920 that makers of caffeinated soft drinks stopped emphasizing their "stimulant qualities," which occurred only when "the federal government investigated the use of caffeine in soft drinks."[21]

There is a striking historical parallel between those drinks and the vogue for cocaine that continued into the early years of the twentieth century. In some previous research on cocaine, I found that the substance could so easily be purchased that in a Philadelphia drugstore in 1903, "regular customers would hold up one finger for "a five-cent powder; two fingers ten cents worth; three fifteen cents, and so on."[22] The attraction of the very name is evident in the fact that one manufacturer named a high-caffeine energy drink "Cocaine" and changed the name to "Censured" only when the FDA issued a warning in 2007.[23]

A basic difficulty for the law in getting a grip on the hazards of caffeine lies in its legal classification. The FDA classifies caffeine as a food, both in foods and beverages that contain it naturally and as an additive; specifically it is "generally recognized as safe when used in cola-type beverages in accordance with good manufacturing practice."[24] By contrast, it has been noted that because dietary supplements are regulated by the Dietary Supplement Health and Education Act rather than the Food, Drug, and Cosmetic Act, sellers of products containing caffeine can "effectively evade FDA regulations" by marketing them as dietary supplements.[25] A further striation in the layers of regulation concerning caffeine resides in the FDA's limitations on the amount of caffeine per dose in over-the-counter pain medicines. As one writer has pointed out, this "tripartite regulatory scheme" has some odd results—for example, the FDA requires pain medications using more than 100 milligrams of caffeine per dose to carry warning labels, but an energy drink with 160 milligrams of caffeine need not provide a warning.[26]

## The Delectable Case of Sugar

Occupying a neighboring peak of critics' concern about things we eat and drink is one of the oldest reliable consumer pleasures: sugar. In a fairly well-established vocabulary, "sugar" means sucrose—beet and cane sugar, from which high-fructose corn syrup, a nutritional culprit for many critics, is often distinguished. For a time, "high-fructose corn syrup was portrayed by the food industry as a healthful alternative" to sugar, even though, as a one writer says, "the two sweeteners are effectively identical in their biological effects," with the chemical difference being that high-fructose corn syrup has a higher percentage of fructose than does refined sugar, in which the glucose is bonded to a molecule of fructose.[27] At least in laboratory animals, when substantial quantities of fructose come into the liver, much of them will be converted to fat. There is evidence that this produces insulin resistance, "which is now considered the fundamental problem in obesity" as well as contributing to heart disease and type 2 diabetes.[28] When one ties these effects with those of caffeine just discussed, many sugar products, especially soft drinks, begin to sound hazardous to health.

Although these purported linkages sound forbidding, the underlying story is one that repeats itself: the lack of certainty about where pleasure merges into dangers to health. In 2010 an Institute of Medicine study underlined a conclusion from a 2005 report that "there is a lack of scientific agreement about the amount of sugars that can be consumed in a healthy diet."[29] The repetitive theme is that, as to the question of how much sugar in how many doses becomes unsafe, one writer says, "We're unlikely to learn anything conclusive in the near future."[30] With sugar, as with many other consumer pleasures, the question is how much tolerance one has for uncertain hazards.

## Bisphenol A

Timid consumers, especially those with children, might be forgiven for thinking that some media were committed to producing a "risk of the month." Beginning around 2005 the chemical bisphenol A (BPA) achieved that status during many months, rather like a novel that moves back and forth on high places on bestseller lists for books. The chemical had many applications in consumer products, from sippy cups to soup cans to corrective lenses, and including dental sealants and water bottles.[31] An important 2005 article built on research that had begun to appear in the late 1990s. The lead author, Frederick vom Saal of the University of Missouri, noted that when he wrote, there were "109 published studies . . . that report significant effects of low doses of BPA in experimental animals, with many adverse effects occurring at blood levels in animals within and below average blood levels in humans." He also said that forty studies had reported "effects below the current reference dose of 50µg/kg [per] day that is still assumed to be safe by the US-EPA and US-EPA in complete disregard of the published findings."[32]

Vom Saal's summary of the "low-dose" literature indicated that "in many tissues in many species, BPA is a chemical with a much higher estrogenic potency than has been acknowledged by chemical corporations and regulatory agencies, since BPA elicits a wide range of effects at doses many orders of magnitude below doses previously predicted to cause no effect."[33] He referred to some "intriguing studies" that suggested that, "in addition to acting as a relatively potent environmental estrogen, BPA can cause some unique types of toxic effects through, as yet, unknown molecular mechanisms." There were, for example, reports "indicating the potential to disrupt thyroid hormone action" and even that "very low part per trillion doses of BPA . . . cause proliferation of human prostate cancer cells," "although higher doses in the part per billion range are without effect."[34]

Vom Saal criticized the EPA in particular for ignoring a recommendation by the National Toxicology Panel to revisit "the current testing paradigm used for assessments of reproductive and environmental toxicity."[35] If there was an edge to his references to federal agencies, there was even more of an edge in his reference to "11 published studies that were funded by the chemical industry, 100% of which conclude that BPA causes no significant effects,"[36] and to his cutting comments on some prior studies. He instanced what he called "misrepresentation[s]" by the American Chemical Council of some research studies that did not find significant adverse effects.[37] In another publication, he referred to "fatal" and "obvious" "flaws" in the latter studies.[38] Acknowledging that there were, "as yet, relatively little published data on human health effects related to exposure to BPA," he noted "two epidemiological studies showing a relationship between blood levels of BPA and ovarian disease and recurrent miscarriage." He concluded that "the weight of evidence based on examination of the published studies concerning low-dose effects of BPA in experimental animals demonstrates the need for a re-evaluation of the prior estimate of the acceptable level of daily human exposure to BPA."[39]

There were reports, or allegations, of many kinds of harmful effects of BPA on the body. A "consensus statement" of a number of scientists, issued in 2006, said that the chemical was causing "organizational changes . . . in the prostate, breast, testis, mammary glands, body size, brain structure and chemistry, and behavior of laboratory animals."[40] Reportedly, animal studies indicated that "exposure during fetal growth affects the development of reproductive systems and, in offspring, can lead to neurological problems."[41] A hypothesized impact of BPA was that it had a "weakly estrogenic" effect,[42] with carcinogenic potential. This inevitably led to a familiar argument about unmerited fright over low dosages of chemicals. The argument stemmed from episodes of the feeding of large dosages of chemicals to laboratory animals, with industry representatives emphasizing that evidence that rats and mice were developing cancer from big quantities was not at all probative of the effects of small doses on human beings. Yet, with respect to BPA, Jerrold Heindel, an expert on the effects of environmental chemicals at the National Institutes of Environmental Health Sciences, pointed out that there could be injurious effects from multiple chemicals with those effects: "If you're being exposed to two-hundred fifty chemicals and only thirty of them have estrogenic activity, but they're each very low, still, thirty of them might add up to be significant."[43]

Reports began to come in about the storage of BPA in the body. The chemical made it to the top of the European hit parade of dangerous substances in 2012 with the publication of what was described as the "first systematic European Union study of chemical in human bodies," which found "traces" of BPA, phthalates—chemicals used as a softening agent in plastics—and triclosan, to be discussed later in this chapter, in "the great majority of people surveyed."[44]

The next year a study in the journal *Pediatrics* reported findings that there were concentrations of BPA in the urine of infants in a neonatal intensive care unit (NICU) that were "16-to-32-fold higher" "in comparison with children in the general population or healthy infants." Given that "respiratory devices were associated with higher urinary BPA concentrations," the investigators wrote that their findings "suggest that medical devices were an important source of BPA exposure for these infants." They did note that these concentrations "were still below" the EPA reference dose (RfD)—that is, the dose "below which no adverse health effects should result from a lifetime of exposure." At the same time, they pointed out there was "ongoing controversy regarding potential health risks of low-dose (ie, below RfD) exposures to BPA" and urged "additional research into other potential determinants in the NICU including the microenvironment of the isolette."[45] There also was evidence that another "estrogen-mimic" like BPA, a flame retardant with the acronym PBB, could cause premature puberty. One study, which followed the accidental contamination of grain, concluded that daughters of women who had eaten and drunk meat and milk containing the substance had "started menstruating earlier than their peers."[46]

A special problem in the world of experimentation on consumers arises when sellers market substitutes for products that have come under suspicion. The problem is that there may be no telling what hazards the substitutes present. As one observer has noted, manufacturers can introduce many chemicals without adequate tests for safety. Specifically with respect to BPA, she observes that a manufacturer can replace that chemical "with another untested compound and get a few years' use out of it before it, too, becomes the subject of health alerts of media attention," with the result that "entire generations" could be affected by harmful side effects.[47]

BPA had become one of the flavors of the decade for consumers concerned about hazards of newer products. The FDA cautiously entered the field of cautionary statements with an "update" published in January 2010. Referring to "recent studies using novel approaches to test for subtle effects," the agency noted "some concern about the potential effects of BPA on the brain, behavior, and prostate gland in fetuses, infants and young children." The sense of an experiment being carried out on consumers in plain sight was evident in the agency's announcement that with the National Toxicology Program of the National Institutes of Health, it was "carrying out in-depth studies to answer key questions and clarify uncertainties about the risks of BPA." Among the "reasonable steps" the FDA said it was taking "to reduce human exposure to BPA in the food supply," it mentioned "supporting industry actions to stop producing BPA-containing baby bottles and infant feeding cups" for the U.S. market.[48]

The FDA's caution about caution was evident in a statement indicating that, as a reporter summarized it, "there was no proof that BPA was dangerous to humans." Sharfstein, the FDA deputy commissioner, said, "If we thought it was unsafe, we would be taking strong regulatory action."[49] A technical legal limitation on the FDA's power was the fact that BPA was classified in the food and drug legislation as a "food additive," a category that makes it complicated to strengthen safety regulations. Dr. Sharfstein said he hoped that the substance could be put into the statutory pigeonhole of "food contact substance," which would give the agency more power and flexibility to regulate it.[50]

Symbolizing the incremental accumulation of data on products on the market was a report in April 2011 that BPA was a skin sensitizer. This was the conclusion on "the weight of the evidence" by the National Institute for Occupational Safety and Health (NIOSH) in a "Skin Notation Profile," which gave the chemical the designation of SK-SEN, which means a "skin notation indicating the potential for immune-mediated reactions following exposure of the skin."[51] Illustrating the fineness of the distinctions involved in the categorization of effects is the study's conclusion that "BPA has limited or no potential of causing direct effects of the skin, including corrosion and irritation."[52] For that reason, the profile did not assign to the chemical the notation of SK-DIR, a notation "indicating the potential for direct effects to the skin following contact with a chemical."

The FDA continued to be in the center of a battleground over the chemical. In March 2012, it denied a citizens' petition for a ban of BPA from food-contact chemicals, although mentioning an "updated safety review" yet to come.[53] The American Chemistry Council, an industry group that represents makers of BPA, asked the agency to ban BPA in plastic baby bottles and sippy cups, a "formal recognition" that "the U.S. marketplace already [had] abandoned those uses," and the FDA adopted such a rule. This being functionally a meaningless action, Consumers Union had urged a ban that extended to food contact materials used by children, ranging from pacifiers to child-sized bowls and including various materials used in breast pumping.[54] But the agency rejected a petition by Congressman Markey to ban the chemical from a number of products, including small, reusable food and beverage containers and coatings for canned foods and beverages.[55] The war carried forward on various fronts. One of these was civil litigation, although a defense lawyer said that defeats to plaintiffs in some lawsuits signaled that few suits would "be filed anytime soon." At the same time, the lawyer said, "consumer marketing pressures" were "encouraging manufacturers to find alternative chemicals."[56]

As debate proceeded in the United States about the risks of BPA, concern about the product had spread to Europe. The European Union had banned its use in baby bottles, and there had been what a reporter termed "more wide-ranging bans on polycarbonate plastics used for food packaging" in countries including France and Switzerland. By 2014 the Risk Assessment Committee of the European Chemicals Agency had given its support to a French proposal to classify the chemical as a "category 1B reproductive toxicant" because of its potential effects on fertility, a category that would classify it as a "substance of very high concern."[57]

In the low-lighted background of the BPA controversy was a consumer product that was even more ubiquitous and carried the special quality of being promoted as a preventive to disease. This was triclosan, a product used to combat bacterial contamination that is used in clothing, kitchenware, toys, and a variety of skin-contact products including antibacterial soaps, mouthwashes, shaving creams, and deodorants. Although not featured in the media as much as BPA, triclosan provides an interesting symbol of controversy, including uncertainty, about a consumer experiment in plain sight.

In April 2010 the FDA published a "consumer update" with a balancing act. The document said, "triclosan is not currently known to be hazardous to humans." However, it noted that "animal studies have shown that triclosan alters hormone regulation" but at the same time pointed out that animal studies did not "always predict effects in humans" and said that "several scientific studies . . . merit[ed] further review" of the product." A positive finishing touch was a reference to "clear evidence" of consumer benefits from the chemical, instancing that as an ingredient in a toothpaste, it prevented gingivitis.[58]

The agency said it would communicate findings of its review "to the public in winter 2012," but the mills of the FDA ground too slowly for the National Resources Defense Council, which in July 2010 sued the agency to force it to issue a final rule on triclosan and triclocarban, also used in many consumer products. Saying that the products had been sold "with no regulatory oversight" for thirty years, the organization asserted that the "hormonal interference" caused by the products had "the potential to cause long-term health problems including poor sperm quality and infertility, and damage to the developing brain leading to poor learning and memory."[59] Two months later, a consumer class action against the maker of Dial soap alleged that the firm's claims about the health benefits of the product were false. The complaint said that in an "extensive and comprehensive nationwide marketing campaign," Dial "knew and purposely misrepresented and failed to disclose to consumers" that the soap had no more antibacterial action than soap and water.[60]

One volley in the battle over the science of the antimicrobials came from Dr. Margaret James of the University of Florida. In a 2010 paper, she concluded from an analysis of sheep placentae that triclosan was a "very potent inhibitor" of estrogen activity, "rais[ing] concern about its possible effects on the ability of the placenta to supply estrogen to the fetus, and in turn on fetal growth and development."[61] By contrast, a lawyer who specialized in defense of toxic tort litigation pointed out that there had not yet been any "peer-reviewed papers . . . which actually demonstrate that triclosan has an adverse effect on human health."[62] Shortly afterward, the *Daily Mail* of London quoted Professor James on the possible effects of triclosan with respect to brain damage to babies in the womb: "We know it's a problem. But we just don't know how much of a problem."[63] This statement illustrates three facets of the Great Experiment. One is the trade-offs that sometimes occur with products that may improve human health but themselves present risks. Another is uncertainty about specific effects of products. Finally, the quotation represents the frequent discussion of product risks in general media with which non-specific consumers are constantly soaked.

Another controversy about something that was supposed to reduce illness involved a type of diet: specifically low-salt diets, much touted as a way to minimize heart disease and decrease blood pressure. A European study, published in the *Journal of the American Medical Association* in 2009, in its own summary "refute[d] the estimates of computer models of lives saved and health care costs reduced with lower salt intake."[64] The authors found a "a weak but consistent inverse association between cardiovascular mortality and the 24-hour urinary sodium excretion at baseline"—that is, that there were more deaths among people whose urine contained less salt over a one-day measurement period.[65] They found weaknesses in prior studies. They said, for example, that those studies "ignored the inconsistency of the association between blood pressure and various indexes of salt intake in observational studies" and made "far-reaching extrapolations from short-term intervention trials in normotensive or hypertensive volunteers to the general population," as well as "the possible adverse effects of an indiscriminate reduction of salt intake." At the same time, the authors were careful to mention the limitations of their study—for example, the relative youth of their survey population and the fact that it "included only white Europeans." They also noted that they had not "assess[ed] sodium sensitivity," pointing out at the same time that "there is no practical clinical test to assess sodium sensitivity in individual subjects."[66]

The publication of this study set off a little firestorm. Officials at the Centers for Disease Control, who did not usually do such things, gave an interview in which one of its medical directors assailed the research. This doctor, Peter Briss, originally pointed to the young average age of the subjects in the study, the relatively small number of them, and the small number of cardiovascular events recorded. With a witticism uncommon in such discussions, he suggested. "At the moment, this study might need to be taken with a grain of salt." Another critic, Dr. Frank Sacks of the Harvard Medical School, said that the study was "problematic" and that "we shouldn't be guiding any kind of public health decisions on it."[67]

One of the most vexing aspects of research on such topics is that it might be impossible to do the kinds of studies that will yield definitive answers. Dr. Michael Alderman, editor of the *American Journal of Hypertension*, said that what was needed was a large-scale study that would randomly assign people to low-sodium diets. But Dr. Lawrence Appel of Johns Hopkins said that kind of study "will never ever be done," noting the impossibility of keeping people on such a diet in an environment with so much sodium in prepared foods. A little side-sniping among experts underlined the difficulty of decision making for ordinary consumers wondering what to do about salt intake. Dr. Briss questioned the wisdom of putting off public health decisions to await results of a study that might not be able to be done. But Dr. Alderman said, "If they can't get people on a low-salt diet for a clinical trial, what are they talking about?" He added, "It will cost money, but that's why we do science." At a time when concerns had emerged about scientific opinions being for sale, a journalist noted that Dr. Alderman had "once been an unpaid consultant for the Salt Institute" but that at the time the controversy erupted, he "did no consulting for it or for the food industry" and took no "money from industry groups."[68]

A constant feature in the background of consumer safety battles is the struggle between the federal government and the states, especially when the states display minds of their own about regulation. With the FDA in caution/cautionary mode, beginning around 2010 a number of states banned BPA for particular uses. Early that year, the Maryland legislature banned the chemical from baby bottles and sippy cups.[69] A few days later, the Wisconsin governor signed a bill that banned the chemical in all cups sold for young children.[70]

The agency's reference to industry actions to stop making child-contact items with BPA was indicative of its tendency, on many occasions, to take producer sensitivities into account. The American Chemistry Council had responded to the controversy with injured innocence. As a press report summarized it, the Council said that "BPA is safe and has been widely used for more than half a century."[71] At the same time, the organization reportedly "called for changes" to the Toxic Substances Control Act "to avoid a hodgepodge of regulations."[72]

While struggles over BPA continued in the United States, in 2013 France banned the chemical in all food-contact food packaging by 2015. The head of Antidote Europe, a health science organization based in France, predicted that the French ban would "provide a springboard" to an eventual ban of BPA throughout the European Union.[73] But an assault on the chemical was at least temporarily repelled in California. The state EPA had added BPA to a list of chemicals "known to cause cancer or reproductive harm,"[74] but a trial court ordered the agency to remove BPA from the list pending an industry suit that opposed that action.[75]

A neighboring battleground featured phthalates. The Chronic Hazard Advisory Panel, the creation of which had been mandated by the Consumer Product Safety Improvement Act, had drafted a report on whether to make a ban on several phthalates permanent, which was to go to a private peer review by scientists nominated by the National Academy of Sciences. The director of a panel that represented American phthalates makers complained that a subsequent rulemaking process would "eliminat[e] further debate."[76]

## A Very Old Story: Cigarettes

Early in the seventeenth century, King James I of England described tobacco smoking as

> A custome lothsome to the eye, hatefull to the Nose, harmefull to the braine, dangerous to the Lungs, and in the blacke stinking fume thereof, nearest resembling the horrible Stigian smoke of the pit that is bottomelesse.[77]

So it has been known for almost four centuries that tobacco is a noxious product. Certainly by the twentieth century it was known that it was a deadly one. I can personally remember being introduced to the phrase "coffin nails" in the late 1940s. And a 1947 hit song, which has been quoted in a judicial decision, sardonically pointed out to smokers,

> Smoke, smoke, smoke that cigarette
> Puff, puff, puff, and if you smoke yourself to death,
> Tell Saint Peter at the Golden Gate,
> That you hate to make him wait.[78]

By 1964, a lengthy government document had made it official: cigarettes are bad for health. A key finding of the publication, written by an advisory committee to the Surgeon General, was that "the mortality rate for male cigarette smokers compared with non-smokers for all causes of death taken together . . . is 1.68, representing a total death rate nearly 70 percent higher than for non-smokers."[79] The report indicated that the more one smoked, "the higher the death rate." Specifically, "for men who smoke fewer than 10 cigarettes a day . . . the death rate from all causes is about 40 percent higher than for non-smokers." The fearsome toll escalated to a point where "for those who smoke 40 or more," the death rate was 120 percent higher than for nonsmokers.[80] The report also pinpointed specific illnesses related to smoking. As to lung cancer, "the magnitude of the effect of cigarette smoking far outweighs other factors." Smoking was "the most important of the causes of chronic bronchitis in the United States, and increases the risk of dying from chronic bronchitis and emphysema."[81] Moreover, although at that point "the causative role of cigarette smoking in deaths from coronary disease is not proven," the committee thought it "more prudent from the public health viewpoint to assume that the established association has causative meaning than to suspend judgment until no uncertainty remains."[82]

Forty-seven years later, despite many years of anti-smoking campaigns and indeed a significant drop in the number of smokers, one estimate put the annual deaths from smoking at 443,000.[83] In 2011, the Centers for Disease Control put several exclamation points on the ravages of cigarettes. Smoking, the CDC estimated, increased the risk of lung cancer twenty-three times for men and thirteen times for women. An agency fact sheet listed no fewer than eleven kinds of cancer caused by smoking. If in 1964 the effects on the heart were still a hypothesis, they were now a fact: "Smoking causes coronary heart disease, the leading cause of death in the United States."[84] By 2014 the CDC reported that cigarette smoking in the United States caused 480,000 deaths annually—including more than 41,000 deaths from secondhand smoke—with a shortening of life that averaged fourteen years for smokers as compared with nonsmokers. Cigarettes, the agency said, caused large numbers of deaths from a range of diseases, including 163,000 deaths from cancer of the lung, stomach, and colon; more than 160,000 deaths from cardiovascular and metabolic disease; and about 100,000 deaths from various respiratory diseases, especially chronic obstructive pulmonary disease (COPD)—for which many television commercials advertised drugs.[85]

The indictment against cigarettes had many counts, including criticisms of particular ingredients of cigarette smoke and specialized kinds of cigarettes. One ingredient is the radioactive isotope polonium, which one writer said would "build up to the equivalent radiation dosage of 300 chest x-rays a year for a person who smokes one and a half packs a day." That critic said that the industry had "known about polonium in cigarettes for nearly 50 years" and had "even devised processes that would dramatically cut down" the concentrations of polonium in cigarettes," but had "consciously decided to do nothing and keep its research secret."[86]

In 2009 Congress gave the FDA power—which it had not done before—to regulate some tobacco products. In the 2009 Family Smoking Prevention and Tobacco Control Act,[87] it banned flavored cigarettes although excluding menthol cigarettes from the ban.[88] It is perhaps a tribute to imaginative marketing that the banned flavors included a menu that ranged from strawberry, grape, orange, clove, and cinnamon to chocolate, cherry, and coffee.

But the exception for menthol in the legislation stuck in the craw of the Tobacco Products Scientific Advisory Committee (TPSAC), which was created by the statute, and which concluded in a 2011 report that "menthol cigarettes adversely affect U.S. public health and . . . there are no public health benefits to menthol cigarettes as compared with nonmenthol cigarettes." The committee's general recommendation was that "removal of menthol cigarettes would benefit public health in the United States."[89] Menthol was a come-on to the taste buds that led people into the cigarette habit. To be sure, existing research "did not support a conclusion that smokers of menthol cigarettes have greater disease risk than smokers of nonmenthol cigarettes." However, two members of the TPSAC summarized "convincing evidence" that the availability of menthol cigarettes "increases number of smokers by increasing the rate of smoking initiation and reducing the risk of cessation, particularly among black Americans." This conclusion drew on a common-sense intuition—the writers called it "biologically plausible"—that menthol cigarettes would lead people to take up smoking: "menthol's cooling and anesthetic properties" "can reduce the harshness of cigarette smoke for new smokers." The trap was a double one—not only would menthol in cigarettes encourage people to start to smoke, but there was an increase in "the likelihood of addiction and the degree of addiction in new smokers." Moreover, there was evidence—some of it from "industry-sponsored studies"—that showed that "some consumers, particularly blacks, hold beliefs about implicit health benefits of menthol cigarettes that may interfere with their quitting."[90]

Menthol cigarettes were thus one small wedge of one of the longest-running consumer experiments in the American economy. A special feature of the cigarette experiment was the phenomenon of trade organizations publishing misleading information and withholding data about product hazards. The Oregon Supreme Court pinpointed the tobacco industry's machinations in a decision that upheld a $79.5 million punitive damages award in a case involving a smoking death. It referred to the defendant Philip Morris's attempts to "spread false and misleading information" "for nearly half a century" in an effort to raise doubts about whether smoking caused illness.[91] More broadly, the tobacco industry engaged in that campaign. As the Oregon court of appeals summarized it, Philip Morris

> and the rest of the industry worked together for more than 40 years to create a public impression that there was a legitimate controversy about whether cigarettes were dangerous to a smoker's health and that resolving that health issue would require further research. Although defendant and the other companies knew throughout most, if not all, of that 40-year period that cigarette smoking was in fact dangerous, they intended that smokers rely on the false impression that the industry created.[92]

Describing "an extensive campaign to counter the effects of negative scientific information on cigarette sales," the court of appeals said that the jury could have found that while that campaign proceeded, "defendant and the other tobacco companies actually had little doubt that cigarette smoking was causally related to a number of diseases." Moreover, it said, Philip Morris "recognized both that nicotine was addictive and that its addictive effect was the primary reason that people continued to smoke" and indeed "spent considerable effort discovering ways to deliver the optimal dose of nicotine in each cigarette without actually adding nicotine to its product." More generally, the court declared that Philip Morris and the industry employed "a large number of methods to create the public impression of a legitimate controversy, despite the lack of supporting scientific evidence." In conducting this battery of activities, Philip Morris and the industry "issued press releases, influenced the content of apparently neutral articles, cultivated opinion leaders, attempted to use their advertising power to get favorable treatment from the print media, and appeared on commercial and public television to put forth that message."[93] As the quotation above from King James indicates, an interesting aspect of the case of cigarettes in the annals of consumer experimentation is that for five centuries, there has been a significant degree of consumer information about the risks of smoking. We noted that the song "Smoke! Smoke! Smoke! (That Cigarette)" goes back to the 1940s. And the first government-mandated warnings on cigarette packages appeared in 1965, when the first statute passed by Congress on the subject required packages to bear the statement, "Caution: The Surgeon General Has Determined That Cigarette Smoking Is Dangerous to Your Health."[94] In 1970, the Public Health Cigarette Smoking Act 1969 made the message more intense: "Warning: The Surgeon General Has Determined That Cigarette Smoking Is Dangerous to Your Health."[95] But the special aspect of the case—as just summarized for judicial decisions—lay in the industry's dedicated and prolonged efforts to combat the very proposition that smoking caused illness, which included the burying of specific data on health effects that had long been becoming recognized by the public in a very general way. It is not a unique phenomenon that product sellers and industry groups will deny the harmful effects of products, but the cigarette industry took the building of its case to a new level of duplicity.

## A Modern Diagnostic Tool

A great continuing experiment has involved millions of American women, and the controversy about it is not about a product but a diagnostic tool: the mammogram. Again there was a lively series of debates among scientists that centered on statistics, but which carried practical meaning for patients. Breast cancer, according to the U.S. Preventive Services Task Force, "is the most frequently diagnosed cancer in women in the United States, not including skin cancer, and is second only to lung cancer as a cause of cancer deaths."[96] The Task Force had issued guidelines in 2002 recommending that women in their forties have mammograms "every 1 to 2 years."[97]

Big science, and science on big medical problems, progresses only in increments over several years. It took until 2009 to collect data on the effectiveness of mammography as a screening device. In recommendations published that year, the Task Force referred to "harms resulting from screening for breast cancer" that "include psychological harms, unnecessary imaging tests and biopsies in women without cancer, and inconvenience due to false-positive screening results." It said also that "one must . . . consider the harms associated with treatment of cancer that would not become clinically apparent during a woman's lifetime (overdiagnosis), as well as the harms of unnecessary earlier treatment of breast cancer that would have become clinically apparent but would not have shortened a woman's life." It noted that "false-positive results are common with mammography and can cause anxiety and lead to additional imaging studies and invasive procedures (such as biopsy or fine-needle aspiration)." It referred to "adequate" evidence that "suggests that the overall harms associated with mammography are moderate for every age group considered," adding that "although false-positive test results, overdiagnosis, and unnecessary earlier treatment are problems for all age groups, false positive results are more common for women aged 40 to 49 years, whereas overdiagnosis is a greater concern for women in the older age groups."[98]

Concluding that for "women aged 40 to 49 years," there was "moderate certainty that the net benefits" of mammography "were small," the Task Force said that "the decision to start regular, biennial screening mammography before the age of 50 years should be an individual one and take into account patient context, including the patient's values regarding specific benefits and harms."[99] This recommendation generated a wave of criticism from groups like the American Cancer Society and various politicians, who chorused, in effect, that it would sentence some women to death from breast cancer.[100]

Data continued to flow. The next year, 2010, a Norwegian study reported that "the introduction of a breast-cancer screening program" indeed reduced the rate of cancer deaths, but that when one "took into account temporal trends in breast-cancer mortality caused by other factors, the apparent effect was considerably smaller than expected."[101] The Norwegian researchers observed that their finding that "only about one third of the reduction in mortality can be directly attributed to breast-cancer screening" was in line with evidence from a British study.[102]

Dr. H. Gilbert Welch of Dartmouth, noting that "well-crafted public health messaging" had created a public perception that screening mammography is "one of the most important services provided by modern medicine," said that the Norwegian data indicated that such messaging must become more balanced." Although saying that "no one can argue that screening mammography is one of the most important services we provide in medicine," he noted that among one thousand women with false positives, "somewhere between 5 and 15 women would be expected to be needlessly treated for a condition that was never going to bother them, with all the accompanying harms." He declared that "by highlighting that the mortality benefit is modest," the Norwegian study "help[ed] confirm that the decision about whether to undergo screening mammography is, in fact, a close call."[103]

In 2014 a Canadian study, conducted over a five-year period, demonstrated that science on important issues may move by leaps and bounds but that sometimes leaps add to existing controversies. The authors concluded that "annual mammography in women aged 40–59 does not reduce mortality from breast cancer beyond that of physical examination or usual care when adjuvant therapy for breast cancer is freely available."[104] The author of the 2010 Norwegian study commented, as a reporter summarized it, that the reason the results of the Canadian study differed from prior results was that "with better treatments"—for example, with the drug tamoxifen—"it was less important to find cancers early" and that "women in the Canadian studies were aware of breast cancer and its dangers" and were more likely to report lumps they would previously have ignored.[105] In a published comment, she said that the "major strengths" of the Canadian study included its "randomized design, intense intervention with five annual mammography screenings, high compliance, and complete follow-up." Although she referred to "potential limitations" of the study, including the lack of quantitative data "on the degree of contamination in the control group or possible confounding by screening mammography after the trial," she agreed with the authors of the study that "the rationale for screening mammography [should] be urgently reassessed by policy makers." She observed that reconsideration of "priorities and recommendations for mammography screening and other medical interventions" was "not an easy task." Indicative of the warfare in many areas of science was her remark that one reason for this difficulty was that "governments, research funders, scientists, and medical practitioners may have vested interests in continuing activities that are well established."[106] Yet reports of the Canadian study stirred a furious response. A comment by the American College of Radiology called it "an incredibly misleading analysis based on the deeply flawed and widely discredited" Canadian screening study.[107]

We note that however arcane the data, in theory the potential consumer of mammography retained the sovereignty of making up her own layperson's mind.[108] This profile simply illustrated a puzzle in consumer choice that runs throughout the vast story of experimentation beyond the laboratory. We want people to be sovereign in deciding about many aspects of their health care, but often meaningful choice requires a degree of statistical sophistication that lies beyond the knowledge of those who are asked to choose.

## Notes

1. Katherine Harmon, "Worts and All," *Scientific American*, Aug. 2010, p. 24.
2. Senate Special Comm. on Aging, Hearing, Dietary Supplements: What Seniors Need to Know, Serial No. 111-18, 111th Cong. 2d Sess., May 26, 2010, p. 6.
3. Ibid., p. 6–7.
4. Ibid., p. 55 (testimony of Charles Bell, programs director, Consumers Union, quoting Dr. Grollman).
5. See ibid., p. 80.
6. Ibid., p. 93 (estimate referenced by Charles Bell).
7. See ibid., pp. 43 and 50.
8. Ibid., p. 57.
9. Ibid., p. 36 (testimony of Tod Cooperman, president of ConsumerLab.com).
10. Ibid., p. 119.
11. See Harmon, supra note 1, quoting Paul G. Shekelle.
12. See James G. Hodge Jr. et al., "The Consumable Vice: Caffeine, Public Health, and the Law," 27 *J. Contemp. Health L. & Pol'y* 76, 77 (2010).
13. Ibid., p. 77.
14. See ibid., pp. 90–91.
15. See ibid., pp. 92–93.
16. Ibid., p. 95.
17. Ibid., p. 96.
18. See ibid., p. 100.
19. See ibid., pp. 97–98.
20. See ibid., pp. 85–86.
21. Ibid., p. 85.
22. Marshall S. Shapo, "Freud, Cocaine, and Products Liability," 77 *B. U. L. Rev.* 421, 424 (1997).
23. See Hodge et al., supra note 12, pp. 88 and 109.
24. See ibid., p. 102.
25. See ibid., p. 104.
26. See ibid., pp. 105–06.
27. Gary Taubes, "Is Sugar Toxic?" *New York Times Magazine*, April 13, 2011, pp. 47–48.
28. See ibid., pp. 50 and 52–53.
29. Ibid., p. 51.
30. Ibid., p. 54.
31. See for example Judith Shulevitz, "The Toxicity Panic," *New Republic*, April 28, 2011, pp. 11–12; Dominique Browning, "Hitting the Bottle," *New York Times*, May 9, 2011, p. A23.
32. Frederick S. vom Saal and Wade V. Welshons, "Large Effects from Small Exposures, II: The Importance of Positive Controls in Low-Dose Research on Bisphenol A," 100 *Environmental Research* 50, 50 (Jan. 2006)(abstract).

33. Ibid., p. 70.
34. Ibid.
35. Ibid.
36. Ibid., p. 50 (abstract).
37. Ibid., p. 70.
38. Frederick S. vom Saal, "Failure of the FDA Risk Assessment Process for Bisphenol A: A Timeline of Bisphenol A-Related Publications by FDA Officials and FDA Regulatory Decisions," http://www.ourstolenfuture.org/Commentary/Opinion/2009/2009-0413fvs-on-bpa.html, from the site Our Stolen Future, printed from the Internet, June 13, 2011.
39. Vom Saal and Welshons, supra note 32, p. 71.
40. Quoted in Shulevitz, supra note 31, p. 13.
41. Summary by Browning, supra note 31.
42. See Shulevitz, supra, p. 11.
43. Quoted in Shulevitz, supra, p. 13.
44. Stephen Gardner, "European Survey Finds Widespread Traces of Hazardous Substances in Humans," 40 *Prod. Safety & Liab. Rep.*(BNA) 1270 (Nov. 5, 2012).
45. Susan M. Duty et al., "Potential Sources of Bisphenol A in the Neonatal Intensive Care Unit," 131 *Pediatrics* 483, 488 (2013).
46. See Elizabeth Weil, "Puberty Before Age 10: A New 'Normal'?" *New York Times Magazine*, March 30, 2012, p. 30 and 34.
47. Browning, supra note 31.
48. FDA, "News & Events," Jan. 2010, printed from the Internet, July 26, 2010.
49. Denise Grady, "F.D.A. Concerned About Substance in Food Packaging," *New York Times*, Jan. 15, 2010.
50. See ibid.
51. "NIOSH Skin Notation Profiles, Bisphenol A (BPA)," CAS No. 80-05-7, p. 5 (April 2011).
52. Ibid.
53. Pat Rizzuto, "FDA Denies Citizen Petition Seeking Ban of Bisphenol A; Safety Review Continues," 40 *Prod. Safety & Liab. Rep.* 411 (BNA) (April 9, 2012).
54. See "Advocates Urge FDA to Ban More Uses of Bisphenol A Than Proposed by Industry," 40 *Prod. Safety & Liab. Rep.* (BNA)(April 30, 2012); Pat Rizzuto, "FDA Grants Chemistry Council Petition, Bans BPA From Baby Bottles, 'Sippy Cups,'" 40 *Prod. Safety & Liab. Rep.* 815 (July 23, 2012).
55. Pat Rizzuto, "FDA Rejects Two of Markey's Three Petitions That Seek Bans on Some Bisphenol A Uses," 40 *Prod. Safety & Liab. Rep.* (BNA) 679 (June 18, 2012).
56. See "Tort Suits Over Bisphenol A Less Likely In Wake of FDA Decision," 40 *Prod. Safety & Liab. Rep.* (BNA) 402 (April 9, 2012).
57. Stephen Gardner, "Higher Toxicity Classification for BPA Recommended by EU Scientific Panel," 42 *Prod. Safety & Liab. Rep.* (BNA) 290 (March 24, 2014).
58. FDA consumer update, "Triclosan: What Consumers Should Know," http://www.fda.gov/ForConsumers/ConsumerUpdates/ucm205999.htm posted April 8, 2010.
59. NRDC Press Release, "Lawsuit Seeks Final Rule on 'Antibacterial' Chemical After 32-Year Delay," July 27, 2010, printed from the Internet.

60. Class action complaint, *Walls v. Dial Corp.*, Civil Action No. 3:10-CV-00734-WDS-DGW (S.D. Ill. Sept. 23, 2010).
61. Margaret O. James et al., "Triclosan Is a Potent Inhibitor of Estradiol and Estrone Sulfonation in Sheep Placenta, 36 *Environment Int'l* 942 (2010) (abstract).
62. Anthony G. Hopp, "Is Triclosan the Next BPA? Probably Not, at Least for Now," 39 *Prod. Safety & Liab. Rep.* (BNA) 62, 62 (Jan. 17, 2011).
63. Pat Hagan, "Toothpaste Fear for Unborn Babies," *Daily Mail*, Jan. 14, 2011, printed from the Internet.
64. Katarzyna Stolarz-Skrzypek, et al., "Fatal and Nonfatal Outcomes, Incidence of Hypertension, and Blood Pressure Changes in Relation to Urinary Sodium Excretion," 305 *JAMA* 1777, 1784 (2011).
65. Id. at 1783.
66. Ibid., pp. 1778 and 1784.
67. Gina Kolata, "Research Questions Benefit of Low-Salt Diet, Drawing Criticisms from C.D.C.," *New York Times*, May 4, 2011, p. A17.
68. Ibid.
69. Meredith Cohn, "Senate OKs BPA Ban in Bottles, Cups for Young Children," *Baltimore Sun*, Feb. 25, 2010, printed from the Internet, July 26, 2011.
70. See Associated Press, "Wisconsin Among First States to Enact BPA Ban," March 3, 2010, Printed from the Internet, July 26, 2011.
71. See ibid.
72. See Shulevitz, supra note 31, p. 15.
73. Rick Mitchell, "French Ban on BPA in Food Packaging Could Have Wide Impact in European Union," 40 *Prod. Safety & Liab. Rep.* (BNA) 1456 (Dec. 24, 2012).
74. Patrick Ambrosio, "California Agency Intends to Add BPA to Proposition 65 List of Harmful Chemicals," 41 *Prod. Safety & Liab. Rep.* (BNA) 148 (Feb. 4, 2013).
75. Carolyn Whetzel, "California Required to Remove Bisphenol A From Proposition 65 List Pending Suit," 41 *Prod. Safety & Liab. Rep.* (BNA) 526 (April 20, 2013).
76. Rachel Boehm, "CHAP Report Will Go Through Private, Not Public, Scientific Peer Review Process," 41 *Prod. Safety & Liab. Rep.* (BNA) 438 (April 8, 2013).
77. The Project Gutenberg EBook of *A Counter-Blaste to Tobacco*, by King James I, printed from the Internet, Aug. 29, 2013.
78. Quoted in *Estate of White v. R. J. Reynolds Tobacco Co.*, 109 F. Supp.2d 424, 433 (D. Md. 2000).
79. U.S. Dept. of Health, Education, and Welfare, "Smoking and Health: Report of the Advisory Committee to the Surgeon General of the Public Health Service," Public Health Service Publication No. 1103, p. 28 (1964).
80. Ibid., p. 29.
81. Ibid., p. 31.
82. Ibid., p. 32.
83. Centers for Disease Control, chart on tobacco data, http://www.cdc/gov/tobacco/data_statistics/tables/index.htm, accessed July 27, 2011.
84. CDC fact sheet "Health Effects of Cigarettes Smoking," http://www.cdc.gov/tobacco/data_statistics/fact_sheets/health_effects/effects_cig_smoking/, accessed July 27, 2011.

85. CDC fact sheet, "Tobacco-Related Mortality," www.cdc.gov/tobacco/data__statistics/fact__sheeets/health__effects/tobacco/related__mor . . ., accessed March 19, 2014.
86. Brianna Rego, "Radioactive Smoke," *Scientific American*, Jan. 2011, p. 79.
87. Pub. L. 111-31 (2009).
88. Ibid. §907(a)(1)(A).
89. Neal A. Benowitz and Jonathan M. Samet, "The Threat of Menthol Cigarettes to U.S. Public Health," 364 *New Eng. J. Med.* 2179, 2180 (2011).
90. Ibid.
91. See *Williams v. Philip Morris*, 127 P.3d 1165 (Or. 2006). After a reversal by a divided U.S. Supreme Court on the punitive damages award (see 127 S. Ct. 1057 [2007]), the Oregon Supreme Court reaffirmed the award (176 P.3d 1255 [2008]), and the case effectively petered out in the U.S. Supreme Court, see 129 S. Ct. 1436 (2009).
92. *Williams v. Philip Morris Inc.*, 92 P.3d 126, 128 (Or. Ct. App. 2004).
93. Ibid., pp. 129–30.
94. Pub. L.89-92, 79 Stat. 282, § 4 (1965).
95. Pub. L. 91-222, 84 Stat. 87, § 4 (1970).
96. U.S. Preventive Services Task Force, "Screening for Breast Cancer updated December 2009.
97. "Screening for Breast Cancer: Recommendations From the U.S. Preventive Services Task Force," 137 *Ann. Intern. Med.* 344 (2002).
98. U.S. Preventive Services Task Force, "Screening for Breast Cancer: U.S. Preventive Services Task Force Recommendation Statement," 151 *Ann. Intern. Med.* 716 (2009).
99. Ibid.
100. See Gina Kolata, "Behind Cancer Guidelines, Quest for Data," *New York Times*, Nov. 22, 2009.
101. M. Kalager et al., "Effect of Screening Mammography on Breast-Cancer Mortality in Norway," 363 *N. Eng. J. Med.* 1203 (2010).
102. Ibid., p. 1209.
103. H. Gilbert Welch, "Screening Mammography—A Long Run for a Short Slide?" 363 *N. Eng. J. Med.* 1276, 1277 (2010).
104. Anthony B. Miller et al., "Twenty Five Year Follow-Up for Breast Cancer Incidence and Mortality of the Canadian National Breast Screen Study: Randomized Screening Trial," 348 *Brit. Med. J.* g366 (2014).
105. See Gina Kolata, "Vast Study Casts Doubts on Value of Mammograms," *New York Times*, Feb. 12, 2014, pp. A-1 and A-3.
106. Matte Kalager et al., "Too Much Mammography," 348 *Br. Med. J.* g1403 (2014).
107. American College of Radiology, "BMJ Article on Breast Cancer Screening Effectiveness: Incredibly Flawed and Misleading," https://www.google.com/?gws_rd=ssl#q=american+college+radiology+BmJ+article+breast+cancer, Feb. 12, 2004.
108. Over the very short term, the Task Force recommendation made very little difference to women and their doctors: "Biennial mammography rates declined by -0.5 percentage points between 2006 to 2009 and 2010" (D. H. Howard and E. K. Adams, "Mammography Rates after the 2009 US Preventive Services Task Force Breast Cancer Screening Recommendation, *Prev. Med.* 55.5, at 485 [abstract] [Nov. 2012]).

# 4

# Red Flags Rising as Products Enter the Market

This book often deals with patterns of injuring events, either established or alleged. One pattern that stands out has this profile: Initially, there is an innovative product idea that requires a lot of time and money to bring to marketable form—in a pill or a medical device, or a complicated mechanical product like an automobile.

Then come hopeful results, in the case of medical products from clinical trials, with the hopefulness becoming optimistic hyperventilation on the part of developers of the product, who already have a psychological as well as financial stake in its success. Now the company puts the product on the general market, often with substantial promotion. The campaign includes a spate of heavy advertising, including direct-to-consumer advertising—even in the case of prescription products, which require a physician's signature. Accompanying the promotion of medical products, with roseate images of customer satisfaction, are rapid summaries of side effects.

After the product (for example, a drug) moves onto the general market, as time goes on, red flags appear at various places on the map—first with anecdotes of harm and then in systematic studies. Data begin to emerge on serious risks, but usually there is a gap of months and years until this data becomes public. Contributing to the time gap are the inevitable tangles of both corporate and regulatory bureaucracy, and the perceived self-interest of marketers in keeping risks quiet. As news about a hazard seeps through the scientific community and eventually into public view, disputes arise about whether the risks of the product are acceptable. These controversies take place among knowledgeable scientists generally, and specifically among scientists—and officials—in regulatory agencies. The maker of the product defends it, first in infighting with the agency, and eventually in public when the problem surfaces in media. While this goes on, sometimes multiple investigations proceed, and often they take a long time.

Political actors enter the stage to spotlight complaints. Companies react in different ways. More often than not, they fight to keep the product on the market. They may acknowledge, to one degree or another, the developing risks associated with the product. They may stonewall regulation—may even conceal negative data.

As struggles over the safety of the product continue within the regulatory agency as well as between the agency and the seller, tort law comes into play. After enough red flags go up on the map, law firms' websites appear that invite potential claimants to come abroad.

## Avandia

A case study on this pattern is the diabetes drug rosiglitazone, brand-named Avandia, which was being taken by approximately a million patients.[1] A central figure in the controversy that arose over Avandia was Steven Nissen, the chair of the department of cardiovascular medicine at the Cleveland Clinic, who had been president of the American College of Cardiology. An important document was an article he published with Kathy Wolski in the *New England Journal of Medicine* (*NEJM*) on the adverse effects of Avandia. It is interesting to consider the background for Nissen's writing of this article. As he described it to a House committee, his interest was piqued by articles in the British journal *Lancet* and the *New England Journal of Medicine* in late 2006 that raised warning signs about Avandia, although neither study reported on enough events to be statistically significant. Nissen and a colleague dug deeper, using—among other sources—clinical data from an FDA website and a website run by GlaxoSmithKline (GSK), the maker of Avandia. They then did a meta-analysis of "all 42 relevant Avandia clinical trials completed before or after drug approval." This analysis showed a statistically significant "43% excess incidence of heart attack in Avandia-treated patients."[2] This calculated excess came from the report in Nissen's *NEJM* article that in the 42 trials reviewed, "there were 86 myocardial infarctions in the [Avandia] group and 72 in the control group," and "there were 39 deaths from cardiovascular causes in the [Avandia] group and 22 in the control group."[3] The data led Nissen and Wolski to the conclusion that "as compared with placebo or other antidiabetic regimens, treatment with [Avandia] was associated with a significant increase in the risk of myocardial infarction and with an increase in the risk of death from cardiovascular causes that was of borderline significance."[4]

The authors were careful to acknowledge "important limitations" of their study—for example, that fact that the trials they surveyed "were not originally intended to explore cardiovascular outcomes," and that because of statistical considerations, there was "considerable uncertainty about the magnitude of the observed hazard." Moreover, since Nissen and Wolski "did not have access to original source data from any of these trials," they "based the analysis on available data from publicly disclosed summaries of events."[5] Despite these qualifications, they declared that the data "point[ed] to the urgent need for comprehensive evaluations to clarify the cardiovascular risk of [Avandia]," saying that the manufacturer should make its "source data for completed clinical trials" "available to an external academic coordinating center for systematic analysis." Laconically, they said that "our data suggest a cardiovascular risk associated with the use of [Avandia]." The public-experimental aspect of Avandia marketing was evident in their statement that "until more precise estimates" of this risk could be made for patients with diabetes, "patients and providers should carefully consider the potential risks of [Avandia] in the treatment of type 2 diabetes."[6]

Nissen's testimony at the House committee hearing was one piece of the puzzle explored there. The committee's chair, the formidable Henry Waxman, launched an attack on GSK because after Avandia had been used by "millions of Americans" during a period of eight years, there still had been no "post-market studies . . . to say conclusively whether Avandia increases or decreases the risk of heart attacks."[7] He noted that the FDA's "primary medical reviewer" had done "everything right," recognizing Avandia's "great promise because of its impact on blood sugar," but also that "there were questions about its side effects that could be answered conclusively only through a properly designed post-market trial." However, he said, "at that point the FDA dropped the ball."[8]

A retort came from Dr. Moncef M. Slaoui, chair of research and development for GSK, who insisted that "when compared with other widely used oral anti-diabetes medicines, Avandia is not associated with an increased risk of death, including death from a cardiovascular event." He insisted that, based on "three large trials" and a "large epidemiological study," "the hypothesis is not accurate that there is an increase in cardiovascular risk associated with the use of Avandia, when we compare it to the two most widely used oral anti-diabetes medicines."

Referring to a study that GSK had published in the *NEJM*, he said that the company found its data "very reassuring," although he noted that it was "interim and therefore not fully conclusive." He criticized editorials published the same day by the *Journal* as "cherry-pick[ing] data points when the data taken as a whole supports the safety profile of Avandia."[9] He referred to a "real world" "balanced cohort study" the firm had done of thirty thousand patients. Acknowledging that that study had the same kind of limitations as meta-analyses, he declared that it "did not confirm that the meta-analyses' signal of a possible increase in ischemic cardiovascular risk was accurate."[10]

The complexity of the decision confronting diabetes patients and their doctors was evident in a statement by Dr. Brian Strom, the chair of biostatistics and epidemiology at the University of Pennsylvania, who called the Nissen meta-analysis "a very weak study,"[11] saying that "ultimately" it might prove "to be correct," but that it "may not be,"[12] and calling for a "large outcomes-related randomized clinical trial."[13] Perhaps most telling on the point of the national experiment that Avandia represented was his declaration that when a "drug is first marketed, physicians, patients, and society need to take into account . . . the substantial probability for as yet unknown adverse reactions." This, he said, argued for limiting "the marketing of a drug in its first years on the market to those patients who truly need it," and for collecting "as much information as possible on their experiences, so that all can learn about uncommon adverse effects as soon as possible."[14] This captures a dilemma of post-marketing experimentation. To market a drug broadly would provide the broadest possible database for adverse reactions, but in the case of a drug that caused adverse reactions, it would produce the most number of injuries. This dilemma is just one example of the complications that abound in the relationship of law and health care. In the sphere of safety regulation, those complications generate hard decisions. A product may work for many people and cause a relatively small number of others to die or suffer serious injuries. Regulators sometimes have to make cost–benefit decisions that keep people from buying products they would like to buy even when they are informed about the risks of those goods.

Accenting the problem from the standpoint of patients and physicians was the FDA's decision in November 2007 to require a new "black box warning" in the labeling for Avandia. This followed the 22 to 1 vote of an advisory committee of experts in July that recommended, as the agency summarized it, "that Avandia stay on the market, pending a review of additional data," but that "additional information of the potential for increased risk of heart attacks should be added to the drug labeling." The new warning included a reference to the "42 clinical studies" in the Nissen meta-analysis, which it said "showed Avandia to be associated with an increased risk of myocardial ischemic events such as angina or myocardial infarction." It also referred to "three other studies" that it said "have not confirmed or excluded this risk." It summarized these studies "in their entirety" as being "inconclusive" on the "risk of myocardial ischemia." At the point of consumer contact the agency's advice was, as is so often the fact, "talk-to-your-doctor" advice. It said that "patients with type 2 diabetes who have underlying heart disease or who are at high risk of heart attack should talk with their health care provider about the revised warning as they evaluate treatment risks" and that doctors should "closely monitor patients who take Avandia for cardiovascular risks."[15]

On the litigation side, often a practical indicator of controversies about drug safety, lawsuits began against GSK. In what became a multidistrict litigation that started in 2007 and had its own website, plaintiffs alleged that the company "knew or should have known of increased risk of heart problems," overpromoted the product, and did not adequately warn of the risks.[16]

By 2009, the organization Public Citizen published a research report that brought the liver into the picture. This study, "accounting for underreporting," concluded that "the number needed to harm . . . for each case of liver failure was 44,000 patient years of exposure for" Avandia,[17] which the lead author, James Floyd, translated to give a "best estimate" that "one case of liver failure occurs for every 44,000 patients who take Avandia."[18]

The governmental hammer descended hard on GSK in 2010. In February came news of a double blow. Two internal reports by two FDA doctors condemned GSK for a new trial by the company, which they called "unethical and exploitative." Although they acknowledged that the trial was "motivated by a desire for definitive answers regarding the cardiovascular safety" of Avandia, a press report said that what concerned the FDA doctors was that patients who used Avandia faced "far greater risks than those who" received the competing drug Actos, "with no promise of any additional benefit." This, one of the doctors' reports said, meant that "the safety of the study itself cannot be assured and is not acceptable."[19] The same week, a 342-page Senate Finance Committee report produced under the direction of the Democratic senator

Max Baucus and the Republican senator Charles Grassley—the latter a long-standing gadfly of the pharmaceutical industry—savaged GSK's marketing of the drug. The report, based on research into a quarter of a million internal GSK documents, concluded that instead of giving warnings about the drug's hazards, "G.S.K. executives attempted to intimidate independent physicians, focused on strategies to minimize or misrepresent findings that Avandia may increase cardiovascular risk, and sought ways to downplay findings that a competing drug might reduce cardiovascular risk." The Senate committee referred to an internal FDA report from 2008 saying that if patients taking Avandia had taken Actos instead, it would have avoided five hundred heart attacks and three hundred cases of heart failure.[20] Baucus, saying that "patients trust drug companies with their health and their lives," declared that "GlaxoSmithKline abused that trust."[21] A press release by Baucus and Grassley said that they had requested the staff report because of concern about the FDA being "too cozy with drug makers" and that the agency had "been regularly outmaneuvered by companies that have a financial interest in downplaying or under-exploiting potential safety risks."[22] Among other things, the report noted that in proceeding with the trial, the company made no references to safety hazards "in the consent form given to patients currently enrolling" in the study. Responding with a metaphor it had previously used, the company said that the Senate report "cherry-picks information from documents which mischaracterizes GlaxoSmithKline's comprehensive efforts to research Avandia and communicate those findings to regulators, physicians and patients."[23] Expressing concern that patients would be scared away from needed treatment, the firm ascribed a "vast majority" of some of the reports to tort litigation.[24]

Characteristically conservative in its conclusions, the *Medical Letter* noted in a March 2010 issue that there still was "no prospective double-blind trial comparing the cardiovascular safety" of Avandia and Actos. It concluded simply that "whether patients who have achieved good glycemic control with [Avandia] and have tolerated it well should stay on it could be decided on a case-by-case basis."[25] But just a few months later, news appeared that lost GSK considerable yardage in public relations. This news was that GSK had covered up a 1999 study that indicated, as a reporter summarized it, that "not only was Avandia no better than Actos," but that there were "clear signs that it was riskier to the heart." It was reported that executives at SmithKline, the corporate predecessor of GSK, had decided not to make more comparisons of the two drugs. The intention to keep bad news secret was evident in an email message from an executive of SmithKline, saying, "Per Sr. Mgmt request, these data should not see the light of day to anyone outside of GSK."[26]

A couple of days after this report surfaced, GSK's public relations problem decidedly became a regulatory problem. A fragmented vote by an FDA panel that combined the Endocrinologic and Metabolic Drugs Advisory Committee (EMDAC) and the FDA's Drug Safety and Risk Management Advisory Committee illustrated a new approach to a type of public information. That is the publicizing of scientific disagreements—where in the past, as *Times* reporter Gardiner Harris put it, this had been "something unheard of just a few years ago, when the F.D.A. nearly always spoke with a single voice." Now the panel spoke with four different voices. Twelve members of the panel said Avandia should be taken off the market, ten said "its sales should be restricted" and label warnings should be "enhanced," seven "voted only to support enhanced warnings," and three would have left the drug on the market with the warnings existing at the time.[27]

Some people who spoke at the meeting of the panel were scathing in their criticism of GSK. Dr. Thomas Marciniak, an FDA team leader, referred to "numerous mistakes" in a drug trial that "served to hide Avandia's risks" and asserted that the company had often "overruled doctors who had concluded that patients had been harmed by Avandia." Accentuating the courtroom-like drama was the chairman's refusal to let a GSK executive respond to Marciniak. Another critic was Dr. William Knowles, the chief of diabetes epidemiology at the National Institute of Diabetes and Digestive and Kidney Diseases, who said that a GSK study was "totally incorrect and deceptive." Dr. Dean Follman, a mathematician at the National Institute of Allergy and Infectious Diseases, was unwilling to use the term "deceptive," but he said, as a reporter summarized it, that because the company "failed to explain why it conducted its analysis so poorly," he "would ignore it, basically." Dr. Nissen, whose meta-analyses had been an important trigger for the Avandia controversy, appeared satisfied on the whole, saying that the panel's vote was "the best he could hope for," opining that "[e]ffectively, this drug is gone."[28]

There were defenses from Avandia prescribers and patients, underlining the fact that large experiments sometimes have complicated roots in the consumer community. Dr. David Capuzzi, a panel member who treated diabetic patients and who voted to keep the drug with no further restrictions, said that doctors should have "as many choices of drugs as possible." Chuck Keyserling, a diabetes patient who had taken the drug for ten years, said that for people who had "flourished on Avandia," a "negative position" on the drug "may be a death sentence."[29]

A sidelight was the issue of possible conflicts of interest. It was reported that Capuzzi had received $14,750 from the GSK speakers' bureau for talks about another drug. Although he emphasized that he had "not given any talks [to doctors' groups] promoting Avandia," a GSK spokesperson said that Capuzzi had "been paid to serve on [an Avandia] advisory board prior to 2008." Another report, about the panel member Dr. Abraham Thomas, provided an interesting comparison. Dr. Thomas, who had voted to remove Avandia from the market, was said to have been paid to speak for the maker of Actos as part of that firm's diabetes speakers' bureau.[30]

The chair of the joint committee, Dr. Clifford Rosen, was moved to write a "Lessons Learned" essay for the *New England Journal of Medicine*. One of his comments noted the opportunity for spin in the new vote—that it could be interpreted "as indicating that the majority wanted to keep [Avandia] on the market or that the majority wanted it either removed from the market or severely restricted in its use."[31] Posing the question of what had "changed in 3 years?," he referred to the discovery of "three lines of evidence since 2007" "suggesting that [Avandia's] cardiovascular risk is significant and that major federal action is now required." These data included "two meta-analyses including 10 new randomized trials" showing that the risk of acute heart attacks was "30 to 80% higher" for Avandia patients than for those taking a placebo; new "observational data," and "several new data sets" showed that the competing drug Actos either "conferred no increased cardiovascular risk or, in some circumstances, protected against" heart attacks.[32] A principal "lesson" Rosen identified was that "although there is evidence that black box warnings"—like those required for Avandia in 2007—and "notifications from the FDA have an impact," there was also evidence that "would argue against limiting new FDA action to the addition of further warnings."[33] Among other things, he noted that "very little" had been said in the panel hearing "about the balance of risks and benefits"—that "though the risks were apparent from the data presentations, there was virtually no discussion of any unique benefits of" Avandia. From this, he drew the lesson that "all committee hearings should be required to include a discussion of the risk-benefit balance." He concluded, "Despite what may have seemed an ambiguous vote . . . EMDAC clearly indicated that the FDA must do more than provide additional black box warnings." He specified just two choices: either "stronger warnings plus the use of informed consent" or "a registry for compassionate use of [Avandia] or removal of the drug from the market." He noted that "the ultimate decision about [Avandia's] fate lies with the FDA."[34]

That decision was not long in coming. In September 2010, the agency mandated that new users could get the drug "only if they are unable to achieve glucose control on other medications and are unable to take Actos," although "current users of Avandia who are benefiting from the drug will be able to continue to use the medication if they choose to do so." The rigor of the new regime was evident in the agency's requirement that "doctors will have to attest to and document their patient's eligibility" and that patients would "have to review statements describing the cardiovascular safety concerns . . . and acknowledge they understand the risks."[35] Dr. Nissen, such a central figure in focusing attention on the risks of Avandia, said that this decision brought an end to "one of the worst drug safety tragedies of our lifetime"; a reporter cited an estimate that in the decade after 1999, "more than 47,000 people taking Avandia needlessly suffered a heart attack, stroke or heart failure or died."[36]

An "extraordinary acknowledgment" that accompanied the agency's order was a statement by Dr. Janet Woodcock, the director of the FDA's drug center: "We know that labels are not often read."[37] This statement not only called into question the agency's reliance "almost exclusively on label warnings"[38] but also a significant wedge of the law of products liability, which tends to assume that warnings will be "read and heeded."[39]

A month later, Dr. Woodcock, joined by the FDA commissioner and deputy commissioner, wrote an essay on the agency's severe action on Avandia, noting that "there was no reliable evidence to refute" the "cardiovascular safety concerns" about the drug.[40] She and her coauthors noted the "remarkable" aspect of the controversy about the drug, embodied in the "strongly held, differing positions on how the agency should respond to emerging safety data, both inside the FDA and in the biomedical community."[41] The ferocity of the infighting had been evident in the fact that as panel chair Clifford Rosen had noted, the joint advisory committee had "met for 20 hours over 2 days."[42] Noting both the "benefits in glycemic control" provided by the drug and that the evidence of its cardiovascular risk was "concerning, but it is not definitive," Dr. Woodcock and her coauthors said that "serious questions" had arisen about the design of a study of the drug done by GSK. Identifying a crucial question for the agency as how it could "prevent such uncertainty about a major risk happening again," she referred to an agency "guidance" document requiring "trials of at least two years' duration" that would compare new drugs "with standard therapy." Emphasizing that the burden was on manufacturers "to demonstrate the safety of medicines,"[43] they said the agency would "continue to review emerging data on" Avandia.

The tort alternative to regulation was in full swing over the period that included the Senate Finance Committee report and the FDA panel's split verdict. Illustrative of the organization of lawsuits on the claimants' side were several websites that reported on Avandia litigation. In July 2010, one of these quoted an article recording that GSK had "agreed to pay about $560 million to resolve a majority of" the lawsuits on Avandia, just as the FDA panel was meeting.[44] A post in February 2011 reported that the company was going to pay $250 million in settlements to 5,500 plaintiffs—at $46,000 per plaintiff, $6,000 more per claimant than the last settlement. The item noted that this was a boon for GSK, because "settlement amounts . . . could have ranged from $500,000 to $1 million if there was concrete evidence that Avandia did cause heart attacks."[45] A post three months later referred to twelve thousand settlements totaling almost $750,000,000 and noted that "the number of lawsuits" on Avandia "shows no sign of slowing down," with "nearly 5,300 cases still pending nationwide."[46] By 2013, the company reportedly had set aside $6.4 billion for "Avandia litigation and settlement costs."[47]

Another set of turns in the Avandia roller coaster came in the fall of 2013. In October, a journal article referred to an "extensive" study by the Duke Clinical Research Institute that the authors said "provided reassurance that rosiglitazone"—the generic name of Avandia—"was not associated with excess cardiovascular risk." Their summary of the evidence, they said, was that Avandia and two other drugs, "from a cardiovascular perspective," "appear to be relatively safe."[48] The next month, the FDA sent out a "safety announcement," saying that it had concluded from "recent data" that drugs with rosiglitazone did not "show an increased risk of heart attack compared to" two "standard type 2 diabetes medicines." The new data, the agency said, came from a large, long-term clinical trial and was supported by what it characterized as the Duke Institute's "comprehensive, outside, expert re-evaluation of the data." The agency noted that it had instituted a "Risk Evaluation and

Mitigation Strategy" specifically for rosiglitazone after the emergence of what it summarized as "previous data from a large, combined analysis of mostly short-term, randomized clinical trials" of the drug that "had suggested an elevated risk of heart attack."

The agency thus decided to "require removal of the prescribing and dispensing restrictions for rosiglitazone medicines that were put in place in 2010." Although it did say that "some scientific uncertainty about the cardiovascular safety of rosiglitazone medicines still remains," it said that its "concern is substantially reduced" and that "distribution of the medicines will no longer be restricted." However, the agency reflected the fact that Avandia-type drugs were still a scientific experiment in progress when it said that "sponsors will ensure that health care professionals who are likely to prescribe rosiglitazone medicines are provided training based on the current state of knowledge concerning the cardiovascular risk of rosiglitazone medicines." A catchall for patients was the agency's statement that "patients with type 2 diabetes should continue to work closely with their health care professionals to determine treatment options that are most appropriate."[49] The victory for GSK does not appear to have been a commercial triumph. One reporter wrote that the FDA action "was unlikely to breathe new life into the drug," which she noted "had been largely discredited in the United States and was withdrawn from the market in Europe in 2010." Ronald Tamler, the clinical director of the Mount Sinai Diabetes Center, said that the FDA's decision was "irrelevant to clinical practice" and that "after years of warnings, patients would not 'abandon their concerns overnight.'" Dr. Nissen, a central protagonist in the development of those concerns, reportedly said that the FDA "was trying to rewrite an embarrassing episode in its history."[50]

## The Pill

Avandia is a relatively late entry on the market. It is interesting to compare with Avandia the story of the oral contraceptive known as "the Pill" from its beginnings, as it evolved from being a new product to its well-established status today. So ubiquitous is its use that one observer pointed out that "among many thousands of drugs, it alone is called 'the Pill.'"[51] G. D. Searle began testing the first version of the Pill, Enovid, in 1956. With increased concern today on drug testing in underprivileged populations, it is worth noting that the first test populations were in Puerto Rico and Haiti. After gaining approval to market the drug for menstrual disorders in 1957, the firm received the FDA's permission to undertake large-scale clinical testing in 1960, although a majority of professors of obstetrics and gynecology did not favor putting it on the market.[52]

The red flags began to appear on the map after the drug proceeded to the general market. An early concern was thrombophlebitis—blood clots. Although an FDA official insisted in a 1966 congressional hearing that the factors involving side effects under consideration were "within the limits of the normal," that year the agency published labeling guidelines that listed clotting episodes as contraindications and said, under the heading "Precautions," that doctors should be "alert to the earliest manifestations of the disease." Other contraindications were "known or suspected carcinoma of the breasts or genital organs" and "undiagnosed vaginal bleeding."[53]

British studies published in 1968 specifically targeted clotting disease, saying that it "seems reasonable to conclude that the risk of death from pulmonary embolism during one year's treatment with oral contraceptives is of the same order as the comparable risk of bearing one child."[54] Over the next decade, concerns arose about heart attacks in women with multiple risk factors, including smoking and high blood pressure. Paralleling data on the heart were reports indicating a significant risk of endometrial cancer in users of postmenopausal estrogens, a chemical cousin of the principal ingredient of the first versions of the Pill. Later came reports on liver tumors.[55]

Over time, Pill makers began to reduce the amount of estrogen in the product, and by the mid-nineties, researchers could report that at least in nonsmokers, "low-estrogen oral-contraceptive preparations do not appear to increase the risk of stroke."[56] An instance of how the adjustment of dosages of a chemical agent can dramatically affect illness rates was the authors' notation of "the virtually exclusive use of oral contraceptives containing less than 50 μg of estrogen"[57]—the original versions of the Pill having contained as much as 150 μg.[58]

By the mid-nineties, the question of breast cancer came into the spotlight. The FDA's consumer magazine was quoting a consumer safety officer for the agency as saying that "the jury is still out" on whether the Pill promoted or accelerated breast cancer. She said, "If a woman has a family history of breast cancer, she might want to use another birth control method or be monitored closely by a physician."[59]

From a consumer perspective, this presented a problem that was quite apart from the problem of laypersons judging uncertainty and the choice of the "ask your doctor" route. An article in the *Journal of the American Medical Association* suggested that the laconic response was too late, if not too little. The authors focused on women who had family histories of breast cancer and who used oral contraceptives before 1975—a date selected because all versions of the Pill sold after 1975 "contain less than 50 μg or less of ethinyl estradiol"—a principal estrogen in the Pill—"and 1 mg or less of several progestins"[60]—the hormones used in the Pill to "oppose" the disease-causing effects of estrogens. The authors found that the use of the Pill "in women with a strong family history of breast cancer may further elevate their breast cancer risk." Specifically, sisters and daughters of such women "who had ever used OCs [oral contraceptives] had a more than 30-fold increase in risk of breast cancer compared with similarly related women who had never used OCs." They further noted that "the elevated risk of breast cancer was most pronounced for women with a first-degree family history of breast cancer who used OCs before 1975,"[61] whereas they found "no association . . . between OC use after 1975 and risk of breast cancer for any category of family history," although noting that their data were limited.[62]

Efforts at innovation moved forward in the next decade, sometimes crawling and sometimes with small leaps and bounds. The developments included the invention of products that altered what had been the standard Pill, with its requirement that women using it must take a furlough from the medicine for seven days out of twenty-eight, which produced in some women various unpleasant side effects including menorrhagia—heavy menstrual bleeding—menstrual migraines, and breast tenderness. These modifications included a pill that would allow four menstrual periods a year. Two commentators observed that "with over 40 brands of COC [combined oral contraceptives] on the market, there are options to fit every woman's needs"—that it was "not a one-pill-for-all situation."[63] Yet for many women, it was not any pill at all; one study showed that "up to 31% of women discontinued taking an oral contraceptives within 6 months of treatment initiation," many because of unwelcome side effects.[64]

In 2010, Bayer Healthcare Pharmaceuticals secured FDA approval to market Natazia, a Pill version that combined an estrogen and a progestin that had not previously been used in the United States. This was a Pill that had to be taken in four stages each month: the estrogen on the first two days and the combination the next five days at two milligrams, the combination for seventeen days at 3 milligrams, the estrogen for two days, and a placebo for two days. The *Medical Letter* summarized research to the effect that this drug "appears to be similar in efficacy to other" Pill versions but "appears to cause less withdrawal bleeding than" the combination of ethinyl estradiol and levonorgestrel, the latter a progestin used in some versions of oral contraceptives.[65] A lay observer might suggest that this was a drug for use only by people with a compulsive attachment to complex pill dosages. Moreover, the adverse effects associated with the drug, perhaps not surprisingly, including menorrhagia and breast pain and tenderness.[66]

At a time when some doctors were prescribing continuous use as an off-label use, the effect of which is to stop menstruation, and some women were using the drug continuously "to avoid inconvenience during a vacation, honeymoon or special event," a North Carolina ob-gyn practitioner, David Grimes, said that he saw "little reason for women to menstruate on a regular basis." However, a Boston ob-gyn practitioner countered that she didn't "know if this is a good idea." She raised as just one question whether there would "be a bump up in breast cancer because we give people more hormones," saying, "This just appalls me. I'm not into fixing things that are not broken."[67] Her cautionary declaration, "We have no idea what we're doing," is a classic capsule statement of what much human experimentation amounts to. It also reflects the uneasy dividing line between medical specialization and consumer desires: here, the consumer decides whether menstruation is a "broken" body process.

A 2009 summary of adverse effects associated with combined oral contraceptives in the *British Medical Journal* was a roundup of suspects from a half century: "increased risk of myocardial infarction, stroke, gallbladder disease, hypertension, glycometabolic imbalance in people with diabetes, carcinoma of the cervix, hepatocellular carcinoma, and—to a lesser degree—breast cancer in current users."[68]

One entry in the field that inspired concern and controversy was the use of the hormone drospirenone, a progestin, in combination products, first approved in the United States in 2001.[69] Drospirenone had a thorny relationship with the FDA through its life as an element of medicines used by women, particularly Bayer's drug Yaz. In one skirmish in this battle of more than a decade, a "Warning Letter" by the agency in 2008 said that Bayer had misbranded the drug by encouraging its use "in circumstances other than those in which" it had been approved, and that it had "over-promise[d] the benefits and minimize[d] the risks associated with YAZ."[70]

By 2011, the agency was publishing a balanced "safety announcement" on drospirenone, reporting on "several epidemiological studies" that found that "the risk of blood clots for women who use birth control pills containing drospirenone is higher than that for women who use birth control pills containing the progestin levonorgestrel." In the same document, the agency noted that "other studies have not reported an increase in risk."[71]

A year later, the agency reported a conclusion that "drospirenone-containing birth control pills may be associated with a higher risk for blood clots than other progestin-containing pills," although it qualified its statement by saying that because of various aspects of the studies at hand, it was "unclear whether the increased risk seen for blood clots in some of the epidemiologic studies is actually due to drospirenone-containing birth control pills."[72] Meanwhile, however, Bayer had taken the risk seriously enough as a legal threat that it had settled U.S. lawsuits on Yaz and the companion drug Yasmin for $142 million, and there was one prediction that it could pay as much as $2.65 billion to settle suits in Europe.[73]

During the first decades of Pill use, non-pill chemical alternatives had been developed—one used by injection and the other by implantation. The principal rationale for the injectable, Depo-Provera, was that because one injection provided contraception for three months, it was a good alternative to oral contraceptives for women who could not be relied on to take pills daily. Warning signs for the drug appeared during a multiyear clinical test that began in 1968. The FDA, although proposing in 1973 to approve Depo-Provera "for a limited and well defined patient population," noted evidence that it "can cause prolonged and possibly even permanent infertility." Moreover, high doses of the drug were shown to cause breast cancer in beagles, and a 1971 report to the National Cancer Institute in 1971 showed that the drug was associated with a risk of carcinoma *in situ* of the cervix that was several times higher than in the general population.[74] It was not until 1992 that the FDA approved Depo-Provera—and that over the objections of groups including the National Women's Health Network and the National Black Women's Health Project.[75] In 2005, the FDA added a black-box warning to the labeling for Depo-Provera, saying that "prolonged use may result in loss of bone density."[76] The "Warnings and Precautions" in recent labeling for the drug include a reference to a "significant loss of bone mineral density" and "reports of serious thrombotic events," although there was no showing of causal association. Accompanying a specific warning against use of the product by women "who currently have or have had breast cancer" was a cautionary note that "women with a strong family history of breast cancer or who have breast nodules should be monitored with particular care."[77]

The implanted contraceptive was Norplant, which has been described as "matchstick-size capsules containing . . . progestin" that are "surgically implanted under the skin of the upper arm," from which gradual release of the progestin achieves contraception. Initially marketed in 1991, the product had gained approval from the FDA in 1995 for "a new campaign" by the maker "to help insure that Norplant patients are adequately informed about" the product.[78]

However, Norplant had begun to generate a series of lawsuits, with one early batch being a class action by women claiming "severe pain and scarring when their doctors removed the . . . capsules."[79] Eventually, thousands of suits wound up in a multidistrict action. In a 2002 opinion, a federal district court granted summary judgment to the manufacturer, Wyeth Ayerst, as to all plaintiffs who had alleged that they had "suffered any of the 26 primary side effects listed in the 'Adverse Reactions' section" of the physician labeling for the product,[80] saying in essence that there was no evidence that different warnings for the product would have changed prescribing behavior by doctors.[81] The court also granted summary judgment to the firm on allegations of "more than 950 other side effects," which were labeled "exotic conditions."[82] However, it denied summary judgment as to plaintiffs who had not alleged any of the twenty-six effects in the labeling.[83]

By the same year, 2002, Wyeth had announced that it "would not resume sales of the implant kits," which had been the subject of a 2000 recall that occurred because of concerns about the lack of contraceptive effects in some lots of the product.[84] This was three years after the distributor of Norplant in the UK had withdrawn it there, blaming "adverse media coverage" and lawsuits for "dwindling demand."[85]

While the large-scale experiment with Norplant proceeded, a very public controversy arose around the use of the drug generally known as "the Pill" as a "morning-after" contraceptive. In the summer of 1996, the FDA's Reproductive Health Drugs Advisory Committee released a "talk paper" that was summarized as approving "certain oral contraceptives . . . for daily use" as "safe and effective as emergency contraceptives." These drugs were Pill versions containing the estrogen ethinyl estradiol and the progestins norgestrol or levonorgestrel.[86] A reporter summarized the committee's unanimous conclusion that these pills "could be used to prevent pregnancy up to 72 hours after unprotected intercourse." The move was an unusual one, because in effect it approved an off-label use, rather than offering a formal approval of a new drug application. The agency's deputy commissioner, Mary Prendergast, explained that this was "as far as we can go without a new drug application," saying that she hoped that publication of a notice about this use in the Federal Register would "calm people's anxieties about using oral contraceptives as morning-after pills" and that "we're still hopeful that someone will come forward to market them."[87]

As it turned out, the agency was behind the curve of off-label practice. A news story reported that "college health specialists, rape crisis centers and some reproductive health clinics" had "increasingly offered" the Pill as a morning-after treatment for "women who were raped, whose method of birth control had failed or who reported that they simply refused to use contraception." The president of the Center for Reproductive Law and Policy, a lawyer by training, asserted that this was "not really an off-label use," but rather "another contraceptive use as a different dosage"—the kind of characterization in which lawyers specialize. She reportedly said that "at rape crisis centers . . . it's become so much the standard of care that there was a malpractice case in California based on failure to offer emergency contraception to a rape victim." A Manhattan gynecologist affirmed this, saying, "We've been using it for many years, knowing it's safe and effective," but said that the FDA action was "like the Good Housekeeping seal of approval."[88]

On the other side, conservative groups weighed in with religion-based arguments. At a hearing before the FDA committee, a representative of the American Life League said that morning-after use was "killing an unborn child before its life is even begun." And one could infer a concern about medical risk in a statement by the Family Research Council that if the Pill were relabeled for morning-after use, "girls and women may forgo other forms of birth control and simply choose to consume larger doses of the pill after sex."[89]

The timing of the announcement of the committee's approval coincided with the eruption of intense controversy about RU-486, a drug originally marketed in France that is chemically named misoprostol. A journal article in 1995 described the scientific literature on the use of a combination of methotrexate, injected into the muscles, and misoprostol, administered a few days later in the vagina. The author concluded that this combination was "both safe and effective" for the termination of pregnancies of no more than two months.[90] Misoprostol became known as a "abortion pill," although it was sometimes confused with the "morning-after" category. A medical editorialist underlined the confusion by pointing out that "if hormonal emergency contraception works largely by interfering with ovulation, it cannot be regarded as an abortifacient," because even a drug administered "within 72 hours after a single act of intercourse cannot dislodge an implanted embryo, because implantation would not have occurred yet."[91] One can only surmise the potential for misunderstanding among women without scientific educations.

Stimulating the argument over RU-486 was the perceived need for contraception alternatives to the Pill. The makers of Depo-Provera had terminated their research on contraceptives in 1995, and although the maker of Norplant reportedly was "committed to contraceptives research," a company official was quoted as saying that the lawsuits filed on the product "could have an impact."[92]

RU-486 met with considerable political opposition to its introduction into the United States.[93] At one point in 1997, the French developer of the drug agreed—under pressure from the Clinton administration—to donate its American patent rights to the Population Council, a nonprofit contraceptive research group in New York.[94]

Backing and filling by the FDA on the efforts to market RU-486 continued until 2000, when the agency approved the drug, but only for use after three visits to a doctor's office, which involved testing and dating of a pregnancy. The treatment began with a dose of the steroid mifepristone, an antiprogestin, followed by RU-486, and was reported to be 92 percent effective in terminating pregnancies.[95]

Following the approval of RU-486, new contraceptive products came on the market; for example, the Ortho Evra patch, first marketed in 1992 by Ortho-McNeil and worn three weeks a month on the skin. Sales of Ortho Evra shot up within a few months, and the product became "the second most popular form of non-oral birth control in prescriptions and sales, behind Depo-Provera."[96] However, by 2006, concerns arose that women purchasing this "once-a-week convenience" were also buying "60% more estrogen in a monthly cycle than women taking" a more typical Pill. A brief 2006 essay in a medical journal, referencing an FDA warning, mentioned concerns about "nausea, breast tenderness and venous thromboembolism [VTE]."[97] In 2008 the agency approved changes to the Ortho Evra label "to include results of a new epidemiology study that found that users of the birth control patch were at higher risk of developing blood clots"—that is, VTE—than women using birth control pills, noting that "VTE can lead to pulmonary embolism." The agency bowed to the physician/patient relationship with a statement that it "believe[d] that Ortho Evra is a safe and effective method of contraception when used according to the labeling, which recommends that women with concerns or risk factors for serious blood clots talk with their health care provider about using Ortho Evra versus other contraceptive options."[98]

Meanwhile, the search for alternative ways to prevent pregnancy bridged the turn of the century. Dr. Allan Rosenfeld, dean of the Columbia University School of Health, noting that many women as young as thirty were choosing sterilization in preference to pills or contraceptive devices, advocated more research on molecular biology. Speaking to a reporter in 1996, he said that although such research would require more initial investment, it was yet "tempting, in a time of budget austerity, to recommend emphasis on investment in downstream, applied research."[99] His reference to "budget austerity" has special force as I write in 2013.

In the years on both sides of 2000, there was an outpouring of hope—often better labeled speculation—about more effective ways of preventing conception. The ideas were varied. Women who considered existing methods to be a product of male-dominated science would have been pleased at the prospect of a hormonal attack on men's production of sperm, for example by "intramuscular injection of an androgen" like testosterone that would lead "to release of the hormone into the bloodstream," with the result that the brain would be "instruct[ed]" "to dampen" hormonal activity that produced sperm. This kind of drug would not be free of several side effects, including lowered levels of HDL cholesterol—the so-called "good" cholesterol. However, one proposed modification echoed developments in the history of female contraception, namely making the drug a cocktail that included a progestin that would lower the required dose of androgen.[100]

A media contributor excitedly reported in 2003 that "a safe, effective and reversible male contraceptive appears to be within reach,"[101] a hope that was repeated over the next years. Authors of a 2009 article summarized an "update on male contraception" with the statement that "male hormone contraception may yet become a reality in the near future."[102]

Yet by 2011 the hope seemed to keep receding. The World Health Organization and the group CONRAD announced that year that they were ending a collaborative study that combined an androgen and a progestin in a male contraceptive. The investigators, whose study population included couples in eight countries, had expected some adverse effects—for example, "acne, increased libido, injection site pain, weight gain [and] mood changes." But they were discouraged by reports of "depression and other mood changes as well as increased libido," "at a higher frequency than anticipated for this combination and not commonly seen with the products when used in their approved indications and dosing regimens." The primary basis for their decision to terminate the study lay in their concern about whether "the drug combination could be successfully developed and marketed as a male contraceptive method."[103]

One commentator called the termination of this study "a major setback in bringing male contraceptives on the market," while noting "difficult ethical questions about how to evaluate side effects in male contraceptive trials." In that connection, the writer noted a list of side effects associated with female contraceptives, including "breakthrough bleeding, mood changes, increased risk of blood-clot formation," and other adverse effects and asked, "Why should we set a different bar for male contraceptives?" This article contained the interpolated, unattributed quotation, "None of the big companies will touch hormonal male contraception again."[104] Before the 2011 termination of the study, a medical journal article spelled out several reasons for the stalling of progress on a male pill: "lack of potential profitability, long-term investment, and medico-legal reasons."[105] Another explanation, identifying a problem that was male-ego rather than chemically oriented, lay in a response by a Dutch woman to an interviewer: "They need a weekly injection in the buttock? Oh, you can forget it. There is no man who will do that. Men are very oversensitive to injections."[106]

It should be noted that as a variety of efforts proceeded with hormonal products, women had had access to nonhormonal contraception for some time in the form of spermicides, a variety of substances used in the vagina to immobilize sperm—in one characterization, "detergents that degrade sperm." Because of various proved and speculated side effects—the latter including irritations of the vaginal wall that facilitated infection—a new idea was described as "chemicals that directly prevent sperm from migrating to or fertilizing an egg," perhaps without the side effect of vaginal irritation.[107] Another possible chemical solution would have "bound tightly to sperm" in the male sperm duct "and remained attached during the journey through the female reproductive tract."[108]

Yet another possibility that could be applied across gender lines was vaccines for both sexes. Most of these chemicals "would prod the immune system to make antibodies able to bind to, and disrupt the functioning of, selected proteins involved in reproduction."[109]

The history of the Pill as a six-decade experiment, as we can now view it, was that this set of drugs had stabilized in a kind of equilibrium of consumer safety and risk, but only after a very long tryout. The development of alternative methods of contraception, therefore, would themselves be likely to require long periods of experimentation on large numbers of women—or men—perhaps resulting in a significant number of injuries. That, arguably, was the lesson of the adventures with many versions of the Pill and also with Depo-Provera and Norplant. It was a lesson strongly implied by the waning of optimism about the possibilities for a safe and effective male Pill. In the near background of the continuing saga was the possibility of what would be an enormous quantitative change in availability, although one that would be quite controversial in many quarters for medical as well as social reasons. This would be the sale of birth control pills over the counter, which according to one report is legal in thirty-five countries and possibly effected in practice in fifty-six others, although a prescription is required in Canada and many European countries in addition to the United States.[110]

## IUDs and Other Devices

An alternative to chemical contraception that had been used by many women is the intrauterine device known as the IUD. Various IUDs have been the subject of lawsuits and are thus representative of the many medical products that have been involved in tort litigation. Just one recent example of litigation on an IUD with a hormonal component involves the Mirena device of Bayer Healthcare, a subject of fifteen hundred suits, including one with the novel claim that the device had migrated from the plaintiff's uterus to her rectum.[111] In 2009, the FDA had told the company that a "live consumer-directed program" promoting the product, which employed the release of the hormone levonorgestrel into the body, "overstates the efficacy of Mirena, presents unsubstantiated claims, minimizes the risks of using Mirena, and includes false or misleading presentations regarding Mirena."[112]

Just a sampling of other devices involved in major litigation includes hip implants and pelvic mesh devices. In 2013, Johnson & Johnson and the claimants' lawyers tentatively announced a settlement of almost

$2.5 billion for eight thousand patients who had to have the company's Articular Surface Replacement removed and replaced, with additions for medical costs involved in remedial surgery.[113] Also in 2014, Stryker Corporation agreed to a $1.43 billion settlement of thousands of claims for its own hip implant device.[114] And a gigantic set of suits was under way on vaginal mesh products used to remedy pelvic organ prolapse and the condition known as stress urinary incontinence. By 2014, as many as forty thousand claims had been filed against several companies, including American Medical Systems, a defendant in fourteen thousand cases, and Boston Scientific Corporation.[115]

## Notes

1. FDA's Role in the Evaluation of Avandia's Safety, Hearing before the Committee on Oversight and Government Reform, 110th Cong., 1st Sess., June 6, 2007, Serial No. 110-76, at 1 (hereinafter Avandia Hearing).
2. Ibid., pp. 90–91.
3. Steven E. Nissen and Kathy Wolski, "Effect of Rosiglitazone on the Risk of Myocardial Infarction and Death from Cardiovascular Causes," 356 *New Eng. J. Med.* 2457, 2459 (2007).
4. Ibid., p. 2467.
5. Ibid., p. 2469.
6. Ibid., pp. 2469–70.
7. Avandia Hearing, supra note 1, at p. 7.
8. Ibid., pp. 8–9.
9. Ibid., pp. 122–23.
10. Ibid., pp. 127–28.
11. Ibid., p. 18.
12. Ibid., pp. 18 and 22.
13. Ibid., p. 18.
14. Ibid., pp. 19–20.
15. FDA news release, "FDA Adds Boxed Warning for Heart-related Risks to Anti-Diabetes Drug Avandia: Agency Says Drug to Remain on Market, while Safety Assessment Continues," Nov. 14, 2007.
16. See "Avandia, Other Drugs Are Bitter Pills for Diabetics, Suits Say," *Trial*, May 2009, pp. 14 and 126, referencing "In re Avandia," MDL No. 1871 (E.D. Pa., consolidated Feb. 28. 2008). The webpage is http:www.paed.uscourts.gov/mdl1871.asp.
17. James S. Floyd et al., "Case Series of Liver Failure Associated With Rosiglitazone and Pioglitazone," vol. 18 no. 12 *Pharmacoepidemiology and Drug Safety* 2338 (Dec. 2009).
18. "Public Citizen Recommends Banning Avandia Because of Risk of Liver Failure, Death," 37 *Prod. Safety & Liab. Rep.* 814, 815 (2009).
19. Gardiner Harris, "Diabetes Drug Harms Heart, U.S. Concludes," *New York Times*, Feb. 20, 2010, pp. A1 and A3.
20. Jessica Coomes, "Senate Committee Investigators Say GSK Knew of Possible Avandia–Heart Attack Link," 38 *Prod. Safety & Liab. Rep.* 190, 191 (March 1, 2010).

21. Harris, supra note 19, p. A3.
22. Coomes, supra note 20, p. 191.
23. Lisa Nainggolan, "New Senate Report Puts Avandia Safety in Spotlight Again," http://www.medscape.com/viewarticle/717322#vp_1 Feb. 22, 2010, last consulted July 6, 2015.
24. Harris, supra note 19, p. A3.
25. 52 *Med. Letter* Issue 1333, March 8, 2010, p. 17.
26. Gardiner Harris, "Drug Maker Hid Test Data, Files Indicate," *New York Times*, July 13, 2010, pp. A1 and A16.
27. Gardiner Harris, "Panel Suggests Limit on Drug for Diabetes," *New York Times*, July 15, 2010, pp. A1 and A23.
28. Ibid.
29. Ibid.
30. Michael O'Riordan, "News Report Links Avandia Panelist to Drug Makers," *Heartwire* July 21, 2010 (summarizing *Wall Street Journal* report). I am grateful to Dr. Morris Schambelan for calling this item to my attention.
31. Clifford J. Rosen, "Revisiting the Rosiglitazone Story—Lessons Learned," 363 *N. Eng. J. Med.* 803, 803 (2010).
32. Ibid.
33. Ibid., p. 804.
34. Ibid., pp. 804–05.
35. FDA news release, "FDA Significantly Restricts Access to the Diabetes Drug Avandia," Sept. 23, 2010.
36. Gardiner Harris, "F.D.A. to Restrict a Diabetes Drug, Citing Heart Risk," *New York Times*, Sept. 24, 2010, pp. A1 and A15.
37. Ibid., p. A15 ("extraordinary acknowledgment" the reporter's characterization).
38. See ibid.
39. A standard formulation of this idea appears in Restatement (Second) of Torts § 402A cmt. j (1965).
40. Ibid.
41. Janet Woodcock, Joshua Sharfstein, and Margaret Hamburg, "Regulatory Action on Rosiglitazone by the U.S. Food and Drug Administration," 363 *N. Eng. J. Med.* 1489, 1490 (2010).
42. Rosen, supra note 31, p. 803.
43. Woodcock et al., supra note 41, pp. 1490–91.
44. http://www.drug-injury.com/druginjurycom/2010/07/avandia-settlement-thousands-lawsuit, July 13, 2010, accessed May 27, 2011.
45. "Avandia Lawsuit Settlement for 5,500 Plaintiffs," www.lawsuitsettlement.lawleaf.com/avandia-lawsuit-settlement-for-5500-plaintiffs, Feb. 12, 2011, accessed May 27, 2011.
46. "Avandia Continues to Settle With Injured Plaintiffs," http://litigationand-settlementnews.com/?p=407, May 12, 2011, accessed May 27, 2011.
47 "Avandia Lawsuit," http://www.drugwatch.com/avandia/lawsuit.php, modified Aug. 8, 2013, accessed Sept. 27, 2013.
48. William R. Hiatt et al., "The Cardiovascular Safety of Diabetes Drugs: Insights from the Rosiglitazone Experience," 369 *New Eng. J. Med.* 1285 (2013).

49. FDA drug safety communication, "FDA Requires Removal of Some Prescribing and Dispensing Restrictions for Rosiglitazone-Containing Diabetes Medications," Nov. 25, 2013.
50. Sabrina Tavernese, "F.D.A. Lifts Some Restriction on Avandia," *New York Times*, Nov. 26, 2013, p. B2.
51. Etienne-Emile Baulieu, quoted by Alexander Theroux in a book review of Bernard Asbell's *The Pill*, *Chicago Tribune*, July 9, 1995, pp. 1 and 12.
52. This history is summarized in Marshall S. Shapo, *A Nation of Guinea Pigs* (The Free Press, 1979), pp. 91–92.
53. See ibid., p. 96.
54. W. H. W. Imnan and M. P. Vessey, "Investigation of Deaths from Pulmonary, Coronary and Cerebral Thrombosis in Women of Child-Bearing Age," 2 *Br. Med. J.* 193, 198 (1968).
55. See Shapo, supra note 52, pp. 117–24.
56. Diana B. Pettiti et al., "Stroke in Users of Low-Dose Oral Contraceptives," 335 *N. Eng. J. Med.* 8, 8 (1996) (abstract).
57. Ibid., p. 12.
58. Ibid., p. 8.
59. Marilynn Larkin, "Estrogen, Friend or Foe,?" *FDA Consumer*, April 1995, pp. 25–26.
60. Dawn M. Grabick et al., "Risk of Breast Cancer with Oral Contraceptive Use in Women With a Family History of Breast Cancer," 284 *JAMA* 1791, 1795 (Oct. 11, 2000).
61. Ibid., p. 1796.
62. See ibid., p. 1795.
63. See Jodi Godfrey and Patricia Sulak, "Toward Optimal Health: Advances in Contraceptive Options," 17 *J. Women's Health* No. 1, pp. 11 and 12–13 (2008).
64. See for example Sandra Kim and Mitzi Wasik, "Contraceptive Treatments: A Review of Current Hormone Options and Newer Agents for Women," 46 *Formulary* 54, 60 (2011), citing M. Rosenberg and M. Waugh, "Oral Contraceptive Discontinuation: A Prospective Evaluation of Frequency and Reasons," 179 *Am. J. Obstet. Gynecol.* 577 (1998).
65. "Natazia: A New Oral Contraceptive," 52 *Med. Letter* 71–72 (Sept. 6, 2010).
66. See for example Kim and Wasik, supra note 64, p. 54.
67. Victoria Stagg Elliott, "Move to Nonstop Use of Oral Contraceptives Stirs Debate," *American Medical News*, July 21, 2000, pp. 26–27.
68. Jean-Jacques Amy and Vrijesh Tripathi, "Contraception for Women: An Evidence Based Overview," 339 *Br. Med. J.* 563, 565 (2009).
69. See for example Tammy Worth, "Birth Control Pill Concerns Bring Lawsuits but Few Solid Answers," *Los Angeles Times*, April 19, 2010.
70. FDA warning letter transmitted to Reinhard Franzen, CEO, Bayer HealthCare Pharmaceuticals, Inc., Oct. 3, 2008.
71. FDA drug safety communication, "Safety Reviews of Possible Increased Risk of Blood Clots with Birth Control Pills Containing Drospirenone," May 31, 2011.
72. FDA drug safety communication, "Updated Information About the Risk of Blood Clots in Women Taking Birth Control Pills Containing Drospirenone," April 10, 2012.

73. Jef Feeley and Margaret Cronin-Fisk, "Bayer Yasmin Lawsuit Settlements Climb to $142 Million," *Bloomberg,* April 26, 2012.
74. See Shapo, supra note 52, pp. 181–84.
75. Committee on Women, "Population and the Environment: Depo-Provera Fact Sheet," Jan. 6, 2007, printed from the Internet June 2, 2011.
76. FDA *Patient Safety News,* Show #36: "New Warning on Depo-Provera Contraceptive Injection," Feb. 2005.
77. Drugs.com, "Full Prescribing Information" for Depo-Provera, http://cwpe.org/node/185 June 2, 2011 last consulted July 6, 2015.
78. "Norplant Devices for Birth Control Safe, F.D.A. Says," *New York Times,* Aug. 20, 1995.
79. See Tamar Lewin, "'Dream' Contraceptive's Nightmare," *New York Times,* July 8, 1994, p. A10.
80. See *In re Norplant Contraceptive Prods. Liab. Litig.*, 215 F. Supp.2d 796, 800, 828, 834 (N.D. Tex. 2002).
81. See ibid., pp. 826–27.
82. See ibid., pp. 800 and 833, where the court says there was no "shred of evidence or expert testimony" showing an association between the product and the conditions.
83. See ibid., pp. 828 and 834.
84. See for example Leslie Berger, "After Long Hiatus, New Contraceptives Emerge," *New York Times,* Dec. 10, 2002.
85. BBC News, "Contraceptive Implant Withdrawn," April 30, 1999, http://news.bbc.co.uk/2/hi/health/331618.stm June 2, 2011, last consulted July 6, 2015.
86. See FDA Talk Paper T96-48, "Emergency Contraceptive Pills Safe and Effective," June 29, 1996, F. D. Cosm. L. Rep (CCH), ¶ 41,497; CNN, "FDA Panel Endorses 'Morning After' Pill," June 29, 1996, https://www.google.com/?gws_rd=ssl#q=CNN+FDA+panel+endorses+morning+after, Oct. 4, 2013, last consulted July 6, 2015..
87. Tamar Lewin, "U.S. Agency Wants The Pill Redefined," *New York Times,* July 1, 1996, p. A1.
88. Ibid., p. A10.
89. Ibid.
90. Richard U. Hausknecht, "Methotrexate and Misoprostol to Terminate Early Pregnancy," 333 *N. Eng. J. Med.* 337, 339 (Aug. 31, 1995).
91. Anna Glasser, "Emergency Postcoital Contraception," 337 *N. Eng. J. Med,* 1058, 1063 (Oct. 9, 1997).
92. Deborah L. Shelton, "The Revolution ... That Never Happened," *American Medical News,* April 15, 1996, pp. 12–13.
93. See for example Warren E. Leary, "Variety of Obstacles Is Blocking New Contraceptives, a Medical Panel Says," *New York Times,* May 29, 1996, p. A13.
94. Tamar Lewin, "Abortion Pill's Legal Woe May Be Nearing an End," *New York Times,* Jan. 25, 1997, p. A6.
95. See for example Tracee Cornforth, "RU 486: The Abortion Pill Approved Mifepristone Mifeprex Pro-Life Pro-Choice," About.com Women's Health, updated March 20, 2010, printed from the Internet June 7, 2011.
96. See Leslie Berger, supra note 84.

97. Eric Wooltorton, "The Evra (Ethinyl Estradiol/Norelgestromin) Contraceptive Patch: Estrogen Exposure Concerns," 174(2) *CMAJ* 154 (2006).
98. FDA news release, "FDA Approves Update to Label on Birth Control Patch," Jan.18, 2008.
99. David L. Wheeler, "A Fresh Direction for Birth Control," *Chronicle of Higher Education*, June 7, 1996, p. A10.
100. See Nancy J. Alexander, "Future Contraceptives," 273 *Sci. Am.*, Sept. 1995, pp. 136–137.
101. John Schieszer, "Male Birth Control Pill Soon a Reality," http://www.nbcnews.com/id/3543478/ns/health-sexual_health/t/male-birth-control-pill-soon-reality/Oct. 1, 2003, Sept, 26, 2013, last checked July 6, 2015.
102. Rajesh K. Naz and Shon Rowan, "Update on Male Contraception," 21 *Current Opinion in Obstetrics and Gynecology* 265, 265 (2009) (summary).
103. CONRAD, "Male Hormonal Contraceptive Study Ending Early," April 22, 2011.
104. Jalees Rehman, "Where's the Male Pill? Many Promising Male Contraceptives Are in Development, but None Has Come to Market. So Why Has It Taken So Long?" *Aeon Magazine*, http://aeon.co/magazine/society/why-is-there-still-no-pill-for-men/Sept. 27, 2013, last consulted July 6, 2015.
105. Naz and Rowan, supra note 99, pp. 268–69.
106. *Chronicle of Higher Education*, item in "Verbatim" column, Nov. 14, 2003, p. A12.
107. See Alexander, supra note 97, p. 139.
108. Ibid.
109. Ibid., p. 137.
110. Reuters, "Most Countries Allow Women Over-the-Counter Access to Birth Control Pill—Without a Prescription," Jan. 2, 2013, http://www.nydailynews.com/life-style/health/world-women-pill-prescription-article-1.1231467, accessed Sept. 27, 2013.
111. See Lacey Louwagie, "Bayer's Mirena IUD Faces Alarming Claim," *Courthouse News Service*, Sept. 22, 2014, http://www.courthousenews.com/2014/09/22/71625.htm, last consulted July 6, 2015.
112. Facsimile transmission from Carrie A. Newcomer on behalf of Cynthia Collins, FDA Division of Drug Marketing, to Fadwa Almanaky of Bayer HealthCare Pharmaceuticals, Dec. 30, 2009.
113. See Barry Meier, "J&J in Deal to Settle Hip Implant Lawsuits," *New York Times*, Nov. 20, 2013, p. B2.
114. Drugwatch, "Stryker Hip Replacement Verdicts & Settlements," Nov. 5, 2014, update last viewed July 6, 2015.
115. Jane Mundy, "Transvaginal Mesh Lawsuits Heating Up," Lawyers & Settlements, Feb. 1, 2014, http://www.lawyersandsettlements.com/articles/transvaginal-mesh-tvt-sling/tvt-sling-transvaginal-mesh-16-19482.html#.VZrKYhTbLcs, Nov. 14, 2014.

# 5

# Profiles of Developing Risk

Cigarettes, BPA, and triclosan all had become embedded in the consumer marketplace, generating questions that were more or less well-aired in public about the level of risk they presented and how to minimize their hazards. Another profile that merits analysis in the taxonomy of large-scale experimentation is the problem that arises, in the consumer perspective, from a surprise. We first analyze here the problem of "mad cow disease," which as consumers would have viewed it, came from nowhere. We then turn to a particular aspect of the problem known as "carpal tunnel syndrome," which involved everyday activities that at first people did not know were causing repetitive stress.

We encounter in these cases an interesting mix of elements: early warning signs that only professionals might recognize, the accumulation of information that requires creative interpretation, the need for scientific detective work, the fashioning of preventive measures accompanied by arguments about the degree of risk aversion that is necessary, industry's resistance to government-imposed precautions, and the question of what constitutes rationality in a world where there are many different kinds of risk that may statistically outrank the problem on which the public becomes focused.

### Mad Cow Disease and Its Human Counterpart

The story of mad cow disease reveals the thinness of the line that occasionally exists between risk aversion and panic, and it presents a parable for our time in the combination of uncertain risk and public perception. Mad cow disease, known more technically as bovine spongiform encephalopathy (BSE), can infect human beings who eat meat from diseased cattle. The version in humans is called Creutzfeldt-Jakob disease. Eating away at the brains of those afflicted, it causes horrible deaths. The disease-causing agents, infectious proteins, are known as prions, and they usually hide out in the brain for years before beginning their vicious attack on its cells.

A doctor who worked with cannibals in New Guinea in the 1950s identified a spongiform disease,[1] but the first identification of the disease in cattle came in 1986 at an agricultural laboratory in England. However, although there was evidence that the disease spread from the use of animal feeds that included "ground-up parts of cows and sheep that included brain, spinal cord, gut, tonsils and spleen,"[2] the British government did not ban the use in feed of meat by-products until 1989.[3] Experiments, it should be noted, include not doing anything. It did appear that the ban on animal by-products in food had some effect: the number of cases of the disease in cows fell from about one thousand a week in 1993 to three hundred by 1996.[4] But social experiments rely on adherence to the rules of the experiment. In the fall of 1995, "surprise random inspections showed that half of the slaughterhouses" in Britain "were in violation of the regulations on animal feed."[5]

With more than one hundred and eighty thousand cases of the disease reported in animals in Britain since 1986, the evidence had accumulated gradually. It was in 1996, however, that the first focus of public attention on the disease came with the death of a twenty-year-old British man who had become a vegetarian but who was thought to have contracted the illness from beef burgers he ate as a child.[6]

One reason the case is symbolic of profiles of developing risk is because of the uncertainty about the disease that existed in the early stages of its discovery. Accounts of the writings of British officialdom in early 1996 on the topic are illustrative. On March 20 of that year, there were reports that the government had said "there may be a link between . . . mad cow disease . . . and a fatal brain disease [that is, Creutzfeldt-Jakob disease] in humans."[7] A reporter labeled this an "embarrassing about-face for the Government," noting that "since 1990, when concern first arose, it had adamantly insisted that there is no link" between mad cow disease and Creutzfeldt-Jakob.[8]

Over the next days, news stories reflected the same uncertainty. For example, they referred both to "only a tentative link"[9] and to the theory that "10 unexplained cases of Creutzfeldt-Jakob disease . . . might have been linked to eating meat from infected cows."[10] Yet with even tentative linkages now being publicized, the British government began trying to make up for lost time—there having been more than one hundred and sixty thousand cases of mad cow disease reported in livestock in Britain since 1986.[11] On April 2, the government proposed to slaughter fifteen thousand "older" cows a week for five or six years, with an eventual total of 4.7 million animals.[12] And the government set up a monitoring system in the 1996 Cattle Passports Order, which, as summarized by an agency document, "prohibits the movement of cattle to or off any holding, or between separately managed herds on the same holding without a cattle passport." It required "any person keeping cattle" to "apply for a cattle passport within 28 days of marking the animals," with applications to "contain the ear tag number, sex and breed of the animal."[13]

An example of the literally painful accumulation of evidence was the publication in early April 1996 of a report indicating that the symptoms of British Creuztfeldt-Jakob patients had "fooled" doctors "into thinking they had psychiatric disorders," as one report put it. Even with a special surveillance unit that started operating in 1990, seven of the first ten patients eventually diagnosed with the disease were not initially classified as having it.[14] Later in April 1996, there was a report of another case, and perhaps two others—all three in Ashford, a farm community in Britain. Although a government spokesman cautioned against premature conclusions, a microbiologist in Leeds called these reports "very bad news," observing that this was "the first instance of the disease's relationship to the early cases of mad cow disease," saying that the significance of the cases in that area was that "they were almost certainly acquired around the time of the first cases of mad cow disease, or a year or two before that."[15]

A particular feature of the mad cow epidemic in Britain was its international consequences. Typically, large-scale social experiments—including experiments in not doing anything—are confined to domestic product markets and fiscs. Internally, the British government had begun a program to compensate farmers for the commercial value of cattle that had to be slaughtered.[16] That, however, was not the half of the government's troubles, which extended into foreign relations. The cattle epidemic exacerbated animosities between Britain and the continent. The European Union imposed a ban on the export of British beef, and its refusal to lift the ban infuriated the British for weeks. Britain retaliated with a policy of "noncooperation," under which it refused to vote on about one hundred decisions of the Union. French farmers, who would learn their own lesson in four years, were leaders in the non-shooting war. Protesting the drop in beef prices in France that was a reaction to the English epidemic, some French farmers blocked passengers from getting off Channel ferries from England. Prime Minister Major's government did reach a deal with the EU that required Britain to slaughter one hundred and twenty thousand cattle, which was three times more than it had wanted to do, and did not specify a date to lift the EU ban.[17]

Meanwhile, the World Health Organization (WHO) tried to put a lock on the figurative barn door with a recommendation against using animal tissues in livestock feed. A report on the WHO recommendation captured the uncertainty inherent in large-scale experiments. David Heymann, a WHO official, said the uncertainty was "very worrisome," observing that "a new disease is frightening."[18] The sifting of evidence, and the attempts to interpret it, went on for weeks and months. From the very beginning of the crisis, there was caution about interpretation of the evidence and risk aversion relating to the appropriate reaction to the developing evidence. At the outset, Britain's "likely explanation "for the ten human cases of Creutzfeldt-Jakob was exposure to mad cow disease. As one report summarized it under the headline "Scant Data Cause Widespread Concern," the cases were "cause for concern" although there was no "direct evidence of a link."[19]

Concern bubbled up in the United States almost immediately when the news arrived about the British cases. Although a Department of Agriculture research facility had been unable to infect an experimental group of cattle with BSE, Paul Brown, medical director of the U.S. Public Health Service, said, "We're playing with fire. We have to worry about things that might happen and prevent them." Given that an FDA proposal to ban sheep parts from cattle feed had not moved forward, a Department of Agriculture spokesman said, "there really aren't any government restrictions."[20] Seeking to correct that state of affairs, the International Center for Technology Assessment swiftly filed a multipurpose petition, including proposals for a ban on "all feeding of mammalian meat and bonemeal to ruminant animals" and a "mandatory antemortem inspection program for cattle . . . to investigate the incidence of TSEs, the acronym for transmissible spongiform encephalopathy."[21]

Industry groups, joined by veterinarians, responded with a voluntary ban on ruminant parts in animal feeds, and the FDA announced it would "expedite regulations" that would enforce such a ban. A spokesman for the National Cattlemen's Beef Association typified a very risk-averse perspective with a declaration that "there is no margin of error here if we are wrong, if we have missed something, and therefore we are going to take this, as some feel, unnecessary and extraordinary step." He said the $60 billion industry could not afford to play "Russian roulette . . . because of a feeding practice that was instituted 200 years ago." He observed, "It will cost us money, but you can't get this industry back if you make a mistake."[22] Later the FDA proposed to add hogs to the list of ruminant animals—basically, those that chew their cud—to the banned list.[23] By mid-1997, it had banned from ruminant feed "any protein-containing portion or mammalian animals," a category that included not only "blood and blood products" but also gelatin and "any product whose only mammalian protein consists entirely of porcine or equine protein."[24]

By the fall of 1996, the search for a link had produced a report in the British journal *Nature* indicating that "'[n]ew variant' Creutzfeldt-Jacob disease (CJD) [also called CJD] has strain characteristics distinct from other types of CJD and which resemble those of BSE"—that is, what had become known as mad cow disease—"transmitted to domestic mice, cat and macaque, consistent with BSE being the source of this new disease."[25] A topical point of departure was what the authors referred to as "the occurrence of a new form of human prion disease . . . in the United Kingdom, affecting unusually young people and having a highly consistent and unique clinocopathological pattern." Analyzing the appearance of this disease in patients who had no "iatrogenic exposure to human prions" (that is, exposure in medical settings), they suggested that "this may indicate the arrival of a new risk factor for CJD in the United Kingdom, with dietary exposure to specified bovine offals"—animal parts, including waste parts—before they had been banned in the country.[26] Their article, laden with charts, tables, and blots of fragments of animal brains, suggested new lines of research on the topic, while noting the expression of concern "that BSE may have been transmitted to, and be surviving in, the sheep population."[27] The authors' findings, said a Cal Tech expert on the cattle disease, was "the first evidence" of the link—that although "most of us felt that the connection was most likely," this finding "strengthen[ed] the presumption." But, as is usual with both natural experiments and human ones, patience was necessary to pin down causes. Dr. Paul Brown, now medical director of an NIH laboratory that did studies of the central nervous system, reportedly said that if cases discovered two years previously were "the start of an epidemic caused when people ate infected cattle, the number of cases should soon explode."[28]

Then a new study complicated the search for a cause. The French authors of this study, led by Dr. Dominique Dormont, questioned the received explanation that prions from diseased cattle entered the human brain, forcing prion proteins there to change into diseased proteins. After a complex series of experiments on mice with progressive use of mad cow proteins and proteins from infected mice, the Dormont authors raised the question of whether the so-called prion hypothesis—that an element of the prion protein (PrPres) "constitutes the infectious agent" in "transmissible spongiform encephalopathies"—was the case, or whether there was a "further unidentified agent" that "may actually transmit mad cow disease.[29]

One piece of the puzzle was that in some mice, the Dormont investigators "could transmit a TSE without detectable PrPres [that is, protease-resistant prion protein] accumulation in the case of interspecies transmission of the BSE agent." This, they suggested, made it "more likely" that there was "an infectious agent in addition to PrPres" and that "this agent may be a nucleic acid." This "transmissible agent," they speculated, "would be tightly associated with PrPres, which would confer enhanced virulence and induce the developing of classical spongiform lesions."[30] Paul Brown of the NIH reflected the continuing scientific uncertainty. Reportedly he said that the Dormont paper did "not disprove the prion hypothesis," noting that there was "not a shred of direct evidence" that "abnormal prion proteins in the brain force normal ones to change their shapes." At the same time, he pointed out, the Dormont group had "not examine[d] every part" of the brains of their test animals, which meant that they might have "inadvertently disregarded" brain tissue containing prions.[31]

Further manifesting the complexity of the problem was a scientific experiment within what had become the broader social experiment involving TSEs. A report on this research appeared in the form of a long letter to the British journal *Nature* in October 1997. The investigators, led by Moira Bruce of the Institute for Animal Health in Edinburgh, injected mice with brain tissue from two sets of human beings who had had CJD. One of these groups, of which the six members included two dairy farmers in Britain, had the variant called spCJD. The others, three persons, had what had become known as "new variant CJD," or vCJD (also called nvCJD) which was the disease that had "been recognized in unusually young people in the United Kingdom," with one case reported in France; this was the group whose illnesses had set off the crisis in Britain.

Brain tissue from people with vCJD was different from that of people with the previously known form of Creutzfeldt-Jakob disease, and it was yet different from that from people with spCJD. What the Bruce team found was that "mice injected with all three vCJD sources have developed a progressive clinical disease very similar to BSE." By contrast, there were "no clinical signs of neurological disease" in mice injected with tissue from the spCJD sources, experiments that had been going on for between six hundred and eight hundred days. The researchers concluded that "vCJD is caused by the same strain or agent that has caused BSE, FSE [a feline spongiform encephalopathy] and TSEs in exotic ruminants," that "vCJD is distinguishable from spCJD," and that the CJD in the two dairy farmers was "of the spCJD type and . . . not linked to the causative agent of BSE." Saying that "epidemiological surveillance continues to indicate that vCJD is a new condition occurring almost exclusively in the UK," the researchers concluded that there was "compelling evidence of a link between BSE and vCJD."[32] An interpretation in line with the Dormont hypothesis was, as a reporter summarized it, that "a virus-like particle or co-factor" was involved in vCJD, which "challenged" the theory that the cause of the disease was prions.[33]

Now the puzzle had deepened, requiring work to be done to establish the connection—and the puzzle generated questions for regulators about the proper degree of risk aversion. Quite concurrently, in September 1997, Paul Brown of the NIH posed the question of why there had not been a BSE epidemic in the United States. One answer he gave was that strains of scrapie (a "fairly natural and fairly common affliction of sheep and goats") in the country were "sufficiently different from those in Great Britain as to be incapable of breaching the species barrier to cattle." Confronting the hypothesis that "we do have an epidemic but have simply not recognized it," he noted that examinations of "5500 brains of cattle dying of neurologic disease since 1990 and . . . almost 1000 downer cattle [cows too sick or weak to stand] have yet to identify a single case of spongiform encephalopathy."[34] His general conclusion on the sought-after connection was that "only through continued surveillance of CJD in Great Britain and other countries," with regional surveillance just having been initiated in the United States, would "the suggested connection between BSE and CJD eventually be proved or disproved." He said, "If cases of nvCJD result from consumption of BSE-contaminated tissue, they may represent a limited group of susceptible individuals within a British population that has been exposed to very low doses of the infectious agent, or (less likely) they may represent the first cases of an evolving epidemic of unknown proportions." He declared, "Statistical modeling suggests that it may take 2 or 3 years of observation before the alternatives become clear."[35]

He added a regulatory agenda—the need for evaluation of "the question of potential risk posed by bovine-sourced biological products ranging from myelin (used in the treatment of multiple sclerosis) to gelatin (used in products from drug capsules to cosmetics)." He concluded that the problem presented "a full plate for government agencies."[36]

However much need there was for more research, the British government leaned strongly to avoidance of risk. Within three months after the publication of the Scottish report and the queries raised by Dr. Brown, the government "banned the sale of most cuts of beef on the bone, including ribs, T-bone steaks and oxtails." A spokesman for the UK's beef industry trade group made the rather caustic comment that to get infected, one would have to eat "all the meat" on contaminated bones, "then the gristle on the bone, and then cut into the bone and [eat] the marrow and bits of bone and in doing so [get] the dorsal root ganglia that might be left there." As he viewed it, the government had "decided that consumer safety was paramount, and that even the theoretical risk was worth the effort of removing all the bones." A news report characterized British beef farmers as "stunned" by the ban on beef on the bone.[37]

While these various scientific arguments proceeded, the U.S. government began to tighten defenses against BSE. In 1997, the FDA proposed a ban on the use of "protein derived from mammalian tissues" in animal food or feed.[38]

By 2000, the British might have had a kind of schadenfreude at the discomfort of their cousins on the continent about spongiform encephalopathy. In September of that year, Italy reported a case of nvCJD, and a Spaniard died from the disease in November. With concern rising in France by October, a supermarket chain there had to recall a ton of beef from thirty-nine stores after the firm learned it had bought an infected cow.[39] By November, a French TV channel aired a documentary on a nineteen-year-old man who was said to be dying of vCJD, with at least two and perhaps as many as four people already having died from the disease. A press story reported that the Loire region, "the biggest beef producer in France," had experienced a halving of its sales after a "massive slump in over-the-counter sales," and many schools ordered their canteens to stop serving beef, especially hamburgers.[40] Illustrative of a wave of suspicion in the country were questions posed by a television anchor as he began a program discussing the problem: "Is the government hiding something? Do they know more than they are telling us?"[41]

BSE moved to North America by 2003, when an eight-year-old cow slaughtered in Alberta was found to have the disease, although Canadian officials did not reveal until May that the cow had the disease. The Canadians said the cow was not slaughtered for human consumption, or they would have reported the news earlier. Although there was no evidence that BSE had been transmitted to the other animals in the cow's herd, they ordered the herd destroyed. When the news came out, the U.S. Department of Agriculture instituted a ban on Canadian cows and meat products. It partially lifted that ban later that year for cattle under thirty months of age and in 2007 permitted imports from Canada of beef from cattle older than thirty months, born after a ban instituted by Canada in 1997.[42]

In December 2003, a cow in the state of Washington was found to have BSE—although, as it turned out, that cow had been imported from Canada.[43] That discovery, predictably, set off new alarms in the United States as well as discussions about the costs of experimentation, including the costs of testing and oversight and involving comparisons with the willingness of other countries to go many miles beyond the United States in testing. The year before the U.S. discovery, Western European countries had tested ten million cows, and Japan tested each of the 1.2 million cows it slaughtered. The comparative figures for the United States were between twenty thousand and thirty thousand cows, out of three hundred million slaughtered annually, a total of about 0.03 percent of American herds.[44]

The Washington cow was a "downer," and there were disputes about downers—how many, and why those animals could not walk. The beef industry claimed that the figure was 60,000 among older animals, the Department of Agriculture estimated 195,000, and some critics extrapolating from European figures said 700,000. Industry representatives said a lot of downers were in that condition because they were "merely lame."

In any event, a significant element of the problem was cost. A former Department of Agriculture veterinarian who had inspected big Pennsylvania slaughterhouses reportedly said that he had rejected "25 to 30 cows a day worth about $500 each" and that plant managers complained that when he stopped the production line, "he was costing them $5,000 per minute." The department's chief veterinarian chimed in that Japan had gone too far in testing every cow slaughtered there, saying that this was "like a doctor testing every patient who comes through the door for prostate cancer"[45]—although a blood test for prostate cancer had become routine in men of a certain age.

In the wake of the concern about the Washington cow, the FDA offered a cautious assessment of "the potential risk to public health from cosmetics made with cattle materials that may be contaminated with the BSE agent." The agency said that transmission of the agent "to humans through intact skin is not likely," but that "cosmetics may be ingested or applied to cut or abraded skin or to mucosal tissue, particularly in the eye, which could provide direct routes for infection." For those who wanted an additional worry bead for their string, the agency made available an electronic version of its assessment that included "an evaluation of the range of possible cattle-derived ingredients that might be used in the manufacture of cosmetics and the likelihood that a contaminated cosmetic results in transmission of the BSE agent to humans."[46] This presumably was not fodder, so to speak, for perusal at the breakfast table.

In 2005, after public comments, the Department of Agriculture issued a new rule that reopened the border to Canadian cattle under thirty months old and beef products from Canadian cattle of all ages. A federal trial court issued a preliminary injunction against the new rule, but the Ninth Circuit disagreed and effectively upheld the fresh importation of young Canadian animals into the United States.[47] As the court of appeals summarized the trial court's reasoning, there were "three ways in which the Final Rule would cause such harm: the increased risk of vCJD to American beef consumers, unspecified environmental injury stemming from USDA's failure to comply with NEPA, and injury to the U.S. beef industry and the U.S. economy that would result from a 'stigma' that tainted Canadian beef would inflict upon the U.S. meat supply."[48] The court of appeals opined that "the district court's calculus overstated the harm that would result from the rule." It referred in part to "the low incidence of BSE in the Canadian herd, the numerous safeguards against BSE in this country, the lack of any Canadian cattle under 30 months of age found with BSE, and the lack of any case of vCJD attributable to Canadian beef," saying that in that context, "any increased risk to human and animal health created by the [rule that overturned the ban] is negligible."[49] It concluded further that " the district court's concern over the possibility of 'stigma' harming the American beef industry appears to be overstated," noting that "following the case of BSE diagnosed in a Washington State cow in 2003"—the animal that it turned out had come from Canada—"consumer demand for, and confidence in, American beef remained strong."[50]

The first decade of the new century had brought a time for some reckoning. First, after three years of investigation, in 2000 the British issued a four-thousand-page report that said that initially the government had seriously downplayed the possibility that BSE could be transmitted to people. Criticizing the "culture of secrecy" it found in the government's response to the problem, the report said that the government had used "an approach whose object was sedation" of the public, an approach born of "a consuming fear of provoking an irrational public scare." Just one example of "sedation" was Prime Minister John Major's statement in the House of Commons, a year before the first human cases were identified, that there was "no scientific evidence that B.S.E. can be transmitted to humans or that eating beef causes it in humans." The report instanced the event of the agriculture minister making a show of feeding hamburger to his four-year-old daughter in 1990 and the declaration of the chief medical officer of the UK in 1996 that he would "continue to eat beef as part of a varied and balanced diet."

Because of the long incubation period for CJD, there were expressions of concern of a substantial toll that was yet to come. The acting head of the British government's advisory committee on the disease, Dr. Peter Smith, said his "own personal belief" was that the number would be "in the region of a few hundred to several thousand more" but that "we can't rule out tens of thousands."[51] By 2010, the British health care organization Bupa reported the number of deaths in Britain from vCJD as 168. The great range of uncertainty remaining about the number of future cases was evident in the organization's statement, "Expert estimates of how many more people are yet to develop the disease range from just tens to thousands of people."[52] This range is only illustrative of similar estimates about many kinds of risks associated with products that are daily tried out on the public.

On the western side of the Atlantic, expressions of concern predated the news about the appearance of BSE in the Alberta cow and the cow in Washington State. Dr. Peter Lurie, the deputy director of the Public Citizen Health Research Group, said in a broadcast in early 2001 that although there was "a safety net in this country," "it has a certain amount of breaches in it and . . . we aren't as well protected as we really could be." Potential breaches included the continued use in vaccines for several years of materials from British cows and the use of such materials in dietary supplements.[53] In the same broadcast, it might be noted, Dr. Paul Brown—who was to raise questions about the link between BSE and CJD—said, "The only thing that we can say for absolute certain is that the human disease called variant Creutzfeldt—variant Creutzfeldt-Jakob Disease—is the result of infection with mad cow disease." He commented, "Everything else about this story is more or less plausible speculation."[54]

With the advent of BSE in North America, a leader in advocacy of strong safety measures was Dr. Stanley Prusiner of the University of California at San Francisco, who had hypothesized in the 1980s that the infectious agent in BSE was prions, and who had won the Nobel Prize in medicine in 1997 for his discovery of the prion. An interesting example of how personal contacts may affect discussion of scientific issues was an encounter between Dr. Prusiner and Karl Rove, the senior adviser to President George W. Bush, after the disease appeared in the Canadian cow. After Prusiner complained to Rove that he had been rebuffed in an effort to have a meeting with Ann Veneman, the secretary of agriculture, he got the meeting, where he told Secretary Veneman "that what happened in Canada was going to happen in the United States"—that "it was just a matter of time." Still complaining—reportedly saying that the secretary "did not share his sense of urgency"—Prusiner said that the advice the secretary was getting from Department of Agriculture scientists was outmoded because it assumed that the cattle disease was "an infection that you can contain by quarantining animals on farms." He acknowledged that cattle could get the disease from eating infected tissues, but he pointed out that prions could arise spontaneously. Although it was "not known whether animals with that form of the disease could pass the disease to humans," Prusiner was reported to say that this was "a risk that greatly worries him." He expressed anxiety that "we just don't know the size of the problem. . . . We don't know the prevalence or incidence of the disease." He reportedly declared that "the only way to learn what the United States is facing" was a solution that had been asserted to be prohibitive—"to test every animal."[55]

As the reckoning proceeded, a different voice criticized "mad cow hysteria." In a 2004 letter, David Gaylor extrapolated from the rate at the time of 16 deaths a year in Britain, added to the then known 140 cases, to come up with a "total number of deaths [of] about 300 in a population of 60 million people." Further extrapolating to the United States, he found "an estimate risk of 5 *per* 10 *million* for the unlikely exposure to BSE-infected meat products for one month." He invoked the comparison of 50 deaths per million as the lifetime risk of U.S. citizens for being killed by lightning. So, he concluded, "the risk of being killed by lightning is 100 times greater than the estimated risk of a susceptible individual consuming BSE-infected meat products for one month."

He also noted that there were an estimated "6,000 deaths per years in the United States due to all food-borne illnesses."[56]

A related question was how much concern—or hysteria—about threats posed to the public is stirred up by media. One group of commentators expressed dubiety that this was a significant problem. In an analysis of the general question published before the first appearance of CJD in Britain, they noted the "usual conviction that 'the media are just interested in sensationalism' or that 'bad news sells papers.'" Their findings, however, were to the contrary—that "*the amount of coverage is predicted only by the objective characteristics of the hazard events*"—that is, "casualties and other measures of damages."[57] Indeed, they said that their "more detailed analyses provide greater support for the view that the media actually de-emphasize the severity of hazard events."[58]

What conclusions can be drawn from this history of an experiment with food products that vaulted across European lines and moved into a U.S. spotlight? We may first ask how consumers, and governments, should react to scares and crises where the threat is a "might" or a "may." I offer some ideas that may be useful in analyzing the sorts of crises that recur as science becomes more able to forecast risks to consumers from the experiments that envelop us in many marketplaces.

Governments should consider responses to risk information with an eye to the drama those responses would provoke, including the jolting effects of crises on consumers. Consumers in advanced modern societies tend to regard the products they eat, ingest, and otherwise use as safe. They do so with good reason, because most of the time, most of those goods are in fact safe. Many are entirely without risk, and others are safe in a relative sense, carrying very small risks. In this connection, it should be noted that regulatory safety initiatives may have their own undesirable costs. It is true that modern governments must sometimes be averse to uncertain, long-term risks. They owe a watchdog attitude to their citizens, who are not in a position to acquire or assess the information about risk that modern science gives us. However, some safety regulations may put people out of work. They may excite more anxiety in consumers than the risks merit. Whatever may have been the nuanced intentions of the British government at the time of the first discovery of CJD in humans, its responses in 1997 after publication of the Scottish report would tend to jolt people from one day's belief in complete safety to a sudden belief the next day that to eat British beef would expose them to a high risk of fatal illness. Arguably, neither of these perceptions would be accurate.

There is, however, a corollary to caution about the publicizing of alarming effects: a principle requiring honesty and forthrightness from the beginning about developing risks. The fact that knowledge about the risk of Creutzfeldt-Jakob disease came into public view in Britain in 1996 simply put a punctuation mark on information that had been building up for some years.

Another point is that both governments and consumers must consider comparative risks. Every time a crisis develops, it is a good idea to ask how the risk in the new spotlight compares with that of other risks that we encounter in ordinary life. Every day a certain number of people die, or become ill, as a result of the most normal risks of everyday living. An easy, common-sense test is to ask, how frightening is this risk as compared with driving to work? More than thirty thousand people die in traffic accidents in the United States every year. Occasionally there is salmonella in the milk or in ground turkey. Now and then an outbreak of *E. coli* occurs in hamburgers. But we don't stop driving, drinking milk, or eating burgers. Again, however, a cautionary note sounds: we should not swallow whole the rhetoric of comparative risk in support of a global argument for a sharp reduction in safety regulation generally. That would paralyze our ability to respond to real risks, even those of relatively small magnitude.

So governments need to maintain not only steadiness at the helm of risk control, but also the appearance of steadiness. This means, in part, that they must be careful about both the quickness and level of response to uncertain risks, and the effect of those responses on public perceptions. *Governments are themselves experimenters when they encounter information about risk that may create a perception of crisis.* A forest fire requires instant response, sometimes even that we burn one person's house to save those of a dozen others. But when reports of illness and deaths escalate from large, risky experiments—processes that those who conduct them may not even think of as experiments—government has a number of tools at its command, including close watches on developing data about hazard and the calm provision of public information.

We simply add that nature itself continues to experiment on the population, with sometimes alarming results. A parallel to prion-caused mad cow disease is the discovery of what investigators called a "consistent and novel prion disease prototype that is associated with chronic diarrhea and hereditary sensory and autonomic neuropathy"—a category of diseases that affect the peripheral nerves—"caused by a novel" mutation.[59]

In an article describing this syndrome, the authors commented that it was "reassuring" that rodent studies "did not show experimental transmissibility," although they said, "This finding does not completely rule out the presence of potentially infections human prions."[60]

## Carpal Tunnel Syndrome

We now offer for comparison a health problem that has developed in a very different setting than the barnyard or the cattle feeding factory that have literally been fertile ground for BSE and ultimately CJD. This problem is carpal tunnel syndrome (CTS), which, by contrast with the diseases just examined, is a creature of the hardware of modern technology. Unlike BSE/CJD, it does not involve an illness that is invariably fatal, but it can make sufferers very uncomfortable, even keep them from performing the jobs that generate the problem. Carpal tunnel syndrome presents a cluster of features that are typical of the experiments in which many people participate every day, and of inquiries concerning the facts—which are not always as they are assumed to be. As with most problems of this sort, it is necessary to identify the problem, collect the data, dispel myths, and fashion solutions that will minimize injury and alleviate suffering.

Carpal tunnel syndrome is named as it is because it involves a "tunnel-like structure" that connects the carpals, small bones in the hand, through which pass some nine tendons that connect "the muscles and the bones they move." Also passing through the tunnel is the median nerve, which "carries signals between the hand and the spinal cord."[61] If the tendons swell up, "the swelling can pinch the nerve," with results that include "numbing, tingling and weakness"—"hallmarks of CTS."[62]

Statistical data on the amount of CTS in the population varies from country to country, which may reflect tendencies among doctors to diagnose it. A study of a region in southern Sweden found a "population prevalence of pain, numbness and/or tingling in the median nerve distribution of 14.4%" with "clinically certain CTS" at 3.8 percent.[63] In the United States, "where CTS is reported most frequently," "the reported prevalence . . . in the general population ranges from 0.7% to 9.2% among women and from 0.4% to 2.1% among men."[64]

For those whose symptoms are not relieved by medication, the solution is surgery, which is fairly big business in the United States—two hundred thousand procedures annually, with "associated direct medical costs" of $1 billion a year.[65] Thus, an important question for public policy is the identification of causes, with the aim of reducing costs in time and money.

Probably the cause that is most in the public mind is the kind of work afflicted people do, and there is evidence on that point. However, it should be noted that there is "a strong association" with overweight and obesity,[66] and that smoking is another culprit, along with "other medical disorders."[67] Although a 1999 study showed an increase in the ratio of CTS in men as compared with women—that is, 1 to 1.4—it still indicated that the prevalence in older women was "almost 4 times that in men, with older women showing the highest age-specific prevalence for confirmed CTS."[68] A study published in 2011 compared "physician-diagnosed CTS and CTR [carpal tunnel release] surgery" in a Swedish country with a county in Minnesota. It found that the recorded incidence of CTS was significantly higher in the Minnesota county—542 per 100,000 women as compared with 324 in the Swedish county, and 303 per 100,000 men in the Minnesota group as compared with 125 in the Swedish group. With the exception of women younger than fifty in Sweden, the rate of surgery tended to be higher in the United States, with double the incidence in the United States for men over fifty.[69]

A watershed on the issue of CTS and working activities came in the late 1970s, a time when one team of researchers noted "there were dramatic increases in productivity in certain industries, and workers began noting an increase in problems involving pain and numbness in the hands." A particular spotlight on the problem came when strikes at meatpacking plants generated press stories that "brought occupational CTS to national and international attention."[70]

A significant amount of public attention has centered on computer use as a villain in CTS, but for average users of keyboards, that hypothesis has been questioned. One study "found no association between keyboard use for more than 4 hours in an average workday and tingling/numbness during the previous week." Danish researchers concluded in a 2003 article that "taken together, previous studies" and research of their own "are in contrast with a common belief that CTS is a frequent disorder among computer users."[71] There was, however, evidence that use of keyboards might be associated with CTS-type symptoms when it approached twenty hours a week and that there was "an elevated risk only among those who used a mouse" for thirty hours a week or more.[72]

Jobs in which work activities significantly generated CTS involved "regular and prolonged use of hand-held vibratory tools." This included such work as rock drilling and chainsaw use by foresters.[73] Moreover, jobs that required "repetitive wrist movement" were also hotbeds of CTS. A summary of the literature showed a "greater than doubling of the risk" among "ski assembly workers employed for an average of 5.1 jobs that entailed 'repeated and/or sustained' flexion, extension or ulnar or radial deviation of the wrist"; auto assembly workers—although with a wide range of statistical confidence; "electrical assembly workers whose jobs involved a precision (pinch) grip and frequent repetition"; and "workers assembling small electrical appliances, motor vehicles and ski accessories." There were also "excess risks" among poultry workers, slaughterhouse workers, and frozen-food packers. Matters of particular concern were risks that increased "5- to-8-fold when . . . self-reported time spent in activities with the wrist flexed or extended" was at least twenty hours a week.[74]

There are many patterns of recognition of the hazards of the experiments that are ubiquitous in our experimental society, and many patterns of social response with varying levels of rationality. In this chapter we have analyzed two cases involving profiles of developing risk—risks that became perceived in different ways in different time frames. The case of BSE/CJD in Britain illustrates widespread fear in a population that arose after a government's initial inclination to keep risk data from the public, followed by a sudden infusion of information into the public sphere. It also illustrates a continuing fear born of uncertainty about what future data will show. The case of CTS shows that sometimes public perceptions of risk are exaggerated, as in the case of normal levels of computer use. But it also shows that when workers in some industries began to discern patterns of pain that accompanied their occupation, they were seeing a statistical reality.

How can a society that prides itself on rationality but also values compassion deal with problems of this kind? Governments can regulate risk-creating conduct. In the case of BSE, they could—and eventually did—set up monitoring procedures for diseased animals and institute trade bans and wholesale slaughter of animals. If there is sufficient political will, governments can enforce rules for working conditions that minimize problems like repetitive stress injuries. Governments can also provide information in as uninflected a way as possible, with the goal of promoting as much public awareness of risk as is possible under conditions of what may be great uncertainty. Finally, the private sector of marketplace societies can go a long way to minimize risk. They can engage in self-regulation, even when it hurts. And they can invent better ways of doing things—as one group of CTS researchers pointed out, "by ergonomic design of tasks and tools, and by appropriate scheduling of work and rest periods."[75]

We are most of us experimenters, on ourselves and on others, in a great big experimental society. How we manage these many processes of trial and error depends on our conceptions of progress, how we value our short-term financial assets, and how we value our fellows.

## Notes

1. See George Johnson, "The Brain Eater," *New York Times* book review, March 16, 1997, p. 9, reviewing Richard Rhodes, *Deadly Feasts: Tracking the Secrets of a Terrifying New Plague* (Simon & Schuster, 1997).
2. See Ray Mosely, "More than Meat At Risk in Beef Crisis," *Chicago Tribune*, March 28, 1996, pp. 1 and 18.
3. See for example Stephanie Strom, "'Mad Cow Disease' Threatens the Farming Life," *New York Times*, March 25, 1996, p. A4.
4. See Philip M. Boffey, "Editorial Notebook: Are the Mad Cows Bad Cows?" *New York Times*, March 29, 2996, p. A14.
5. See John Darnton, "The Logic of the 'Mad Cow' Scare," *New York Times* review, March 31, 1996, pp. 1 and 5.
6. See Heather Timmons, "Britain Has Learned Many Harsh Lessons in a Long Effort to Combat Mad Cow Disease," *New York Times*, Dec. 26, 2003, p. A31.
7. John Darnton, "Britain Ties Deadly Brain Disease to Cow Ailment," *New York Times*, March 21, 1996, p. A1.
8. Ibid.
9. See Lawrence K. Altman, "U.S. Confident on Mad Cow Disease," *New York Times*, March 27, 1996, p. A8.
10. See Sarah Lyall, "Britain's Daunting Prospect: Killing 15,000 Cows a Week," *New York Times*, April 3, 1996, pp. A1 and A5.
11. See Altman, supra.
12. See Lyall, supra.
13. Department for Environment, Food and Rural Affairs, "Summary of Cattle Passports Order 1996," http://adlib.everysite.co.uk/adlib/defra/content.aspx?doc=18281&id=18283, last consulted July 6, 2015.
14. See Lawrence K. Altman, "British Study Says Brain Patients Had Psychiatric Symptoms," *New York Times*, Apri1 5, 1996, p. A5, reporting on *Lancet* study.
15. Associated Press, "New Cases of Infection Linked to Cow Disease Seen in Britain," *New York Times*, April 27, 1996, p. A2.
16. See Edwin Unsworth, "Mad Cow Disease Scare Threatens U.K. Farmers," *Business Insider*, April 1, 1996, p. 23.
17. See Alan Cowell, "Britain Incensed as Europe Keeps Ban on Beef Exports," *New York Times*, April 4, 1996, p. A4; John Drnton, "War Over British Beef," *New York Times*, June 24, 1996, p. A5.
18. See Lawrence K. Altman, "W.H.O. Seeks Barriers Against Cow Disease," *New York Times*, April 4, 1996, p. A4.
19. Clair O'Brien, "Scant Data Cause Widespread Concern," *Science*, March 29, 1996, p. 1798.
20. See Tara Gruzen, "U.S. Never Banned Suspect Feed," *Chicago Tribune*, March 28, 1998, sec. 1, p. 19.

21. Citizen Petition No. 96P-0106/CP1, filed with the FDA, summarized, F.D. Cosm. L. Rep. (CCH) ¶ 41,354 (April 22, 1996).
22. Lawrence K. Altman, "Voluntary Rules on Feed After Cow Disease," *New York Times*, March 30, 1996, p. A9.
23. See Marian Burros, "New Steps Urged Against Cow Disease," *Washington Post*, March 26, 1997, p. A15.
24. 21 CFR ¶ 589.2000, F.D. Cosm. L. Rep. ¶ 66,291 (June 16, 1997).
25. John Collinge et al., "Molecular Analysis of Prior Strain Variation and the Aetiology of 'New Variant' CJD," 383 *Nature* 685, 685 (1996) (abstract).
26. Ibid., p. 685.
27. See ibid., p. 689.
28. Gina Kolata, "More Evidence By British Ties Cow Illness to Humans," *New York Times*, Oct. 24, 1996, p. A5 (reporter's summary).
29. Corinne I. Lasmezas et al., "Transmission of the BSE Agent to Mice in the Absence of Detectable Abnormal Prion Protein," 275 *Science* 402, 402 (1997).
30. Ibid., pp. 403–04.
31. See Gina Kolata, "Study Questions Top Theory on Cause of Mad Cow Illness," *New York Times*, Jan. 17, 1997, p. A9 (some quotations are paraphrases of remarks of Dr. Brown).
32. M. E. Bruce et al., "Transmissions to Mice Indicate That 'New Variant' CJD Is Caused By the BSE Agent," 389 *Nature* 498, 499–501 (1997).
33. See Sandra Blakeslee, "New Evidence Said to Link Mad Cow Disease to Humans," *New York Times*, Sept. 30, 1997, p. A6.
34. Paul Brown, "The Risk of Bovine Spongiform Encephalopathy ('Mad Cow Disease') to Human Health," 278 *JAMA* 1008, 1010 (Sept. 1997).
35. Ibid., p. 1011.
36. Ibid.
37. Sarah Lyall, "Mad Cow Alert: British Ban Beef on the Bone," *New York Times*, Dec. 4, 1997, p. A16.
38. 62 Fed. Reg. 30976 (1997).
39. Sarah Veysey, "Mad Cow Fears Are Creating E.U. Losses," *Business Insurance*, Dec. 4, 2000, p. 1.
40. Patrick Bishop, "CJD Nightmare Causes Consumer Panic in France," *The Telegraph*, Nov. 7, 2000, http://adlib.everysite.co.uk/adlib/defra/content.aspx?doc=18281&id=18283, last consulted July 6, 2015.
41. Suzanne Daley, "Living With Mad Cows: The French and Fear Itself," *New York Times*, Nov. 19, 2000, review section, p. 5.
42. See "BSE Found in Canadian Cow, Herd Destroyed," F.D. Cosm. L. Rep. (CCH), Report Letter No. 2115 (2003), p. 2; USDA Economic Research Service, "Beef Trade," updated Nov. 7, 2012, http://www.ers.usda.gov/topics/animal-products/cattle-beef/trade.aspx Oct. 19, 2013.
43. See Christopher Drew et al., "Despite Warnings, Industry Resisted Safeguards," *New York Times*, Dec. 28, 2003, p. A19.
44. See ibid.; Donald G. McNeil Jr., "Mad Cow Case Leads Government to Consider Greater Meat Testing," *New York Times*, Dec. 26, 2003, p. A1.
45. See ibid., p. A31.
46. FDA notice, "Risk Assessment for Cosmetics and Potential Contamination with Bovine Spongiform Encephalopathy Agent, Availability," 69 Fed. Reg. 42191 (2004).

47. See *Ranchers Cattlemen Action Legal Fund United Stockgrowers of Am. v. U.S. Dept. of Agriculture*, 415 F.3d 1078 (9th Cir. 2005).
48 Ibid., p. 1104.
49. Ibid.
50. Ibid., p. 1105.
51. See Sarah Lyall, "British Wrongly Lulled People on 'Mad Cow,' Report Finds," *New York Times*, Oct. 27, 2000, p. A8.
52. Bupa, "Creutzfeldt-Jakob Disease (CJD)," published May 2010https://global.ihi.com/alarm+service/health+fact+sheets/creutzfeldt-jakob+disease.aspx August 4, 2011.
53. "Is the U.S. Safe From Mad Cow Disease? Could We Be Safer?" excerpts from *Newshour* broadcast of Jan. 26, 2001, in 17 *Health Letter* No. 3, pp.1–2 (March 2001).
54. Ibid.
55. Sandra Blakeslee, "Expert Warned That Mad Cow Was Imminent," *New York Times*, Dec. 25, 2003, p. A1.
56. David Gaylor, "Letter to the Editor Regarding Mad Cow Hysteria," 23 *Risk Analysis* No. 3, p. 513 (2004).
57. William R. Freudenberg et al., "Media Coverage of Hazard Events: Analyzing the Assumptions," 16 *Risk Analysis* No. 1, pp. 31 and 39 (1996).
58. Ibid., p. 40.
59. Simon Mead et al., "A Novel Prion Disease Associated with Diarrhea and Autonomic Neuropathy," 369 *N. Eng. J. Med.* 1904, 1905 (Nov.14, 2013).
60. Ibid., p. 1913.
61. See JAMA patient page, "Detecting Carpal Tunnel Syndrome," 282 *JAMA* 206 (1999); Keith T. Palmer et al., "Carpal Tunnel Syndrome and Its Relation to Occupation: A Systematic Literature Review," 2007 *Occup. Med.* 57, 64.
62. See "Detecting Carpal Tunnel Syndrome," supra; Alfred Franzblau and Robert A. Werner, "What Is Carpal Tunnel Syndrome?" 282 *JAMA* 186, 187 (1999).
63. Isam Atroshi et al., "Prevalence of Carpal Tunnel Syndrome in a General Population," 282 *JAMA* 153, 155 (1999).
64. See Anderson et al., supra, p. 2966.
65. Franzblau and Werner, supra, p. 186.
66. See Atroshi et al., supra, p. 157.
67. See Johan Hviid Andersen et al., "Computer Use and Carpal Tunnel Syndrome: A 1-Year Follow-Up Study," 289 *JAMA* 2963, 2963 (2003).
68. See Atroshi et al., supra, p. 157.
69. Isam Atroshi et al., "Incidence of Physician-Diagnosed Carpal Tunnel Syndrome in the General Population," 171 *Arch. Internal Med.* 943, 943 (2011).
70. R. Gelfman et al., "Long-Term Trends in Carpal Tunnel Syndrome," 72 *Neurology* No. 1, at 33, 39 (2009).
71. Andersen et al., supra, pp. 2968–69 (citing sources and authors' conclusions).
72. See ibid. See also Palmer et al., supra, note 59, p. 64 ("The balance of evidence of keyboard and computer work does not indicate an important association with CTS.").
73. See Palmer et al., supra, p. 63.
74. See ibid.
75. Palmer et al., supra note 59, p. 64.

# 6

# Product Images as Lenses for Experiments

A vital aspect of mass experimentation that touches the lives of individuals concerns people's knowledge of the features and qualities of activities or products. The case of products is especially illustrative of this knowledge element. Product sellers always seek to differentiate their goods. Each advertisement for a new product tries to present some aspect of it that will make people want to buy it. Truly, each new product offering is in some sense experimental, because the seller is trying out on consumers the features of the product that it extols in an effort to show that the product brings some novelty to the market. One might think that, accustomed to various kinds of promotional campaigns, consumers would be increasingly immune to such blandishments. But the remarks of a Louisiana appellate court in 1969 may be as applicable to today's presumably jaded consumers as they were a half-century ago: That court spoke of a "consumer . . . romanced with Madison Avenue warranties ranging from such guarantees as taking the guess-work out of heretofore vexing problems to providing one with instant status and prestige."[1]

On the other side of sales promotions, each purchase of a product—at least of a new or newly advertised product—is an experiment for the consumer. Thus, we may view representations made for products as lenses for consumer choice—for consumers to choose to subject themselves to these miniature experiments.

It is important to note that representations can be communicated—or absorbed without written or oral communication developed by the speaker to the recipient—in various ways. For example, the packaging of a product can be part of its portrayal to the consumer. This was evident in a federal decision in a setting of massive experimentation on workers, that of asbestos products, in a case in which a worker in a plant that made construction materials sued for illness that he attributed to asbestos dust that was visible in his work zone. The trial court imposed strict liability on a company that mined asbestos for "failure to warn of asbestos's dangerous qualities" and for its "defective packaging of asbestos." The Sixth Circuit agreed with the defendant that it "could not be held strictly liable based upon the failure to warn," but it affirmed a judgment for the plaintiffs on liability for a design defect, for "failure of the product to meet the consumer-expectation standard." It said that "the failure to warn, as well as the defective packaging, were part of"—here it quoted the trial court—"the totality of the circumstances which make [the] product defective."[2] Specifically, the court commented that "the packaging of a product is also an element to consider when determining whether the consumer would reasonably expect the content of the package to pose the danger it did."[3]

A powerful, more general observation on the legal relevance of product appearance is a statement by Justice Traynor of California, a leading judicial inventor of the modern law of products liability, in a case involving a power tool that injured its purchaser. "Implicit in [a] machine's presence on the market," Justice Traynor declared, there was a "representation" "that it would safely do the jobs for which it was built." He placed the representational background of the product in a broad frame, saying that "it should not be controlling whether plaintiff selected the machine because of the statements in the brochure, or because of the machine's own appearance of excellence that belied the defect lurking beneath the surface, or because he merely assumed that it would safely do the jobs it was built to do."[4]

The opera *L'Elisir d'Amore* features a traveling vendor who sells a love potion to gullible citizens, but his sales pitch was limited to audiences in little town squares. In a day of mass media, the wide range of product representations may have broad legal consequences. An Ohio appellate decision captures some of these effects, although it was reversed on grounds related to the target audience for the representations. The case involved a statewide class action on behalf of patients who had been prescribed the powerfully addictive painkiller OxyContin. In concluding that the patients could bring a class action, the appellate court referred to "common issues of fact regarding whether [the defendant drug makers] negligently promoted or marketed OxyContin, and whether [the defendants] knowingly concealed material facts about the nature and qualities of OxyContin from [the plaintiffs] and the classes of persons they represent." Specifically, the court mentioned evidence that the defendants "engaged in a common, class-wide course of conduct, inasmuch as they failed to issue warnings regarding such matters as OxyContin's addictive nature, the inappropriateness of using OxyContin for certain ailments like arthritis pain . . . [and] the danger of crushing OxyContin tablets," and evidence about "false and misleading promotional materials."[5] The overruling decision of the Ohio Supreme Court implicitly accepted the widespread nature of the defendants' promotions of the drug, but rather focused on the ideas that, as it paraphrased a precedent, "addiction to the drug is an individualized question of fact" and that the principal audience of drug promotion of prescription drugs—physicians—"were adequately warned of the powerful dosage of OxyContin relative to morphine." Since patients must get prescriptions from physicians, who are called "learned intermediaries," the "learned intermediary doctrine" of the law of products liability "discharges the duty to warn from the manufacturer to the physician."[6]

The potential breadth of dissemination of product claims and the range of targets of those claims is evident in the very different context of a suit against an aircraft maker for misrepresenting that the plane complied with federal regulations. At issue was the craft's ability to fly at certain altitudes, when the plaintiffs had to pay for modifications that would allow flight at altitudes specified in the regulations. The defendant manufacturer prevailed in the trial court on its theory that the purpose of the regulations was "to promote safety of flight" and that they were "not intended to protect buyers of aircraft from economic loss caused by faulty design."[7] However, the appellate court reversed, saying that there was "no reason a purchaser should not be allowed to recover where the damages are the result of changes required to render the aircraft safe, rather than the result of physical injury due to the aircraft's unsafe condition." The appellate court noted that the state precedents did "not limit liability for fraudulent misrepresentations to situations in which the party making the fraudulent misrepresentation *intended* that the misrepresentation be communicated to the plaintiff" but that "rather, they extend liability to situations in which the plaintiff was within the class of persons whom the maker of the fraudulent statement 'ha[d] *reason to expect* to act or refrain from action in reliance upon the misrepresentation.'"[8]

There are some technical nuances in the law on this topic, as is evident in a decision in an attempted class action involving a diet drug,

Xenadrive RFA-1, promoted as a "Clinically Proven Fat Loss Catalyst," where the plaintiff proposing the class claimed that the product had caused an "acute psychotic break." The court refused to certify a class on a fraud claim, which was based on the idea that "every class member suffered harm because they paid for a product that differed from what it was represented to be, and thereby incurred a financial injury equal to the amount they paid for the product." The court pointed out that the class had "allegedly suffered only financial harm as a result of having purchased a product that was not accurately described at the time of sale" but had "suffered no physical or psychological injuries" from the drug.[9] By contrast, however, the court upheld a class action claim for "unjust enrichment" based on claims that it "was unjust for the Defendants to retain the benefit" of their profits "in light of the fact that the product purchased by the class members was not what it was purported to be."[10] It also allowed claims under the state consumer sales practices act, on the grounds that allegations that the defendants had "engaged in unfair, deceptive or unconscionable practices or acts" would qualify as a "cognizable injury" because the statute was "intended to redress" "the financial harm resulting from the unfair or deceptive transaction."[11]

The lesson of these decisions is that under some legal doctrines, representations may be crucial for liability in large-scale product experiments on the public. Illustrative are the case of OxyContin—known as "hillbilly heroin," where poor persons are vulnerable to misstatements for an analgesic that may catch them up in a web of addiction—and the case of the diet drug, where the target audience is people who are psychologically vulnerable to claims that they can quickly lose weight.

The market for prescription medical products involves ongoing experiments on millions of persons. Exactly because the product requires a prescription, manufacturers defending suits involving their products rely on the learned intermediary doctrine employed by the Ohio Supreme Court in the OxyContin case summarized above, which essentially immunizes manufacturers on the basis that it is the consumer patient's physician who makes the relevant decision on risk. But with respect to certain kinds of products, courts have sometimes recognized that the experiment takes place without mediation.

An example of experiments unmediated as a practical matter is a case that arose from the perforation of the plaintiff's uterus by an intrauterine contraceptive device, an IUD, for which there was a patient brochure but which the plaintiff said she had never received. In concluding that it was not enough for the manufacturer to warn the plaintiff's doctor and that she was "entitled to be personally warned" of the dangers of the device, the court emphasized that with respect to methods of birth control, "the treating physician generally does not make an intervening, individualized medical judgment in the birth control decision." Because of the patient's "independent decision" on that question," the "final choice" was hers. Moreover, the court noted that the defendant had "marketed the product with the idea of convincing women to choose the CU-7." Its refusal to apply the learned intermediary doctrine placed the plaintiff front and center as a choice-maker, in what was in essence an experiment on herself, about a particular product. Linking promotion through the mass media to the result was the court's declaration that "IUD manufacturers, through mass advertising and merchandising practices, generated a general sense of product quality, making it difficult for consumers to fully understand the risks involved with the use of an IUD."[12]

The precise character of media representations may be crucial with respect to very specific attributes of seemingly innocuous, commonly used products. A domestic kitchen illustration is a case involving a woman who was burned when she lost control of a roasting pan, originally made in France, when she was cooking a twenty-pound turkey. Although the pan had originally been sold as "an all-purpose cooking dish without handles," an American company added some small handles to it when it was asked to do so by the television home-shopping channel QVC for purposes of a Thanksgiving promotion. The statement in the promotion that the pan could be used for a twenty-five-pound turkey was the foundation for a holding by a federal appeals court in favor of the plaintiff. The court threaded its way through New York legal theories on products liability. The trial court had charged the jury that "[a] product is defective if it is not reasonably safe[;] [t]hat is, if the product is so likely to be harmful to persons that a reasonable person who had actual knowledge of its potential for producing injury would conclude that it should not have been marketed in that condition." Given that instruction, the appellate court concluded that the jury could have found for the defendant because the pan was a "multi-use product" that, in addition to roasting turkeys, it "could also be used to cook casseroles, cutlets, cookies, and other low-volume foods" and that therefore it "did not fail the risk/utility test." However, since "the pan was advertised as suitable for a particular use--cooking a twenty-five-pound turkey," the court also decided that under state law, "a general charge on strict products liability based on the risk/utility approach does not suffice." It opined that the jury also could have found "that the product was nonetheless unsafe for the purpose for which it was marketed and sold—roasting a twenty-five-pound turkey—and, as such, was defective under" another state law test—"the consumer expectations test"—and thus justified a separate instruction on a breach of warranty theory.[13] In a very different context than that of the IUD discussed above, the information available to the consumer put her front and center in an unwitting small-scale experiment in her kitchen.

Thus, in the world beyond the laboratory, the way an experiment is presented to those who will be its subjects is significant, and it may even be crucial. The modes of presentation are diverse, as are the technical legal theories that provide foundations for civil liability. Decisions have referred to sources including "advertising on radio and television, in newspaper and magazines, and in brochures made available to prospective purchasers,"[14] and to "representations in video tapes, brochures, and literature."[15] The representation-based doctrines applied to support liability in those cases include express warranty, implied warranty, and negligent misrepresentation. The theory of express warranty is the most direct doctrine of this group. The core definition in the Uniform Commercial Code, applicable in both consumer and commercial transactions, is that of "any affirmation of fact or promise made by the seller to the buyer which relates to the goods and becomes part of the basis of the bargain."[16]

The presentation of products, and indeed of activities involving products that will affect consumers, may influence courts to impose liability on theories that are not directly based on representations. This is evident in cases involving the most mundane products, including baby oil and cotton swabs. In a very sad case, a fifteen-month-old boy got hold of a container of baby oil and began to drink it. When his mother yelled as him to stop, he gasped and inhaled some of the product into his lungs. His mother, believing that he had only drunk the product and at worst would suffer diarrhea, did not seek medical attention. Later, however, he developed breathing difficulties attributable to the effects of the oil on his lungs, which reduced the circulation of oxygen to his blood. The effects were tragic: cardiac arrest, resulting brain damage, and severe retardation and seizures.

There was no warning on the product about the dangers of aspirating it, as contrasted with swallowing it. The court referred to a medical journal article that warned about those "unique dangers," in which the authors said that "the latent danger of this substance needs to be publicized, along with the potentially grave prognosis accompanying aspiration of large amounts of this product." The court referred to "uncontroverted evidence" that "demonstrate[d] the danger of aspirating baby oil." It "recognize[d] that other oils may be equally as dangerous, and that other products may have attributes that render them no less dangerous than baby oil." However, it said that "what makes baby oil unique . . . is that baby oil is intended for use *on babies*."[17] This led the court to reject the defendant's argument that the incident was unforeseeable. In a case based on strict liability for failure to warn, it upheld verdicts for the plaintiffs that totaled $2.5 million for what might have seemed an unlikely product for a lawsuit.

A case involving another seemingly innocuous product, the cotton swabs branded as Q-Tips, reinforces the lesson. In an unpublished Missouri case, a five-year-old boy tore his eardrum and dislocated bones in his inner ear when he used a Q-Tip in an attempt to clean his ear. The court adduced the child's testimony that "he had heard about Q-Tips from television commercials and did not know they could cause injury." It also appeared to accept his assertion that, as it summarized it, "he would not have attempted to clean his ears with the Q-Tips if he knew they could hurt him." It referred to testimony by a product manager for the defendant that "the primary selling points for Q-Tips were their 'purity, safety, and softness,' her declaration that "they were the 'softest and safest swab,'" and her conclusion "that the number of injuries to children was too small to warrant toning down the safety aspects of its marketing strategy or including a warning on the Q-Tip packaging." In a decision that favored the plaintiffs' negligence claim, the court referred to the defendant's "extensive marketing activity" that emphasized the "safety of Q-tips," indeed saying that the company had "strenuously promoted" the swabs as "soft and safer" but did not "inherently alert a user to their potentially destructive capacity."[18]

The lesson of this group of cases may be generalized to a variety of products and activities. It is as if goods that do not provide warnings come to medical facilities or the supermarket shelf with a sign around them that is—in the language of the Uniform Commercial Code—an "affirmation" of safety that induces consumers to participate in the experiments we unthinkingly do with products every day.

The more precise the affirmation, the more likely it is that courts will impose liability on those who make representations—and this is so even when the consumer sues for what he was not told in the context of something he was told. Illustrative is an opinion of the Iowa Supreme Court, answering questions from a federal court in a suit by a smoker against several cigarette manufacturers. In the background of the case were "advertisements, statements or representations suggesting that there are no risks associated with smoking, including addiction." The precise question was whether, in that context, the defendants' failure to disclose information about the risks of smoking could be held to be fraud.[19] Quoting precedent, the Iowa court pointed to a state rule that "the failure to disclose material information can constitute fraud *if* the concealment is made 'by a party under a duty to communicate the concealed fact.'"[20] It concluded that "a manufacturer who makes statements for the purpose of influencing the purchasing decisions of consumers has a duty to disclose sufficient information so as to prevent the statements made from being misleading, as well as a duty to reveal subsequently acquired information that prevents a prior statement, true when made, from being misleading."[21]

Other decisions in cigarette litigation have gone further to favor smokers. In a hard-fought California case, the allegations—part of a pattern in such litigation—were that the defendant "knew that there was no valid scientific controversy concerning the adverse health effects of smoking, that it carefully avoided conducting or sponsoring research that might reveal the health hazards of smoking and concealed the results of research conducted in Germany on its behalf, and that it sought to maintain the false controversy and to make its cigarettes more addictive in order to increase sales." The court rejected the defendant's argument that the plaintiff had "failed to prove that she actually relied on particular statements," saying that claimant she did not have to "prove that he or she directly heard a specific misrepresentation or false promise to establish actual reliance." Rather, it said, "actual reliance is established if the defendant made a misrepresentation to a third party, the defendant intended or had reason to expect that the substance of the communication would be repeated to the plaintiff and would induce the plaintiff's reliance, and the plaintiff was misled when the substance of the communication was repeated to the plaintiff." Specifically, it referred to evidence "tending to show that Philip Morris for many years engaged in a broad-based public campaign to disseminate misleading information and create a false controversy concerning the adverse health effects of smoking with the intention of causing smokers and potential smokers to rely on the substance of that misinformation, and that the substance of the misinformation reached [the plaintiff] indirectly through various means and media sources and caused her to begin and to continue smoking."[22]

The conduct of the tobacco companies in the cases just summarized is simply representative of a most dangerous experiment that continues to be conducted on millions of people. The response of the courts we have quoted only confirms that the principal sets of data on those experiments have long since been collected, if not publicized, by the sellers of cigarettes. An important element of problems involving dangerous products and activities, spotlighted in these cases, is that of trust, and trust may be extrapolated broadly to the attitudes of people generally. There are many experiments that go on around us at all times—in the natural environment, in workplaces, in the consumption of new and established products, and in direct encounters with providers of services, including health care providers. Tied closely to trust is reliance, and the tendency of people to rely on the statements of others—providers of goods and services, and even politicians—about both risks and benefits of proposed courses of action. If trust diminishes, the inclination of people to rely on others is likely to diminish.

An important issue involving trust in experimentation, including the interstitial experimentation that occurs in many everyday episodes of medical treatment, concerns the relationship between doctor and patient. The concept of "informed consent" in medical jurisprudence tends to focus on the autonomy of the patient. A famous pronouncement of Cardozo nearly a century ago has a distinctly modern ring: "Every human being of adult years and sound mind has a right to determine what shall be done with his own body."[23] An interesting commentary on the concept of a "firmly individualistic form of autonomy" suggests that that idea gives insufficient weight to a concept of "relational autonomy," which takes into account a broader idea of "beneficence," defined as "the welfare or best interest of the patient."[24] Presenting this view, Sheila A. M. McLean observes that "it seems counterintuitive to suggest" that the "firmly individualistic" approach "*necessarily* ignores the link between those participating in a caring interaction based in trust—that is, the patient and the healthcare provider."[25] She summarizes recent case law from the United States and Commonwealth countries to the effect that "the law on consent is concerned to strike a balance between competing, and sometimes conflicting, claims and interests."[26] She says, "Whatever patients want to receive, the courts have traditionally and consistently distanced the issue from *that* patient's interests, whether by focusing on what doctors believe is good medical practice or what some imagined patient might have wanted."[27] She suggests that "a good interaction would result in the negotiation of a relationship that is more equal, but which would include respect for the individual's right to make his or her own decisions in a self- rather than other-regarding manner."[28] Her criticism of the current state of the law is that although "the claim that consent and autonomy are brethren under the skin may have served a purpose in leading healthcare professionals away from their traditional preference for paternalism and towards closer engagement with patients' rights . . . it has not resulted, and probably cannot result, in prioritizing patients' interests."[29]

The more precise the language of the portrayal of a product or service—even the images the portrayal projects—the more inclined courts will be to hold the representer to its language, thereby enforcing the trust that specific words build. Thus, a statement that a roof was "bondable up to 20 years" could be evidence of an express warranty, as "an explicit reference to future performance."[30] Perhaps most remarkably, in the rough and ready days of the nineteenth century, the Supreme Court found grounds for liability in representations that a mine was "rich in gold," with "veins . . . disseminated throughout the whole formation, in threads of from two to six inches wide." The Court said there could be liability "even if the party innocently misrepresents a fact by mistake."[31] The Court's declaration that such a misstatement "operates as a surprise and imposition on the other party" could be generalized to sales of products generally. One of the most famous assurances to consumers is the Good Housekeeping Seal of Approval, backed up by the statement, "We have satisfied ourselves the products and services advertised in Good Housekeeping are good ones and the advertising claims made for them in our magazine are truthful." One California decision concluded that this statement, together with the seal, supported a claim for negligent misrepresentation.[32]

An Oregon case involving a rollover of a vehicle, the Toyota 4Runner, highlights the power of colorful images to induce consumer reliance. The appellate court, in affirming a judgment for the plaintiff, referred to "print and television advertising" of that model "containing specific representations of 4Runners engaged in sharp steering maneuvers." The court noted that "the 'anti-lock brake system' section of the . . . marketing brochure contains a computer graphic illustration of a 4Runner traveling on a two-lane road," with dotted lines indicating "that the 4Runner's successful course of travel involves swerving left to avoid an obstacle in the right lane of travel and then swerving back to the right to avoid an obstacle in the left lane of travel." The court instanced a print advertisement "depicting a 4Runner traveling on a paved, two-lane road" indicating that "the 4Runner successfully travels across a small body of water or ice in the right lane, and then, just on the other side of that obstacle . . . veers sharply into the left lane to avoid debris from a landslide." It also referred to a television ad that "contained numerous images of 4Runners engaging in sharp turns and maneuvers," with a narrator saying that 4Runners "adapt quickly to changing environments" and another ad that "cut back and forth between images of people enjoying recreational activities and images of 4Runners making sharp turns."

The appellate court said that although the defendant had not "explicitly represented that the 1994 4Runner would not roll over under the exact circumstances" of the plaintiff's accident, the jury could have found that "an ordinary consumer would reasonably expect a 1994 4Runner traveling at legal speed not to roll over following foreseeable evasive maneuvers, such as three sharp turns on a flat, dry, paved highway."[33] The Oregon Supreme Court affirmed the plaintiff's judgment, although focusing on the design of the vehicle rather than its representational background.[34]

At all levels, experimentation assumes reliance, because reliance intimately ties in with trust. An important element of the reliance issue is that of materiality. This concept has been defined in different ways, but a good simplified summary of the essence of the question of whether a representation is material is whether it has a tendency to influence a decision to undertake a course of conduct—for example, to subject oneself to a medical procedure or to buy a product. One who chooses to be the subject of an experiment—a formal one under laboratory-type conditions or a mass-market experiment—might have chosen as she did because of an uninformed assumption that the experiment was not hazardous.

Certainly scientists and physicians conducting controlled drug experiments have a fiduciary duty to their subjects. The standard may be less stringent when experimentation occurs in the realm of commerce, but sellers of products on the market must be careful about language indicating the efficacy of their goods. In one case, a distributor of carburetors sued the manufacturer for loss of customer goodwill when the devices did not function well, adducing evidence that the defendant's own sales manager had complained that "the Acucarb was untried and uncalibrated as it was released to production, it was not tested and proven enough to be sold." Specifically, his testimony indicated that the defendant had chosen to start "producing units," rather than "to go into full test program." The plaintiff distributor testified that he had "relied upon brochures distributed by" the defendant, one of which said that "this new system is designed, developed, *thoroughly tested* and produced by the recognized leader in LP-gas carburetion." Another brochure said that the defendant had developed the carburetor after "three years of intensive research and testing, both in the lab and over the road" and that the carburetor was "the result of a comprehensive developing and testing program." Moreover, advertisements by the defendant in trade publications said that "the carburetor was 'the result of over three years of intensive research and development—in the lab and in the field' and was '*thoroughly tested*.'"[35] The Sixth Circuit's decision in the case included an intramural disagreement on whether state law provided a cause of action for negligent misrepresentation. However, the panel agreed that the trial court was wrong in concluding that the plaintiff had presented "no evidence that statements made by [the defendant] and its agents were either false or 'made recklessly thereby inducing action on the part of the plaintiff.'" The court concluded that the plaintiff had "produced clear and convincing evidence from which the jury might have inferred that [the defendant] did not thoroughly test the relevant version" of the carburetor and that the defendant "made its statements with knowledge of, or at least reckless disregard for, their falsity"—that is, that it might have committed fraud.[36]

Even an advertisement for one optional product feature may color the background for the lack of that feature on the product. An example is a case in which a nine-year-old boy suffered severe injuries when a truck hit his motorbike as he turned from an unpaved country road onto a highway. The plaintiff argued that the cycle was defectively designed because it lacked a safety flag. Over the defendant's objection, the trial court admitted an advertisement that offered a free "WindWhip," which it called "a safety flag for everyone," for cycle purchasers at Christmas. The advertisement also said that "besides being crazy and fun, the WindWhip ma[de] younger riders easier to spot" and "help[ed] older street riders stand out and be seen in traffic." The trial court admitted the ad "as evidence of the availability of wind flags and of Honda's use of wind flags on similar models," and the appellate court ratified that decision as "probative evidence of the value of a flag on the motorbike."[37] The decision is an example of the exercise of judicial control of ongoing experiments—in this case a product design within the context of an advertising campaign—through civil litigation.

Sometimes the implicit limitations of a representation leave the consumer on his own. An example is a case in which a St. Louis dentist, who performed at "the highest level in competitive tournament play" in racquetball, suffered a severe injury to his eye when a shot hit him there. An advertisement for the maker of the lensless eye guard he was wearing had an ad in a racquetball magazine that included the words, "PUT YOUR HAND OVER ONE EYE AND READ THIS. . . . This is a test. To show you what it would be like if you lost your eye in a racquetball accident. . . . [T]o be brutally frank, it's possible. The ball travels at speeds clocked as high as 142 m.p.h. And it can do a lot of damage if it hits your eye just right." The ad also said that the eye guard was made from a "tough, virtually indestructible polycarbonate" and will "stop a lot of accidents." The court, however, fixed on the fact that "there was no claim in the advertisement . . . that the eye guard would prevent all accidents." It also noted that the jury, which gave a verdict for the defendant, could have properly inferred from the plaintiff's own testimony about his proficiency at racquetball that "he must have known of the hazards that existed notwithstanding his use of the eye guard."[38]

Another limit on liability for representations is the category of "seller's puffs." A counterweight to decisions favoring smokers is a case involving cigarette ads that showed a man and two women with the statement "Guard Against Throat Scratch," a picture of Santa Claus smoking along with that same statement, and a picture of a male soldier talking to a woman, accompanied by the statement that the defendant's cigarettes would "lessen throat irritation." The court concluded that the ads "were probably not representations of fact as a matter of law" that that "even if they were, they were representations of mildness or comfort, taste or enjoyment, not health or safety."[39]

Generally, experimenters—formal and informal—know things about at least potential hazards that, at least initially, their subjects do not know. The outcome in lawsuits will often turn on what they do or do not tell their subjects. When what they say is skewed well beyond the facts, courts may term their behavior fraudulent. And the boundaries of the definition of fraud are somewhat elastic. According to a much-cited test articulated by the House of Lords in a nineteenth-century case that involved allegations of what today we would call securities fraud, the definition of fraud includes not only false statements made "knowingly" or "without belief in [their] truth," but also statements made "recklessly, careless whether [the statements] be true of false."[40] This definition sweeps in not only cases like the carburetor case discussed above,[41] but also some cigarette cases.[42]

The cases in which the experimenter does not communicate hazards or potential hazards to the public span a range over many activities and products. Episodes we have described concerning risks associated with nuclear power plants and atomic testing highlight the difficulties in communication about risks that may be low-probability but that could be very serious if they come to fruition. In the case discussed in Chapter Two involving fallout from the atomic tests in the western United States, the plaintiffs claimed, among other things, that the government had not told them about the health risks from exposure to radioactive materials. In such cases, there exists both knowledge—at least knowledge about a range of potential risks—and a possibility of communicating it. In other cases, of which the most profoundly tragic and far-reaching results stemmed from the impact on a Japanese nuclear plant by the tsunami and earthquake of 2011, it may be practically impossible to communicate the risk in advance to a potentially affected population. Part of the problem may lie in the mistaken belief of the very people who create the risk that they have prepared for the worst contingency.

Sometimes a part of the problem is the vastness of the population that may be affected. An analogy appears in the case law on the duty of makers of products to notify purchasers or to recall goods that begin to manifest safety problems after they have been marketed. Some decisions have found a duty, with respect to products ranging from a snowthrower[43] to a helicopter engine.[44] They have been most sympathetic to plaintiffs where the defendant knows, or reasonably could discover, the identities of owners of its products.[45] They have been more reluctant to impose a duty when there is "an over-the-counter sale of a generic product for use by an unknown consumer."[46] However, even in a case involving millions of products—cigarettes—the Maryland Court of Special Appeals declared that "what constitutes reasonable notice" of health hazards "would be a question of fact for the jury."[47]

A South Dakota case where keeping information from the public proved dangerous to a product maker's economic health featured more than one layer of concealment. The maker of a control on a water heater was informed by a water heater manufacturer that some of its knobs had begun to stick, leading to explosions. Although the maker of the control began using tougher materials on the knobs, for a time it did nothing to rectify the problem with the ones on the market and for some years did not report the problem to the Consumer Product Safety Commission, although a federal statute required that sellers "immediately" report any "substantial product hazard." And although it eventually launched a recall campaign with the Commission's approval, the response rate on that campaign was "poor," and it did not follow through with dealers who did not respond to its original notice. The South Dakota Supreme Court affirmed a plaintiff's judgment, including a punitive award, for "fraudulent concealment."[48]

Courts frequently face the question of how much room for maneuver they should afford experimenters, including those who are trying out products and activities on the public at large. A classic statement that limits maneuvering room appears in a 1913 fraud case in in which the Missouri court indicated that it would provide little leeway of that sort. Saying that "fraud is kaleidoscopic, infinite," the court observed, "Messieurs, the fraud-feasors, would like nothing half so well as for courts to say they would go thus far, and no further in its pursuit." Given that attitude, the court declared, "Accordingly definitions of fraud are of set purpose left general and flexible, and thereto courts match their astuteness against the versatile inventions of fraud-doers."[49]

We have sketched a legal framework of which experimenters must be aware with respect to how they represent their products and activities when they know, or have reason to know, of dangers they are creating for the public. Beyond that, one of the most difficult questions for courts in this area is who should pay when no one knew, or could have known, of a hazard at the time that an experiment was conducted. An experimenter averse to liability risks could routinely provide a notice that unforeseen and uncertain dangers may arise from its product or activity. However, a steady dose of such cautions might dull consumer sensitivity to those warnings to a point where they become meaningless. Experimenters may contend, with justice, that it is unfair to require them to pay for injuries caused by risks unknowable at the time an experiment was conducted. Yet it is always the experimenter who is the initiating actor, usually with some sort of profit in mind; for example, commercial profit or academic glory. In that case, it often will seem more just to place the burden of injury on experimenters, requiring them to spread the cost of their risky activities and signaling them that they should make advance provision for shouldering that burden.

## Notes

1. *Ducote v. Chevron Chem. Co.*, 227 So.2d 601, 605 (La. Ct. App. 1969).
2. *Adkins v. GAF Corp.*, 923 F.2d 1225, 1228 (6th Cir. 1991) (partly quoting 706 F. Supp. 559, 565 [S.D. Ohio 1988]).
3. Ibid.
4. *Greenman v. Yuba Power Prods Co.*, 377 P.2d 897, 901 (Cal. 1963).
5. *Howland v. Purdue Pharma L.P.*, Prod. Liab. Rep. ¶16,694, at 59,857-59,858, 2003 WL 21637968, pp. 4–5 (Ohio Ct. App. 2003).
6. *Howland v. Purdue Pharma L.P.* 821 N.E.2d 141, 145-47 (Ohio 2004) (quoting in part *Wethington v. Purdue Pharma L.P.* 218 F.R.D. 577, 588-89 [S.D. Ohio 2003]).
7. *Learjet v. Spenlinhauer*, 707 F. Supp. 44, 49 (D. Me. 1989).
8. *Learjet Corp. v. Spenlinhauer*, 901 F.2d 198, 201-02 (1st Cir.1990).
9. *Delahunt v. Cytodyne Technologies*, 241 F.Supp.2d 827, 833-34 (S.D. Ohio 2003).
10. Ibid., p. 836.
11. Ibid., pp. 835–36.
12. *Hill v. Searle Labs.*, 884 F.2d 1064, 1070-71 (8th Cir. 1989).
13. *Castro v. QVC Network, Inc.* 139 F.3d 114, 119-20 (2d Cir. 1998).
14. See *Whitaker v. Farmhand, Inc.*, 567 P.2d 916, 920-21 (Mont. 1977).
15. *Keller v. A.O. Harvestore Prods., Inc.*, 819 P.2d 69, 72 (Colo. 1991).
16. UCC § 2-313(1)(a).
17. *Ayers v. Johnson & Johnson Baby Products Co.*, 818 P.2d 1337, 1342-43 (Wash. 1991).
18. *Strothkamp v. Chesebrough-Pond's, Inc.* 1993 WL 79239, at 5-9, Prod. Liab. Rep. (CCH) # 13,456, at 41-879-41,880 (Mo. Ct. App. 1993) (not for publication).
19. *Wright v. Brooke Group Ltd.*, 652 N.W.2d 159, 163 (Iowa 2002).
20. Ibid., p. 174.
21. Ibid., p. 176. To be sure, there is case law indicating that a consumer may not advance a claim for a failure to warn of "known product dangers" when he did not know of misleading statements until the time he brought suit. See *Burton v. R. J. Reynolds Tobacco Co.* 397 F.3d 906, 913 (10th Cir. 2005).
22. *Bullock v. Philip Morris USA, Inc.*, 71 Cal.Rptr.3d 775, 791-92 (App. Ct. 2008). Another California appellate court said that "it was sufficient that the statements were issued to the public with the intent that they reach smokers and potential smokers and that [the plaintiff], as a member of the intended target population, heard them" (*Whiteley v. Philip Morris Inc.*, 11 Cal.Rptr.3d 807, 845 [App. Ct.2004]). See also *Williams v. Philip Morris Inc.*, 48 P.3d 824 (Or. Ct. App. 2002) (on the cigarette industry's efforts "to encourage the impression there was a genuine and continuing controversy" on causation of cancer, with industry relying on "criteria for proof of causation that the scientific community generally either had never accepted or have since discarded"), *aff'd*, 127 P.3d 1165, 1177 (Or. 2006) (focusing on defendant's knowledge that "smoking caused serious and sometimes fatal disease," but that the company "nevertheless spread false or misleading information to suggest to the public that doubts remained about that issue") (later history on punitive damages, extending to United States Supreme Court, omitted).

Other language from the Oregon courts' decisions appears in Chapter Three, text accompanying notes 91–93.

23. *Schloendorff v. Society of New York Hosp.*, 105 N.E. 92, 93 (N.Y. 1914).
24. See Sheila A. M. McLean, *Autonomy, Consent and the Law* (Routledge-Cavendish 2010), e.g., pp. 39, 9, 57, and 65.
25. Ibid., p. 39.
26. Ibid., p. 217.
27. Ibid., p. 226.
28. Ibid., p. 39.
29. Ibid., p. 227.
30. *Safeway Stores, Inc. v. Certainteed Corp.*, 710 S.W.2d 544, 548 (Tex.1986). Cf. *Cummings v. HPG Int'l, Inc.*, 244 F.3d 16, 22 (1st Cir. 2001) ("representation that their roofs would last twenty years was specific and verifiable, not a mere expression of opinion or estimate," although court ultimately rejects claim for fraud and negligent misrepresentation for lack of showing of requisite culpability).
31. *Smith v. Richards*, 38 U.S. (13 Pet.) 26 (1939).
32. *Hanberry v. Hearst Corp.*, 81 Cal.Rptr. 519, 522 (Ct. App. 1969).
33. *McCathern v. Toyota Motor Corp.* 985 P.2d 804, 817-19 (Or. Ct. App. 1999).
34. See *McCathern v. Toyota Motor Corp.*, 23 P.3d 320, 332 (Or. 2001).
35. *Miller's Bottled Gas, Inc. v. Borg-Warner Corp.*, 955 F.2d 1043, 1045-48 (6th Cir.1992) (italics the court's).
36. Ibid., p. 1051–54.
37. *Morales v. American Honda Motor Co., Inc.* 151 F.3d 500, 516-17 (6th Cir. 1998).
38. *Williams v. Pro-Tec, Inc.*, 908 F.2d 345, 347 (8th Cir. 1990).
39. *Gunsaulus v. Celotex Corp.*, 674 F. Supp. 1149, 1159 (E.D. Pa. 1987).
40. *Derry v, Peek*, 14 App. Cas. 337 (H.L. 1889).
41. *Miller's Bottled Gas, Inc. v. Borg-Warner Corp.*, 955 F.2d 1043, 1051 (with evidence that the defendant tested its carburetors "only spottily and hastily in view of the need to market [them] before gasoline prices fell," a jury could have found "at least reckless disregard" for the falsity of the representations).
42. See cases discussed in text accompanying notes 19–22 supra.
43. *Dixon v. Jacobsen Mfg. Co.*, 637A.2d 915, e.g., at 923-24 (N.J. App. Div. 1994) (reversing judgment for defendant on issue of "warning defect").
44. *Walton v. Avco Corp.*, 557 A.2d 372, 377-80 (Pa. Super. 1989), *aff'd* for the plaintiff on failure to warn issue, 610 A.2d 1992, 459-60 (Pa. 1992).
45. See for example Dixon, supra.
46. The court describes the facts this way in a case involving a hay baler, *Birchler v. Gehl Co.*, 88 F.3d 518, 521 (7th Cir. 1996) (quoting a precedent).
47. *Hollingsworth & Vose Co. v. Connor*, 764 A.2d 318, 333-34 (Md. Ct. App. 2000).
48. *Holmes v. Wegman Oil Co.*, 492 N.W.2d 107, 112 (S.D. 1992).
49. *Stonemets v. Head*, 154 S.W. 108, 114 (Mo. 1913).

# 7

# Experiments Generating Defects

We may have an image of experimenters as inventors of chemical products with beakers, Bunsen burners, and vials, but that is not one-tenth of the story of products whose life on the market is a grand set of experiments. From time to time, consumers attribute injuries to certain features of innovative products that their sellers not only intend to incorporate in those products but in which they take pride. In a large number of litigated cases, products of this sort present the question of whether those features can be judged to make those products "defective." This chapter uses as illustrations of this issue a small number of those cases, which are a very small fraction of the large number of experiments with consumer products that sometimes adversely affect the lives of consumers at work and leisure.

Some of these products are things most people would not think of as vehicles for injury. Consider, for example, the baseball bat, historically made of ash, birch, or maple. Now think specifically about that relative newcomer to the diamond, the aluminum bat. Who might have thought that because of its physical characteristics, it would be the subject of an injury suit? But that was exactly the case with an action brought by Andrew Sanchez, a pitcher for the California State University Northridge team, who was hit in the head by a ball that rocketed off an aluminum bat at what an expert witness said was a speed of more than one hundred miles per hour. The witness testified that the nature of such bats "significantly increased the inherent risk" that a line drive would injure a pitcher, as compared with the wooden bats of yore. Andrew, it should be noted, had competed with some form of aluminum bat since he was six years old. That, however, did not prove an insuperable obstacle to his suit. A California appellate court concluded that, as a subject of the ongoing experiment with these bats, Andrew had raised a factual question about whether the design of the bat "substantially increased" the "inherent risk" that he faced.[1]

Both sellers and consumers are experimenting all the time with many kinds of products. They march along different kinds of slopes, sometimes slippery ones, always testing out the footing. As the process of experimentation proceeds, all kinds of factors come into play. The question of whether there are different ways of achieving the same consumer goal arises; for example, are there alternative designs for risky products? What consumer profile do we assume with respect to knowledge of risk? To expectations of risks and benefits? How much meaningful choice do consumers have about whether to encounter a product, including the ability to choose among alternatives?

The emergence of new technologies across a broad front of products presents the issue of when sellers must be responsible for the failure to bring goods up to attainable technological levels. In one case in which the court gave manufacturers a push toward that goal, vertically stacked wire containers fell on a forklift operator from the forks of the machine, causing permanent paralysis of his limbs. The plaintiff argued that the lift truck should have had an overhead guard. In affirming a substantial jury verdict for him, the court took note of the manufacturer Hyster's argument that when it made the machine in 1965, "it did not, or could not, make an overhead guard standard equipment due to low-clearance problems encountered in loading and unloading the vans of semi-trailer trucks." However, the court also observed that "in 1966 Hyster did in fact make such guards standard" on the model forklift the plaintiff was operating, and "strengthened this policy in 1970, while still facing those same low-clearance problems which had existed in 1965." It said that the defendant's apparent decision in 1965 not to make at least non-retractable guards "standard due to low clearance problems, while at the same time realizing this machine could and would be used in high-stack areas," was "a conscious marketing choice." It concluded that a verdict for the plaintiff was appropriate "if the jury found that the lack of a guard on such a machine, despite the low-clearance problems, was an unreasonably dangerous condition which led to plaintiff's injuries." It said "the existence of a retractable guard, while something which the jury could consider, is not vital to such a finding."[2]

A particularly tense presentation of the problems presented by developing technologies appears in a pair of opinions by the noted federal judge Jack Weinstein in a case involving injuries to a two-and-a-half-month-old child attributed to a whole-cell DTP vaccine. In an opinion initially denying summary judgment to the manufacturer, he viewed the situation as one in which, "while [the defendant] lagged, a Japanese company, applying the available technology," brought to market another design, an acellular vaccine. He referred to expert testimony for the plaintiff that if the defendant had "not abandoned research and development" on the acellular vaccine, it could have marketed such a product by the time the plaintiff suffered her injury. Although the defendant submitted evidence that "this would have been an impossible feat," Judge Weinstein concluded that the jury could have found that whole-cell vaccine "was a defective product at the time plaintiff received her DTP inoculation."[3]

As the case developed at trial, Judge Weinstein pointed out that the "pioneering efforts of the Japanese" had produced "the recipe for an effective acellular vaccine" in 1979, the year the plaintiff was inoculated. But he also noted some facts that weighed in favor of the defendant: the Japanese vaccine standards at the time were "less stringent" than the U.S. standards; the acellular product had been approved only for use in children above two years; and American pediatricians had "overwhelmingly" recommended the whole-cell vaccine for very young children at the time. As he summarized it, it would have taken yet "more years of further development and testing" to produce a "more advanced vaccine for two-month-old infants" in the United States. He decided that the jury could not have concluded that at the time the plaintiff received her inoculation, "the defendant could have developed, produced and proven to the FDA's satisfaction the efficacy and safety of an acellular vaccine" for a child of the plaintiff's age. Of particular relevance to our topic was his comment that "the case illustrates some of the strengths and weaknesses of the American system for marketing drugs"—that "requiring strict proof of safety—both to comply with FDA regulations and to avoid tort liability—slows the availability of new products," with a possible result being "that dangers will be enhanced during the necessarily extended developmental period." He observed that "these results are attributable to the way in which scientists usually solve problems—through incremental, peer reviewed experiments—and to the regulatory system, not to any delict on the part of this defendant."[4] These comments captured the congruence of the uncertainties in science as it is practiced with the uncertainties inherent in many kinds of continuing experiments done on human beings in various types of marketplaces.

The process of innovation that confers great advantages on consumers often brings along with it knowledge on the part of sellers of hazards that might not have been evident at the beginning of product development. Illustrative is a case in which the vehicle in which the plaintiff was riding slammed into the trailer of a truck made by the defendant. The plaintiff sued on the basis of the "underride hazard" presented by the height of the bumper on the trailer, which was a 1987 model. The plaintiff offered expert testimony that "national tests and demonstrations as early as 1969 and 1970" indicated that a clearance of that height "expose[d] . . . a significant proportion of the vehicle population to serious underride accidents." The court upheld a jury finding for the plaintiff on the issue of the design of the bumper.[5]

It should be noted that a manufacturer that responds to a known problem must be sure to do so adequately. The maker of a water pump system used by firefighters found this out in a case involving a "runaway" pumping machine that crushed the plaintiff between the cab door of the machine and a fence. Knowing about the problem of runaways, the defendant had installed a green light "OK to Pump" system that was to signal to the operators of fire trucks "whether a shift out of 'ROAD mode' and into 'PUMP mode' had been successfully completed." However, the plaintiff provided evidence that the defendant "received continuous information" about runaway trucks "from the time it introduced the green light in 1976 through the time it manufactured" the system at issue in 1989. The court thought that this was "evidence from which a reasonable jury could infer that the system did not work to effectively prevent runaway fire trucks" and concluded that there was sufficient evidence of a design defect to deny summary judgment to the defendant.[6]

A parable of the computer age is a New Jersey case involving a truck driver who had an accident while he was putting data into an onboard computer made by the defendant. The plaintiffs, with whose car the trucker collided, argued that the potential for distraction presented by the fact that the computer could be operated while the truck was moving was a design defect. At the technical heart of the case was a provision in the state products liability law that provided a defense in design defect cases when "the harm was caused by an unsafe aspect of the product that is an inherent characteristic of the product and that would be recognized by the ordinary person who uses or consumes the product." However, there was a statutory exception to the defense for products whose danger "can feasibly be eliminated without impairing the usefulness of the product." Although the jury found that there was no defect, the appellate division reversed, granting a new trial for the plaintiffs against the computer maker, and the New Jersey Supreme Court upheld the appellate division.

Justice Garibaldi's opinion for the supreme court acknowledged that entering data while the truck was in motion "may be an 'inherent characteristic' of the computer that is recognized by the ordinary [driver] who uses . . . the product with the ordinary knowledge common to" drivers. However, she disagreed with the trial court "that the proofs were sufficient as a matter of law to establish that making the [computer] inoperable in whole or in part while in motion would so impair the usefulness of the product that an instruction on the 'impairing the usefulness' exception to the . . . defense was unnecessary." Instead, she concluded that "whether [the defendant] could have—without impairing the usefulness of the computer—eliminated the dangers posed by the [computer's] being operable while in motion is a question of fact" for the jury. That question, she specified, was "whether operability of all functions while in motion is an inherent characteristic of the [computer] and whether or not eliminating that feature in whole or in part would significantly diminish its intended use."[7] The case indicates the potential breadth of the inquiry that innovators may have to make about how their products are used.

Advancing technology—the epitome of experimentation—has been a boon to consumers in the most varied applications. We explore here a diverse group of products, ranging from cigarette lighters to motor vehicles to medical gloves with latex components.

The case of the cigarette lighter is laden with irony. While tobacco companies were experimenting for decades on the lungs of millions of consumers, a little piece of hardware came into being that made it easier to light up. The cigarette lighter has its origins in the nineteenth century, apparently with a device invented in 1823 that had an unfortunate tendency to "unexpectedly explode," using hydrogen as it did with platinum as a catalyst.[8] Apparently a quantum leap occurred in 1903 with the invention by an Austrian chemist named Carl Auer von Weisbach of a lighter that used an alloy combining iron and cesium as a flint.[9]

Besides providing an efficient boost to a habit that proved toxic to various organs of smokers, modern lighters had a more direct negative effect—they became a very dangerous toy in the hands of young children. A raft of decisions in so-called "childplay lighter" cases reflect a complicated legal picture concerning the effects of a technology for which ongoing experiments in households have proved deadly to occupants.

A concentrated example of judicial disagreement on such a case appears in opposed opinions in a Seventh Circuit case in which a four-year-old used a Bic lighter that set off a fire in a two-year-old's bedroom that proved fatal to the younger child.[10] So drawn out was the case, which took two hearings by the entire Seventh Circuit, that a dissenting judge said he doubted that "few, if any, cases that have been decided during recent years have consumed the number of judge-hours that this case has cost this court."[11]

Judge Manion's opinion for the majority upheld a decision for Bic on the basis of a "consumer contemplation test" that served as a standard for design defect cases in Illinois. He acknowledged that "the ordinary consumer expects that if a lighter's flame is put to some other combustible objects, a larger fire ensues," which indeed was what made "a lighter dangerous." But he said that this did "not make a lighter unreasonably dangerous under the consumer contemplation test." He posited that "children are not ordinary consumers under the consumer contemplation test" and declared that it would work an "absurdity to abandon the ordinary consumer standard for [a] foreseeable user standard, especially where children are concerned." He reasoned that since "children lack knowledge about consumer products," "they should not be the standard to measure consumer expectations." Rather, he said that since "the ordinary consumer—if not a four-year-old child—is deemed to expect that lighters cause fires," "lighters are not unreasonably dangerous."[12]

Judge Cudahy observed in dissent that, given that "in the case of products like lighters and knives, injury to some children is perhaps inevitable," "the issue ought to be what party is best able to bear and distribute the cost of this inevitable injury—the child or the manufacturer." He said, "It is not clear to me whether employing a regime of tort law is preferable to requiring potential victims (or their parents) to go into the marketplace and buy insurance to guard against the cost of unavoidable accidents." Favoring a risk-utility test rather than the consumer contemplation test on which Judge Manion relied, he acknowledged that it might be "patronizing to deny consumers the opportunity to purchase 'riskier' products at a lower price," but said this was not the court's "choice to make," and that he saw "nothing irrational in Illinois' choosing the course it thinks most sensible and socially appropriate."[13]

Other courts weighed in to favor the risk-utility test. The Ohio Supreme Court adduced statistics indicating that there were 5,800 annual episodes of residential fires caused by children playing with lighters, with a toll of 170 deaths and a national cost of at least $300 million. The court said that the policy of "promot[ing] public safety" advanced by the strict liability doctrine "nowhere applies with more force than where it comes to the protection of our children."[14] Another court cited similar data in a case in which the plaintiff, a three-year-old, used a lighter to set fire to a pile of clothes. Noting a comparison of injury costs to the cost to lighter makers of making all lighters child-proof, the court concluded, on a defective design claim, that the defendant sellers had not proved "as a matter of law that they did not owe a duty" to the plaintiff.[15] In yet another lighter case, the defendant "conceded the feasibility of childproofing the lighter" for purposes of the motion before the court. The Third Circuit combined the "high gravity" and "considerable probability of risk" with the "high social value placed on the safety of people and property" and "the likelihood of a reasonably available alternative" in concluding that those factors "may outweigh BIC's interest in producing its lighters without childproofing features."[16]

A federal court added a wrinkle in a lighter case with a statement that Bic had shown that it had "no duty to make the lighter childproof." However, it said that the characteristics of the product, which included the facts that it "permit[ted] butane gas to escape in large quantities, and to pool against clothing and persons in such a manner as to explode . . . [or] to cause a large and sudden flame and to engulf clothing or objects in flame," did not restrict a claim on negligent design "to persons who are young, or to children." It said that the defendants had not shown that there was "no genuine issue concerning the product design in regard to people generally."[17] The Texas Supreme Court partly reasoned in the same track in saying, in answer to a certified question, that "a manufacturer's intention that its product be used only by adults does not insulate it from liability for harm caused by a child who gains access to the product," although "liability standards must be applied in the context of the intended users." Responding to a question it summarized as "whether a defective-design claim can be maintained under" stated circumstances, the Texas court responded that "it can, depending on the evidence, but there will also be cases—the present case may or may not be one—in which a claim cannot be maintained as a matter of law."[18]

The results in these cases differ, but overall they do send messages to innovators. As manufacturers continue to refine the design of their products, they must take into account not only the potential population of users—even juveniles who, from the standpoint of firms, misuse their goods—but also the overall costs of predictable injuries as compared with the costs of making products safer, including choice of alternative designs and foregone profits. An interesting legal twist emerges from the battle between advocates of a "consumer contemplation" test—which intuitively one might think tilts toward plaintiffs—and supporters of a "risk-utility" test, which ordinarily might seem to favor defendants. Results in some of the childplay lighter cases reverse these intuitions.

The problem of vehicle rollovers yielded a plaintiff-oriented result in a case in which the Sixth Circuit drew on both tests. The case involved an SUV, a Ford Bronco II, driven by a man who had never driven the vehicle before, who felt it "jerk" or "overcorrect" during a lane change and, in "trying to regain control of the vehicle . . . may have turned the steering wheel as much as a full revolution." In its analysis of the stability index of the Bronco, a Ford report "listed five alternatives to increase the index." Three of those it "did not choose provided for a wider track and a higher stability index than the proposal chosen." As the court summarized it, "The increased track width was a problem because it would have required a sheet metal design change with a minimum one-year delay in production, and because Ford planned to sell the vehicle in Japan." On what it termed the "risk-benefit" axis of the case, the court said, in affirming a verdict for the plaintiff, that "if reasonable minds could conclude that stability index is relevant to rollover propensity, they could also conclude that [the] alternative designs would pose less risk than the design Ford adopted" and that "reasonable minds could reach different conclusions on whether the foreseeable risks of the Bronco II's design outweighed its benefits." At the same time, the court said that "even if the jury did not conclude that the Bronco II had a design defect under the risk-benefit analysis, it could have found a design defect if the vehicle was more dangerous than an ordinary consumer would expect when used in a reasonably foreseeable manner" and that the two-wheel lift of the vehicle as the driver changed lanes "was more dangerous than an ordinary consumer would expect."[19]

Another case, indirectly involving a product, raises a design question that most consumers would never think about. The product was a refrigerated meat trailer, and the design feature involved the hanging of meat from the ceiling. The plaintiff suffered crippling injuries when a trailer carrying 36,742 pounds of beef quarters suspended that way overturned on his pickup and crushed him. The availability of alternative designs—including the tying of meat to the floor of the trailer and the installation of partitions "to restrict the swinging motion of the meat"—was central to the court's affirmance of a judgment for the plaintiff.[20]

A medical product provides an excellent illustration of a consumer good, undreamed of in prior eras, that confers blessings at the expense of serious injuries to a significant number of users. This product is latex gloves, which were in widespread use and were indeed quite useful for their purposes but had unfortunate side effects on a substantial number of users. Just one victim of the damage these gloves could do was Linda Green, a CT scan technologist at a Milwaukee hospital, who used up to forty pairs of the gloves in a single work shift. She experienced a spreading rash and "chronic cold-like symptoms" that escalated into "an acute shortness of breath, coughing, and tightening of the throat" and required hospitalization. Eventually what was diagnosed was a latex allergy that brought on asthma.

Green's case reached the Wisconsin Supreme Court. Its response to a product that was widely used—in effect a broad-scale experiment within the health care market—raised the question of how far ordinary people could be assumed to make judgments about technologies in which they are not expert. Expert witnesses for Green testified that the latex proteins in the defendant's gloves could cause allergic reactions in 5 to 17 percent of health care workers nationally who used the products. The defendant argued against the plaintiff's reliance on a "consumer contemplation" test on the grounds that the test was inappropriate for "complex products" because "ordinary consumers may not know of or fully understand the technical or mechanical design aspects of" such products. The supreme court, however, said that test did "not inevitably require any degree of scientific understanding about the product itself" but instead "requires understanding of how safely the ordinary consumer would expect the product to serve its intended purpose." The court said that the jury could reasonably have found that the gloves "contained an ingredient that can cause an allergic reaction in a 'significant number' of consumers" and that at the time of Green's sensitization, the "ordinary consumer" did not know of the statistical magnitude of the risk. It rejected the defendant's argument that using a "consumer contemplation" test without consideration of the risks and benefits of a product would drive "many useful products" off the market. The court said that "if, even in light of warnings or instructions, a product remains defective and unreasonably dangerous to the ordinary consumer," it saw "no reason that the product should remain on the market."[21]

In the same year, a California appellate decision on latex gloves captured the intensity of the struggle over legal doctrine. In a case involving several plaintiffs, the court bundled together the complexity of the product with its rejection of the consumer expectations test, which it acknowledged could "be applied even to very complex products" but said that should be done "only when the circumstances of the product's failure are relatively straightforward." That description, as the court viewed it, did not apply to "the alleged circumstances of the . . . failure" of the latex gloves in the cases at issue, which "involve[d] technical and mechanical details about the operation of the manufacturing process, and then the effect of the product upon an individual plaintiff's health." Noting that the effect of the "particular material" in the gloves and their "particular manufacturing process[es]" might "well . . . create in their users many degrees of allergic reactions," the court said that the understanding and assessment of "responsibility for such . . . reactions" was "a matter that is driven by the science of the manufacturing the preparation procedures, as well as the medical aspects of the individual's reaction to various substances." It found a material inconsistency between the plaintiffs' effort to focus "on the overall product performance" in terms of the "basic safety measure" of using the gloves as a "protective device" and their "complex and technical approach to proving the alleged design defect." Saying that "plaintiffs are seeking to prove that their conditions were caused by more than a natural allergy to a natural substance, such that a product defect or a wrongdoing by a defendant could have been causative factors," the court declared that "the complexity of this task makes it inappropriate to apply the consumer expectations test for design defect."[22]

The lessons these opposed decisions provide for innovators are as complex as the technology of latex gloves. Different courts dip into different barrels of the legal test for design defect—consumer expectations and risk-utility, sometimes combining them in a capacious dual test. This means that the prudent innovator will pay attention not only to whatever estimates it can make about the economic value of its product and the costs its dangerous characteristics may inflict, but also to what the hypothetical reasonable consumer may anticipate about the injuries it may cause.

One balm for producers is that at some point, the experimental becomes the everyday, and consumers are expected to know about the hazards of products unknown to their grandparents. People who did home improvements two generations ago did not use high-speed power saws, but their descendants know that "to accomplish its purpose," a tool of that kind must whirr at as many as seven thousand revolutions a minute. Given that knowledge and "no practical means of stopping [the] blade, or shielding it with a fool-proof mechanical guard," it has been held that such a saw is not defective.[23] Analogously, and sadly, a two-and-a-half-year-old child cannot pin a design defect label on a lawn dart hurled by an eight-year-old, because the dangers of that object "should be obvious even to children of the tender age of eight."[24]

Also obvious is the danger posed by hot water. In a suit against the maker of a heater brought on behalf of a fifteen-month-old child, the court observes that "the ordinary purpose of the . . . water heater was to heat water for residential uses *and* for residential appliances" and that the heater at issue "performed in the exact manner in which it was expected to perform when it was used in the customary, usual, and reasonably foreseeable manner."[25] Echoing this decision in another water heater case in which an infant was severely burned, the court, in affirming a judgment for the maker of a thermostat, said, "An ordinary person is fully aware of when water is too hot for his liking, and can protect himself accordingly."[26] In both of these cases, the court relied on the risk-utility test.

Inevitably, we are brought to that favorite of critics of tort law: hot coffee. A federal district court captured the argument for the defense in its declaration, "One of the qualities of 'good' coffee is that it be 'hot.'"[27] The same goes for tea. As an Ohio court put it in a suit against McDonald's, "A hot cup of tea is still a hot cup of tea."[28] The Seventh Circuit put a numerical point on the idea in a case in which the holding temperature of a carafe on the hot plate of a coffee maker was 179 degrees. Although noting that "coffee at 180° F is considerably more likely to cause severe burns than is coffee at 135° to 140° F, the maximum at which [the plaintiff] believes that coffee should be served," the court said that "without evidence that a holding temperature of 180 degrees F is of little worth to consumers, plaintiffs cannot show that the choice of a high temperature makes coffee defective."[29]

Yet despite the expression that hot food should be eaten hot, restaurants may still beware, at least where children are involved. In a Louisiana case, a waitress brought extra cups of heated dipping sauce for a family that was eating breadsticks. The family's three-year-old spilled some sauce on his legs, resulting in second-degree burns. When the waitress testified "that she was aware that the sauce was hot enough to burn someone," the court affirmed a plaintiff's judgment on a verdict that the restaurant was 70 percent negligent, the parents having been found 30 percent negligent.[30]

One should also note that the possibility of an alternative design may advance the case for someone who slips even near an object that is obviously sharp. Illustrative is the case of a man who walked by a slicing machine that was running unattended and reached out "to grab something to steady himself," suffering serious injuries when his hand contacted the blade. When there was evidence that "when the slicer in question was produced, it could readily have been manufactured with an interlock," the court said that "a reasonable jury could not rationally have reached any conclusion other than that, because of the omission of a blade interlock, the . . . slicer was defectively designed." The court concluded that it was not an error to use the consumer expectations test: "A swimming pool can be used satisfactorily without diving, but a delicatessen slicing machine cannot be used satisfactorily without frequent and thorough cleaning of its blade."[31]

In sum, innovators face liability risks based on a combination of several factors. One is the comparison of the risks and benefits of their products. Another is the expectations of consumers about risk, which includes sub-issues about what consumers ordinarily can be expected to know and the ability of consumers to make meaningful choices. Some of these factors inhere in the everyday use of products for generations. Hot coffee has been a consumer staple for a long time. However, many of our grandparents did not have hot water heaters, nor did they have power tools that spun at several thousand revolutions a minute. As makers of those products refine their designs—an experimental process that is as ongoing as the demand of consumers for more kinds of products—they sometimes learn of injuring events in consumers' use of products that are even more surprising to the consumers than to the manufacturers themselves.

We continue our analysis of product innovation with another varied group of products used in many forms of human activity, from lighting up cigarettes to driving different kinds of vehicles and including the firing of various types of weapons and the employment of specialized hardware in medical care. Among the products and activities in this group that have been established for the longest time are smoking and the use of firearms. Among the relatively newer ones are motor vehicles and devices used in patient care in hospitals. In all of these cases, sellers push forward in the effort to develop and expand markets—an enterprise involving experimentation on the run that often, but not always, produces net gains in consumer welfare.

The case of cigarettes presents one of the most interesting battlegrounds in the law of products liability, as well in the broader world of regulation. We have noted a condemnation of tobacco by a seventeenth-century monarch—King James I, who referred to "a custome lothsome to the eye" and "dangerous to the lungs."[32] Jumping centuries, three going on four, we find a series of government documents detailing the vicious health effects of smoking.[33] People at large were more—or less—aware of those effects. A popular song of the 1940s had a verse including the words "puff, puff, puff, and if you smoke yourself to death."[34] Yet it was not until the 1950s that consumers who suffered from smoking-caused illness began to bring tobacco companies to court. A great struggle between the companies and plaintiffs' lawyers has gone on since then, consuming considerable amounts of court time. One technological improvement that was at least initially an improvement—from the companies' point of view—was the introduction of additives to the basic tobacco used in cigarettes. A litigant in a Florida case gave evidence that the defendant, Philip Morris, had "used as many as 110 to 115 total additives and that some additives changed the form of the nicotine to freebase nicotine," a product "absorbed into the cells much faster and [that] can lead to greater nicotine addiction."[35] But if additives spelled addiction and therefore more sales, they also generated liability risks for cigarette makers. The plaintiff in the Florida case provided "evidence that the use of 'flue-cured' tobacco, i.e., tobacco that had been exposed to toxic exhaust fumes from propane heaters, increased by as much as ten times the level of carcinogenic tobacco-specific nitrosamines in the tobacco." The court in that case affirmed a judgment for the plaintiff.[36]

A much-quoted pronouncement in a comment to the Restatement (Second) of Torts had effectively immunized "good tobacco" from suit,[37] but a federal court was an unwilling consumer of that characterization, saying, "Although 'good tobacco,' without any additives or foreign substances, may not be unreasonably dangerous, that does not automatically mean that all tobacco-containing products are not unreasonably dangerous." A particularly interesting sentence in the opinion captured the status of practically all goods on the market, save products from farmers' markets: "The cigarettes sold by defendants are manufactured products and . . . the court finds that they are subject to design, packaging, and manufacturing variations which may render them defective even if the tobacco used in their manufacture was initially unadulterated."[38] This court denied the defendants' motion to dismiss.

The Sixth Circuit held some tobacco companies' feet to the metaphorical fire of their cigarettes in a case in which the defendants, although "largely admitting that they engaged in pervasive tactics to distort the dangers of smoking," argued that "the health risks of cigarette smoking have been 'common knowledge' for decades" ("Puff, puff, puff that cigarette"). The focus of the case was a particular disease, the lung cancer from which the plaintiff's decedent suffered. The court rejected the defendants' contention that "as long as the public knew that tobacco was dangerous, it is irrelevant if it did not appreciate the specific maladies that might attend its use." It referred to an expert's testimony that at the time the plaintiff's decedent smoked, there was "no reason to believe" that the public "had any understanding of the nature of [the] connection" between cigarettes and lung cancer, an understanding the witness described as "hypothetical." It referred to the expert's statement, based on "extensive data, including federal government reports," that "as far as I know, people thought cigarette smoke was simply as dangerous as breathing city air." Acerbically, the court said, "It is one thing to be aware generally that a product might have an attenuated and theoretical connection with a deadly disease like lung cancer; it is another altogether to comprehend that it is the cause of an overwhelming majority of lung cancer cases." It declared, "The 'common knowledge' requirement is emasculated if a defendant may show merely that the public was aware that a product presented health risks at some vague, unspecified, and undifferentiated level."[39] Thus, a lack of precise information on the part of consumers was central to liability issues in an episode of one of the longest-running consumer experiments of all time.

Firearms, from handguns and assault weapons to BB guns, provide another very long-running experiment that has involved thousands of deaths—by design or by accident. Guns have been a target of litigation for years, but plaintiffs have not often been successful. The Fifth Circuit concisely described the case for the defense when it said that because the kind of guns at issue "functioned precisely as they were designed, and because the dangers of handguns are obvious and well-known to all members of the consuming public," the plaintiffs could not recover under either a consumer expectations test or a risk-utility test.[40]

As I have observed elsewhere, this seems a macabre reference to the consumer expectations test, since the ultimate "consumer" of ammunition is the victim of a shooting. But the strength of judicial opposition to imposing liability on sellers of handguns is evident in a Washington appellate case involving a so-called Saturday night special, a .22-caliber low-end product "generally characterized by short barrels, light weight, easy concealability, low cost, use of cheap quality materials, poor manufacture, inaccuracy and unreliability."[41] Referring to a statutory definition of design defects that referred to the "burden on the manufacturer to design a product that would have prevented . . . harms" and "the adverse effect that an alternative design that was practical and feasible would have on the usefulness of the product," the Washington court said that it was "'difficult to comprehend how any operable handgun, no matter how different from the one that paralyzed [the plaintiff], 'would have prevented those harms.'"[42] Courts have even extended the argument that consumers are well aware of the danger of shot projectiles to a paintball gun[43] and a BB gun.[44] Thus, courts ratify the long-time social experiment with guns and gun-like devices, which users view as contributing to consumer welfare.

Improvements in technology that yield an alternative design, but one that coexists with an original design that remains in use, are at the heart of an Illinois death case involving a connector attached to intravenous devices or catheters used in hospitals. The defendant Baxter's first model of such a device, a "luer slip connector," had been used for about forty years. It was defined by the company as a product that, "when properly inserted, must provide a reasonably secure friction fit that will not leak or easily slide out of the catheter." For twenty years, Baxter had also sold a "luer lock connector," which, as the company defined it, "would provide a secure lock such that non-intentional separation of the Luer adapter from catheter . . . could not occur." Under industry standards, the slip connectors had to "withstand five and one-half pounds of separation force before disconnecting, and luer lock connectors must withstand eight pounds of force." After luer lock connectors came on the market, all makers of IV sets, "including Baxter, made all female fittings with flanges so these fittings could accommodate either luer slip or luer lock male fittings." The plaintiff's decedent died when an air embolism went to her brain after her catheter became disconnected from an intravenous tube. Her surgeon "acknowledged luer slip connectors can easily disconnect," testifying that "he had seen such disconnections a 'few times' and 'quite often so many times'" before the accident at issue. The plaintiffs' suit basically attacked the sale of tubing without a luer lock connector. The complaint alleged, *inter alia,* that:

> (1) the tubing was unreasonably dangerous because it was designed, manufactured, and sold without a Luer-lock connection; (2) the friction-fit connection failed when the product was used in a reasonably foreseeable manner; and (3) Baxter failed to warn of the likelihood of unintentional disconnection and the need to use tubing equipped with the Luer-locking device.

A Baxter vice president admitted that the firm was aware of failures associated with use of the slip connectors but said that the firm "did not encourage sales representatives to recommend Luer-locks for central line applications" but rather "simply made both products available to its customers." A group product manager for the firm, insisting that "both luer slip and luer lock connectors were safe products," said,

> You have customer preference. And if a customer prefers one versus the other, they're both safe products, so you offer them what they want, you know, clinically what they decide that they need. So it's just like anything else. You offer a variety of products to fit the customer's requirements.

She concluded, "There are obviously customers that wanted friction fit. It was selling in the marketplace."

The Illinois Supreme Court affirmed its appellate court's affirmance of a large judgment against Baxter. The supreme court noted that various personnel at the hospital, including "the nurse responsible for the actual purchase and distribution of medical supplies" and doctors involved in the care of the plaintiffs' decedent, did not know about differences between the two types of connector. It concluded that the patient, "who was conscious after surgery, could have reasonably expected that her IV catheter connection, if properly designed and manufactured, would be safe to use for its intended purpose," noting the obvious—that "she was the person who would be harmed if the device failed." The supreme court also concluded that the verdict against Baxter "based on application of the risk-utility test was not against the manifest weight of the evidence."[45]

Over a period of two decades, Baxter and its hospital customers had in effect used patients as experimental subjects for two models of IV connectors. As a general product category, those connectors surely were a boon to medical care. But as a practical matter, the decisions of the Illinois courts delivered a sharp message to innovators: When a new product clearly dominates an older one for safety—at least in broad applications—the inventor must remove the older product from the market or suffer expensive legal consequences.

In the 1950s, Ronald Reagan began to serve as a spokesman for the General Electric Theater on television, intoning over and over that "progress is our most important product." The idea that motor vehicles must be "crashworthy" provides another legal manifestation of the fact that those who make technological progress must sometimes make parallel progress with safety. Congress's passage of the National Traffic and Motor Vehicle Safety Act in 1966[46] implanted in federal law the idea that vehicles must have a reasonable ability to withstand the millions of collisions that take place in traffic every year. The Eighth Circuit's landmark decision in *Larsen v. General Motors Corporation* in 1968 confirmed that "while automobiles are not made for the purpose of colliding with each other," their manufacturers must take into account that such events were "a frequent and inevitable contingency of normal automobile use."[47] This case, backing up the congressional statute, has provided the basis for a separate cottage industry for lawyers.

Two decisions by the Fourth Circuit, one favoring an autoworker and the other favoring representatives of a deceased driver, capture a spectrum of the efforts of courts to define the "crashworthiness doctrine." A 1974 case involved a Volkswagen microbus, an almost legendary vehicle with a lot of room for passengers that had a rear engine and very little front-end protection. The vehicle in this case hit a telephone pole at more than forty miles an hour. The plaintiff, injured in the accident, claimed that the defendant should have provided "sufficient energy-absorbing materials or devices or 'crush space' . . . so that . . . the integrity of the passenger compartment would not be violated," arguably minimizing her injuries. The court refused what it viewed as the plaintiff's effort to redesign a vehicle that was "a special type" that had been "uniquely developed in order to provide the owner with the maximum amount of either cargo or passenger space in a vehicle inexpensively priced and of such dimensions as to make possible easy maneuverability." It noted that the lack of collision-absorbing space on the front end of the microbus "was readily discernible to anyone using the vehicle; in fact, it was . . . the unique feature of the vehicle," and added that "the usefulness of the design is vouchsafed by the popularity of the type." With this view of the innovation achieved by the vehicle, the appellate court overturned a trial court decision for the plaintiff based on negligent design.[48]

Almost a quarter century later, the Fourth Circuit overturned a summary judgment for Ford in a case in which a fatal fire erupted in a van, driven by a man with high blood alcohol content, which hit a tree at a speed of forty to forty-seven miles an hour. The plaintiffs claimed that the car could have been made more resistant to that kind of fire if the fuel system had been better designed—for example by using steel parts rather than the plastic parts used in the decedent's van. The court said that in light of the use of steel parts in other Ford vehicles, the plaintiffs were "entitled to the reasonable inference that the costs of making the van safer were not prohibitive." Although it considered the argument that the injury under these circumstances was unforeseeable, the court opined that that it could not "say that a car crashing into a tree at as high as 47 miles per hour is 'unquestionably bizarre.'" It observed, "The same 40–47 mile per hour single car collision could have been produced by a myriad of other events, such as a car veering off the road to avoid an oncoming collision, or a car losing control on a patch of ice or because of drowsiness." It added that the fact that the decedent was drunk "does not make the physical aspects of the crash any more bizarre."[49]

These decisions on auto design by a single federal appellate court, both logically argued, teach a lesson that is more generally apparent in the substantial body of crashworthiness cases involving theories of design defect. Innovators must keep up with the technologies in their product areas, especially when they have been generating safety improvements themselves, although their obligations to do so are somewhat subject to consumer preferences. The case of the Volkswagen microbus discussed above and the luer connector case provide some definition of their zone of choice. Where there is a clearly available, safer alternative for a product in repetitive use in defined circumstances, manufacturers must choose that alternative and put its less safe, if useful, predecessor model on the shelf or risk liability. However, where there is a wide range of consumer preferences among a great variety of product features, with a corresponding spectrum of safety choices, they may elect to provide a range of options for that variegated market. At least this is so when the dangers of the less safe alternative are clear to the eye or they are adequately communicated. That is the way the law demarcates the sovereignties of experimenters on both the producer and the consumer sides.

## Notes

1. See *Sanchez v. Hillerich & Bradsby Co.*, 128 Cal.Rptr.2d 529, 531, 538 (Ct. App. 2002).
2. *Christopherson v. Hyster Co.*, 374 N.E.2d 858, 868 (Ill.Ct.App. 1978).
3. Jones ex rel. *Jones v. Lederle Labs*, 695 F. Supp. 700, 708 (E.D. N.Y. 1988).
4. Jones by *Jones v. Lederle Labs*, 785 F. Supp. 1123, 1127 (E.D.N.Y. 1992).
5. *Detillier v. Sullivan*, 714 So.2d 244, 249 (La. Ct. App. 1998), writ denied.
6. *DeLeon v. Northrop Grumman Systems Corp.*, 2004 U.S. Dist. Ct. Lexis 27350, at 9, Prod. Liab. Rep. (CCH) ¶17,077 2004 WL 3186504 (D. N.M. 2004).
7. *Roberts v. Rich Foods, Inc.* 139 N.J. 365, 383-84, 654 A.2d 1365, 1374-75 (N.J. 1995).
8. Frank Dutton, "A Brief History of Matches and Lighters," http://www.toledbend.com/VCL/articles/index.asp? request=lighterHistor, last consulted July 6, 2015.
9. See ibid.
10. *Todd v. Societe Bic*, S.A., 21 F.3d 1402, 1403 (7th Cir. 1994).
11. Ibid., p. 1415 (Ripple, J., dissenting).
12. Ibid., pp. 1408–09.
13. Ibid., pp. 1413–14 (Cudahy, J., dissenting).
14. *Perkins v. Wilkinson Sword, Inc.*, 700 N.E.2d 1247, 1252 (Ohio 1998).
15. *Robins v. Kroger COO*, 982 S.W.3d 154, 164 (Tex. Ct. App.1998). The court came to the same conclusion in a later decision, 80 S.W.3d 641, 647 (Tex. Ct. App. 2002).
16. *Griggs v. BIC Corp.* 981 F.2d 1429, 1436-37 (3d Cir. 1992).
17. *Eads by Eads v. Bic Corp.* 740 F.Supp. 1433, 1435 (W.D. Mo., 1989). In another case that focused in part on the characteristics of a lighter, in which the court declared that "Bic has a duty to design a child-resistant lighter," the court noted that the product "projects a fairly large-size flame when its throttle is fully open" (*Bondi v. BIC Corp.*, 739 F. Supp. 346, 349-50 [E.D. Mich. 1990]).
18. *Hernandez v. Tokai Corp.* 2 S.W.3d 251, 260-61 (Tex.1999). A federal district court had given summary judgment to the defendant in the case, but after the appellate court received the Texas Supreme Court's answer to the certified question, it vacated and remanded the trial court's decision (189 F.3d 489 [5th Cir. 1999]).
19. *Clay v. Ford Motor Co.* 215 F.3d 663, 671 (6th Cir. 2000).
20. *Mitchell v. Fruehauf Corp.*, 568 F.2d 1139, 1144-45 (5th Cir. 1978).
21. *Green v. Smith & Nephew AHP, Inc.* 629 N.W.2d 727, 742-43, 754-55 (Wis. 2001).
22. *Morson v. Superior Court*, 109 Cal.Rptr.2d 343, 356-58 (App. Ct. 2001).
23. *Bundie v. Skil Corp.*, 489 F. Supp. 19, 20 (E.D. Pa. 1980).
24. *First Nat'l. Bank of Dwight v. Regent Sports Corp.* 803 F.2d 1431, 1437 (7th Cir.1986).
25. Gonzalez by *Gonzalez v. Morflo Indus., Inc.*, 931 F. Supp. 159, 167 (E.D. N.Y. 1996).
26. *Williams v. Briggs Co.*, 62 F.3d 703, 707 (5th Cir. 1995).
27. *Brown v. Tennessee Donut Corp.*, (1978–1979 Transfer Binder) Prod. Liab. Rep. ¶ 8148, at 16,848 (Tenn. Ct. App. 1978).
28. *Immormino v. J & M Powers, Inc.* 698 N.E.2d 516, 519 (Ohio Ct. Com.Pl. 1998).

29. *McMahon v. Bunn-O-Matic Corp.*, 150 F.3d 651, 659 (7th Cir. 1998).
30. *Lavergne v. America's Pizza Co.*, 838 So.2d 845, 848 (La. Ct. App. 2003).
31. *Mettinger v. W. W. Lowensten, Inc.*, 678 A.2d 1115, 1123-24 (N.J. App. Div.1996).
32. See supra, Chapter 3, text with note 77.
33. See supra, Chapter 3, text with notes 79–85.
34. See supra, Chapter 3, text with note 78.
35. *Philip Morris USA, Inc. v. Arnitz*, 933 So.2d 693, 695 (Fla. Dist. Ct. App. 2006).
36. See ibid., pp. 698–99.
37. Restatement (Second) of Torts § 402A, cmt. i (1965).
38. *Burton v. R. J. Reynolds Tobacco Co.* 884 F. Supp. 1515, 1522 (D. Kan. 1995).
39. *Tompkin v. American Brands*, 219 F.3d 566, 572-73 (6th Cir. 2000).
40. *Perkins v. F.I.E. Corp.*, 762 F.2d 1250, 1275 (5th Cir. 1985).
41. See *Kelley v. R. G. Indus., Inc.*, 479 A.2d 1143, 1153-54 (Md. 1985).
42. *Knott v. Liberty Jewelry and Loan, Inc.*, 748 P.2d 661, 665 (Wash. Ct. App. 1988), review denied.
43. *Clark v. Brass Eagle, Inc.*, 866 So.2d 456, 461 (Miss. 2004) (the plaintiff "offered no proof that the paintball gun used in the incident failed to function as expected and offered no feasible design alternative which, to a reasonable probability, would have prevented what happened to him").
44. *Moss v. Wolohan Lumber Co.*, 1995 WL 348144, at 2, Prod. Liab. Rep. ¶ 14,302 (N.D. Ill. 1995) (both the plaintiff and the shooter "testified that the BB gun worked as they expected").
45. This summary comes from the appellate court decision, *Hansen v. Baxter Healthcare Corp.*, 723 N.E.2d 302, 305-08 (Ill. Ct. App. 1999) and the supreme court decision, 764 N.E.2d 35, 38, 42, 44-46 (Ill. 2002).
46. Pub. L. 89-563 (1966).
47. 391 F.2d 495, 502 (8th Cir. 1968).
48. *Dreisonstok v. Volkswagenwerk, A.G.*, 489 F.2d 1066, 1073-74 (4th Cir. 1974).
49. *Binakonsky v. Ford Motor Co.* 133 F.3d 281, 287-88 (4th Cir. 1998).

# 8

# Long-Running Public Health Catastrophes

We turn now to two examples of products that inflict serious harm on large populations over long periods of time. First we briefly amplify the case of cigarettes, introduced in prior chapters. Then we focus on asbestos, exposure to which has frequently been tied to smoking as a source of illness. The analysis of these products, especially grim and especially symbolic because of the large number of illnesses involved, provides a powerful set of illustrations of the belated responses of the legal system to long-term, uncontrolled, and unconsented experiments on millions of people.

## I. Cigarettes

We set out the terrible statistics of illness caused by cigarettes in Chapter Three, ranging beyond four hundred thousand premature deaths per year.[1] We have noted that courts have tended to impose liability on cigarette makers as their representations of safety become more precise.[2] We also noted that the addition to leaf tobacco of various substances has inclined some courts to support claims that cigarettes were defective products.[3]

Claims for failure to warn of the dangers of cigarettes encountered some obstacles in the Supreme Court's interpretation of the Public Health Cigarette Smoking Act of 1969, because those claims necessarily attacked the sufficiency of federally mandated cigarette health warnings. In the *Cipollone* case, decided in 1992, an opinion of Justice Stevens (representing a four-justice plurality of the Court) concluded that the 1969 statute was preemptive of claims for failure to warn to the extent that they alleged that "post-1969 advertising or promotions should have included additional, or more clearly stated, warnings."[4] Specifically, Justice Stevens said that the 1969 act preempted "claims based on a failure to warn and the neutralization of federally mandated warnings to the extent that those claims rely on omissions or inclusions in respondents' advertising or promotions."[5]

However, three other justices argued that Congress had not intended to preempt any common law damages actions under state law. [6] Moreover, the overlap of failure to warn with the character of manufacturers' promotions was evident in the plurality's declaration that the 1969 act did "not pre-empt [the plaintiff's] claims based on express warranty, intentional fraud and misrepresentation, or conspiracy."[7]

A 2005 decision by the Ninth Circuit drew on *Cipollone* in concluding that a "failure-to-warn claim is not preempted" by the amended congressional legislation on the subject, which included the 1969 act and its predecessor, the Cigarette Labeling and Advertising Act of 1965. As the appellate court viewed it, the plaintiff was not challenging "the warnings Philip Morris actually gave pursuant to the legislation" but that "rather, his claim addresses smoking harms outside the Act's reach, about which Philip Morris gave no warnings at all, but could have, through means other than advertising and promotion." The court said that the plaintiff's failure-to-warn claim was predicated on a state "common law duty that requires manufacturers to advise consumers of their products' dangers, a warning which is not necessarily required to be given through advertising or promotion." Since the state in question, Nevada, did "not specify how manufacturers should warn consumers," the court said, the plaintiff's "failure-to-warn claim is not preempted as long as it (1) does not challenge a substantive warning issued pursuant to the Act, and (2) is not based on Philip Morris' packaging, advertising, or promotional material."[8]

On the substantive law, replying to the defendant's argument that "as a matter of law . . . the dangers of smoking were commonly known by 1969," the Ninth Circuit chose a contrary position, introduced by reference to other cases in Chapter Seven. It found "a basis to conclude that Nevada courts would narrow the inquiry and distinguish between knowing about general health risks of smoking and knowing about specific risks, like lung cancer or addiction, caused by tobacco products." This inquiry, the court said, presented "a question of fact to be decided by a jury." It declared, "The common knowledge inquiry should have been narrowed to whether the link between cigarette smoking and lung cancer was common knowledge, not simply whether the link between smoking and general health hazards was well-known."[9]

Then, in 2008—sixteen years after *Cipollone*—Justice Stevens delivered an anti-preemption blow to cigarette makers in a case in which the plaintiffs based a fraud claim on the companies' "message that their 'light' cigarettes deliver less tar and nicotine to consumers than regular brands despite [the defendants] knowledge that the message was untrue." He took note of the defendants' argument that the plaintiff's claim was "more analogous to the 'warning neutralization' claim" that the plurality had found preempted in *Cipollone*. He described the heart of the claim in *Cipollone* as being "the defendants' failure to warn, as it was 'predicated on a state-law prohibition against statements in advertising and promotional materials that tend to minimize the health hazards associated with smoking.'" By contrast, he said "As was true of the claim in *Cipollone,* [the plaintiffs'] claim that the deceptive statements 'light' and 'lowered tar and nicotine' induced them to purchase petitioners' product alleges a breach of the duty not to deceive." He acknowledged that "the presence of the federally mandated warnings may bear on the materiality of [the defendants'] allegedly fraudulent statements," but said, quoting a prior appellate opinion, that "that possibility does not change [the plaintiffs'] case from one about the statements into one about the warnings."[10]

The sum of the complex bundle of judicial holdings on cigarette litigation is that inaccurate statements about the health effects of cigarettes, as well as the addition of other substances to tobacco leaf, may support civil claims for cigarette- caused illness, and that so long as a claim with elements of a failure to warn also is based on misrepresentations, it is not barred by the legislation on cigarette promotion or advertising. The theme of consumer information as a key to consumer sovereignty thus carries forward in the vast national experiment with the marketing of cigarettes.

We also introduce another perspective, one from a broad viewpoint of public health, on a product that has brought such painful illness to so many. During a period that included the enactment of two federal statutes and the issuance of many judicial opinions, including some competing opinions in two cases decided by the Supreme Court sixteen years apart, the promotion of cigarettes continued, if in somewhat limited fashion. And if one credits the surgeon general's statistics, during that period millions of lives were shortened by the smoking of cigarettes.

## II. Asbestos

While the vast market trial of cigarettes created a public health epidemic over many years, a parallel, uncontrolled national trial emerged from the mining of asbestos and the industrial and military use of asbestos products. Those activities and uses of asbestos constituted a colossal experiment on American workers—and members of the general public—throughout the twentieth century. This section describes how that experiment proceeded in a largely unregulated fashion for decades, and then it analyzes the efforts to respond to the frequently horrible effects of asbestos by controlling its use and imposing money judgments for those effects. The story is one of society trying to catch up with the effects of a very broad experiment on people who were largely ignorant of its nature—and indeed of the fact that an experiment was in progress.

The history of asbestos-caused disease is a long-running saga with roots as ancient as the first century; Paul Brodeur reported this history in a remarkable, influential article published in 1968.[11] Evidence that asbestos fibers caused illness began to surface two millennia later, in the late nineteenth century.[12] By the late 1920s, British researchers had accumulated "a whole literature" on the disease asbestosis,[13] a chronic inflammation of the lung that builds up scar tissue, leading to shortness of breath and a host of complications. No later than the mid-1930s, a South Carolina medical professor identified a case of cancer caused by asbestos.[14]

Over the course of the twentieth century, industries found thousands of applications for asbestos—which is not one, but as many as five different kinds of substances, the fibers of which have a range of effects on the human body. Many of these uses arose from the special capacity of asbestos to resist heat and fire, and others from its "great powers to absorb and to filter."[15] Among other large-scale usages was the employment of asbestos in many parts of naval ships during World War II. Besides its other usages in many kinds of buildings, both commercial and residential, it found applications in a varied set of consumer products. For example, several American and Japanese firms patented uses of asbestos in "tampons, sanitary napkins, and diapers,"[16] with one patent for diapers or sanitary napkins being issued as early as 1959.[17]

The health hazards of asbestos were a shared concern among many officials in the industries that produced these products as early as the 1930s—although the executives did not often share their concern with people outside the industry. Perhaps the most famous, or notorious, examples were dredged from a cache of documents that became known as the Sumner Simpson papers. Totaling almost six thousand documents, these were discovered in the 1970s in two locations at the asbestos firm Raybestos-Manhattan. The magnificently named

Mr. Simpson, who had been president and board chairman at the firm, was a methodical saver of papers—including "various letters, newspaper clippings, articles from publications, correspondence, and other documents relating to the health hazards of asbestos to workers in the mining and manufacture of asbestos products."[18] The first letter in the famous batch was sent in September 1935 to Simpson by A. F. Rossiter, the editor of the magazine *Asbestos*. He wrote to Simpson that the magazine had respected Simpson's wishes concerning "publish[ing] nothing" about "asbestosis and the work which has been, and is being done, to eliminate or at least reduce it," but he said that the magazine "would like very much to review the whole matter." Within a month, Simpson effectively responded in a letter to Vandiver Brown, a lawyer for Johns-Manville, another asbestos firm. Enclosing Rossiter's letter, Simpson did not beat around the bush: "I think the less said about asbestos, the better off we are." He noted that *Asbestos* had been "very decent" about not reprinting articles on asbestos dust control and asbestosis that had been published in English magazines. Brown immediately replied, "I quite agree with you that our interests are best served by having asbestosis receive the minimum of publicity."[19]

Simpson's active interest in the topic extended to the possibility of civil litigation against the company. It is illustrative of both that interest and of concerns that were arising in the government about asbestos hazards that in 1936 the Public Health Service asked for permission to examine employees at a South Carolina plant of Raybestos-Manhattan. Simpson wrote a couple of letters to the plant manager on the subject, in one of which he said that the manager "may advise the Public Health Service that they may take" chest X-rays of the employees, "with the understanding that they are not available for any purpose whatsoever except public health information." Tellingly, he told the manager, "You want to stress the fact that we do not want them given to shyster lawyers and doctors so as to be the subject of suits, for, as you know, we have had enough adjustments for any one company."[20]

Another twinning of a recognition of the dangers of asbestos with a condemnation of trial lawyers appeared in a 1937 article in the *New England Journal of Medicine* by Dr. John B. Hawes Jr. Dr. Hawes said that there was "not the slightest doubt" in his mind that "asbestos dust is the most dangerous of all dusts," but at the same time he also condemned "unscrupulous and mercenary lawyers."[21]

There is evidence that during the next two decades, a cover-up of the dangers of asbestos proceeded. One person identified as participating in this process from the thirties to the fifties was A. J. Lanza, at one point a Metropolitan Life medical official who was accused of delaying for four years the publication of the results of a company study completed in 1931,[22] and was accused in the 1950s by a scientist with the National Cancer Institute of forcing the discontinuance of "field work on environmental cancer," specifically "in "workers employed in the chromate industry."[23] According to one account, in 1951 Lanza was instrumental in getting an order sent down to the NCI scientist "to cease contact with private and governmental organizations that had clinical data on industrial agents suspected of causing cancer."[24]

A leading scholar has pointed out that with the vast number of uses for asbestos from the 1930s onward, "most of those persons expected to contract cancer from asbestos were not asbestos miners, milling, or manufacturing workers" or insulation workers.[25] There was "medical evidence" on asbestos exposure from "thermal insulation, brake linings, vinyl asbestos flooring, drywall patching compounds, asbestos clothing, gaskets, asbestos-cement sheet, and perhaps a few more" products.[26] Up through the late 1980s, a total of fifty thousand metric tons of asbestos were used annually in brake shoes and brake linings.[27]

It was not only identifiable direct exposure that created potential health hazards. Even by 1960, one researcher had found "asbestos bodies" in 25 percent of the autopsied bodies of five hundred "ordinary urban dwellers," with a prime candidate for the source of these exposures being asbestos dust from brake lining and asbestos clutch facings; other sources were "the continuous disintegration of asbestos products" in floor tiles and roofing materials and "the demolition of buildings containing numerous other asbestos products."[28]

In some cases, the hazards extended even to the playground. A graphic example appears in a book about the impact of a mining operation for the substance vermiculite that was run by W. R. Grace Company in Libby, Montana. (Author's disclosure: I served as an expert witness for personal injury claimants in litigation involving the W. R. Grace bankruptcy.) Because there was a deposit of asbestos at the mine, "the vermiculite from Libby was contaminated with asbestos."[29] The writer of the book reports a statement by Gayla Benefield, a local resident, about what the author calls "the baseball diamonds and piles of vermiculite that surrounded Grace's expanding plant." Ms. Benefield recalled watching baseball games: "Heck, just about everybody who lived here went down to those ball fields at one time or another. The children who were too young to play baseball used to play beyond the outfield fence in the piles of vermiculite dust. It was worse even than the ball fields. It was filled with asbestos dust."[30]

Research did began to catch up, but as is so in many areas of medical investigation, responsible science takes a long time to pin down causation in cases of experiments that have been conducted on the public for a generation and more. A landmark was a 1955 study by the British epidemiologist Richard Doll. In a study of the autopsies of 113 men who had been exposed to asbestos dust for at least twenty years, he found eleven "excess deaths from lung cancer," as contrasted with expected deaths of less than one in "the whole male population."[31]

One of the most dedicated researchers on the topic was Irving Selikoff, for many years the chief of environmental medicine at Mount Sinai School of Medicine in New York. Originally drawn to the problem of asbestos-related deaths by his observations of insulation workers who came to a New Jersey clinic in the 1950s, he doggedly pursued the question over a decade. The result was a paper with two coworkers that appeared in the *Journal of the American Medical Association* in 1964. Surveying more than fifteen hundred insulation workers in the New York City area, these authors found that in each of four periods of five years, "far more deaths from cancer of the lung and pleura occurred among the asbestos workers than would have occurred had their death rates from these diseases been the same for all US white males."[32] For lung cancer, the increase was "six to seven times the expected incidence."[33] The Selikoff group also introduced, on the basis of "fragmentary" data, the specter of the dreaded lung tumor mesothelioma.[34]

Almost two decades later came the publication of a remarkable document in the scientific annals of asbestos, one that has proved statistically prophetic. This was a paper by William J. Nicholson, George Perkel, and Selikoff that became known as the Nicholson study.[35] This paper, which analyzed groups of workers exposed to asbestos in "a number of occupations and industries and occupations," concluded that the population potentially exposed to asbestos from 1940 through 1979 was 27,500,000. The authors presented projections of "approximately 8,200 asbestos-related cancer deaths" then "occurring annually," a number that would "rise to about 9,700 annually by the year 2000" and then decrease "but still remain substantial for another three decades."[36] A later paper by Rand Corporation authors noted that these numbers did not account for "workers exposed to asbestos after 1979 who subsequently develop asbestos-related disease"—a population that itself might be fairly numerous, because 112 million pounds of asbestos was still being produced in 1987 and 13.2 million pounds in 1999.[37] With specific reference to mesothelioma, the Rand authors said, "If one assumes that almost all cases of mesothelioma in the United States between 1985 and 2009 have occurred (or will occur) within the worker cohorts exposed to asbestos identified by Nicholson . . . the numbers . . . validate Nicholson's estimates," although those estimates would be "too high" if the assumption was that "many cases of mesothelioma have occurred (or will occur)" in that period "among persons not in Nicholson's asbestos-worker cohort."[38]

Whatever disputes there might be on statistical projections, there was widespread agreement on the vast numbers of people exposed to asbestos. A New York School of Medicine professor told a Senate hearing in 2007 that he estimated that "23 million Americans have been occupationally exposed [to asbestos] over the last 50 years and are now at risk for health problems."[39] Red pins of disease continued to appear all over the national map. In the same year, a report on preliminary X-ray findings indicated that "at least 15 people who worked at or lived near a West Dallas vermiculite plant suffer from symptoms of asbestos-related illnesses."[40] Another discovery that surfaced in 2007 detailed "an additional 35 cases" of mesothelioma among people who worked in "iron ore mining and processing" and the manufacture of ceiling tiles containing asbestos in northeastern Minnesota. These cases brought "the total number of mesotheliomas among workers residing in Minnesota" to 58.[41]

The national litigation docket was a rough indicator of the number of cases of illness caused by asbestos. By 2002 came a report of a new flood of asbestos cases—at least ninety thousand new claims in 2001, with eighteen companies filing for bankruptcy in the prior two years.[42] By 2005, Rand researchers were estimating that seven hundred and thirty thousand asbestos tort cases had been filed.[43]

A landmark case in the civil litigation was that of Clarence Borel, who had been an insulation worker for thirty-three years. As the Fifth Circuit summarized it in affirming a judgment for Borel for the defendant's failure to warn of the dangers of asbestos, Borel said that "at the end of a day working with insulation material containing asbestos his clothes were usually so dusty he could 'just barely pick them up without shaking them.'" He testified that "You just move them just a little and there is going to be dust, and I blowed this dust out of my nostrils by handfuls at the end of the day, trying to use water too, I even used Mentholatum in my nostrils to keep some of the dust from going down in my throat, but it is impossible to get rid of all of it. Even your clothes just stay dusty continually unless you blow it off with an air hose."

The problem of imbalances in information between producers and consumers was evident in Borel's statement that he "knew the dust was bad" and that the insulators "used to talk 'about' it . . . could it give you TB, could it give you this, and everyone was saying no, that dust don't hurt you, it dissolves as it hits your lungs." He said, "There was always a question, you just never know how dangerous it was. I never did know really. If I had known I would have gotten out of it." After Borel acknowledged, "I knew I was working with insulation," he was asked whether he knew that it contained asbestos. His response was, "Yes, sir, but I didn't know what asbestos was."[44]

Over the course of a generation, as the dust of asbestos drifted through the court system, it permeated through many major areas of legal doctrine. We summarize several of these effects here as illustrations of how theories of liability construct a legal frame for very dangerous experiments on large populations. One set of applications of legal doctrine to asbestos arises from the way products are represented to, or in some way appear to, consumers and workers.

Sometimes representations, although imprecise about the specific qualities of a product, provide a powerful background for findings of liability. As I have written elsewhere about product advertising, it "occupies both background and foreground in our daily existence."[45] But it is not only advertising, as conventionally defined, that provides this backdrop. Product appearance may underlie judgments of liability based on theories of liability. A good example is a case in which the plaintiff Curtis Adkins had unloaded railroad cars that brought asbestos fiber in burlap and paper bags to his employer, creating an environment in which asbestos dust "was visible in the air of his breathing zone." In Adkins's suit for asbestosis, the Sixth Circuit finely tuned liability theories. The appellate court agreed with the trial court that Adkins could not recover under a strict liability theory for failure to warn. However, it affirmed a verdict for him based on a "consumer expectation test" for design defect. The appellate court said that "the failure to warn, as well as . . . defective packaging," were part of what the trial court had called "the totality of the circumstances which make [the] product defective." Citing precedents, the appellate court said, "The presence or absence of a warning is a factor to consider when evaluating what an ordinary consumer would expect when using the product." To be sure, the asbestos in the bags the plaintiff handled might not fit the everyday definition of a product for purposes of the theory of strict liability. However, noting that "liability was premised on" the role of the defendant—a firm that "crushed, processed and packaged" raw asbestos for resale to users—as "the supplier of a product to the consumer," the court said that "asbestos fiber which had been extracted from rock, processed, and packaged, was clearly a product within the definition of section 402A" of the Restatement (Second) of Torts.[46]

In the foreground of the way products appear to the consumer are direct representations about their qualities that turn out to be inaccurate. In an Illinois case, thirty-four public school districts sued seventy-eight firms that "either mined, manufactured, installed or sold" asbestos for reimbursement for the replacement of asbestos products in school buildings. There were some differences of opinion between the appellate court and the Illinois Supreme Court on claims that amounted to conspiracy among the defendants to defraud. In upholding this set of counts, the appellate court noted, among other allegations, that the defendants had "obscured data on the relationship between asbestos exposure and disease" and "conspired to deprive plaintiffs of this data." The appellate court found these allegations sufficient on the theory that the "defendants intended to deprive the public and plaintiffs of the medical and scientific data." The appellate court also rejected the defendants' argument that the allegations of conspiracy were inadequate, saying that "conspiracies by their very nature do not allow the allegation of specific details of defendants' acts" and that "the exact role of each defendant cannot always be spelled out in the complaint."[47] On this point, the Illinois Supreme Court disagreed, saying that the complaints' references to "numberless and nameless" parties that "partook in this fraudulent activity" had not "alleged with specificity, certainty and particularity the facts necessary to state a cause of action in fraud."[48] However, the supreme court said that with respect to either strict products liability or negligence theories, "the plaintiffs should be given a chance to prove that friable asbestos exists within the buildings if they met certain technical requirements."[49] Further concluding that the plaintiffs had sufficiently alleged negligent misrepresentation, the supreme court said that "the plaintiffs also might have stated causes of action in fraudulent misrepresentation, and breach of express and implied warranties, if the pleadings had been more specific" or if the plaintiffs had measured up to particular state statutory requirements.[50]

A theory of liability that resides next door to direct representations is indeed that of implied warranty, a doctrine advanced in favor of a claim in an asbestos case in which the plaintiffs were firms that ordinarily would be thought to be defendants. In the background of this claim, which ultimately proved unsuccessful, was the extraordinary number of shipyard workers—some 4.5 million—who were engaged in building up the phalanx of ships used by the United States in World War II. The gist of a complaint by Johns-Manville, then a leading producer of asbestos products, was that the government had breached an implied warranty for asbestos products used in building ships. Johns-Manville argued, as the court summarized it, that "manufacturers of dangerous or defective asbestos-containing products [were] forced to manufacture [them] during the World War II effort" and that "the implied warranty of specifications more narrowly signifies that the products manufactured to customized government specifications will result in satisfactory performance in that the manufacture of the products will not increase the manufacturer's costs of performance." This theory posited "not a 'reverse warranty,' based on subsequent use of the product, in any sense of the term, but a warranty based on the parties' shared knowledge of the risks inherent in the production of asbestos-containing products according to government specifications." Perhaps responding to what a layperson might think of as the chutzpah of this claim—the Court of Claims referred to the fact that Johns-Manville had "gingerly approach[ed]" it—the court noted that the plaintiffs had not presented any "case from the law on contractual indemnity that stands for the proposition that a breach claim can be based on an implied warranty running to the manufacturer that the purchaser or user of a product will use it in a safe manner." It said that the fact that "the Government allegedly drafted customized specifications, mandated performance, tested the products, knew of the defects, supervised the products' use, and failed to enforce its own safety standards" had "not been viewed as factors that give rise to any duty the Government, as user of the products, to asbestos manufacturers."[51]

Our review of theories of liability in asbestos cases now focuses on negligence, the mainstay of personal injury law. For experiments both large and small, negligence usually requires knowledge of a risk, either actual or constructive—a traditional formulation requires a showing that a defendant "knew or should have known" of the risk. We have noted the evidence from the 1930s in the Sumner Simpson papers that officials of asbestos firms were cognizant then of the hazards of the fibers.[52] In fact, a number of decisions have fixed the 1930s as the time when asbestos firms had the duty to know of those dangers.

An example is a case in which the Porter Hayden Company, a predecessor of which had been "founded by former members of Johns-Manville," was a defendant. In this case, the Maryland Court of Special Appeals referred to testimony about a 1930 article on pulmonary asbestosis in *Asbestos* magazine. The court referred to testimony that "a number of companies that mine[d] and manufacture[d] asbestos products, including Johns-Manville, had advertised in that issue" of the magazine. The court said it believed that "a reasonable inference could . . . be drawn that Johns-Manville knew or should have known of the contents of this article." Referring to a witness's notation that Porter Hayden's predecessor "generally acquired its asbestos-containing materials from Johns-Manville," the court said that a jury could have inferred that "Porter Hayden could have discovered this information about the hazards of asbestos 'by utilizing the peculiar opportunity and competence which [it] has or should have as a dealer in' asbestos-containing products."[53]

A few years later, in a case in which some plaintiffs were family members exposed to fibers carried home by asbestos workers, the same court referred to testimony by the same witness—an expert on asbestos history—about articles published as early as 1933 and 1934 that were "nonobscure" on "diseases suffered by asbestos workers." The court said it was for a jury to decide "whether it could be inferred from the publications, which concerned users of asbestos-containing products rather than bystanders," as well as from a 1939 workers' compensation law that "made asbestosis an occupational disease" that "asbestos-containing products posed a danger to bystanders as well as users."[54] Moreover, a federal district court concluded on the basis for jury findings that as early as 1935, the asbestos firms before it "had a duty at that time to inform all asbestos users and their household members of the dangers associated with exposure to the Defendants' asbestos-containing products."[55] And in a 2002 decision in the W. R. Grace bankruptcy, the court referred to "common knowledge for twenty to perhaps thirty years" that exposure to asbestos "would lead to long-term, serious, health effects with long latency periods."[56]

One should note, however, a range of judicial opinion about the time that companies possessed knowledge about the health hazards of the fibers. On the one hand, in a case in which the "state of the art" was an issue, the Fifth Circuit referred to testimony of the medical director of Johns-Manville—"the industry's largest member"—on that firm's knowledge of the dangers of asbestos at the time of a plaintiff's exposure, from 1957 to 1966, as indicating that "the same risks were scientifically discoverable by other asbestos corporations."[57] By contrast, the Sixth Circuit referred to testimony that at the time the plaintiff was exposed to asbestos, "the medical community understood that a particular concentration of particles per cubic foot"—five million—"was a safe level of exposure for insulation installers," testimony confirmed by an expert for the plaintiffs.[58]

Sometimes experimenters can be shown to have been more than cognizant of the risks they create for others. Decisions in asbestos cases have sometimes reached to categories of culpability more extreme than negligence. These categories include "wanton, willful and reckless conduct" and the "intentional torts" for which the minimum requirement is a showing of a defendant's "knowledge of substantial certainty" that an injury will occur. In the extreme—conduct meriting punitive damages—courts use a variety of verbal standards, which range upward from recklessness to "egregious" behavior. In a case in which Johns-Manville and another company were the defendants, a New Jersey appellate court referred to the Sumner Simpson papers in saying that it was "appalling . . . that Johns-Manville had so much information on the hazards to asbestos workers as early as the mid-1930s and that it not only failed to use that information to protect these workers but, more egregiously, that it also attempted to withhold this information from the public."[59] The state supreme court approvingly quoted this language in affirming a punitive damages award while commenting, "We cannot imagine that the conduct proven in this case would have been viewed as any less egregious in the 1940s, when the exposure commenced, than it is today."[60]

The most unforgiving doctrine that experimenters with the safety of others face is that of strict liability—liability that may be imposed without foreknowledge of the risk at issue. In theory, strict liability focuses on the type of danger that inheres in a product rather than on the defendant's culpable conduct that is the grist of negligence law. In affirming a judgment on the basis of strict liability for failure to warn in the *Borel* case mentioned above, the Fifth Circuit effectively approved instructions by the trial court "that strict liability could be imposed only if the product was unreasonably dangerous to the user or consumer at the time it was sold." At the same time, the trial court employed a definition of "unreasonably dangerous" that included a hint of negligence doctrine. It spoke of products "dangerous to an extent 'beyond that contemplated by (an) insulation contractor or insulator (i.e. asbestos insulation worker) with knowledge available to them as to the characteristics of the product," but the instruction also included a statement that "the danger 'must have been reasonably foreseen by the manufacturer.'" Responding to the defendant's argument that it was error for the trial court not to instruct the jury "that liability could not be imposed if the utility of the product outweighed the danger involved," the appellate court pointed out that the trial court "did tell the jury that liability could not be imposed unless the product was 'unreasonably dangerous,' a concept that necessarily implies a balancing of a product's utility against the danger." Moreover, mixing a duty to warn into strict liability based on the characteristics of the product, the court said that "even when such a balancing leads to the conclusion that marketing is justified, the seller still has a responsibility to inform the user or consumer of the risk" and that "the failure to give adequate warnings in such circumstances can render the product unreasonably dangerous." That failure, the court indicated, "was precisely the contention of the plaintiff in this case."[61]

The *Borel* decision, as we have indicated, was a landmark—forty years after Sumner Simpson's expression of concern about "shyster lawyers," a plaintiff's lawyer used facts to establish the hazards to health that asbestos posed, even though the strict liability standard applied in the case had overtones of negligence. This was the first reported case in an avalanche of litigation that led to dozens of bankruptcies of companies involved in the mining, processing, and sale of asbestos.

Beyond the failure to warn at the heart of *Borel* and many other decisions, there is some case law indicating that it is appropriate to apply strict liability on the basis of the inherent characteristics of a product rather than the failure to communicate its hazards to users. In a leading decision on this topic in an asbestos case, the Louisiana Supreme Court said, "A product is unreasonably dangerous per se if a reasonable person would conclude that the danger-in-fact of the product, whether foreseeable or not, outweighs the utility of the product." The court stressed the theoretical distinction between product and conduct: "This theory considers the product's danger-in-fact, not whether the manufacturer perceived or could have perceived the danger, because the theory's purpose is to evaluate the product itself, not the manufacturer's conduct." Underlining this point, the court emphasized that "the fact that a risk or hazard related to the use of a product was not discoverable under existing technology or that the benefits appeared greater than they actually were are both irrelevant."[62] A Missouri opinion took the case against the dangers of asbestos even further, in rejecting a defendant's argument that it should have received a "risk-benefit" instruction. In this case the court remanded a plaintiff's judgment because of insufficient proof that the defendant's product had caused the plaintiff's illness, but it was firm on the idea that the case "presents no issue of weighing benefits against dangers." It pointed out, "Although asbestos once was widely used as an insulating material it is now considered so dangerous that insulation products containing asbestos have not been marketed since the early 1970s and widespread asbestos removal projects have been undertaken."[63]

Matching this foray into strict liability in the sense of the "design" of asbestos was the unusual New Jersey decision in *Beshada v. Johns-Manville Products Corporation,*[64] which applied strict liability to a failure to warn in a most vigorous way—a way that itself comprehended the inherent dangers of asbestos. Given the background we have sketched about asbestos firms' knowledge of the hazards of the products, it may seem odd that the defendants should cling to the argument that, as the court summarized it, "it is unreasonable to impose a duty . . . to warn of the unknowable." The court acknowledged that "failure to warn of a risk which one could not have known existed is not unreasonable conduct." But it then drew a distinction based on the fundamentals of strict liability. Noting that the defendants' argument was "based on negligence principles," it emphasized, "We are not saying what defendants should have done. That is negligence." Rather, the court said,

> We are saying that defendants' products were not reasonably safe because they did not have a warning. Without a warning, users of the product were unaware of its hazards and could not protect themselves from injury. We impose strict liability because it is unfair for the distributors of a defective product not to compensate its victims.

It declared, "As between those innocent victims and the distributors, it is the distributors—and the public which consumes their products—which should bear the unforeseen costs of the product." [65]

*Beshada* initially arose from suits by more than fifty claimants, many of whom had worked with asbestos "for various periods between 1930 and 1981." A large group of these plaintiffs sued on exposure to asbestos beginning around 1935.[66] Whatever one views as the year that asbestos firms were on notice about the dangers of their products, the decision represents a judicial policy judgment concerning the problem we address here—injuries that become recognized after long periods of exposure to products and eventually become epidemic. Even if one views the court's reasoning as casuistic, it follows rigorously the logic of strict liability with reference to a lack of information on the part of those exposed to dangerous products.

That lack of information would appear relevant to the fact that many employees who worked with asbestos did not take the precautions that an informed rationality would dictate. Illustrative of this seeming insouciance was a letter to a W. R. Grace official from a company lawyer who said he had "only seen one person wearing a respirator" in Grace's Montana dry mill.[67] A plausible explanation for this kind of encounter with a serious risk is that the people encountering the risk did not know about it. In one case of mesothelioma, which afflicted an endocrinologist who worked at a medical college, a worker at the college said that neither he nor his coworkers "knew what asbestos was; they simply called it 'dust.'" He said that over a period of a dozen years, "every employee was required to have a physical, which included an X-ray," but that "they were never told why the X-ray was part of the physical."[68]

*Scope of Duty*

In the developing universe of illness caused by asbestos, a cluster of legal questions has risen about how far into the chess match of fact and law a company must be able to see. The issues relate to both the range of predictability and questions of justice that arise in the midst of experiments with the safety of large numbers of people. In a case involving a shipyard worker, the Washington appellate court was unsympathetic to an asbestos firm's argument that the government's failure to provide safeguards for employees was a "superseding" cause of the plaintiff's disease that cut off the firm's responsibility. The story was a familiar one: the plaintiff often worked on vessels "while in close proximity to other workers using asbestos insulation," "never wore a respirator," and was never "instructed regarding the hazards of asbestos exposure or precautions that could be taken to avoid exposure." The court said that "the actions of the government through its management of [the shipyard] were not unexpected or extraordinary, since the procedures for using asbestos products" there "were similar or identical to those followed elsewhere" and noted that "indeed, the procedures for use of asbestos cloth were so widely known that [the defendant] found it unnecessary to issue instructions for its use."[69]

A different issue, on which there has been some difference of opinion, arises with respect to the scope of an asbestos firm's duty when a family member suffers an asbestos illness because of contact with dust brought home by a worker. The sad facts of one such case were that from the age of eight or nine, the plaintiff, who suffered from mesothelioma, had washed her stepfather's work clothes, which were covered with asbestos dust. Rejecting the defendant's argument that her illness was unforeseeable, the court adduced testimony from an expert that it was "known in the industry since 1930 . . . that it is important for workers not to bring toxic substances home on their clothing and thereby expose their families to it." Invoking a state law rule imposing liability for failure to warn people "in the foreseeable zone of danger," the court said that the defendant "could reasonably foresee that the use of its product, which results in asbestos dust becoming airborne and soiling insulators' clothes, may result in workers wearing their asbestos-covered clothes home and exposing their households to harms associated with asbestos dust."[70] By contrast, in a case involving the mesothelioma death of a woman who washed her husband's work clothes, the Tenth Circuit said that the defendants "could not have foreseen that [the decedent] would be exposed to their products in the manner in which she was," noting that it was undisputed that she "was never exposed to asbestos as a user or present where the product was used."[71]

People with asbestos-caused illnesses have continued to press at the boundaries of duty. The issues are varied. Apart from the problems of family members of asbestos workers are questions related to the type of harm that has occurred—in one set of cases, emotional harm, and in another, types of injury to property.

The Supreme Court has defined a blurry boundary in two cases involving asbestos. One of these involved a pipefitter for a railroad who was a member of the group of workers known as "the Snowmen of Grand Central." The label derived from the plaintiffs' labors beneath the Grand Central Terminal, where "without any protective gear," they "would hammer, slice, and pull . . . insulation material" containing asbestos, "which broke apart as it was removed, scattering dust particles into the air." The men "would emerge from their work in the tunnels covered from head to toe with white dust." After the plaintiff Michael Buckley attended an "asbestos awareness" class, he developed a fear that he would develop cancer—a fear that Justice Breyer's opinion for the Court said had some foundation, especially given the fact that Buckley had for some years indulged in the habit that begins this chapter—smoking. At the time he sued, though, periodic medical checkups had not shown signs of "cancer or any other asbestos-related disease." The Court denied recovery in his suit for negligently inflicted emotional distress, which has been a somewhat narrowly constructed category of tort liability. It referred to a list of restrictive policy reasons in a precedent, which included the unpredictability of calculating liability for such injuries and "the 'potential for a flood' of comparatively unimportant, or 'trivial,' claims." It rejected the argument that the "physical contact" of the dust with the plaintiff was sufficient to justify liability, pointing out that "contacts, even extensive contacts, with serious carcinogens are common." On that point, interestingly, it found support in the figures on the exposures of large populations to asbestos in the Nicholson study mentioned earlier, as well as in statistics on the number of children exposed to tobacco smoke in the home. Although Justice Breyer admitted that "we do not have the answers" to many of the questions involving uncertainty (for example, "the problem of 'unlimited and unpredictable liability'"), he could find no basis for departing from what he called "the current common-law consensus" on "certain classes of negligently caused harms."[72]

Six years later, the Court drew a lawyer's distinction in a case in which the plaintiff already suffered from asbestosis and claimed for "his asbestosis-related 'pain and suffering'" that included "damages for fear of developing cancer." For this fear, the Court was willing to award "mental anguish damages." Justice Ginsburg's opinion for the Court referred to evidence, including an admission by the defendant's own expert, that established cases of asbestosis were significantly associated with an increased risk of developing lung cancer. This helped Justice Ginsburg to find that the Snowmen case did not control this one, because in that case, the Court "sharply distinguished exposure-only plaintiffs from 'plaintiffs who suffer from a disease.'" She noted that in the Snowmen case, the Court had "stated, unambiguously," that "the common law permits emotional distress recovery for [the latter] category."[73]

A parallel group of cases involve "asbestos in buildings." In this category, differences in result have flowed from differences in the character of asbestos products, in varied judicial views of technical tort rules, and in levels of liberality in reading complaints. The exact character of the fibers involved led the Tenth Circuit to reject a school district's claim that focused on vinyl asbestos floor tile (VAT), which for many years had been "widely used, both commercially and residentially" until its use was discontinued because of the "health dangers associated with exposure to respirable asbestos fibers." The main danger of respiration with asbestos came from "friable" materials that could, when dry, "be crumbled, pulverized, or reduced to powder by hand pressure." However, given that "properly maintained VAT does not readily fit this definition," the court rejected what it summarized as the claim that "the mere presence of VAT in [the plaintiff school district's] buildings damages those buildings because it requires the School District to incur additional costs in conducting renovations in the vicinity of the VAT where the renovation might cause the VAT to become friable." Applying a rather general rule that opposes the award of tort damage for economic loss, the court said, "While the presence of asbestos in VAT may well impose increased renovation costs, any additional expense is best characterized as economic loss—consequential damages resulting from the failure of VAT to meet the School District's economic expectations in terms of performance."[74]

A different slant appears in an Illinois case, summarized above with respect to its treatment of other legal issues. The plaintiffs were several school districts that sought to comply with state laws that required "schools throughout the State to identify, contain and remove all asbestos materials that constitute a significant health hazard, and to repair or maintain asbestos materials that do not pose a significant health hazard in the schools." In upholding a complaint grounded in several theories of liability, the Illinois Supreme Court referred to a distinction that courts often draw between "property damage," to which tort law clearly is properly applied, and "economic loss," the category often fenced out from tort recovery. Taking as true on their face allegations "that friable asbestos exists in plaintiffs' buildings and asbestos has been released throughout the schools," the court concluded that "it would be incongruous to argue there is no damage to other property when a harmful element exists throughout a building or an area of a building which by law must be corrected and at trial may be proven to exist at unacceptably dangerous levels."[75]

An adjoining category of the law focuses on a phenomenon of significant importance in an experimental society: the case of multiple producers of the same type of product, in situations where it may be impossible to identify the one firm that made the product that injured a particular claimant. An interesting, and controversial, theory advanced for claimants in this type of case is the "market share" theory. Originally developed by the California Supreme Court in a case involving the hormone product DES,[76] this theory posited that in the case of multiple manufacturers of a product for which the plaintiff could not identify the maker of the exact unit of the product that caused her illness or injury, liability could be imposed on the major producers of the product on a proportionate-share basis. Courts have been wary about applying this concept beyond the case of DES, but there are a few decisions in the asbestos area where the courts have split on result. A California appellate decision refused to apply a general order developed by a trial court that barred the application of the "market share" theory to asbestos cases in a case brought by plaintiffs who alleged exposure to asbestos products when they were working with brake pads. The court, noting that the plaintiffs had alleged that "the 'vast majority' of their exposure to brake dust came from used brake pads which were unidentifiable at the time because their trade names and trademarks had been worn off," said that "the peculiar facts presented by exposure to asbestos fiber from brake pads" made it appropriate to apply the market share theory.[77]

By comparison, a few years later, another California appellate court refused to apply that type of theory in an asbestos case, saying that it would be "unfair" to impose liability on a single supplier when there were "hundreds of possible" defendants among "the multitude of asbestos suppliers" and "only a remote possibility that any of a handful of joined defendants caused plaintiff's injury."[78] And the Tenth Circuit, directly opposing use of the market share theory in asbestos cases, pointed out that unlike the cases involving DES, "the injury does not arise at a specific time which can be related to a known ingestion of a dangerous substance." Acknowledging that "plaintiffs in asbestos related injury cases may not be able in all cases to identify potential defendants," the court declared that "the public policy favoring recovery on the part of an innocent plaintiff does not justify the abrogation of the rights of a potential defendant to have a causative link proven between that defendant's specific tortious acts and the plaintiff's injuries where there is a lack of circumstances which would insure that there was a significant probability that those acts were related to the injury." Underlining the fact that civil litigation by individual asbestos claimants presents a question of great quantitative significance, the court said, "The creation of a program of compensation for victims of asbestos related injuries *as a matter of policy* is a matter for the legislative body and not for the courts."[79]

Whatever one's view of the substantive question of the applicability of market share liability, the problem of asbestos captures the symbolism of these fibers in the wider world of national experimentation with dangerous products in more than one way. It represents the complexities of a world of multiple producers of similar products, the difficulties in assessing causation in the development of many diseases, and the tension between the tort approach and comprehensive legislative compensation solutions.

Tort litigation on asbestos, in fact, has been an exemplar of the difficulties of controlling large-scale experiments related to the problems of acquiring and assessing causation data. In a world that lacked current general views of ethics and morality, it might be possible to set up large-scale prospective experiments in which one used nonconsenting people as experimental animals. One could expose them to all kinds of substances, like asbestos fibers, and measure their development of disease over time as compared with control groups. As we noted in Chapter One, this has in fact been done by experimenters whose mental screens filtered out notions of conventional ethics; the case of the Tuskegee syphilis study is a notable, stark example.

Ethical principles, not to mention the expense of doing such experiments, assured that this would not be done with asbestos. To be sure, as the twentieth century went on, data collection on a massive scale proved—with remarkable predictive precision in the case of the Nicholson data—the deleterious health effects of exposure to asbestos fibers. Yet in individual civil cases, the question of causation has generated a battleground of trench warfare. This warfare reached all the way to the Supreme Court, where a majority sent back to the court of appeals a case in which the plaintiff had won a decision from the appellate court rejecting summary judgment in favor of an asbestos firm. At issue was the allegation that the plaintiff's late husband had been exposed to the defendant's asbestos products. There was controversy about the strength of documents submitted by the plaintiff on the question of exposure, including a deposition of her late husband and a letter from an official of one of his employers. Noting that the defendant, Celotex, had argued that these documents were "inadmissible hearsay," the Supreme Court majority essentially viewed the case as involving a failure of proof on the plaintiff's allegations.[80]

The argument turned out to be a prolonged one, however. The court of appeals, to which the case was remanded, concluded that it was improper to grant summary judgment against the plaintiff. Judge Kenneth Starr, writing for the majority, found that several documents—including documents that he italicized as having been "*submitted by Celotex*"—had established "an unbroken chain" that linked the decedent to a particular asbestos product and linked that product to the defendant. He said that while the documents "provide less than overpowering support for [the plaintiff's] position, their cumulative effect is . . . sufficient to defeat the summary judgment motion."[81]

The particularity of the kinds of judgments that have had to be made about exposure to specific asbestos products is evident in a wave of cases, figuratively containing millions of particles of asbestos, that have washed over federal and state courts. We compare just two cases out of dozens. In an Eleventh Circuit case, the defendant again was Celotex, which was a successor to the Philip Carey Manufacturing Company. A pipefitter named Baker testified that he "recalled working in proximity to" to a man he thought was the plaintiff's late husband, Bennie Lee Odum, in a boiler room in a barracks and that "during one two-day period Baker was working on plumbing in and around a 25′ by 25′ boiler room while Odum was rewiring a condensation pump and performing other electrical work inside the same room." Baker said that during that job, "he and Odum would have been exposed to dust from . . . Philip Carey pipecovering and cement being installed in the boiler room" by pipefitters employed by the naval air station where they worked. Baker "recall[ed] that the pipefitters threw the boxes of Philip Carey pipecovering material out of the boiler room onto the floor." Although he "admitted that he himself did not use the Philip Carey products and that he was not sure that the Philip Carey products he observed contained asbestos, he believed that they did." Saying, "There appears to be no genuine issue as to the fact that Philip Carey manufactured a number of pipecovering materials during the relevant time period," the court said that it was for the jury to decide on "the truth in the conflicts" in Baker's testimony.[82]

In the other case, decided by the Seventh Circuit, the plaintiff's late husband said that he had "used 'Kaylo,' an asbestos-containing product manufactured by Owens-Illinois," but the court said that "a review of his testimony indicate[d] that he used that term generically, rather than as a brand name." The court also noted that "when asked specifically about Owens-Illinois at the job site, the most [the decedent] was able to offer was a recollection that he had seen boxes of Owens-Illinois material present at the job site." Pointing out that he had not testified "that he worked with or was exposed to Owens-Illinois products," the court concluded that he had not presented enough evidence "to create a material issue of fact regarding causation."[83] From the perspective of consumers and workers, part of the problem of the experimental society is that they usually cannot record data about exposures to dangerous products as weeks and months go along, in part because they are unaware of the dangers.

The great experiment with asbestos has yielded a finely tuned set of technical questions with respect to causation of illness. These questions turn on judgments about the numerical thresholds that claimants must meet. Illustrative of the problem are the arguments in a set of opinions in a case in which the plaintiff attributed her husband's death from colon cancer to his exposure to asbestos. Originally a jury held for the plaintiff, but the district court set aside that verdict and gave judgment as a matter of law for the defendant. A focal issue was the question of what "standard mortality ratio" (SMR) was the benchmark for showing causation—SRM being the amount of increase in the incidence of a disease that is attributable to exposure to a particular substance. On one appeal, the Second Circuit effectively rejected the idea that the plaintiff must show an SMR of 2.0—a doubling of the risk of colon cancer associated with exposure to asbestos. It quoted a prior case on the idea that a "physician or other such qualified expert may view the epidemiological studies and factor out other known risk factors such as family history, diet . . . or other factors which might enhance the remaining recognized risks, even though the risk in the study fell short of the 2.0 correlation."[84]

However, when the district court reviewed the case after a remand and another jury verdict for the plaintiff, it insisted that the plaintiff must establish an SMR of 2.0.[85] Additionally, the district court noted that there were several other factors that had to be considered with respect to establishing a causal relationship. Those included the "consistency of the association" and the dose-response relationship between the alleged causative agent and the disease, as well as the "'confounding' or alternative factors or conditions" that could contribute to the development of the disease in the plaintiff.[86] The court noted, among other things, that the New York county where the plaintiff's husband had resided had "a cancer mortality rate substantially higher than that of the rest of the United States." Reviewing a complex body of evidence, including statistical studies, the court concluded that the plaintiff's proof on causation "simply [did] not justify the conclusion that just because a person who has been exposed to asbestos develops colon cancer, the asbestos 'clearly . . . played a role' in the development of that cancer."[87]

But now the appellate court took another turn at the problem, and in the framework of the intervening landmark Supreme Court decision on scientific proof in *Daubert v. Merrell Dow Pharmaceuticals,*[88] it essentially reiterated its former position on SMRs. The Second Circuit concluded that "the district court overstepped the boundaries set forth in *Daubert,*" given testimony that there were "a number of studies listing SMRs for asbestos/colon cancer ranging from 1.14 to 1.47" that were "statistically significant when taken together." The appellate court observed that the district court "cited no authority for the bold assertion that SMRs of less than 1.50 are statistically insignificant and cannot be relied upon by a jury to support a finding of causation." It said that "although perhaps a floor can be set as a matter of law, we are reluctant to adopt such an approach" and that it thought "it would be far preferable for the district court to *instruct* the jury on statistical significance and then let the jury decide whether many studies over the 1.0 mark have any significance in combination."[89] Moreover, it noted that reports of OSHA and the EPA—"conspicuously absent from the district court opinion"—had "concluded, upon their review of available epidemiological studies, that a strong causal link does exist between asbestos exposure and gastrointestinal cancer." It declared that "a rational jury could have decided that these agencies' conclusions bolstered" opinions of experts for the plaintiff "that the epidemiological evidence does establish a causal connection between asbestos exposure and colon cancer." It found cause for concern in the district judge "supersed[ing] the opinions of the expert witnesses with his own lay judgment," and it found "especially troubling" the district court's omission of "any consideration of agency reports backing up the claims of plaintiff's experts and supporting the jury verdict" for the plaintiff.[90]

This intramural controversy between federal courts simply symbolizes the difficulty of defining the facts—the scientific facts—about the consequences of broad-scale experimentation with hazardous products. Those controversies—let alone the facts—are, without expert testimony, beyond the ken of laypersons, and indeed they are grounds for stormy arguments among experts. These arguments take place not only about the "facts" of the measuring standard—is the ratio 1.14, or 1.47, or 2.0?—but also about what the cutoff is for judgment against the existence of a correlation—is it 2.0, or 1.5, or less . . . and is the number different for civil litigation and public regulation? A further complication for societal oversight of experimentation lies in the multiple levels of the legal process. Just the case summarized above demonstrates the intersecting roles of both trial and appellate courts and the unique role of juries.

*Time Limits on the Right to Sue*

Because asbestos-connected illnesses usually take many years to manifest themselves, important issues of justice arise when victims of those diseases bring suit a long time after their first exposure. The legal problem resides in the barrier posed to litigation by statutes of limitation, which bar suits brought a certain amount of time after an injury occurs.

A major judicial tool used to defeat the application of these statutes in cases involving injuries that come to light only after first use of a product is the "discovery rule," which permits suit by parties at a date measured from the time when they could reasonably have discovered the role of a product in causing an illness. Illustrative is a mesothelioma decision from 1979, in which the plaintiff's decedent had been exposed to asbestos dust in a job in which he sawed and planed asbestos boards made by the defendant, Johns-Manville. Drawing on precedents applying the discovery rule in medical malpractice cases, the court said application of the discovery rule was the "just result in a products liability case involving exposure to asbestos."[91] It drew on language in academic commentaries, one of them written by an author who was to become a leading defense lawyer, for a statement that could well be generalized to a range of products: "The clear trend, in most jurisdictions in cases dealing with drugs, chemicals and asbestos has been to apply some variation of the discovery rule which is based on equitable considerations. Courts have felt that the injured party should be allowed to have his day in court when his injury was of an inherently unknowable nature."[92]

The discovery rule has been applied to property damage as well as physical injury. One example is a case in which in 1971 and 1972, the University of Vermont sprayed Mono-Kote 3 (MK3), a fireproofing product made by W. R. Grace, on an old field house it was converting into a central heating plant. The university did not discover asbestos in the fireproofing of the plant until 1985 and sued the next year for damages that included the cost of removing the asbestos from the building. The state supreme court employed the discovery rule to overcome a six-year statute of limitations. It quoted a prior opinion on the ideas that "one cannot maintain an action before one knows there is one" and that "to say to one who has been wronged, 'You had a remedy, but before the wrong was ascertainable to you, the law stripped you of your remedy,' makes a mockery of the law."[93] In language particularly relevant to asbestos, the court said that these views were "especially persuasive in suits to recover the costs of removing asbestos, a material used extensively in construction before its dangers fully came to light—or at least before manufacturers warned purchasers of its hazards." It said it was "unwilling to turn the statute of limitations into . . . an unjust and inflexible tool."[94]

To be sure, some courts have refused to create a discovery rule on their own. In a case involving a chemical injected into the plaintiff's body during diagnostic experimentation, the New York Court of Appeals said in a brief opinion that the matter was "best reserved for the Legislature, and not the courts."[95] Yet it is interesting that eventually the New York legislature adopted a discovery rule.[96]

A continuing battleground on statutes of limitations has featured what can be an achingly human issue—the combined question of fact and law of whether the plaintiff has been sufficiently "diligent" in discovering the cause of his illness. The bitterness of battles over this issue is evident in a Pennsylvania case in which the state supreme court was equally divided about whether the plaintiff had exercised reasonable diligence in suing for her husband's death from mesothelioma, which was first diagnosed in January 1985, although her husband "repeatedly denied" to a doctor that he had been exposed to asbestos. After hospitalizations during the next two months when the diagnosis was confirmed, the plaintiff's husband died on March 31. His widow filed a worker's compensation claim in August of that year, ascribing the death to occupational exposure to asbestos, but did not file a tort action until March 1987. An opinion supporting the tort claim noted that for the sixty days between the initial mesothelioma diagnosis and his death, the decedent was "engaged in the dying process." This judge said he thought "a jury could easily find the decedent's failure to discover the cause of his injury during this difficult period was due to 'blameless ignorance' rather than 'somnolence.'" Thus, he concluded that "this is not a case where reasonable minds could not differ" and that it was error for the trial court to find "a lack of reasonable diligence as a matter of law."[97] However, another opinion stressed that the plaintiff "had approximately 22 months after the decedent's death to investigate the specific causes of the injury and to commence an action." This judge said that "to decide otherwise would be to hold that the limitations period commences not with the occurrence of the injury, but at an indeterminate time thereafter, allowing a reasonable time to cope with the effects of the injury."[98] His opinion, rejecting the application of the discovery rule, prevailed because the court was equally divided.

Wrangling over the question of what constitutes due diligence for purposes of statutes of limitations is just one facet of the human side of asbestos litigation. Most wrenching is the suffering that flows from asbestos-caused illness, and quite as poignant are judicial efforts to establish the outer limits of the dollar values of that suffering.

Emblematic of the degree of suffering in asbestos cases was the testimony of a physician who suffered from mesothelioma, who referred to his "painful stomach distension" from injections of artificial nutrition and said that chemotherapy had made him feel "poisoned" and "scalded."[99] A sardonic capturing of pain came from another mesothelioma victim, a woman who heard a W. R. Grace executive comment that his company had had a "good day" at congressional hearings. She commented that "she'd like to tell them what a 'good day' was for her."[100]

A case that reached a federal appellate court embodied both pain and the difficulty of valuing it. The plaintiff's husband, John Consorti, who had been a pipe insulation worker, died from mesothelioma. As Judge Leval described Consorti's suffering for a Second Circuit panel, Consorti had "developed a tumor which gradually enveloped his spine" and "pressed against his vocal cords, causing him to lose his voice and choke"; the tumor "interfered with eating, swallowing, even breathing." Added to this was the fact that his pain was "deepened by the certainty of imminent death."[101]

A jury valued Consorti's agony at twelve million dollars. However, although the appellate court took "it as a given that reasonable people of his age, in good mental and physical health, would not have traded one-quarter of his suffering for a hundred million dollars, much less twelve," it found itself required to reduce the award. It was operating in a local legal environment filled with precedent on damage amounts in mesothelioma cases—specifically, awards that had been given by Helen Freedman, a state trial judge who had handled all the New York asbestos litigation. Drawing on the range of awards Judge Freedman had made in cases over a spectrum ranging from three to thirty-four months of suffering, Judge Leval concluded that the maximum permissible award for Consorti's pain and suffering was $3.5 million.[102] This decision was symbolic of the difficulties involved in reducing the terrible effects of experiments gone wrong to dollars, against the dollar-oriented background of the benefits conferred by useful but toxic products.

* * *

Even by the second decade of this century, research reports came in about the pernicious breadth of the effects of asbestos on the human body. A British study of asbestos workers published in 2012 concluded that there were "significantly higher" numbers of deaths from heart disease and cerebrovascular disease—which often leads to stroke—in that group as compared with the general population.[103]

Many attempts have been made over the years to solve the problem of asbestos compensation by legislation. In the background of these efforts was the creation of sixty private trusts organized for some of the approximately one hundred companies that went into bankruptcy, at least in part because of asbestos liabilities. In the years between 1988 and 2010, these trusts paid about $17.5 billion on around 3.3 million claims.[104] The enormity of the problem generated various bills in Congress, generally labeled the Fairness in Asbestos Injury Compensation Act—the so-called FAIR Act. These proposals would have created a $140 billion compensation trust fund, with about $90 billion of the money to come from defendants, $46 billion from their insurers, and the rest from existing asbestos trust funds. The bills generated substantial opposition, much of it from the property/casualty insurance industry, and as of this writing had gone nowhere, despite bipartisan support.[105]

As efforts to solve the problem in Congress stalled, industry groups turned to state legislatures, focusing on versions of a proposal called the Furthering Asbestos Claims Transparency (FACT) Act, modeled on draft legislation of the Americana Legislative Exchange Council (ALEC). The legislation included requirements that claimants provide statements of all claims against asbestos trusts within thirty days of filing suit, and that they and their lawyers attest that their statements were based on a "good-faith investigation" of all such claims. Wisconsin passed a FACT-type bill in 2014 after Ohio and Oklahoma had enacted that kind of law in the preceding two years. A representative of the plaintiffs' bar condemned the statutes as "assist[ing] the asbestos industry in vilifying the victims in the media, misleading the public with propaganda and working to eliminate accountability."[106]

Legislative battles over compensation for illness caused by asbestos—in is inception, a creature entirely of tort litigation—simply underline the breadth and depth of the public policy issues that underlie vast social experiments that expose large numbers of the public to serious health risks. The inability of Congress to resolve the problem, and the episodic efforts in state legislatures to cabin liability—one observer said that in many states there was "little appetite for change"—simply accentuates the potential magnitude of suffering inherent in such far-reaching experiments, many of them at first heralded for their social and economic benefit. For many years, asbestos was the fiber of the future. Now it is the fiber of the past: a vast experiment that failed.

## Notes

1. See supra, Chapter Three, text with notes 79–93.
2. See supra, Chapter Six, text with notes 19–21.
3. See supra, Chapter Seven, text with notes 35–38.
4. *Cipollone v. Liggett Group, Inc.*, 505 U.S. 504, 524 (1992).
5. Ibid., pp. 530–31.
6. See ibid., pp. 531–42 (Blackmun, J., concurring in part and dissenting in part).
7. Ibid., p. 531.
8. *Rivera v. Philip Morris, Inc.*, 395 F.3d 1142, 1148 (9th Cir. 2005).
9. Ibid., pp. 1152–53.
10. *Altria Group, Inc. v. Good*, 555 U.S. 70, 81-83, 129 S.Ct. 538, 546 (2008).
11. Paul Brodeur, "Reporter At Large: The Magic Mineral," *New York Time*, Oct. 12, 1968, p. 117.
12. Ibid., p. 120.
13. Ibid., p. 126.
14. Ibid., p. 131.
15. Ibid., pp. 117–18.
16. Barry Castleman, *Asbestos: Medical and Legal Aspects*, 5th ed. (Aspen 2005), p. 352.
17. See Ibid., p. 353.
18. *Lohrmann v. Pittsburgh Corning Corp.* 782 F.2d 1156, 1159 (4th Cir. 1986).
19. *Lockwood v. AC & S, Inc.* 744 P.2d 605, 614 (Wash. 1987).
20. See Castleman, supra, note 16, pp. 156–57.
21. See ibid., pp. 157–58, referring to J. B. Hawes, "Dangerous Dusts," 216 *N. Eng. J. Med.* 162 (1937).
22. See ibid., pp. 147–48.
23. See ibid., pp. 72–73.
24. See ibid., p. 865 (timeline).
25. Ibid., p. 728.
26. Ibid., p. 350.
27. Ibid., p. 451.
28. Brodeur, supra, p. 138.

29. EPA, "Vermiculite," http://www.epa.gov/asbestos/pubs/verm.html, accessed May 4, 2012.
30. Michael Bowker, *Fatal Deception* (Touchstone, 2003), p. 26.
31. Richard Doll, "Mortality from Lung Cancer in Asbestos Workers," 12 *Brit. J. Indus. Med.* 81, 86 (1955).
32. Irving J. Selikoff, Jacob Churg, and E. Cuyler Hammond, "Asbestos Exposure and Neoplasia," 188 *JAMA* 22, 24 (1964).
33. Ibid., p. 25.
34. See ibid., pp. 25–26.
35. William J. Nicholson, George Perkel, and Irving Selikoff, "Occupational Exposure to Asbestos: Population at Risk and Projected Mortality—1980–2030," 3 *Am. J. Indus. Med.* 259 (1982).
36. See ibid., p. 306.
37. Stephen J. Carroll et al., Rand Inst. for Civil Justice, "Asbestos Litigation" (2005), p. 139. http://www.rand.org/pubs/monographs/2005/RAND_MG162pdf.
38. Ibid., p. 145.
39. "Asbestos: Still Lethal, Still Legal," Hearing Before the Subcommittee on Employment and Workplace Safety, Senate Committee on Health, Education, Labor, and Pensions, 110th Cong., 1st Sess., c. p. 23 (March 2, 2007) (statement of Dr. Harvey Pass).
40. Ed Mayberry, news summary for Aug. 16, 2007, http://www.houstonpublicmedia.org/news/21290/, Houston Public Media, Aug.16, 2007, printed from the Internet June 19, 2014.
41. Chronic Disease and Environmental Epidemiology Section, Minnesota Dept. of Health, "Mesothelioma in Northeastern Minnesota and Two Occupational Cohorts: 2007 Update," (Dec. 7, 2007), p. 2.
42. Alex Berenson, "A Surge in Asbestos Suits, Many by Healthy Plaintiffs," *New York Times*, April 10, 2002.
43. "Asbestos Litigation," supra note 37, p. xxiv.
44. *Borel v. Fibreboard Paper Products Corp.* 493 F.2d 1076, 1082 (5th Cir. 1973).
45. *Shapo on the Law of Products Liability* §1.01[B], (CCH 2013), pp. 1–4.
46. *Adkins v. GAF Corp.*, 923 F.2d 1225, 1227-29 (6th Cir. 1991).
47. *Board of Educ. of City of Chicago v. A, C and S, Inc.*, 525 N.E.2d 950, 961 (Ill. Ct. App. 1988).
48. *Board of Educ. of City of Chicago v. A, C and S, Inc.*, 546 N.E.2d 580, 594 (Ill. 1989).
49. Ibid., p. 591.
50. Ibid., p. 600.
51. This summary incorporates material from *Johns-Manville Corp. v. U.S.*, 12 Cl.Ct. 1 (1987) and *Johns-Manville Corp. v. U.S.*, 13 Cl.Ct. 72 (1987).
52. See supra, text accompanying notes 18–19.
53. *Eagle-Picher Industries, Inc. v. Balbos*, 578 A.2d 228, 247-48 (Md. Ct. App. 1990).
54. *A C and S, Inc. v. Abate*, 710 A.2d 944, 980-81 (Md. Ct. App. 1998).
55. *Cimino v. Raymark Industries, Inc.*, 739 F. Supp. 328, 331 (E.D. Tex. 1990).
56. *In re W. R. Grace & Co.* 281 B.R. 852, 862 (Bkrtcy. D. Del. 2002).
57. *Dartez v. Fibreboard Corp.* 765 F.2d 456, 461 (5th Cir. 1985).
58. *Murphy v. Owens-Illinois, Inc.*, 779 F.2d 340, 342-43 (6th Cir. 1985).

59. *Fischer v. Johns-Manville Corp.*, 472 A.2d 577, 587 (N.J. App. Div. 1984).
60. *Fischer v. Johns-Manville Corp.*, 512 A.2d 466, 476 (N.J. 1986).
61. See *Borel v. Fibreboard Paper Products Corp.*, 493 F.2d 1076, 1087-91 (5th Cir. 1973).
62. *Halphen v. Johns-Manville Sales Corp.*, 484 So.2d 110, 114 (La. 1986).
63. *Hagen v. Celotex Corp.*, 816 S.W.2d 667, 673-74 (Mo. 1991).
64. 447 A.2d 539 (N.J. 1984).
65. Ibid., p. 549.
66. See ibid., p. 543.
67. Letter from Gary A. Graham to Jay W. Hughes re *Carl E. & Marian Craig v. W. R. Grace* (Sept. 27, 1999), p. 2, attached as Exhibit 16 in *In Re W. R. Grace & Co. et al.*, No. 01-1139 (Bankr. D. Del. April 2, 2001) (referenced in author's expert testimony, mss. at 74 n.320).
68. Motley Ness, profile of Dr. William Blackard (last updated Aug. 25, 2005), attached as Exhibit 5 in W. R. Grace bankruptcy litigation, supra (referenced in author's expert testimony, mss. at 75 n.321).
69. *Hoglund v. Raymark Indus., Inc.*, 749 P.2d 164, 170-71 (Wash. Ct. App. 1987), review denied.
70. *Anchor Packing Co. v. Grimshaw*, 692 A.2d 5, 33-36 (Md. Ct. App. 1997).
71. *Rohrbaugh v. Owens-Corning Fiberglass Corp.*, 965 F.2d 844, 846-47 (10th Cir. 1992).
72. *Metro-North Commuter R. Co. v. Buckley*, 521 U.S. 424, 433-36 (1997), partly quoting *Consol. Rail Corp. v. Gottshall*, 512 U.S. 532, 557 (1994).
73. *Norfolk & Western Ry. Co. v. Ayers*, 538 U.S. 135, 154-56 (2003), in part quoting *Metro-North*, supra, 521 U.S. at 436.
74. *Adams-Arapahoe School Dist. No. 28-J v. GAF Corp.*, 959 F.2d 868, 872 (10th Cir. 1992).
75. *Board of Educ. of City of Chicago v. A, C and S, Inc.* 546 N.E.2d 580, 588 (Ill. 1989).
76. *Sindell v. Abbott Labs*, 607 P.2d 924 (Cal. 1980).
77. *Wheeler v. Raybestos-Manhattan*, 11 Cal.Rptr.2d 109, 111-13 (App. Ct. 1992).
78. See *Lineaweaver v. Plant Insulation Co.*, 37 Cal.Rptr.2d 902, 907-08 (App. Ct. 1995).
79. *Case v. Fibreboard Corp.*, 743 P.2d 1062, 1066-67 (Okla. 1987). For similar language, see *Blackston v. Shook and Fletcher Insulation Co.* 764 F.2d 1480, 1486 (11th Cir. 1985) ("the problem is one better suited for solution by state legislatures, state courts, and Congress rather than through the creation of some federal 'presumption' by federal courts sitting in diversity cases only").
80. See *Celotex Corp. v. Catrett*, 477 U.S. 317 (1986).
81. *Catrett v. Johns-Manville Sales Corp.*, 826 F.2d 33, 39-40 (D.C. Cir. 1987).
82. *Odum v. Celotex Corp.*, 764 F.2d 1486, 1488-89 (11th Cir. 1985).
83. *Shine v. Owens-Illinois, Inc.* 979 F.2d 93, 97 (7th Cir. 1992).
84. *In re Joint E. & S. Dist. Asbestos Litig.*, 964 F.2d 92, 97 (2d Cir. 1992), quoting *Grassis v. Johns-Manville Corp.*, 591 A.2d 671, 675 (N.J. App. Ct. 1991).
85. See *In re Joint E. & S. Dist. Asbestos Litig.*, 827 F.Supp. 1014, 1028 (S.D.N.Y. 1993).
86. Ibid., pp. 1037–38.
87. Ibid., p. 1048.

88. 509 U.S. 579 (1993).
89. *In re Joint E. & S. Dist. Asbestos Litig.*, 52 F.3d 1124, 1132, 1134 (2d Cir. 1995).
90. Ibid., pp. 1135–36.
91. *Louisville Trust Co. v. Johns-Manville Products Corp.*, 580 S.W.2d 497, 498, 500-01 (Ky. 1979).
92. Id. at 501, quoting Sheila Birnbaum, "'First Breath's' Last Gasp: The Discovery Rule in Products Liability Cases," 13 *FORUM* 279 (1977).
93. *Univ. of Vermont v. W. R. Grace & Co.*, 565 A.2d 1354, 1357 (Vt. 1989), quoting *South Burlington School District v. Goodrich*, 382 A.2d 220, 225 (Billings, J., concurring and dissenting).
94. Ibid.
95. *Thornton v. Roosevelt Hosp.*, 391 N.E.2d 1002, 1003 (N.Y. 1979).
96. McKinney's N.Y. CPLR Law § 214-c (updated 2013) (time of limitation "shall be computed from the date of discovery of the injury by the plaintiff or from the date when through the exercise of reasonable diligence such injury should have been discovered by the plaintiff, whichever is earlier").
97. *Baumgart v. Keene Bldg. Products Corp.*, 666 A.2d 238, 245 (Pa.1995) (Montemuro, J.).
98. Ibid., pp. 240–41 (Zappala, J.).
99. *Ness, Motley, Loadholt, Richardson & Poole, Profile—Andrew Allen Patrick* (last updated Aug. 25, 2000), p. 2, attached as Exhibit 10 in W. R. Grace bankruptcy litigation, supra note 67 (referenced in author's expert testimony, mss. at 73, n.312).
100. Letter to Jay Hughes from Meredith J. Johnson, Mayor, Day, Caldwell & Keeton, re: *Brenda Bright, et al. v. Owens-Corning et al.* (Sept. 14, 2000), including excerpts from deposition of Brenda Bright, attached as Exhibit 11 in W. R. Grace bankruptcy litigation, supra (referenced in author's expert testimony, Mss. at 73, n.313).
101. *Consorti v. Armstrong World Indus., Inc.*, 72 F.3d 1003, 1009 (2d Cir. 1995).
102. See ibid., p. 1015.
103. Anne-Helen Harding et al., "Cardiovascular Disease Mortality among British Asbestos Workers (1971–2005)," 10 *J. Occup. & Environmental Med.* 1136 (2012).
104. See for example GAO, "Asbestos Injury Compensation: The Role and Administration of Asbestos Trusts," GAO 11-819 (Sept. 2011), http://www.gao.gov/products/GAO-11-819.
105. See for example Patrick Hanlon and Anne Smetak, "Asbestos Changes," 62 *N.Y. U. Surv. Am. L.* 525, 580–82 (2007); Mark A. Hofmann, "Insurers Denounce Asbestos Fund Bill: Lack of Financial Finality Criticized," *Business Insurance*, Jan. 23, 2006, p. 4; Mark A. Hofmann, "Asbestos Reform Plan Raises Concerns About Fiscal, Legal Challenges," *Business Insurance*, June 12, 2006, p. 3.
106. Michael Bologna, "Business Groups Target States in Effort to Rein in Asbestos Litigation," 82 *U.S. L. Wk.* 1472 (April 1, 2014).

# 9

# Elements of Decision Making

Decisions on whether to experiment—whether on our own bodies or on the body politic—involve several elements. An important question involves attitudes toward risk—both individual attitudes and public attitudes.

## I. Worlds of Risk

### *A. Definitions and Perceptions of Risk*

A threshold question is how to define risk, a definition that affects decision making at every turn. John D. Graham and Lorenz Rhomberg have offered a definition that starts with lay language and then becomes more technical: "We speak of the 'risk' of an adverse outcome . . . because, in any particular instance in which the possible causative risk factors are present, the adverse outcome may or may not occur as a matter of chance." Those factors, they wrote, "skew the probabilities of different adverse outcomes, but there is no rigid relationship between cause and effect that manifests itself identically in every observation of the process in question."[1] Thus, decision making on the whole range of social and individual experiments requires some understanding of the risk factors, and also an understanding of the uncertainty of making causal judgments.

There is a field of study called "risk analysis," and not surprisingly there are arguments about the proper definition of its breadth—arguments that shape the discourse on what types of experiments should even be thrown into the hopper of decision making. In a speech in 1984, James J. Short, the outgoing president of the American Sociological Association, asserted that the field had been too narrowly defined. He said that "scientific and social-policy analyses of risk" typically "focus on a very limited range of things people value: their health but not usually their mental health . . . their economic well-being in aggregate, but not in individual or distributional terms; the physical environment but neither the social values associated with it nor ecological scarcity."[2]

Daily, the media reflect continuing disputes about the proper breadth of risk analysis, and three decades later those disputes seem to reflect Short's statement that "a coherent sociology of risk has yet to emerge."

How do people judge risk? It has now become commonplace that the answer to that question usually depends on how specific questions about particular risks are put. One example of the need for specificity is a fairly early study of one group of test subjects asked to rate the lethality of twenty different causes of death, including a large number of illnesses and the category of auto accidents. The respondents had a "fairly high" degree of agreement on death rates, the number of people who died from each cause and the number who survived, but "rather low agreement" about survival rates.[3] The investigators commented that the survival rate "mode was incompatible with subjects' natural mode of thought"—requiring, as it did, "a translation process that took much effort and added noise to subjects' judgments."[4] They hypothesized that "people might respond quite differently to a threat if they assess its lethality by thinking about the survival rate or the number of survivors" so that "[a] public health official could 'conclude that people underestimate or overestimate lethality, depending upon the question asked."[5]

A similar range of puzzlement is evident among scholars—as Brendon Swedlow and a group of coauthors writers put it, "When different scholars study different sets of regulatory cases of unknown and unestimable representativeness, they more likely than not will arrive at nongeneralizable and frequently contradictory conclusions."[6] The study summarized just above included responses to twenty different causes of death, but the universe of risk—as Swedlow and his collaborators broke it down—is much larger, almost a gigantic caricature of things to worry about. Including every study they could find "of risk perceptions and every risk-taking exercise published in the United States or Europe since 1970" in an article published in 2009, they derived risks "from 403 risk lists from 252 sources."[7] They condensed an initial list of almost 12,000 "verbatim risks"—"risks described exactly as on the list from which [they were] taken"—into a list of 2,878 "unique risks" spread over 18 categories ranging from "crime and violence risks" and "alcohol, tobacco and other drug risks" to ecogeological risks" and "occupational risks."[8] And this was only an overview of the "risk matrix—a nearly comprehensive list of risks"[9]—that they developed.

Elizabeth Barrett Browning could not have put even a supercondensed list of these lists into all her *Sonnets from the Portuguese.*

Yet this spectrum of threats to various forms of human existence confronts those who make decisions about the experiments in which we all engage every day—on the job, in our homes, and in doctors' offices and hospitals.

Among the ongoing controversies about perceptions of risk are arguments about the rationality of the public. Cass Sunstein, a law professor who became President Obama's "regulatory czar," viewed the so-called precautionary principle—discussed more fully below—as being "closely connected to current controversies about fear and rationality—about whether individuals and societies do, should, follow conventional accounts of rational behavior."[10] As summarized in a critique by Dan Kahan and his coauthors, a "rational weigher" model—distinguished from an "irrational weigher" model—posits that "if people left to their own devices generally make choices that maximize their well-being, then devising legal regimes and institutions to regulate risk-taking is largely unnecessary and indeed ultimately destructive of societal wealth and individual freedom."[11] This view flies in the face of such social experiments with individual self-experiments as Mayor Michael Bloomberg's proposal to limit the size of sugared soft drinks. By contrast, as summarized by Kahan, the "irrational weigher" model draws on "a vast array of cognitive limitations and defects that distort popular perceptions of risk," including both overestimation and underestimation of risk.[12]

There is ammunition for both sides in various factors that distort people's perceptions. These include the "availability heuristic," which arises from images that people may have of catastrophic events. Today this would include the meltdown of the Fukushima Daiichi reactor in Japan. Emotional responses to certain kinds of events that are far out of proportion to their statistical danger may set off panic responses in the public. One example of such events, discussed in Chapter Five, is the public concern over "mad cow" disease.[13]

From another angle came the criticism that "the quantitative appearance of cost-benefit analysis lures unsuspecting (and even suspecting) decisionmakers to believe that it offers far more than it can actually deliver." These authors refer to a number of problems of calculation: the "substantial uncertainty in calculating both costs and benefits of most responses to most significant threats," the difficulty of monetizing noneconomic costs and benefits, and "temporal issues and discounting"—for example, the discounting of the value of future lives.[14]

### *B. Risk and Culture*

A counterpoint appears in the emphasis that Kahan his coauthors place on differing views of risk rooted in culture. Drawing on a survey they did as well as on prior scholarship, they posit two sets of basic "attitude scales." One is "egalitarian and solidaristic," which includes a category of people who tend to hold high levels of concern "about global warming, nuclear power, and pollution generally." By contrast, a "hierarchical and individualistic" group has "less concern" about these issues.[15]

I have constructed a parallel set of categories. One of these includes the "rights-seekers," who "insist on skeptical scrutiny of claims that injured person have exercised free will in confronting risks." This group "mix[es] what can be an almost prophetic anger at the harmful consequences of risky activities, including their emotional consequences, with an empathy for injured persons."[16] Into the other category fall "preservationists," who stress "law as a social conservator," who emphasize "law and order" and hold views that "seem to feature a certain resignation about the human condition." Yet I have noted the irony in the fact that the preservationists, with their love for law and order, tend also to the idea that in the game of life, we should "let 'em play," with the consequence that the law "should stay out of the daily encounters in which millions of people in society are bumping up against one another."[17] Obviously none of these categories is airtight, but I would note that there is an irony in the pairing of "hierarchical" and "individualistic" qualities that Kahan and his coauthors combine. This category, it would appear, combines the Wild West cowboy with a preference for a military command structure.

In any event, as Kahan and his colleagues point out, "conflicts in perceptions of risk . . . reflect individuals' adherence to competing visions of how society should be organized."[18] Those perceptions heavily influence the determination of whether there are even decisions to make about subjecting people to a myriad of experiments. We may borrow from Franklin Roosevelt's great first inaugural address in which he inveighed against "nameless, unjustified, unreasoning fear." Throughout this book we give examples of fears that may be "unreasoning," but for many people, including those who buy products and vote, those fears may not be "unjustified."

### *The* Challenger *Launch*

A leading case study in decision making did not involve the thousands, even hundreds of thousands, of lives at risk in many choices about risk. But because the seven people killed were astronauts in a well-publicized event, the 1986 explosion of the space shuttle *Challenger* has become a focal point for education in risk management. The *Challenger* "blew up 73 seconds after its rockets were ignited," a "flicker of flame" having "emerged from [a] leaky joint" where the craft's O-rings burned through about fifty-nine seconds after launch.[19]

A particularly poignant aspect of the disaster was the fact that during the evening before the launch, "for hours, the rocket engineers and managers considered the question: *Will the rubber O-rings fail catastrophically tomorrow because of . . . cold weather?*" The temperature was predicted to be 26 to 29 degrees, with the coldest launch before that having been at 53 degrees.[20]

Engineers for Thiokol, the rocket manufacturer, had "prepared 13 charts to make the case that the *Challenger* should *not* be launched the next day," given the temperature forecast. However, after criticisms of "serious weaknesses in the charts," despite the fact that the Thiokol managers had made no recommendations against launches in twelve years, they "changed their minds and decided that they now favored launching the next day."[21] In his critical analysis of the decision making process, Edward Tufte focused on the visual display of the charts, saying that the chart makers "had reached the right conclusion," having "the correct theory and . . . thinking causally," "but that "they were not *displaying* causally."[22] The problem was that "clutter generated by the outlines of . . . 48 little rockets" was "the strongest visual presence in [the] graph," effectively overcoming what should have been the focus—"a possible link between damage and temperature." As Tufte summarized it, "As presentation graphics, the displays failed to persuade government officials that a cold-weather launch might be dangerous." He put the matter in aphoristic form: "*There are right ways and wrong ways to show data; there are displays that reveal the truth and displays that do not.*"[23] Diane Vaughn, the author of a book on the event, summarized her view of "how unseen history, culture, and structure undermined decisionmaking that night"[24] and concluded that "the previously shared values about rule following, authority relations, and technical rigor the participants automatically invoked on the eve of the launch did not work in the best interest of safety."[25]

An interesting side critique by Tufte concerned a dramatic media event, testimony to the commission investigating the accident by the famed physicist Richard Feynman. Feynman did an experiment for the commission with a small clamp he bought at a hardware store, a piece of rubber from an O-ring, and a glass of ice water. He demonstrated that "when you undo the clamp, the rubber doesn't spring back"—that "for more than a few seconds, there is no resilience in this particular material when it is a temperature of 32 degrees." Tufte noted that Feynman "was aware of the problematic experimental design and that Feynman himself had said at a later session of the hearing that "*this is not the way we do such experiments.*" Saying that Feynman's presentation was "deeply flawed, committing the same type of error of omission that was made in the 13 pre-launch charts," Tufte pointed out that a "credible experimental design requires at least two clamps, two pieces of O-ring, and two glasses of water (one cold, one not)." Pointing out that "presumably only the cold ring will show reduced resiliency," he said, "In contrast, the one-glass method is not an experiment; it is merely an experience."[26] His general conclusion was that "if displays of data are to be truthful and revealing, then the logic of the display design must reflect the analysis."[27]

It was government managers who made the launch decision for the *Challenger,* but some lessons derived from the disaster apply equally to managers of private firms. One lesson, drawn by Diane Vaughan, focused in part on a decision-making process in which "by virtue of position, supervisors had access to information that crossed disciplinary boundaries and so allegedly knew 'more,' but without hands-on knowledge of lab work, they also knew 'less.'"[28]

The pressures that this kind of decision places on officials are evident in comments by the White House Council on Environmental Quality, within four months after the *Challenger* exploded, on a regulation that required agencies to "evaluate the reasonably foreseeable potential impacts of an action," including those "which have a low probability of occurrence but which would be expected to result in catastrophic consequences" if they did.[29] The Council commented that "worst-case" analyses "breed endless hypothesis and speculation" and insisted that agencies should have to consider only low-probability effects that were "reasonably foreseeable" and "supported by "credible scientific evidence."[30] The Council chair acknowledged that "legitimate people will disagree that this is the best approach."[31]

### *C. Knowledge of Risk*

A constant problem for decision makers, not to mention the people they represent, is ignorance, which includes a lack of knowledge about risks that one might not conceive at all. One set of risks constantly in the background of modern life is the hazards of multiple chemical exposures. Fully three decades ago, a National Academy of Sciences panel generalized a response to a Coast Guard request for information on the exposure of its inspectors to a variety of chemical vapors. A summary of the report said that "although exposure to multiple chemicals and stresses prevails in many industries and environments, the problems associated with toxicological interactions have been ignored."[32]

A current repetition of concern about the problem, accompanied by arguments in response, appeared in a study by a team of researchers for the Silent Spring Institute ,which reportedly "analyzed concentrations of nearly six dozen chemicals in 213 'conventional' cosmetic, personal care, cleaning, and other products and the concentrations of those chemicals in 43 'alternative' products," which "were advertised as being 'green.'"[33] The team, which found "26 chemicals at levels above the detection limit," said its study, titled "Endocrine Disruptors and Asthma-Associated Chemicals in Consumer Products," was "one of the first to look for a large and varied suite of compounds of product types." They wrote that "the presence of chemicals in multiple commonly used products 'highlight[s] the importance of considering the cumulative toxicologic effects of combined exposures'" and stressed the need for disclosure of ingredients to consumers.[34] An official of another organization said that because of multiple exposures, "going through our normal routines and current labeling isn't accurate enough for consumers to avoid even some of the most well-known toxins." The American Safety Cleaning Institute countered that "detailed safety assessments are conducted by companies throughout the life cycle of a product" and that the Silent Spring study "wrongly raises unfounded safety concerns over cleaning products and ignores enhanced efforts to communicate with consumers about product ingredients."[35] And the Centers for Disease Control reportedly "did not find detectable levels of newly tested chemicals," including new data on thirty-four chemicals not previously reported—"in the vast majority of human subjects who were sampled."[36]

It should be emphasized that the lack of foreseeability of risks is not limited to the general public but is also a problem for industry. Purely illustrative is a confession of ignorance on the part of Boeing concerning metal fatigue on older 737 jets, in the wake of the opening of a five-foot hole in a Southwest Airlines plane in 2011. A senior Boeing engineer, Paul Richter, reportedly said that "the company had thought that the jets would not be vulnerable to serious cracks in their skin until 'much, much later'" and that "it was surprised that its safety projections were so far off the mark." Implicitly making the collateral point that products do wear out was his statement that the company thought it only had to worry about cracks after sixty thousand cycles of takeoffs and landings, whereas the Southwest jet had only had about forty thousand cycles.[37] The economics of discovering problems in long-term use of products is evident in a statement by John Goglia, who was a member of the National Transportation Safety Board for several years, about the dangers in older planes that had gone through thousands of takeoff-and-landing cycles. Observing that the metal fatigue problem had been identified before—two decades earlier a roof section on a 737 had ripped open and a flight attendant had been sucked out of the craft—he said, "We're talking about the same issues today, and we're proposing the same fixes." He suggested that what was needed was "to take a few of these high-cycle airplanes and run them through a very vigorous inspection program and see where we can identify deficiencies, and see whether there is anything different than what the manufacturer thought there would be." However, he said he did not "see that happening because it is expensive."[38]

### *D. Ways of Weighing Risk*

The law has identified different ways to weigh risk. One method is to compare the cost of injurious effects caused by an activity with the costs of avoiding harm. Take the case of a particular chemical used in a food product—for example, a chemical sweetener—that may cause a certain number of cancers. However, it may also reduce the number of cases of diabetes. This poses the question of how the cost of prohibiting use of the product compares with the cost of the injuries it will—or may—cause. A constant problem with this comparison, which extends to all the comparisons discussed in this section, is that it will often be very difficult—sometimes impossible—to place the right dollar value on either cost. There may be great controversy about how may cancers the product causes, because there are so many factors potentially involved in the development of cancer; in fact, the factors thought to be causative may vary with respect to particular forms of cancer. A similar set of difficulties attends the calculation of the number of cases of diabetes that will be avoided by use of the sweetener. And just one example of the behavioral complexities involved in such calculations is the case of the consumer who drinks only diet drinks and then gorges on pie.

### *E. The Precautionary Principle*

For more than a generation there has been spirited discussion, bridging the Atlantic, of an idea called the "precautionary principle." This discussion has been focused largely on environmental risks, with a principal statement of its role as "part of a system of rules designed to guide human behavior towards the ideal of an environmentally sustainable economy."[39]

A historical basis for the idea lies in the German concept of *Vorsorge,* which has been abstractly defined as "an interventionist measure, a justification for state involvement in the day-to-day lives of the citizen in the name of good government."[40] Commentary on the precautionary principle describes it as "a culturally framed concept that is constructed from changing social judgments about the appropriate roles of science, economics, ethics, politics and law in anticipatory environmental protection and management."[41]

Writers have offered many definitions of the idea. One summary of sub-principles includes the proposition that regulatory action should be taken in cases of uncertain risk where "there is neither the data nor the modelling accuracy to do the job" but "where the burden of evidence falls on the side of possible harm." This catalog includes the idea that regulators should give particular respect to "the most vulnerable and marginal" members of society. In the operation of the legal system, this means that "the balance of proof falls on the initiator to show that particular interests will not be harmed at all."[42] An operational consequence of this is "the application of the safe minimum standard in the setting of regulations, building in biases of safety in risk determinations."[43]

Embedded in this risk-averse idea is a certain skepticism of expert judgments, even a lack of trust in such judgments that is a "rational and prudent response to be expected of anyone outside their field of expertise." Fueling this type of response are various examples of "what are seen as 'expert' mistakes," including episodes involving asbestos, DES infertility treatments, DDT, and BSE.[44] The positive assessment of the role of nonexperts includes the beliefs that they "see problems, issues/and solutions that experts miss by thinking more broadly and not being bound by disciplinary constraints," that "lay judgments reflect a sensitivity to social and political values and common-sense that experts' models do not acknowledge," and that "the lay public may have a better capacity than experts alone for 'institutionalizing regret,' accommodating uncertainty and correcting errors."[45]

One sweeping statement of the principle is that "where the environmental risks being run by regulatory inaction are in some way uncertain but non-negligible, regulatory inaction is unjustified."[46] A general statement of its potential for broad application is that it requires "acting in advance of scientific proof of harm to address uncertain but potentially significant risks."[47] Another, in a "Guidance Paper" issued by a European commission in 2000, is that the principle "covers those specific circumstances where 'scientific evidence is insufficient, inconclusive or uncertain and there are indications through preliminary objective scientific evaluation that there are reasonable grounds for concern that the potentially dangerous effects on the environment, human, animal or plant health may be inconsistent with the high level of protection chosen for the community."[48] A parallel, contemporaneous statement, issued in 1998 by the Wingspread Conference, said, "Compelling evidence that damage to humans and the worldwide environment is of such magnitude and seriousness that new principles for conducting human activities are necessary," and declared that "when an activity raises threats of harm to human health or the environment, precautionary measures should be taken even if some cause and effect relationships are not fully established scientifically." It further asserted, "In this context the proponent of an activity, rather than the public, should bear the burden of proof."[49]

The precautionary principle is an effort to minimize risk in conditions in which the assessment of probability of risk is made difficult, if not impossible, by uncertainty, and sometimes even by ignorance. One definition of uncertainty in this discourse is "a condition under which there is confidence in the completeness of the defined set of outcomes, but where there is acknowledged to exist no uniquely valid theoretical or empirical basis for the assignment of probabilities to these outcomes." Ignorance, by contrast, describes a situation in which "there not only exists no basis for the assigning of probabilities (as under uncertainty) but where the definition of a complete set of outcomes is also problematic." Under this definition, "it is not only impossible to rank the options but even their full characterization is difficult," and "it is always possible that there are effects (outcomes) which have been entirely excluded from consideration."[50]

As critics see it, the set of ideas bundled with the precautionary principle, "taken to its logical conclusion," "would mean an end to innovation."[51] My own analysis recognizes that experimentation, on both large and small scales, necessarily assumes uncertainty and sometimes may proceed in ignorance. Further recognizing that no facet of life is free from these elements of indeterminacy as our daily experiments with risk proceed at many levels, it seeks to develop ideas that will enable both policy makers and consumers in making everyday decisions to do so as wisely as possible.[52]

### *Key Supreme Court Decisions*

An epic judicial struggle over the precautionary principle, folded into an issue of statutory interpretation, erupted in the early 1980s in a pair of Supreme Court decisions. The first of these cases, *Industrial Union Dept., AFL-CIO v. American Petroleum Institute,*[53] involved an OSHA regulation that, among other things, placed a limit of one part per million parts (ppm) of air on airborne concentrations of benzene. That substance, of which "11 billion pounds were produced in the United States in 1976," was "used in manufacturing a variety of products" ranging from motor fuels to detergents, and is one to which "the entire population of the United States is exposed in small quantities."[54]

In the spotlight were two provisions of the Occupational Safety and Health Act. One was section 3(8), which defined occupational safety and health standards as standards that required workplace conditions or methods "reasonably necessary or appropriate to provide safe or healthful employment and places of employment." The other was section §6(b)(5), which focused on "toxic materials or harmful physical agents," and which directed the secretary of labor to "set the standard which most adequately assures, to the extent feasible, on the basis of the best available evidence, that no employee will suffer material impairment of health or functional capacity." Justice Stevens, writing for a plurality of the Court, summarized the secretary's position as that "no safe exposure level can be determined and that §6(b)(5) requires him to set an exposure limit at the lowest technologically feasible level that will not impair the viability of the industries regulated."[55] He concluded that the "evidence in the administrative record of adverse effects of benzene exposure at 10 ppm"—ten times the amount of the limit OSHA had set—was "sketchy at best,"[56] saying that the rationale for the 1 ppm level was based on "a series of assumptions indicating that some leukemias might result from exposure to 10 ppm and that the number of cases might be reduced by reducing the exposure level to 1 ppm."[57]

The heart of the policy argument lay in Justice Stevens's declaration, with reference to the language of section 3(8), that "'safe' is not the equivalent of 'risk-free'" and his argument that "a workplace can hardly be considered 'unsafe' unless it threatens the workers with a significant risk of harm."[58] He concluded that the secretary had "relied squarely on a special policy for carcinogens that imposed the burden on industry of proving the existence of a safe level of exposure, thereby avoiding the Secretary's threshold responsibility of establishing the need for more stringent standards."[59] Justice Powell's concurring opinion complained that the record had no "adequate documentation" that the agency had justified the "substantial costs" of the regulation.[60]

Justice Rehnquist's concurring opinion identified the problem as "one of the most difficult issues that could confront a decisionmaker: whether the statistical possibility of future deaths should ever be disregarded in light of the economic costs of preventing those deaths." His technical conclusion was that Congress had "improperly delegated" the choice at issue to "the Secretary of Labor and, derivatively, to this Court."[61] Arguing that Congress had provided a "standardless delegation,"[62] he said that "the legislative history demonstrates that the feasibility requirement, as employed in §6(b)(5), is a legislative mirage" that would "assum[e] any form desired by the beholder."[63]

Justice Marshall's dissent inveighed against what he termed the Court's requirement of a "threshold finding of 'significance.'" Although he acknowledged that "the magnitude of the risk cannot be quantified at the present time," he pointed out that the secretary had "found that exposure to benzene at levels above 1 ppm posed a definite albeit unquantifiable risk of chromosomal damage, nonmalignant blood disorders, and leukemia." He declared that the Court's approach "would place the burden of medical uncertainty squarely on the shoulders of the American worker."[64] He strongly argued against the effort to introduce a cost-benefit analysis into section 6(b)(5), noting that "no cost-benefit analysis is referred to at any point in the statute or its legislative history."[65] In what were essentially precautionary-principle terms, be pointed out that "risks of harm are often uncertain, but inaction has considerable costs of its own" and observed that "the agency must decide whether to take regulatory action against possibly substantial risks or to wait until more definitive information becomes available—a judgment which by its very nature cannot be based solely on determinations of fact."[66]

The very next year, the Court turned toward a precautionary perspective, in *American Textile Manufacturers Institute v. Donovan.*[67] This

1981 case involved a standard for permissible exposure levels (PELs) for cotton dust, a standard devised by OSHA to minimize the occurrence of byssinosis, "brown lung" disease, which afflicted many thousands of cotton mill workers. As Justice Brennan summarized it for a majority, OSHA had "interpreted the Act to require adoption of the most stringent standard to protect against material health impairment, bounded only by technological and economic feasibility."[68] He rejected what he characterized as the industry's position that not only must OSHA "show a significant risk of material risk impairment," but that it must also show "that the reduction in risk of material health impairment is significant in light of the costs of attaining the reduction."[69] Focusing on section 6(b)(5) and drawing on a court of appeals summary of legislative intent in the case, he said, "Congress itself defined the basic relationship between costs and benefits, by placing the 'benefit' of worker health above all other considerations save those making attainment of this 'benefit' unachievable."[70]

Justice Rehnquist, now in dissent, drew on his concurring opinion in the *Petroleum Institute* case. Arguing that Congress had "abdicated its responsibility" to decide the "fundamental and most difficult policy choice" about weighing prevention costs against "the statistical possibility of future deaths,"[71] he referred to the debate in the Senate "about the extent to which the Secretary should be authorized to create a risk-free work environment." He declared that the statutory words in section 605(b)(5) "to the extent feasible" "were used to mask a fundamental policy disagreement," and that "if Congress had been required to choose whether to mandate, permit, or prohibit the Secretary from engaging in a cost-benefit analysis, there would have been no bill for the President to sign."[72]

There has been controversy about whether the United States or Europe has been more attached to the precautionary principle. Some have argued that "Europe is more risk-averse and precautionary, whereas the United States is seen as more risk-taking and optimistic about the prospects for new technology." Others have suggested that "the United States is more precautionary because its regulatory practice is more legalistic and adversarial."[73] To discover which hypothesis is more accurate has taken a great deal of effort, and the answer has been gray rather than black and white. A group of researchers, after developing "a comprehensive list of almost 3,000 risks identified in the literature" over three decades beginning in 1970, focused on a randomly selected group of one hundred ecological, health, and safety risks in their search for information "on the stringency of regulation" on both sides of the Atlantic.[74] This laborious enterprise yielded the overall conclusion that "the degree of precaution exhibited in European and American risk regulation is very similar."[75] Writing in 2005, the authors did find "some limited support [for] the flip-flop hypothesis—that the United States was more precautionary than Europe in the 1970s and 1980s, but Europe has become relatively more precautionary than the United States." However, they found that "the magnitude of the shift is quite modest." Acknowledging their "inability to obtain full information about regulations in each region," they concluded that "equal precaution remains the modal pattern." They said that although "the change is more often toward greater relative precaution in Europe," there were "many cases [that] show the opposite result," noting that "the direction of movement was toward greater relative precaution in Europe for 21 cases, and toward greater relative precaution in the United States for 14 cases." Their quest for general answers yielded only a set of specifics: "Regulation is highly contextual, with policy choices that are specific to the particular risk."[76]

*F. Comparisons With Risk*

Similar problems occur when the focus is on comparison of risk with risk and of risk with benefit. A brace of controversies from 1992 captures some of the problems that arise with different standards. An almost bizarre episode in that year pivoted on a request by the Office of Management and Budget to the Labor Department to "assess comprehensively the net health benefit of a regulation on workers' health" that would set "permissible exposure limits for hundreds of hazardous substances." An OMB official said that the agency's "preliminary analysis tells us that [the effect of the OSHA rule] may be negative"—for example, by leading to higher unemployment or reduced wages—and that "thus, on balance, workers' health may be adversely affected." OSHA had proposed its rule under the strictures of the 1981 decision in the *Textile Manufacturers* case that effectively prohibited the agency from using a cost-benefit test for health standards. In testimony before the Senate Governmental Affairs Committee, the OMB official said that OSHA's failure to conduct a risk-risk analysis was "an important omission." This statement drew hostile fire from Democrats on the committee. John Glenn, the committee chairman—no stranger to risky employment himself—said that the OMB's position "seems to stand logic on its head—to say that controlling a dangerous substance in the workplace makes an increased health hazard to the worker." He declared that "the same tortured logic would seem to say that increasing dangerous materials in the workplace (i.e., making it cheaper to conduct business and the chance of increased wages) would mean better health for the workers."[77] An assistant secretary of labor replied softly, saying that the Department of Labor would "begin to study the questions you've raised as expeditiously as possible." Some other comments were harsher. Senator James Jeffords, a Republican, said he was "disappointed that OMB has not thought it wise to kind of pull this thing back and bury it somewhere, it's so absurd." Even less kind was a comment from a lawyer for the Public Citizen consumer group, who declared, "Clearly the inmates are running the asylum."[78]

Contemporaneously, in the pigeonhole of risk-benefit analysis, arguments arose about the Environmental Protection Agency's approach to regulation of pesticides under the Federal Insecticide, Fungicide, and Rodenticide Act, which effectively requires a weighing of risks and benefits.[79] The executive director of the National Coalition Against the Misuse of Pesticides attacked what he labeled as the agency's assumption "that new pesticides to be registered have benefits." He criticized what he termed a laissez-faire approach that allowed the market to judge what the benefits of the products were. An EPA official countered that the agency's job was "to capture what the world would be like if we take regulatory action on a chemical." He reportedly said that the assessment of benefits always confronted a changing world—for example, the occurrence of pest resistance—creating a situation in which the public would not "wait for new data on benefits."[80]

The increasing sophistication of science potentially has a profound effect on judgments about large-scale experimentation on the public because of how the uses of new technologies can affect the definition of acceptable risk. Illustrative was a 1996 proposal by the EPA for changes in determinations of causation of cancer by various chemicals—specifically, the use of tools from molecular biology rather than the administration of large doses of chemicals to laboratory animals. It had been argued that animal testing of that kind tended to "overstat[e] risks from some chemicals because it tends to ignore how the chemicals behave in people, particularly at low exposures." Underlining the difficulty of decision making in this area were comments by EPA scientists, and others outside the agency who took part in an EPA review, that it was "impossible to say whether more chemicals would be added to or taken off" the agency's list of carcinogens. A Berkeley scientist, Dr. William Pease, reportedly said that the EPA was "inviting delay and obfuscation by setting its scientific aim too high given the shortage of data on the vast majority of suspected cancer agents." He said, "We don't have the kind of data that is needed for 90 percent of these compounds" and that his "experience as a scientist" was "that no one can agree on these issues." He asserted that one didn't "need to analyze everything to death before you begin to take public health decisions about potential carcinogens."[81]

*G. People's Judgments About Risk*

In an experimental society, a crucial set of questions concerns how people make judgments about risk. There is a spectrum of viewpoints on these issues. In a 1984 article, one group of commentators decried the exercise of judgment by scientists "reduced to employing the same *quasi-rational* cognitive processes that laypersons must use, with much the same consequences, uncertainty, misunderstanding, and persistent dispute that leads to personal animosity—epiphenomena which frustrate, delay, and often misdirect the development of public policy."[82] Confronted with a controversy about the risks of plutonium discharges from the Rocky Flats nuclear plant (RFP), these writers fashioned an "analytical principle" based on plutonium exposure and dosages and smoking habits: "If the amount of respirable plutonium in the atmosphere downwind from RFP is known, then persons living in that area who know . . . the make of cigarette they smoke each day" could make judgments about their risk from smoking.[83]

Although the acquisition of such specific information surely is helpful in the effort to establish a depoliticized zone of science, often that kind of information is difficult to acquire or the data are in controversy. And there are problems well beyond that. Charles Yablon has observed that in the area of hazardous products, determining the "true risk" of products is a task "fraught with difficulties."[84] Summarizing a distinguished literature on the topic, he discerns a developing debate "over how the law should deal with the malleability and ad hoc nature of the perception of product risk by most consumers." He identifies major players in this debate as "the educators and the 'protectors.'" The "educators" emphasize the provision of "clear, vivid, comprehensible and accurate information about . . . risks," with a premise being the "assumption that most people can be educated to make 'sound decisions,' which are presumably those based on accurate probability assessments." A contrasting position places stress on the idea that "risk assessments are not only manipulable but that there are powerful and sophisticated market actors with the ability and incentives to manipulate them—namely product manufacturers."[85] Importantly, both of these positions involve normative judgments, as Yablon summarizes the views of their advocates. For Kip Viscusi, as Yablon encapsules his position as an "educator," this "entails an emphasis on the greater choice, product innovation and individual responsibility that would result from a fault-based liability regime emphasizing warnings and availability of information, whether or not such warnings were effective in promoting 'rational' product choice and use by most consumers." By contrast, as Yablon needs commentators like Jon Hanson and Douglas Kysar, they would "privilege protection over choice," saying that "it does not matter whether consumer demand for [a] product was based on risk preference or cognitive error."[86]

Paralleling these arguments in Yablon's summary is what is, "at least in part, a debate over the objective reality of risks." On the one hand is "a theory of the regulatory state," closely associated with Cass Sunstein, "that recognizes that peoples' perceptions of risk will often be distorted by heuristics and biases," with "many of the demands on policymakers (as well as their responses)" being "not only irrational, but based on mistaken probability judgments."[87] On the other hand is the conclusion that "there is a strong subjective element to risk perception"—in part "because such perception involves considerations of values as well as facts." A very strong articulation of this position lies in the view that "risk does not exist 'out there,' independent of our minds and cultures, waiting to be measured." Rather, "human beings have invented the concept of risk to help them understand and cope with the dangers and uncertainties of life."[88]

An important practical aspect of Yablon's analysis has to do with the idea that "the theory of subjective probability began as an attempt (primarily by philosophical economists) to give empirical content to probability judgments applied to single nonrepeat events."[89] When one is judging events that occur with relative frequency, "accurate probability judgments can often be made on an objective and empirical basis." But "when judging the probability of individual, unique events . . . there are no objective facts that can conclusively determine the accuracy of such judgments, and the relevance of statistical evidence is unclear and contestable."[90] One might comment that the more experimental a product or process, the more a person's encounter with that product or process tends to become a unique event.

Another dimension of the problem lies in the fact that tests of products may not have sufficient sensitivity to pick up hazards. The case of thalidomide, a drug associated with thousands of serious birth defects, is illustrative. It appeared, after the fact, that rats and mice used as experimental animals in teratology tests of the drug were "less sensitive than other animals" but that some test rats were more sensitive, with indications that embryos were resorbed in their uteruses. There also were defects observed in macaques and marmosets.[91] Two analysts who made this point declared, "The sign of teratogenic activity in rodents, even though merely fetal resorption, should have stimulated . . . more expensive studies on primates."[92] Further, although the disease-causing propensities of asbestos were well established when they wrote in 1983, they argued for using analogy to adopt a risk-averse approach to the "premature" substitution of other fibers. They stated as their "hypothesis and consequent analogy" that "the risk of exposure to any fiber is the same as the risk of exposure to asbestos in the same concentration, fiber length, and aspect ratio (or shape)." "This analogy," they declared, "should enable precautions to be taken in the use of other fibers and should prevent premature switching from asbestos to fibers whose action is not understood."[93]

### *H. Behaviors Toward Risk*

There has been an increasing literature on the issue of how people behave in fact, which surely is crucial to the decision making of individuals about risk. An important question is how inclined people are to make judgments on the basis of their rational expectations of the utility of their behavior. Summarizing prior studies, one observer has referred to the apparent anomaly that "models that assume individuals behave rationally perform so well describing behavior in market experiments" whereas "individuals behave irrationally in psychology experiments."[94] One of his suggestions is that "variants of subjective expected utility could prove fruitful in explaining demand for information (to reduce ambiguity)" and that "timid behavior that looks like risk aversion but disappears over time" may be "ambiguity aversion instead."[95] One explanation for seemingly irrational decisions, taken from a much-cited source, is the "'loss aversion' assumption": that "losses are more painful than equally sized gains are pleasurable."[96] Another is that "people treat errors of commission, or action, as more blameworthy than errors of omission, or inaction."[97] These hypothesized behavioral realities are foundations for this commentator's assertion that "the continued use of EU [expected utility] can only be justified in two fairly narrow ways."[98]

Many studies have illuminated various crevices in the assumptions of economic theory about decision making. One paper, focusing on ecological risk perception and cautiously presented because its research base was only sixty-eight university students, finds that "natural hazards rate relatively low on the hierarchy of perceived risks to nature," with the investigators saying that "the relatively benign evaluation of natural forces in ecological risk perception parallels the benign view of nature as a contributor to human health risk."[99]

Another study, also using students as subjects, found that different results were obtained if people confronted with risk choices were given comparisons of risks from other activities or products. Specifically, the investigators asked their subjects how they would vote on the location of a toxic waste incinerator in a "small town with many economic problems."[100] The earmark of the study was that it appeared "to be the first to provide a direct, quantitative comparison between a statistical summary of risk and one in which the risk is 'placed in context' by means of a risk comparison"[101]—in this case, the health risks of cigarette smoking. The subjects were told that a representative of the company that wanted to build the incinerator said that "the odds of a really serious accident or health risk . . . 'are incredibly small—only about one in a million.'" In another stage of the study, the hypothesized company representative said that the risk of the incinerator was "less than the risk of smoking a couple dozen cigarettes." Interestingly, "the risk comparison involving cigarettes actually produce[d] more hostility toward the incinerators than [did] the 'one in a million' terminology" and, "if anything, the risk comparison would actually increase the tendency to vote against the proposed incinerator."[102] Although "the effect of the one-in-a-million information" yielded only "mildly positive" results and the "risk-comparison results [were] mildly negative," the difference between the two was "statistically significant." Carefully qualifying their interpretation, the authors suggested, "If spokespersons are perceived as having 'something to sell' . . . the nature of the situation may quickly shift toward increased suspicion and distrust."[103]

Another study carried the lesson that the way that risks are scaled may significantly affect people's perceptions. These authors constructed a "risk ladder" in a study of the responses of New Jersey homeowners to questions about the risks associated with radon and asbestos, providing study subjects with comparisons to smoking. They concluded that risk perceptions differed depending on a subject's "position on the risk ladder and the risk represented at the ends of the scale."[104] Their lesson for strategists in risk communication was that "to construct a risk ladder intentionally is to make judgments about the risk perceptions that are likely to be encountered and the risk perceptions that are appropriate to encourage." They gave examples of ways to manipulate perceptions:

> Are people likely to underestimate the risk at all levels? Extend the ladder downward so all levels are near the top. Do they exaggerate the risk at all levels? Extend the ladder upward so all levels are near the bottom. Do they ignore important differences between high and low levels?" Truncate the ladder at both ends so high levels are near the top and low ones are near the bottom.[105]

These strategic suggestions for interested parties indicate the difficulty of discovering the meaning of decisions by consumers to confront or avoid risk. One reason that it is not easy being the subject of a broad social experiment is that one is often unaware of the traps that even a dispassionately conceived experiment may contain.

Folded closely within these issues is the question of how rational people are about alleged hazards to health. What are the attitudes to health risks among the general population? German researchers provided some answers to this broad question based on "a sample of roughly 22,000 individuals," which included questions that included "'willingness to take risks, in general' on an 11-point scale" and questions "about willingness to take risks in specific contexts: car driving, financial matters, sports and leisure, career, and health."[106] Among other findings, the authors noted that "any single measure" in any of these contexts was "a significant predictor of several of the behaviors, providing further validation of their behavioral relevance," but that "the only measure to predict all of the behaviors is the general risk question."[107]

Among the specific findings was that "individual differences" in the survey population were "partially explained by differences in four exogenous factors: willingness to take risks is negatively related to age and being female and positively related to . . . height and parental education." However, although these factors "have a qualitatively similar impact on risk attitudes in most contexts," their "magnitude differs across contexts," and "an age profile . . . raise[d] questions about the stability of risk preferences over time." They speculated, among other things, that "differences in risk attitudes over the life cycle could . . . be socially constructed, e.g., risky behavior in driving, sports, and health could be condoned at an early age but frowned upon later in life."[108] Incidentally, the authors concluded that a "standard measure of risk preference, in which respondents indicated willingness to invest in a hypothetical asset with explicit stakes and probabilities," called into question "the practice of exclusively using lottery questions to predict risky behavior in all contexts." In this connection, they noted that "the hypothetical lottery does not predict smoking, migration, or self-employment and predicts public sector employment with the 'wrong' sign." Quite specifically, they observed that "the best predictor of behavior in a given domain is typically the question incorporating context specific to that domain"—"for example, willingness to take risks in health matters is a better predictor of smoking than the hypothetical investment question, or the general risk question, or any other domain-specific question."[109]

Layered upon the question of individual attitudes to risk is the issue of how governments should respond to those attitudes when there is no significant scientific basis for them. One commentator, Howard Chang, puts the question of whether governments should "respond to public fears with regulations designed to reduce . . . feared risks if a risk assessment fails to identify a significant risk at stake."[110] He acknowledges that "it may not be easy to dismiss such fears as irrational" and that "the fear of these risks imposes real social costs that risk regulations can reduce, which suggests that it should always be appropriate to consider reductions in these fears a social benefit militating in favor of regulation."[111] However, although sympathetically noting the "real welfare loss" imposed "on those who experience those fears,"[112] he concludes generally that regulation responding to fears that "fail to reflect risk assessments" is undesirable.[113] He focuses on a controversy in which the United States contested a European Community ban on imports of beef from cattle fed with growth hormones, and on a ruling against the EC by the Appellate Body of the World Trade Organization. That ruling cited an international agreement requiring a foundation for health and safety regulations that took into account "risk assessment techniques developed by the relevant international organizations," although the Appellate Body referred to "the intense concern of consumers" about "the quality and drug-free character of the meat available in [their] internal market." Ultimately, Chang suggests that there is "some scope for domestic regulations to respond to consumer anxieties that may seem excessive from the perspective of the technocrat, when "those anxieties derive some support from risk assessments."[114]

*I. Utility and Morality*

Running parallel to these questions are issues involving tradeoffs between a morally neutral risk-utility matrix of decision and a set of concepts that emphasize moral considerations. As one author summarizes the familiar arguments for utilitarianism, that strategy "allocate[s] resources among protecting health, providing for more jobs, and increasing social income in such a way as to secure the community good or, in technical terms, to maximize utility for everyone in the community."[115] This author, Carl Cranor, contrasts a combination of views of Norman Daniels "graft[ed]" onto the great book *A Theory of Justice* by John Rawls. As Cranor summarizes it, Daniels extrapolates Rawls's ideas into the notion that "health care protections have a special places in the lives of people and they should receive special protections in distributive theories."[116] As Cranor further develops the idea, "justice requires securing equal opportunities for people in a community, and receiving equal opportunity requires the securing of . . . environmental health protections," which become "a requirement of justice." In the perspective presented here, the constant experimentation with human health that occurs throughout the workplace and in other environments may "undermine opportunities in morally arbitrary ways" when it involves "human practices or institutions *that could be modified*."[117] Building on these ideas, Cranor criticizes an outcome produced by utilitarianism: that "minor benefits for many . . . can take precedence over severe harms to a few because each person's wants or, more important, each person's *needs,* including healthcare needs, are seen as just another way of producing community utility."[118] The practical effect of such a state of affairs is that the injury victim's good health is "taken from him and converted to the benefit of others."[119]

Cranor's preferred approach to "scientific evaluation of evidence in the tort law and administrative regulations" is the adoption of a "distributively sensitive consequentialism" that "permits one to take into account the overall effects of one's actions in addition to" their distributional effects. These "distributively sensitive theories" will "assign considerable moral weight" to "health harms to the public," a concern with "special urgency for the public."[120]

## II. Standards for Decision

### *A. The Problem of Proof and the Role of Experts*

An ongoing war is in progress about the stringency of standards used for proof of causation in toxic tort cases, a war that is symbolic of the vast experiment with chemicals that takes place on the American public every day. A stark presentation of opposing viewpoints on the proof issue occurred between two distinguished lawyers who represented plaintiffs and defendants, respectively, in such cases. On one side, the claimants' lawyer, Thomas Henderson, insisted that "policy considerations" could support judgments of liability "even where scientific inquiry and knowledge are not certain or not complete."[121] By contrast, the defense lawyer, Bert Black, argued that once a causation question had been framed, "the analysis becomes a policy-free factual inquiry."[122]

Professor Cranor criticized Black's attack on an "expressed certainty" standard for expert testimony,[123] arguing that a standard of "proof to a reasonable degree of medical certainty" should be sufficient to meet the plaintiff's burden of production of evidence in toxic tort suits.[124] Cranor premised that "in such suits there is often considerable uncertainty, dispute and controversy concerning the factual conclusions at issue" and referred to the possibility that "there may be no well-established consensus in the community against which to measure the scientific validity of a particular legal judgment."[125] He suggested that the use of a relatively stringent criminal law-type standard for proof would tend to "distort tort law error rates"—particularly the problem of "false negatives"—with the result of there being "even greater odds by chance alone of failing to detect an association between exposure and disease when it exists."[126] Arguing against what functionally would be a criminal law standard of a persuasion burden—as contrasted with a burden of production—he said that this was "surely a substantial and unfair barrier to plaintiffs." He insisted that in tort cases, such a persuasion burden "substantially distorts the balance of interests between plaintiff and defendant."[127] He underlined the difficulty of obtaining valid epidemiological data, because of the expense of research on large groups,[128] and he generally emphasized that relatively stringent rules tilt against plaintiffs' access to tort remedies.[129] He concluded that judges should allow juries a fairly broad range of judgment in deciding the worthiness of causation testimony, saying that "while judges can and certainly have made judgments about scientific acceptance of scientific theories and facts," it was "not clear juries cannot make similar judgments when presented with much the same information."[130]

A very different perspective came from Michael Gough in an essay in the book *Politicizing Science: The Alchemy of Policymaking*. Gough, painting with a broad brush, summarized other writers' descriptions of a process that yields politically generated conclusions on matters of science, with "scientists masking policy decisions as 'scientific'" and "politicians labeling politically driven decisions as scientific, attempting thereby to place them outside the realm of political discussion, debate, and compromise."[131] A key part of this process was the "burnish[ing] of images" of risk by "government agencies, businesses, and environmental organizations" that "can lead immediately to calls for government action to control the risks."[132] The fashioning of these "images" of risk would not adduce data. Rather, Gough's conspirators, like agencies and environmental organizations, would first assert the existence of risk and then "demand evidence to set the assertion aside, no matter how flimsy the evidence for it."[133] One element of Gough's attack on opponents of the so-called precautionary principle was the use of "consensus" scientific panels—which he said "almost always include people who made the assertion" and who "usually steer a careful, centrist path through scientific information," with it being "not unusual . . . to conclude that the risk is not as big as some asserted, but that it can't be rejected, and that more research if needed." "'Splitting the difference' or 'finding a consensus,'" Gough said scornfully, "is not science."[134] He cautioned that once data are collected, what he viewed as an anti-science process was "dependent on policy decisions and professional judgments."[135]

Two observers, writing somewhat prophetically in the 1980s, turned their camera angle on disagreements in the public on risks allegedly imposed "on a large group."[136] Focusing on nuclear power plants, they noted a phenomenon we have mentioned previously: "Uncertainty is ubiquitous."[137] The "potential for conflict" would arise in choosing particular risk paths, because in such contexts, "risk is not a purely private choice," and "if preferences differ, each individual cannot obtain a facility corresponding to his or her particular attitude toward risk"; thus, such risks have "a fundamentally *public* aspect."[138] Typically such situations would require decisions that generate both winners and losers, and "the usual democratic institutions do not deal" with such situations "very well." Choosing the solution that reflected "the preferences of the median voter" would leave "many people . . . vastly unhappy with any solution."[139] The best compromise that could be put together was to develop "a policy that would give compensation to those most unhappy with the policy choice."[140] If this seemed highly impractical, with the competing demands for public resources that have come to the fore in recent years, the authors at least had identified some thorns in the bush of policy making.

### *B. Proof in Injury Cases: Daubert and Its Offspring*

The courts have been a principal battleground in the war over proof, with decisions at the top of the judicial pyramid—the Supreme Court—radiating into many decisions in lower courts.

The Supreme Court set the pace with three decisions in the 1990s. The flagship case, decided in 1993, was *Daubert v. Merrell Dow Pharmaceuticals.*[141] The case arose from allegations that the anti-nausea drug Bendectin, taken by pregnant women, had caused birth defects in their children. Refusing to adopt a 1923 court of appeals decision that required "general acceptance" of scientific principles,[142] the Court fixed on Federal Rule of Evidence 702, which then allowed testimony from expert witnesses "if scientific, technical or other specialized knowledge will assist the trier of fact to understand the evidence or to determine a fact in issue." In spotlighting the "helpfulness" standard of the rule, the Court referred to a group of four factors that could "bear on the inquiry" regarding scientific evidence. These included "whether a theory or technique . . . can be (and has been) tested," whether it had been "subjected to peer review and publication," and the "known or potential rate of error." The Court did conclude with a bow to "general acceptance" as something that "can yet have a bearing on the inquiry."[143] Confronted with conflicting expert testimony on whether Bendectin caused birth defects, the court reversed a court of appeals decision for the maker of the drug because that court had "focused almost exclusively" on the "general acceptance" test.[144] Judge Kozinski of the court of appeals responded sardonically, pointing out that "none of the plaintiff's experts has published his work on Bendectin in a scientific journal or solicited formal review by his colleagues" and saying, "It's as if there were a tacit understanding within the scientific community that what's going on here is not science at all, but litigation."[145]

The Supreme Court, having staked out a somewhat liberalized field for scientific testimony in *Daubert,* then began to set limits. In *General Electric Co. v. Joiner,*[146] the Court reversed a court of appeals opinion favoring a plaintiff who alleged that his exposure to the chemicals known as PCBs had promoted his small-cell lung cancer and whose expert testimony had been rejected by the trial court. Chief Justice Rehnquist said for the Court that studies that involved direct injections of "massive doses of PCBs" into infant mice were "so dissimilar to the facts presented" in the litigation—he noted that the plaintiff was "an adult human being whose alleged exposure to PCBs was far less than the exposure" of the mice—that "it was not an abuse of discretion for the District Court to have rejected the experts' reliance on them." After rejecting epidemiological studies on which the plaintiffs relied, he drove home his disapproval of the plaintiffs' evidence in two quotable sentences. In one, he said that "nothing in either *Daubert* or the Federal Rules of Evidence requires a district judge to admit opinion evidence that is connected to existing data only by the *ipse dixit* of the expert." In another, he declared, "A court may conclude that there is simply too great an analytical gap between the data and the opinion proffered."[147]

A third decision by the Court refused to draw a distinction between "scientific" knowledge and "technical" or "other specialized" knowledge. In this case, which involved the failure of a tire, the Court concluded with respect to the deposition of an expert in tire failure analysis that a trial court had "the same broad latitude when it decides *how* to determine reliability as it enjoys in respect to its ultimate reliability determination." In doing so, it reversed a court of appeals ruling that the deposition fell "outside the scope of *Daubert*."[148] The result in the particular case was to empower the trial judge to exclude the expert's testimony.

This trilogy of Supreme Court decisions eventually found its way into a revision of Evidence Rule 702. That rule now limits expert evidence to testimony "based on sufficient facts or data" that is "the product of reliable principles and methods," and when "the witness has reliably applied the principles and methods to the facts of the case."[149]

In one sense clarifying, the *Daubert* body of law gave rise first to an underbrush and then a forest of argument. I summarize here just a few cases, from many dozens in the area, to illustrate the vegetation that has grown up in the area.

*Bendectin controversies.* A graphic presentation of polar positions appeared in litigations over birth defects that the plaintiffs ascribed to Bendectin, the very drug that had been at issue in the *Daubert* case. In one federal case, the plaintiffs used chemical analysis and animal studies to support a finding that the drug caused birth defects, although the defendants—as in the Supreme Court case—used as many as thirty-five epidemiological studies offered by the defendants to oppose the causation hypothesis. The trial court concluded that at an early stage of litigation, it could not give summary judgment to the defendant, citing the "lin[ing] up" of experts "on both sides" and the existence of "many questions concerning the scientific studies proffered" by both sides. Although noting a "profound frustration with hired-gun experts" in prior decisions in Bendectin cases, the court said it could not "at this stage of the proceedings adopt a general rule precluding all testimony of plaintiffs' experts."[150]

Sharpening the issue were opposed results in Texas appellate courts in a case in which the jury found for the plaintiff, in a verdict challenged by the drug maker on the ground that there was no evidence that the drug had caused the limb reduction defects sued upon. Rather remarkably in view of its ultimate conclusion, the Texas appellate court noted that "all of the [plaintiffs'] witnesses admitted that none of the authors of the animal or epidemiological studies concluded that Bendectin caused limb reduction defects" and that they all "agreed that they were not primary researchers into Bendectin and its effect on developing fetuses." Yet it found that, based on "animal studies, *in vitro* studies, and epidemiological studies," those witnesses had provided "some evidence"—the phrase it used for three of the experts—that supported the plaintiffs' case on causation.[151] Emphasizing that the defendant's lawyers had been able critically to explore the testimony of the plaintiff's witnesses through cross-examination, the court presented a remarkable theory of trials in affirming the plaintiffs' judgment. It posited that it was "critical to distinguish the search for truth in law and in science." It acknowledged that "the purpose of any legal inquiry" was "to resolve a dispute between the parties" under "a body of rules" that "may well impede evidence of the truth," but it said that "these shortcomings and compromises have been accepted when put in balance with other considerations." Then the court let loose a paean for jury verdicts: "In the quest for justice, we say we are engaged in a search for truth, and we accept the jury's verdict as true except in very limited circumstances. This determination by citizens of the crucial facts of the case is the bedrock of our jurisprudence, however wrong its conclusion is in the eye of God or objective reality." The court added,

> We accept the legitimacy of the verdict if the rules of evidence and procedure have been followed because this is the way our history has accepted as the best way for determining truth in the courtroom, especially when contrasted with the earlier methods of oath, ordeal or combat.

It then reemphasized its point about truth by saying, "What the jury finds may not be really true, but we will accept it as true in order to resolve the dispute."[152]

The Texas Supreme Court recoiled from this view of truth-seeking in litigation. It contrasted the more than "thirty published, peer-reviewed epidemiological studies on the relationship between Bendectin and birth defects" that rejected the plaintiffs' hypothesis on causation with the fact that "none of the findings offered by the [plaintiffs'] five experts in this case have been published, studied, or replicated by the relevant scientific community." Taking a stand with the idea that causation analysis should be free of policy considerations, the supreme court rejected the argument that "liability should not be allocated only on the basis of reliable proof of fault because legal rules should have the goals of 'risk spreading, deterrence, allocating costs to the cheapest cost-avoider, and encouraging socially favored activities,'" and because "consumers of American justice want people compensated." It also rejected the associated ideas that "for some cases that very well may mean creating a compensatory mechanism even in the absence of clear scientific proof of cause and effect" and that "deferring to scientific judgments about fault only obscures the core policy questions that are addressed by the laws that the court is applying." It concluded that by invoking the traditional rule that "claimants prove their cases by a preponderance of the evidence," which led it to the declaration that "the law should not be hasty to impose liability when scientifically reliable evidence is unavailable."[153]

Courts have now developed a complex set of factors to be considered in determining reliability. Just two illustrations are a district court opinion that lists nine "indicia of reliability"[154] and another that lists seventeen questions it says would be "germane" to the so-called gatekeeping function of courts deciding *Daubert* issues.[155]

*Breast implant controversies.* A parallel set of science wars erupted in several decisions on illnesses attributed to silicone gel breast implants. A Nevada decision took a fairly liberal stance toward the ability of juries to sort out scientific evidence when Charlotte Malhum claimed that the rupture of an implant caused an autoimmune disease, offering testimony by an immunologist and a rheumatologist in addition to that of a neurologist who treated her. The immunologist hypothesized that liquid silicone that "bleeds" from a breast implant finds it way into the lymph nodes, from which it "travel[s] to other organs, including the heart, the lungs, the nerves, and the brain." He opined that the plaintiff "suffered from a multiple-sclerosis-like disease and progressive dysfunction of the nerves, resulting from exposure to silicone." The treating neurologist, "although he did not provide specific testimony that silicone caused Malhum's illnesses," said that the plaintiff's "symptoms corresponded to multiple-sclerosis-like autoimmune disease, axonal neuropathy, and demyelinization, all of which are caused by antibodies attacking her nervous system." He juxtaposed the plaintiff's problems with "other silicone breast implant patients" he had treated who "experienced similar nervous system disorders and autoimmune diseases." The rheumatologist, who observed the plaintiff's symptoms, drew on "his training and experience in treating over one hundred women who had silicone gel breast implants" in testifying that they "were caused in large part by exposure to silicone." Again essentially reasoning by analogy, he said that the plaintiff's symptoms, many of which were shared with "other women who have silicone gel breast implants," were part of what he termed "atypical autoimmune disease," which he "believe[d] can be caused by silicone gel breast implants."[156] The Nevada court concluded that based on this evidence, "a reasonable jury could conclude that but for the breast implants, Malhum would not have suffered from myriad illnesses."

Two levels of Oregon appellate courts also accepted causation testimony on silicone gel breast implants, although the plaintiff's experts were not precise in identifying the causal linkage between the implants and the plaintiff's disease. The plaintiff's expert testified, based on his survey of the literature and his evaluation of fifty patients, that "95 percent [of the patients] had two neurologic symptoms in common: inner ear dysfunction and a loss of sensation in the extremities" and that this "combination of symptoms presented a 'unique pattern' that he had not seen previously in his medical practice." He concluded that "there's unquestionably a very strong correlation," although he said that while he did not "understand the mechanism yet," he was "working on" that issue.[157] In deciding that this testimony was admissible, the Oregon appellate court rejected the defendant's argument that it should have been excluded because the expert's "study has not been published or subjected to peer review" and thus "lacks general acceptance." The court said that although the expert's "hypothesis (the exposure of human tissue to silicone produces neurological injuries) appears to be novel, it is based on his own experiences and observations as well as on scientific methodology" and noted that he had "eliminated other potential causes through differential diagnoses, another generally accepted form of scientific methodology used in medical treatment."[158]

In affirming the appellate court, the state supreme court said, "Publication or lack thereof in a peer-reviewed journal is a relevant, though not dispositive, consideration in assessing the scientific validity of a particular technique or methodology on which an opinion is based." It placed the admissibility of such evidence on a broader foundation when it said, "A conclusion about causation ultimately is a qualitative decision." It cited the *Reference Guide on Epidemiology* on the idea that "while the drawing of causal inferences is informed by scientific expertise, it is not a determination that is made by using scientific methodology" and said that there were "many generally accepted hypotheses in science for which the mechanism of cause and effect is not understood fully." It concluded that the expert's "inability to explain the mechanism of plaintiff's condition" went to the "weight" of his testimony and "not to admissibility."[159]

Two federal appellate courts carried forward the proof war on the implants. The Tenth Circuit, in rejecting testimony of experts for a plaintiff, focused on a lack of epidemiological evidence. It adduced the testimony of an immunologist for a National Science Panel, convened by a federal court, that there was "'no reproducible[,] reliable data' supporting the theory that silicone gel breast implants cause any immune system dysfunction" as well as similar testimony by an epidemiologist and a rheumatologist for the panel. It also referred to a statement in a study by the Institute of Medicine that "there was not 'even suggestive evidence' that silicone breast implants caused systemic disease." Although noting the "impressive credentials" of the plaintiff's expert rheumatologists, the court said, "Their reliance on differential diagnosis without supporting epidemiological evidence is misplaced and demonstrates the unreliable nature of the testimony." Declaring that "observations cannot define a disease" the court said that the plaintiff's witnesses had "completely ignored or discounted without explanation the many epidemiological studies which found no medically reliable link between silicone breast implants and systemic disease." It stressed that it could not "find a single case in which differential diagnosis that is flatly contrary to *all* of the available epidemiological evidence is both admissible and sufficient to defeat a defendant's motion for summary judgment."[160]

By contrast, the Ninth Circuit accepted testimony from three expert witnesses for a plaintiff. It noted that one of these, a toxicologist, was "a recognized expert on the immunological effects of silicone in the human body" who had based his opinion on "his review of medical records and [the defendant's] studies, and his general scientific knowledge of silicone's ability to cause immune disorders as established by animal studies and biophysical data." The court pointed out that one of two physician witnesses testified that his opinion favoring the causation hypothesis "was based on scientific studies he authored, his participation in a preliminary epidemiological study involving over 200 women, and his examination of [the plaintiff] during which he discovered evidence of silicone in her tissue and detected symptoms consistent with exposure to silicone." It noted that the other medical witness, a rheumatologist, had based his opinion "on medical records, his clinical experience, preliminary results of an epidemiological study and medical literature." The court concluded that the "experts' opinions were based on scientific techniques that satisfied the requirements established in *Daubert*." [161]

These battles of experts in civil trials over the specific question of whether silicone breast implants caused autoimmune disease thus reflected the broader arguments over the issue of how specific the evidence must be to justify regulation in the broader world of injuries. The conflicts in these tort cases closely resembled the disputes in the regulatory arena between those who demand relatively concrete data on casual connection and those, emphasizing a risk-averse perspective, who would err on the side of precaution.

We add the common-sense point that one problem in the evaluation of evidence is the overlooking of the obvious. A good example from the political world is a case in which authorities removed the body of a former ambassador to Switzerland, M. Larry Lawrence, from Arlington National Cemetery because they initially had ignored the obvious—namely that a transcript revealed that he was in college at "precisely the time he claimed to have suffered a head injury during a German torpedo attack on a merchant marine ship on which he served." One hypothesis was that Lawrence, a "leading Democratic fund-raiser," had faced relatively lenient scrutiny for his ambassadorial nomination; but this fact on a printed record did not rise to the attention of "more than a dozen 'vetters,' including retired members of Federal law-enforcement and intelligence agencies" during "a 25-day background check."[162]

## *C. Control Points and Choke Points*

A major control on the level of public experimentation is the passage of regulatory legislation. Congressional hearings and committee reports reveal the differing stimuli that produce these laws. The basis for safety legislation varies considerably with respect to the incidence of injuries and threats of injury. One example on the deadliest end of the spectrum is the statistical background of the initial legislation on regulation of cigarette advertising and labeling, which included hundreds of thousands of deaths and lives shortened annually. By comparison, some safety laws owe their genesis to relatively small numbers of injuries. One example is the 1937 episode in which the drug Elixir Sulfanilimide caused a little over one hundred deaths, triggering the passage of the 1938 Food, Drug, and Cosmetic Act.

Although regulatory laws and rules typically have their genesis in reports of injury from products and environments, one should note that there are episodes involving outcry against relatively tight regulation that have led to modifications that decrease the level of regulation. An example is the history of the FDA's 1987 regulations for the approval of Investigational New Drug (IND) applications for drugs that included medications designed to combat AIDS. The agency sought in these regulations to balance the desire of sufferers for access to drugs that were alternatives to those in the formal investigational process with a desire to enforce "a requirement for sufficient scientific evidence on the basis of which experts could reasonably conclude that the drug may be effective in the intended patient population."[163] Unsatisfied with the restrictions that these regulations placed on their ability to choose unapproved drugs, AIDS "activists" went to the point of trapping agency officials in this headquarters. That move appeared to have inspired a new regulation for "expedit[ing]" new therapies, but one that still required placebo testing—a sticky point for the activists—"where no therapy has been shown to be effective." After the development of a "gray market" in one of the drugs, more pressure from sufferers, and a "community based treatment trial" that "show[ed] a dose response," the FDA gave approval to the drug.[164] This series of events demonstrated the flexibility of a politically defined concept of "good science" in a situation of consumer pressures.

The history of the investigation of AIDS drugs is an unusual one, but most medical products are subject to various screening processes before they come to market. One is the prescription list itself. Many people would be surprised to know that the prescription list came into existence only in the early 1950s. After the 1938 law and then the restriction that the prescription list placed on a rough-and-ready marketplace—indeed one that in the early twentieth century had included the availability of cocaine in drugstores[165]—there came, by degrees, formal structures for the approval of prescription drugs, and eventually of medical devices. An important step in this tightening of regulation was the adoption in 1962 of the New Drug Application (NDA) process, which required a showing of effectiveness as well as safety demonstrated through "adequate and well-controlled investigations, including clinical investigations." That law provided the basis for the Investigational New Drug process, which required drug makers to go through three stages of testing of their products on human beings.

A complement to regulation that we have discussed is the way that private law—basically tort law—provides screens against hazards that are products of marketplace experiments. The prospect of successful tort litigation does serve to make experimenters on mass markets more cautious about the risks they might impose on consumers. In particular, the prospect of "mass tort" litigation is likely to force businesses to be especially careful about such risks. Successful "mass tort" cases may prove literally to be ruinous to companies. The trail of gasping victims of asbestos-caused illness has led to a trail of bankruptcies by companies associated in one way or another with asbestos. The range of firms that have been sued has continued to expand, now including firms whose products did not contain asbestos but were used with those that did. This expansion, it was predicted in 2013, would include many thousands more asbestos claims over "the next few decades."[166] It may finally be noted that plaintiffs' personal injury lawyers, condemned by some for their alleged rapacity, themselves provide an informal screen against consumer claims that have no basis in scientific fact.

## Notes

1. John D. Graham and Lorenz Rhomberg, "Uncertainty and Risk Assessment: How Risks Are Identified and Assessed," 545 *Annals* 15, 16 (1996).
2. James F. Short, Jr., "The Social Fabric At Risk: Forward the Social Transformation of Risk Analysis," 49 *Am. Sociological Rev.* 711, 711 (1984).
3. Baruch Fischoff and Donn MacGregor, "Judged Lethality: How Much People Seem to Know Depends Upon How They Are Asked," Vol. 3. No. 4 *Risk Analysis* 229, 231 (1983).
4. Ibid., p. 232.
5. Ibid., p. 235.
6. Brendon Swedlow et al., "Theorizing and Generalizing About Risk Assessment and Regulation through Comparative Nested Analysis of Representative Cases," 31 *Law & Policy* No. 2 at 236, 237 (2009).
7. Ibid., p. 240.
8. See ibid., pp. 240 and 244–47.
9. Ibid., p. 239. For an earlier comprehensive study of risks, see James K. Hammitt et al., "Precautionary Regulation in Europe and the United States: A Quantitative Comparison," 25 *Risk Analysis* 1215 (2005), in

which the authors conclude that "the most common pattern" in their data shows that "the United States and Europe are equally precautionary over the 35-year period" between 1970 and 2004, ibid., p. 228. The authors find "some limited support" for the hypothesis "that the United States was more precautionary than Europe in the 1970s and 1980s but Europe has become relatively more precautionary than the United States." They find "a slight shift toward greater relative precaution in Europe from about 1970 through 2004" but that "the magnitude of the shift is quite modest." Id. at 1227.

10. Cass Sunstein, *Laws of Fear: Beyond the Precautionary Principle* (Cambridge Univ. Press, 2005), p. 4.
11. Dan Kahan et al., "Fear of Democracy: A Cultural Evaluation of Sunstein on Risk," 119 *Harv. L. Rev.* 1071, 1074-75 (2006).
12. See ibid., p. 1075.
13. For other brief references, see Sunstein, supra note 10, p. 94; Kahan, supra note 11, p. 1092.
14. See Gregory Mandel and James Thuo Gathii, "Cost-Benefit Analysis Versus the Precautionary Principle: Beyond Cass Sunstein's Laws of Fear," 2006 *U. Ill. L. Rev.* 1037, 1045-52.
15. See Kahan et al., supra note 11, 119 *Harv. L. Rev.*, p. 1087.
16. *Marshall S. Shapo, Tort Law and Culture* (Carolina Academic Press 2003), p. 299.
17. See ibid., p. 300.
18. Kahan et al., p. 1108.
19. See Edward Tufte, *Visual and Statistical Thinking: Displays of Evidence for Making Decisions* (Graphics Press LLC, 1997), p. 28.
20. See ibid., pp. 39 and 42.
21. See ibid.
22. Ibid., p. 44.
23. See ibid., pp. 45–48.
24. Diane Vaughn, *The Challenger Launch Decision* (Univ. of Chicago Press 1996), p. 417.
25. Ibid., pp. 418–19.
26. See Tufte, supra, pp. 50–52 and marginal note 48 on p. 52.
27. Ibid., p. 53.
28. Vaughn, supra, pp. 358–59.
29. Council on Environmental Quality, final rule on preparation of environmental expert statements, 51 Fed. Reg. 15618, 15621 (April 28, 1986).
30. Ibid., pp. 15620, 15621.
31. See Cass Peterson, "Worst Case Environmental Rule Scrapped," *Washington Post*, April 28, 1986, p. A3.
32. "Risks from Multiple Chemical Exposures Not Sufficiently Known, NAS Panel Says," *Chem. Reg. Rep.* (BNA), April 3, 1981, p. 19.
33. Pat Rizzuto, "Chemicals in Consumer, Household Products Should Be Disclosed, Research Team Says," 40 *Prod. Safety & Liab. Rep.* (BNA) 311 (March 12, 2012).
34. Robin E. Dotson et al., "Endocrine Disruptors and Asthma-Associated Chemicals in Consumer Products," 120(7) *Environ. Health Persps.* 935 (2012).
35. Pat Rizzuto, supra n. 33, p. 312.

36. Patrick Ambrosio, "CDC Update Includes Exposure Data for 34 New Chemicals, Pesticides," 40 *Prod. Safety & Liab. Rep.* (BNA) 312 (March 12, 2012) (reporting on CDC, *Fourth National Report on Human Exposure to Environmental Chemicals*).
37. Christopher Drew and Jad Mouawad, "Boeing Says Jet Cracks Are Early," *New York Times*, April 6, 2011, p. B1.
38. Ibid., p. B7.
39. Essay by James Cameron, "The Precautionary Principle and International Law," p. 113 in Tim O'Riordan, James Cameron, and Andrew Jordan (eds.), *Reinterpreting the Precautionary Principle* (London: Cameron May, 2001) (hereafter, *Reinterpreting).*
40. Ibid., p. 11.
41. Ibid., p. 9.
42. See ibid., pp. 19–20.
43. Ibid., p. 23.
44. See ibid.
45. Ibid., p. 207.
46. Ibid., p. 116.
47. Ibid., p. 143.
48. This language appears in slightly different forms in "Communication from the Commission on the Precautionary Principle: Summary," paragraph 3 and Annex III, introduction paragraph (Eur-lex #52000 DC 0001, 2000).
49. "Wingspread Statement on the Precautionary Principle" (Racine, Wisconsin, Jan. 20, 1998), http://www.sehn.org/wing.html, last conulsted July 6, 2015.
50. O'Riordan et al., supra note 39, p. 78.
51. Ibid., p. 35 (summarizing arguments).
52. Professor Sunstein scolds two authors for "prefer[ring] to replace cost-benefit analysis with a European-style precautionary principle," saying that "in many contexts, that principle is worse than unhelpful: it is utterly incoherent," and pointing out that "risks are found on all sides of social situation, and risk reduction itself produces risks." He says, "It is unhelpful to say that regulators should be 'precautionary.' The real question is how precautionary to be." (Cass Sunstein, "Your Money or Your Life," *New Republic*, March 15, 2004, pp. 27 and 29–30, reviewing Frank Ackerman and Lisa Heinzerling, *Priceless: The Price of Everything and the Value of Nothing* (New Press).
53. 448 U.S. 607 (1980).
54. Ibid., p. 615.
55. Ibid., p. 613.
56. Ibid., p. 631.
57. Ibid., p. 634.
58. Ibid., p. 642.
59. Ibid., p. 658.
60. Ibid., p. 670 (Powell, J., concurring in part and concurring in the judgment).
61. Ibid., p. 672 (Rehnquist, J., concurring in the judgment).
62. Ibid., p. 676.
63. Ibid., p. 681.
64. Ibid., pp. 690 and 713 (Marshall, J., dissenting).
65. Ibid., p. 719.
66. Ibid., pp. 722–23.

67. 452 U.S. 490 (1981).
68. Ibid., p. 503.
69. Ibid., p. 506.
70. Ibid., p. 509.
71. Ibid., p. 547 (Rehnquist, J., dissenting).
72. Ibid., pp. 545–46.
73. See James K. Hammitt et al., "Precautionary Regulation in Europe and the United States: A Quantitative Comparison," 25 *Risk Analysis* 1215, 1215-16 (2005).
74. See ibid., pp. 1216 and 1218–19.
75. Ibid., p. 1227.
76. See ibid.
77. "OMB Defends Cost-Benefit Theory in Testimony Before Senate Committee," 21 *O.S.H. Rep.* (BNA) 1418 (March 25, 1992).
78. "Labor Department Says it Will Explore 'Validity' of New Risk Analysis Approach," 16 *Chem. Reg. Rep.* (BNA) 7 (April 3, 1992).
79. See 7 U.S.C. §136(bb) (the term "unreasonable adverse effects on the environment" as meaning, *inter alia*, "unreasonable risk to man or the environment, taking into account the economic, social, and environmental costs and benefits of the use of any pesticide").
80. "Benefits Assessment Miscalculated Due to Lack of Guidance, NCAMP Charges," 16 *Chem. Reg. Rep.* 16 (April 3, 1992).
81. John J. Cushman Jr., "E.P.A. Plans Radical Change in Calculation of Cancer Risk," *New York Times*, April 16, 1996.
82. Kenneth R. Hammond et al., "Improving Scientists' Judgment of Risk," 4 *Risk Analysis* No. 1, 69, at 70 (1984).
83. See ibid., pp. 72–77.
84. Charles Yablon, "The Meaning of Probability Judgments: An Essay on the Use and Misuse of Behavioral Economics," 2004 *Ill. L. Rev.* 899, 943.
85. Ibid., pp. 948–49.
86. See ibid., pp. 952–53.
87. Ibid., p. 937.
88. Ibid., pp. 938–39 (partly quoting Paul Slovic, "Trust, Emotion, Sex, Politics and Science," pp. 392–93 in Paul Slovic [ed.], *The Perception of Risk* [2000]).
89. Ibid., p. 946.
90. Ibid., pp. 965–66.
91. See Myron Fiering and Richard Wilson, "Attempts to Establish a Risk by Analogy," 3 *Risk Analysis* No. 3, at 207, 213 (1983).
92. Ibid., p. 214.
93. Ibid., p. 211.
94. Colin Camerer, "Individual Decision Making," in John H. Kagel and Alvin E. Roth (eds.), *The Handbook of Experimental Economics* (Princeton Univ. Press, 1995), pp. 587 and 674.
95. Ibid., p. 676.
96. Ibid., p. 668, citing Amos Tversky and Daniel Kahneman, "Loss Aversion in Riskless Choice: A Reference-Development Model," 106 *Quarterly J. Econs.* 1039 (1991).
97. Ibid., citing Ilona Ritov and Jonathan Baron, "Reluctance to Vaccinate: Anissian Bias and Ambiguity," 3 *J. Behav. Decision Making* 263 (1990).

98. Ibid., p. 642. Those ways are when the "EU is not so badly violated in choosing over gambles with the same set of possible outcomes . . . or with probabilities well above 0 and below 1—though it is still statistically rejectable," and "where parsimony is *very* highly valued compared to predictive accuracy (but even then EV [expected value] is often just as good").
99. Timothy McDaniels et al., "Characterizing Perception of Ecological Risk," 15 *Risk Analysis*, 575, 587 (1995).
100. William R. Freudenburg and Julie A. Rursch, "The Risks of 'Putting the Numbers in Context': A Cautionary Tale," 14 *Risk Analysis* 949, 951 (1994).
101. Ibid., p. 956.
102. See ibid., pp. 951–52.
103. Ibid., pp. 953 and 956.
104. Peter M. Sandman et al., "High Risk or Low: How Location on a 'Risk Ladder' Affects Perceived Risk," 14 *Risk Analysis* 35, 42 (1994).
105. Ibid., p. 44.
106. Thomas J. Dohmen et al., "Discussion Paper, Individual Risk Attitudes: New Evidence from a Large, Representative, Experimentally Validated Survey," Centre for Economic Policy Research, ISSSN 0265-8003, online at http:ftp.i2a.org/dp1730.pdf, offprint on p. 1.
107. Ibid., pp. 1 and 5.
108. Ibid., pp. 34–35.
109. See ibid., pp. 1 and 5.
110. Howard F. Chang, "Risk Regulation, Endogenous Public Concerns, and the Hormones Dispute: Nothing to Fear but Fear Itself?" 77 *S. Calif. L. Rev.* 743, 744 (2004).
111. See ibid., p. 774.
112. Ibid., p. 749.
113. See ibid., p. 775.
114. See ibid., pp. 745 (n.7) and 750.
115. Carl Cranor, *Regulating Toxic Substances* (Oxford Univ. Press. 1993), p. 163.
116. See ibid., pp. 168–69.
117. Ibid., p. 170.
118. Ibid., p. 175.
119. Ibid., p. 176.
120. See ibid., pp. 177–78.
121. See Thomas Henderson, "Causation in Toxic Litigation," 1 *Courts, Health Science & the Law* 331, 333 (1991).
122. See Bert Black, "A Complete Picture of Causation," 1 *Courts, Health Science & the Law* 1, 327, 327 (1991).
123. Carl Cranor, supra note 115, p. 61.
124. See ibid., p. 79.
125. See ibid., p. 62.
126. See ibid., p. 76.
127. Ibid., pp. 78 and 81–82.
128. See ibid., pp. 74 and 77.
129. See ibid., p. 79.
130. Ibid., p. 70.
131. Michael Gough, "Introduction: Science, Risk, and Politics," p. 3 in *Politicizing Science: The Alchemy of Policymaking* (Hoover Institution Press 2003).

132. Ibid., p. 6.
133. See ibid., pp. 9–13.
134. Ibid., p. 14.
135. Ibid., p. 10.
136. Lester B. Lave and Thomas Romer, "Specifying Risk Goals: Inherent Problems with Democratic Institutions," 3 *Risk Analysis* 217, 218, 226 (1983) ("we expect the controversies to intensify").
137. Ibid., p. 218.
138. Ibid., p. 220.
139. See ibid., pp. 222–25.
140. Ibid., p. 226.
141. 509 U.S. 579 (1993).
142. *Frye v. United States*, 293 F. 1013 (1923).
143. Ibid., pp. 593–94.
144. See ibid., p. 597.
145. 43 F.3d 1311, 1318 (9th Cir. 1995).
146. 522 U.S. 136 (1996).
147. Ibid., pp. 144–46.
148. *Kumho Tire Co., Ltd. v. Carmichael*, 526 U.S. 137, 142 (1999).
149. Fed. R. Evid, 702 (Westlaw 2001).
150. *Longmore v. Merrell Dow Pharmaceuticals, Inc.* 737 F.Supp. 1117, 1121 (D. Idaho 1990).
151. See *Merrell Dow Pharms. Inc. v. Havner*, 907 S.W.2d 535, 554-57 (Tex. Ct. App. 1995).
152. Ibid., p. 553.
153. *Merrell Dow Pharmaceuticals, Inc. v. Havner*, 953 S.W.2d 706, 726, 728 (Tex. 1997).
154. *Milanowicz v. Raymond Corp.*, 148 F. Supp.2d 525, 533-36 (D.N.J. 2001).
155. *Williams v. Daimler Chrysler Corp.*, 2008 WL 4449558, at 3-4 (N.D. Miss. 2008).
156. *Dow Chemical Co. v. Malhum*, 970 P.2d 98, 108-09 (Nev. 1998).
157. *Jennings v. Baxter Healthcare Corp.* 954 P.2d 829, 833 (Or. Ct. App. 1998).
158. Ibid., p. 834.
159. *Jennings v. Baxter Healthcare Corp.*, 14 P.3d 596, 608-09 (Or. 2000).
160. See *Norris v. Baxter Healthcare Corp.*, 397 F.3d 878, 884-87 (10th Cir. 2005).
161. *Hopkins v. Dow Corning Corp.* 33 F.3d 1116, 1124-25 (9th Cir. 1994).
162. See Clifford Krauss, "State Department Concedes Flaws in Investigation of Envoy," http://www.nytimes.com/1997/12/13/us/state-department-concedes-flaws-in-investigation-of-envoy.html*New York Times*, Dec. 13, 1997.
163. 52 Fed. Reg. 19466, 19468 (1987).
164. See for example Marshall S. Shapo, *Experimenting With the Consumer* (Prager 2009), pp. 38–41.
165. See for example Marshall S. Shapo, "Freud, Cocaine, and Products Liability," 72 *B.U.L. Rev.* 421, 424 (1997).
166. See Perry Cooper, "As Asbestos Litigation Enters Sixth Decade, New Approaches to an Old Problem," originally in 41 *Prod. Safety & Liab. Rep.* (BNA Bloomberg), Feb. 4, 2013.

# 10

# Different Kinds of Lawmaking: Experiments in the Workplace Environment

## A. Overview: Societal Processes for Sifting Out Facts and Philosophies of Risk

Society's oversight of mass experiments on Americans, through law, occurs in several stages and in several compartments. At any time, many kinds of investigations are going on about the risks of particular products and activities. Some are epidemiological studies, both prospective and retrospective, that investigate the possible relationship between specific illnesses and the ingestion or inhalation of certain products in particular kinds of work. Prospective studies are themselves deliberate experiments on significant numbers of people—sometimes very large numbers. Many formal studies of that kind are carried on across the country on particular products, especially drugs and devices. Generally these studies are subject to some degree of supervision by institutional review boards (IRBs), which, among other things, scrutinize the consent forms given to patients on whom products are being tested. In a much broader setting are the informal experiments that take place every day in workplaces and consumer markets, when investigators retrospectively calculate the risks and benefits of exposure to particular working conditions and to specific products.

The risks and injuries that arise from these experiments sometimes move to the foreground of the various kinds of lawmaking that bear on the many facets of our experimental society. Chief among these kinds of lawmaking is legislation, both federal and state. There are many triggers for laws designed to regulate consumer and worker safety. Sometimes the stimulus for a piece of legislation will be a discrete series of incidents involving illnesses or adverse reactions to products. We have mentioned the episode in 1937 when more than one hundred people died from Elixir Sulfanilomide, which led to the passage of the Food and Drug Act of 1938. Another is the appearance of limb defects in the children of mothers treated with the morning sickness drug thalidomide in the late 1950s, which was a principal inciting incident for passage of the Drug Amendments of 1962. Recognition of the number of deaths that could be attributed to the failure of automobiles to withstand collisions combined with a notable piece of journalism—Ralph Nader's book *Unsafe at Any Speed*—to bring the National Traffic and Motor Vehicle Safety Act into the statute books.

On occasion these laws may be fairly specific about the risks they regulate. One illustration, in which the statute names several types of risks, is the Federal Hazardous Substances Act, which specifies, among other things, products that are "toxic," "corrosive," "strong sensitizer[s]," and "flammable or combustible."[1] Often such laws cast their descriptions of the risk to be regulated or prevented in rather abstract language. The motor vehicle act defines "motor vehicle safety" to mean protection of the public "against unreasonable risk of accidents occurring as a result of the design, construction or performance of a motor vehicle" and "against unreasonable risk of death or injury to persons in an accident."[2] The "general duty" clause of the Occupational Safety and Health Act requires "each employer" to "furnish to each of his employees employment and a place of employment which are free from recognized hazards that are causing or likely to cause death or serious physical harm to his employees."[3] Writing in 1993, Carl Cranor identified no fewer than twenty-one statutes that "may be used to regulate carcinogens."[4]

## B. The Workplace As a Paradigm of Experimentation

The effects of these various constraints on experimentation differ with respect to how much they restrain harmful experimental conduct—and I stress that, drug by drug, workplace by workplace, and outdoor environment by environment, we are all frequently conducting, and having conducted upon us, experiments in risk. We may consider, as one example of the impact of safety regulation, the work of various federal agencies that deal with workplace safety. A principal decision maker in the area is the Occupational Safety and Health Administration (OSHA), which is confronted daily with mini-experiments in which employers push the margin of safety with respect to hazardous working conditions. The subject is laden with data and disputes, often politically rooted, over the interpretation of data.

A good point of departure is the one case that has gone to the Supreme Court on a dangerous condition in the workplace; the fact that there has been only one case may be symptomatic of the difficulties workers face in their attempts to limit on-the-job risk. The case, *Whirlpool Corp. v. Marshall,*[5] involved a screen welded to iron frames in Whirlpool's Marion, Ohio, manufacturing plant. The screen was used to catch objects that would otherwise fall to the floor of the plant. The mesh in one part of the screen was weak, and a maintenance employee fell though it to his death. That event resulted in an OSHA citation requiring "immediate abatement of the hazard" and a proposal of a money penalty against the employer—all of $600. It took five years for the agency to affirm that citation, and only then it gave the employer "six months to correct the unsafe condition."[6] One day two maintenance employees complained about continuing safety problems with the screen. The next day their foreman ordered them "to perform their usual maintenance duties on a section of the old screen." They refused and were sent to the personnel office, where they were told to punch out and that they would not be paid for the six hours that remained on their shift.

The case reached the Court on the question of whether the employees' "refusal to work" was justified by an OSHA regulation that permitted an employee to refuse to work when there was an immediate choice "between not performing assigned tasks or subjecting himself to serious injury or death resulting from a hazardous condition."[7] In upholding the employees' refusal, the Court referred to several sections of the OSHA statute that pertained to "imminently dangerous" workplace conditions, provisions that, among other things, allowed employees to bring suit to compel the secretary of labor to seek an injunction against the employer. Beyond its reliance on these specific provisions, the Court pitched its decision on broader language in the statute. It referred to language in the preamble to the Act that declared a purpose "to assure so far as possible every working man and woman in the Nation safe and healthful working conditions."[8] It stressed the "prophylactic" purpose of the Act. Noting that the statute did "not wait for any employee to die or become injured," the court said it would be "anomalous" to interpret the law in a way that prohibited a worker from withdrawing "from a workplace that he reasonably believes is highly dangerous." It also invoked the broad "general duty" section of the Act, quoted above.[9]

The subsequent history of the OSHA legislation is a river filled with crosscurrents of politics running through and around a range of issues that grow out of mini-experiments in worker safety, like the one in the Whirlpool plant where the foreman pushed the envelope of risks. A substantial wedge of the problem existed at the trench level of enforcement. In a statement made in a House hearing, the pro-labor Democrat George Miller charged that under the administration of George W. Bush, "OSHA's regulatory function shut down," with "only one significant health and safety standard" being promulgated during that time and the agency "significantly weakened."[10] The hearing featured a staple of such events, individual stories of deaths in the workplace—just one illustration being the case of a worker crushed under an automotive lift.[11] Against the background of an estimated four million work-related injuries annually,[12] hard numbers in the enforcement area included an average penalty for fatal accidents of only $11,000[13] and a significant decline in the number of OSHA compliance officers per million workers—from 10.2 in the administration of the first President Bush to 6.4 in 2007.[14]

A lawyer who represented industry clients sought to put the problem in comparative perspective of other sources of risk: "The data suggests you have twice as great a chance of dying in your home and six to eight times the chance of dying on the highway as in the workplace."[15] Yet, as an academic witness pointed out with a separate comparison, it was "only a 6-month misdemeanor" when a worker died from "a willful violation of safety laws," whereas when "the same employer who commits that violation goes out over the weekend and shoots a deer without a state permit" and "transports that deer across state lines, it is a 5-year felony."[16]

Another House hearing focused on the enforcement problem in the construction industry. Congresswoman Lynn Woolsey pointed out that there were "2,094 inspectors for the 8 million work sites" in the nation.[17] The acting building commissioner of New York City pointed out that in the city alone, there were "approximately 7,500 active new building construction sites and 8,000 additional major alterations," and he observed that "OSHA has a minimal number of compliance officers" who "simply cannot cover enough ground."[18] A very specific problem was accidents involving cranes. Reflecting the specialized nature of workplace problems, and of interest groups, was testimony by the executive director of the National Commission for the Certification of Crane Operators. Referring to a number of crane accidents, he noted that "only 15 states and five (5) cities require crane operators to be certified or licensed" and that "only two (2) states require crane inspectors to be licensed."[19] If one views the subjection of workers to risk as an experiment, this is a striking, if mundane, example of unsupervised experiments.

Symbolic of the tensions in enforcement was a controversy that erupted in the hearing about what one witness characterized as OSHA's refusal to rescind items in an agency compliance directive "that removed safety provisions and created unsafe working conditions for ironworkers." Just one illustrative case involved an ironworker who fell fifty-nine feet to his death on a Las Vegas construction project, when the compliance directive had eliminated a requirement of a decked floor "every two floors or 30 feet, whichever is less." A witness, brother-in-law of the deceased worker, referred to "OSHA photos of his crushed and lifeless body" in intimating that his brother-in-law would have survived if the regulation that existed before the directive had been in force.[20] Congresswoman Shelley Berkley from Las Vegas, noting the "unprecedented growth of a construction boom" there, grilled Edwin Foulke, an assistant secretary of OSHA, on the directive. Foulke said that he had advised union representatives that he "would begin to review the situation and determine what, if anything, would be done." Queried as to what his conclusion was, he replied, "We are still reviewing the information." Congresswoman Berkley's tart rejoinder was to ask, "How long is it going to take?" She declared, "I don't want to turn on my television in Las Vegas and hear that another worker at one of these sites . . . has fallen to their death."[21] To be sure, those sophisticated in the statistics of injury may say that deaths and serious injuries are a standard part of construction projects and that a single death, although worthy of journalistic notice, is just a single data point in the broad scheme of things. I simply observe that the case of this compliance directive shows that specific government regulations of workplace safety can themselves constitute experiments in data collection on injuries.

The workers suffering injuries on the job ranged across a broad arc of employment. Particularly poignant as I write in 2014, in the midst of street demonstrations following the death of two African American individuals, was a research report indicating that 16 percent of police officers "scored at or above a critical level of depression" as defined by a scale that included components "such as depressed mood, feelings of guilt, helplessness, loss of appetite, and sleep disturbance."[22] Their general conclusion was that "compared to populations of similar age," police officers had "higher reported rates of depression and PTSD."[23]

The health care environment had its own special set of risks. Medical interns, long viewed as a source of fatigue-related accidents, had significantly greater risks of needlestick injuries and lacerations "associated with extended work duration and nighttime shifts."[24] Specifically with reference to extended hours, the rate of such injuries was 1.31 per one thousand opportunities for such injuries as against 0.76 for non-extended work.[25]

A crucial question about the facts of workplace accidents concerns the accuracy of the count of injuries. A physician who is also an epidemiologist testified at a 2008 hearing that "there is no disagreement in the medical literature that an undercount exists and that this undercount is significant." He referred to research of his own indicating that "the current system misses 66 percent of work-related injuries and illnesses in Michigan." He also cited a study that concluded, as he summarized it, "the current system misses 33 to 69 percent of all non-fatal work-related injuries" and another estimate, based on data from six states. that "the current system misses up to 50 percent of non-fatal work-related injuries and illnesses."[26] A counter to these estimates came from a lawyer representing the U.S. Chamber of Commerce, who suggested that there was disagreement over "the subjective area of pain" and the complexity of a "recording scheme that has 46 sections and 200 pages of frequently asked questions"—although he insisted that "the steadily declining injury rates provided by OSHA and the Bureau of Labor Statistics are and must be substantially reliable."[27]

The next year, the General Accounting Office issued its own conclusion that underreporting was a constant feature of the landscape of workplace injuries. One explanation given by the GAO report was, as a journalist summarized it, employer reluctance to "avoid reporting workplace injuries and illnesses for fear of jeopardizing workers compensation premium discounts." Another was a reluctance on the part of workers who feared being fired or didn't "want to let their co-workers down by losing rewards for maintaining safety."[28] Reports of undercounting led the Bureau of Labor Statistics to announce an effort to improve its surveys of injuries and illnesses. A BLS official noted, among other things, the difficulties of "counting long-term work-related illnesses."[29]

A Senate hearing brought into the spotlight the contrast between penalties for workplace safety violations and for violations of other regulatory schemes. Senator Kennedy, chairing the hearing, contrasted the $320,000 penalty for violation of the South Pacific Tuna Act with the $70,000 penalty for causing a workplace fatality.[30] Margaret Seminario of the AFL-CIO referred to what appeared to be a focal set of incidents for members of Congress: the deaths of ten workers at Las Vegas construction sites, pointing out that penalties that had "started out at $7,000" were "reduced to zero—zero—in these workers' deaths."[31]

An interesting feature of this hearing, which was titled, "When a Worker is Killed: Do OSHA Penalties Enhance Workplace Safety?" is that most of the conclusions in the testimony were basically inferential. It appears that it was difficult, if not entirely impossible, to get empirical data on the question. However, the witnesses referred constantly to examples of lenient enforcement, suggesting that the answer to the question posed for the hearing was no—that OSHA penalties were not strong enough to enhance worker safety.[32]

One of the most precise causal linkages appeared in testimony by David Uhlmann of the University of Michigan, who summarized the "net result" as "a worker safety program where most violators—even willful violators—will face only administrative violations and relatively modest penalties if they are cited." His conclusion was that this state of affairs made it "easy for companies to put profits before compliance and to view any penalties that may result as a 'cost of doing business.'"[33]

Reinforcing the point was Ms. Seminario's argument that there was "nothing in the law" indicating "that there are really serious consequences for actions that put workers in danger." She concluded that "there is no message."[34] A freshman senator from Illinois, Barack Obama, underlined the argument. He said that "slap[s] on the wrist" and the "slash[ing]" of fines for employers "invite employers to cut costs, even if it means putting their employees' lives at risk, with the assurance that the watchdog agency will not bite."[35]

An interesting coda to these statements came from a Republican senator, Johnny Isakson of Georgia, who cited his experience in running "a company for 33 years" and his recognition, every morning when he got up, that "if I had an accident or I had a worker hurt, it was not in the best interest of the worker, but it sure as heck was not in the best interest of the company either." What was noteworthy was that, in a way that might sound naïve to sophisticated analysts of accident data, this Republican legislator declared that his goal was "to accelerate" "to 0" the rate of accidents to one hundred thousand full-time-equivalent employees.[36]

Thus, zero deaths, an unattainable grail in many medical experiments, became a goal at least in political discussion of the ongoing experiment with worker safety.

We have noted that on occasion, the sympathetic presentation of a single fatality or a few deaths may seem to have a disproportionate effect on risk analysis in the political world. Yet a remark by Congressman John Sarbanes at the hearing captures an important ethical issue of policy wrapped up in many cases of broad experimentation: "My impression is that there is a certain dimension of viewing this workforce as kind of a disposable workforce."[37]

A specialized workplace problem of considerable quantitative importance involves employers with plants scattered across the country. A House hearing in 2008 focused in large part on Cintas, "the largest uniform supplier in North America with more than 400 facilities, employing more than 43,000 people."[38] A central incident discussed in the hearing involved the death of a washroom employee dragged by a conveyor into a drier that "continued to operate for 20 minutes at 300 degrees before he was discovered."[39] There was evidence that both the company and OSHA were aware of hazards of the sort involved in the worker's death but that no initiatives were taken to eliminate those risks at the facility where it occurred.[40] One congressman said he was "appalled" at the "total lack of responsibility" taken by the company for the accident.[41]

An interesting feature of the testimony at this hearing, which I discovered after initially writing what I did above about a lack of empirical data, was a statement by Randy Rabinowitz, a lawyer who represented unions. She said that there was "very limited empirical evidence" on the question of whether "OSHA enforcement works better than voluntary programs" and said that "OSHA spends a lot of money on something they don't know whether it is working or not."[42]

Other testimony exhibited controversy on what worked and what didn't. An official of an international consulting firm said that even multi-site "companies that work diligently to comply with OHSA standards will not necessarily have an effective process for assuring that findings of non-compliance in one facility will be made known across the organization and addressed at other facilities."[43] By analogy, one may at least raise the question of how much uniformity of practices exists in multi-institution investigations of medical products. In another medical arena, an analogy appears in the much-discussed question of standards for the prevention of infection in thousands of hospitals. A counterpart is the great differentials in the frequency of performance of certain kinds of surgical procedures. The variation of practice in many areas of activity is a facet of our daily, countrywide experimentation on human beings.

A different rendering of the workplace environment appeared in testimony of a lawyer who represented employers in occupational safety cases. He pointed out that as of the time of the 2008 hearing, workplace fatalities were "roughly one-third" of their pre-OSHA number.[44] He declared that with respect to "multiple employers who are operating at multiple sites," "the present act and the tools OSHA has developed over its 37 years of existence are adequate to assure that the statutory goal is met and that while not perfect . . . we are working towards that goal."[45]

These pieces of workplace history and the diverse conclusions that various witnesses draw from them are simply illustrative of the constant process of setting the parameters of workplace experimentation with safety. This is a process that occurs in the context of considerations of profit margins, public relations, and politics, and it includes public perceptions of issues with humanitarian elements.

While the images of worker injuries that may have been uppermost in the minds of the members of Congress who voted for the OSHA legislation may have been those of broken bones and mangled limbs, a growing problem has been that of illness attributable to substances used in the workplace. By 1990, a group of researchers were summarizing data on such illnesses as asbestos-caused disease, silicosis—which they described as "the most prevalent chronic occupational disease in the world and stubbornly resistant to eradication in the United States"—and on a "broad array of natural and synthesized chemicals" with potential for causing asthmatic conditions. They also referred to the identification of organic solvents as "potentially important causes of acute and chronic glomerular disease," an inflammation of the kidneys that degrades their ability to remove wastes from the body. Moreover, they instanced then-recent research on "a strong linear dose-response relation between benzene and leukemia."[46]

A companion article, which swept more broadly over different kinds of hazards and different kinds of physical effects, displayed the experimental character of chemicals to which workers are exposed. With respect to neurological problems, the authors' review of the literature concluded that "almost a decade of prodigious effort has not yielded clear answers about the pattern and extent of solvent-induced neurologic dysfunction." However, they said, "Putting all the discrepant facts together, it seems most prudent to presume that repeated and heavy exposure to solvents can lead to chronic neuropsychological dysfunction, which may become irreversible in patients who are not removed from exposure soon after the onset of symptoms."[47]

The theme of a lack of data, so characteristic of the experimental society, appeared in their statement that with respect to endocrine and reproductive effects of chemicals, "adequate information exists only for a handful of agents." However, despite the limitations of the data, they found "some credible associations," including depressed sperm counts related to exposure to lead and carbon disulfide, a solvent, and a "predict[ed]" "likelihood" of effects on sperm from "a variety of other solvents . . . pesticides . . . metals, and alkylating agents."[48]

Data on causation of cancer were "mixed," with "newer estimates of the total influence of workplace exposure on the U.S. cancer rate" ranging from 4 to 10 percent. Again reflecting the unexplored nature of the terrain, research on patterns of disease in a number of industries "demonstrated the elevated risk of certain cancers in identified populations without revealing the causal factor or factors."[49] Another puzzle lay in the problem of "multiple chemical sensitivities," where, once more, data were "sparse" and although there was "real controversy," the authors said that "most practitioners remain unaware of the problem or are skeptical, and little constructive investigation has been reported."[50] However, at that point the authors suggested that public fears about one product associated with public "dread of the chemical environment" might have been exaggerated. This was the defoliant Agent Orange used in Vietnam. Findings that were "far from definitive" indicated that "other than a possible excess of soft-tissue sarcoma or lymphoma, neither cancer nor any other cause of death seems to be occurring in excess."[51]

For good measure, beyond chemical hazards, the authors briefly summarized the literature on musculoskeletal stresses. With specific reference to carpal tunnel syndrome, the sum of studies using "quantified biochemical measures and videotaped documentation of work practice" was that "force, repetition and vibration" were "the most relevant occupational risks."[52]

Emphasizing the difficulties in minimizing industrial illness is the case of hexavalent chromium, which was identified by the California Air Resources Board in 1986 as a "human carcinogen for which there is no safe threshold exposure level."[53] Yet it was not until 2006 that the Department of Labor, responding to a court order, announced that it would order a standard for worker exposure to the chemical—a statement accompanied by predictions that the standard would "spark a number of lawsuits."[54]

Graphic stories abounded on industrial accidents as well as illnesses. OSHA officials with on-the-ground experience told of incidents involving construction accidents that would be data points in a study of the ongoing set of experiments that are the workplace. One example involved a worker with a blood alcohol level of .09 who fell from a forklift that was improperly being used as a personnel elevator. Other cases involved unauthorized modifications to a crane, including the addition of "a homemade counterweight and homemade jib that was overbuilt at 26 feet," with the result that the hydraulic cylinder on the crane failed, and the jump-starting of a grader that violated two sets of warnings. These cases and others involving workplace violations could be registered in the category of "equipment misuse, unauthorized structural modifications, improper training or lack of experience."[55]

Paralleling the direct regulation of OSHA with respect to workplace injuries is the indirect regulation provided by civil tort suits for products liability against makers of workplace machines. As indicated above, incident reports under OSHA indicate that misuse of equipment is a recurrent cause of injuries to workers. There are many decisions on the topic, with varying results. We note two interesting pairs of cases.

A Montana case involved a "trained and licensed groundman," Gerald Lutz, and his supervisor, a crane operator, who were trying to retrieve drilling pipe that had spilled from a semi-trailer. They had discussed the potential for electrocution in the process they were using, and they set up a board "to delineate between the safe and unsafe 'pick' areas." Unfortunately, this precaution failed when a taut, uninsulated crane cable, "apparently no longer directly beneath the tip of the crane's boom, contacted [a] power line," conducting "electricity from the power line to the pipe" and electrocuting Lutz.

The maker of the crane argued that that Lutz had misused the crane "by sideloading, or dragging the load, from beneath the power lines." However, the Montana Supreme Court relied on the concept of "reasonably foreseeable misuse" in rejecting this defense. It noted that there "really [was] no factual disagreement that cranes are often operated in close proximity to live electrical lines and that, as the evidence here indicates, sideloading is a not an uncommon, albeit improper, practice of crane operators and groundcrews." It further noted that there were "2,300 crane/power line contacts in the United States each year" and that "crane/power line electrocutions are the fifth leading cause of work-related deaths in the United States." Moreover, it pointed out that the crane maker "admit[ted] that the cranes which it manufactures can be misused through sideloading" and knew "that if sideloading occurs in the vicinity of power lines, the possibility exists that its crane cables might contact power lines." Having observed that insulated cable links were "readily available and . . . commonly used," the court concluded that "as a matter of law, the affirmative defense of unreasonable misuse is unavailable to" the defendant.[56]

A contrast appears in a Fifth Circuit decision holding against a car owner who sued an automaker for injuries that occurred when a tire jack provided by the defendant collapsed on him while he was under the vehicle. There were two warnings in documents—including one in the owner's manual provided by the defendant—not to go beneath the car. Reversing a panel decision that favored the plaintiff, a majority of the full appellate court undertook a complicated linguistic analysis of the concept of "use" as applied to the jack. It concluded that the plaintiff had not produced evidence that his "use of the jack in contravention of a warning was nonetheless reasonably anticipated" and that thus he had not met his burden "to show that [his] damage arose from a reasonably anticipated use of the jack."[57] The court was at pains to point out that its holding did "not mean that an adequate warning will *always* be dispositive of reasonably anticipated use" but emphasized that "merely because" the state products liability act "includes an adequate warning as one ingredient in the 'unreasonably dangerous design' test does not mean that a court is precluded from considering an adequate warning in relation to other areas of the Act." It said that its holding meant "only that a warning against a product *misuse* is relevant to assessing what uses of its product a manufacturer reasonably anticipates" and that "when, in the face of such a warning, a plaintiff presents no evidence about whether the manufacturer should have reasonably expected users to disregard the warning, the plaintiff fails to meet the burden imposed on him" by the state statute.[58]

Paralleling these doctrinal arguments about foreseeability of particular uses of products are disputes that arise when a product manufacturer claims that alterations or other unintended uses of its product, rather than its design of the product, are responsible for an injury. The Fifth Circuit reversed a summary judgment for a firm that made a top drive system used on an offshore drilling vessel on which the plaintiff's crew was trying to change a valve. In the course of these efforts, during which an obstacle to success was a frozen shaft connection, the crew used a set of tongs that were pulled beyond their rated capacity and which failed, with the result that a piece of the tongs broke off and injured the plaintiff. The maker of the top drive system, which had denied that it was negligent, argued that "even if the connection was overtorqued as a result of" its negligence, "the accident occurred not because of the overtorqued connection but because" the senior toolpusher of the plaintiff's employer "knowingly chose to exceed the rated capacity of the tongs." The maker of the drive system offered testimony by the toolpusher that at his instruction, "the tongs were pulled in excess of their rated capacity and the tongs broke because they were 'stressed out.'" Although the court said that the toolpusher's testimony might "support the conclusion that the negligence of" of the employer and the owner of the drilling vessel "contributed to the accident which led to [the plaintiff's] injuries," it concluded that evidence was "insufficient to establish, as a matter of law, that [the drive maker's] actions were not a legal cause of [the plaintiff's] injuries." It also noted that there was "a fact question as to causation because" of evidence indicating "that the events that led to [the plaintiff's] injuries were placed into motion only after" a connection made by the top drive froze, "and the [employer's] crew attempted to break it."[59]

By contrast, the Seventh Circuit turned down a claim by a worker who sued Caterpillar for injuries that occurred when he was using a forklift on which a dealer had placed a deadman's switch that was not on the machine when Caterpillar sold it to the dealer. In denying recovery, the court emphasized that the switch, which the dealer added to the machine at the request of the plaintiff's employer, had been "placed into the stream of commerce by [the dealer] after [the dealer] had substantially altered the forklift truck and subsequently delivered it to" the employer. Premising that "liability depends upon foreseeability," the court opined that the addition of the switch was a "substantial change" or "alteration" of the product that exonerated the maker of the forklift.[60]

Holdings of this sort, on the foreseeability of particular types of uses and the effect of additions to products after their original design and sale, are micro-responses of the court system to the efforts of product users to push the frontiers of product capacity: mini-experiments on the job. We note that those users include both corporations and individuals like the man who got under the jacked-up car.

Besides tort suits, another parallel to OSHA as a legal mechanism bearing on workplace accidents is workers' compensation. This giant system provides more than $50 billion per year in payments for workplace injuries, without requiring a showing of fault on the part of employers and not allowing reference to the carelessness of employees. The compensation function of workers' compensation is clear, but whether the existence of the system affects the frequency and severity of workplace accidents is not. There is relatively little data on the question. A study published in 1980 concluded, with reference to the hypothesis that employees systematically underestimate hazards on the job, that "we still do not know whether imposing workers' compensation reduces that underestimate, leaves it unchanged, or increases it."[61]

Data on the effects of workers' compensation on employee behavior mirrored the complexities and uncertainties of the evidence about employers. One study found that states that paid at least as many benefits as those recommended by the National Commission on State Workmen's Compensation Laws had higher rates of accident but lower rates of severity of injury than states that did not have that level of benefits.[62] A contemporaneous study indicated that although it was "generally true" that increases in workers' compensation benefits "will increase safety investments," there were several situations in which increases in benefits either had no effect on safety investments or even were associated with decreases in such investments. Those situations included periods of rapid inflation in the price of safety investments and payments of significant premiums for hazardous work.[63] Another article, published in 1989, suggested that "if [workers' compensation] benefits were nonexistent, the average fatality rate would rise by 1.5 per 100,000 workers, or an increase of 22%."[64] The authors concluded, "Workers' compensation represents so far the most influential government program for reducing workplace fatalities." They also asserted that "complaints voiced by firms with respect to escalating workers' compensation premiums may be overstated, since they neglect the substantial wage offset resulting both from the risk reduction induced by workers' compensation and the trade-offs workers make between *ex post* insurance compensation and *ex ante* wage compensation."[65]

We may conclude that if one viewed the law's treatment of workplace injuries as a series of clinical experiments, the data about the effects of the law would leave social planners with a significant degree of uncertainty about what revisions, if any, should be made to the workers' compensation regime.

## Notes

1. 15 U.S.C.A., §1261(f)(1)(A),
2. 49 U.S.C.A. § 30102(8).
3. U.S.C.A. § 654(a)(1).
4. Carl Cranor, *Regulating Toxic Substances* (Oxford, 1993), p. 104.

5. 445 U.S. 1 (1980).
6. See ibid., p. 6, n. 4.
7. The regulation then was 29 CFR §1977.12, quoted in 445 U.S. at 4 n.3.
8. 29 U.S.C.A. § 651(b).
9. See ibid., pp. 12–13, referring to § 29 U.S.C.A. § 654(a)(1), which is quoted above, in the text accompanying note 3.
10. "Are OSHA's Penalties Adequate to Deter Health and Safety Violations?" Hearing before the Committee on Education and Labor, House of Representatives, Serial No. 111-16, 111th Cong., 1st Sess. (April 28, 2009), at 2.
11. See ibid., p. 24.
12. See ibid., p. 30 (prepared statement of Margaret Seminario, AFL-CIO director of safety and health).
13. Ibid., p. 29 (statement of Seminario).
14. See table, ibid., p. 38.
15. Ibid., p. 43, statement of Lawrence P. Halprin.
16. Ibid., p. 49, statement of David M. Uhlmann, director of the Environmental Law and Policy Program, University of Michigan Law School.
17. "Is OSHA Failing to Adequate Enforce Construction Safety Rules?" Hearing Before the Committee on Education and Labor, Serial No. 110-98, 110th Cong., 2d Sess., p. 5 (hereafter, "Is OSHA Failing?").
18. Ibid., p. 24, testimony of Robert Limandri.
19. Ibid., p. 9, testimony of Graham J. Brent.
20. See ibid., p. 20–22, testimony of George Cole.
21. See ibid., pp. 55–56, exchange between Congresswoman Berkley and Edwin Foulke.
22. John M. Volanti et al., "The Buffalo Radio-Metabolic Occupational Police Stress (BCOPS) Pilot Study: Methods and Participant Characteristics," 16 *Ann. Epidemiol.* 148, 154 (2005).
23. Ibid., p. 148 (abstract ).
24. Najib T. Ayas et al., "Extended Work Duration and the Risk of Self-Reported Percutaneous Injuries in Interns," 296 *JAMA* 1055,1061 (2006).
25. Ibid., p. 1059.
26. Testimony of Kenneth Rosenman in "Hidden Tragedy: Underreporting of Workplaces Injuries and Illnesses," hearing Before the Committee on Education & Labor, pp. 30–31, Serial No. 110-97 (2008).
27. Testimony of Baruch Fellner, ibid., pp. 24–25. Indeed, workplace deaths had been declining—in 2009 to 4,551, down from 5,214 in 2008, and at a rate of 3.5 deaths for every one hundred thousand workers, the fourth consecutive year of decline in that rate. See Bruce Rolfsen, "Fatality Rate at All-Time Low for 2009: Transport Accidents Claimed Most Lives," 41 *OSH L. Rep.* 441 (May 19, 2011).
28. See Jeff Casale, "GAO Faults OSHA's Workplace Injury Data Collection System," *Business Insurance*, Nov. 23, 2009, p. 4. There also was testimony from railroad workers that they had been harassed and intimidated, and sometimes even fired, after reporting injuries. See Ellen Byerrum, "Workers Tell House Panel of Injuries Followed by Harassment, Intimidation," 37 *OSH L. Rep.* 967 (Nov. 1, 2007).
29. See Michael Rose, "BLS Plans to Study Disconnect Between Injury Data, Workers' Compensation Data," 39 *OSH L. Rep.* 1004 (Nov. 26, 2009).

30. "When a Worker Is Killed: Do OSHA Penalties Enhance Workplace Safety?" Hearing of the Senate Committee on Health, Education, Labor and Pensions, 110th Cong. 2d Sess. (April 29, 2008), p. 3.
31. See ibid., pp. 12–13, testimony of Seminario.
32. One set of examples is that presented by Seminario, ibid., pp. 14–19. In 2006, an official of an international human resources firm suggested that OSHA had fallen behind in the worldwide experiment with workplace safety. See Ellen Byerrum, "OSHA Has Become Secondary Player in Global Job Safety Issue, White Says," 36 *OSH L. Rep.* 453-54 (May 18, 2006).
33. Ibid., p. 31, testimony of David Uhlmann.
34. Ibid., p. 47, testimony of Seminario.
35. Ibid., p. 56, statement of Obama.
36. See ibid., p. 8, statement of Isakson.
37. Hearing, "Is OSHA Failing?" supra note 17, p. 50, remarks of Representative Sarbanes.
38. "Improving Workplace Safety: Strengthening OSHA Enforcement of Multi-Site Employers," hearing before the Subcommittee on Workforce Protections of the House Committee on Education and Labor, 110th Cong. 2d Sess., Serial No. 110-88 (April 23, 2008), p. 2.
39. See ibid., p. 1.
40. See ibid., p. 2.
41. See ibid., p. 7, Congressman Hare.
42. Ibid., p. 68, statement of Randy Rabinowitz.
43. Ibid., p. 40, statement of Frank A.White.
44. Ibid., p. 43, testimony of Ron Taylor.
45. Ibid., p. 44.
46. See Mark R. Cullen et al., "Medical Progress: Occupational Medicine (First of Two Parts)," 322 *N. Eng. J. Med.* 594, 595-96, 598-99 (1990).
47. Mark L. Cullen et al., "Medical Progress: Occupational Medicine (Second of Two Parts)," 322 *N. Eng. J. Med.* 675, 675 (1990).
48. See ibid., p. 676.
49. See ibid., pp. 677–79.
50. See ibid., pp. 680–81.
51. See ibid., pp. 679–80.
52. Ibid., p. 677.
53. California Air Resources Board, "Hexavalent Chromium Regulatory History," http://arb.ca.gov/toxics/chrome/history.htm last updated June 17, 2004, last checked on the Internet July 3, 2015.
54. See "Court-Ordered Hexavalent Chromium Rule to be Issued in 2006 After Delays," *O.S.H. Rep.* (BNA), Jan. 12, 2006, p. S-5.
55. See "Misuse, Modifications, Misconceptions Often Lead to Heavy Machinery Accidents," 35 *O.S.H. Rep.* (BNA) 165 (Feb. 24, 2005).
56. *Lutz v. National Crane Corp.*, 884 P.2d 455, 457-60 (Mont. 1994).
57. See *Kampen v. American Isuzu Motors, Inc.* 157 F.3d 306, 318 (5th Cir.1998)
58. Ibid., p. 314.
59. *Donaghey v. Ocean Drilling & Exploration Co.* 974 F.2d 646, 650-51 (5th Cir.1992).
60. *Leon v. Caterpillar Indus., Inc.*, 69 F.3d 1326, 1338-41 (7th Cir.1995).

61. Linda Darling-Hammond and Thomas J. Kniesner, *The Law and Economics of Workers' Compensation* (Rand R-2716-ICJ, 1980), p. 59.
62. See Chelius, "The Influence of Workers' Compensation on Safety Incentives," 35 *Indus. & Labor Relations Rev.* 235, 242 (1982).
63. Richard B. Victor, Linda R. Cohen, and Charles E. Phelps, *Workers' Compensation and Workplace Safety* (Rand R-2918-ICJ 1983), p. 50.
64. Michael J. Moore and W. Kip Viscusi, "Promoting Safety Through Workers' Compensation: The Efficacy and Net Worth of Injury Insurance," 20 *Rand J. Econs.* 499, 511 (1989).
65. Ibid., p. 513.

# 11

# Different Kinds of Lawmaking: Consumer Products and Other By-Products

The vast experiments on workers in diverse workplaces have counterparts in the wide world of consumer products and in the overlapping worlds of the highway and the broad environment. Efforts to deal through law with injuries caused by these experiments have included safety legislation and legislative proposals aimed at compensation, and lawsuits seeking payment for injury—the latter sometimes generating collisions between private law and safety legislation.

## I. Products That Are Ingested or Have Close Contact With the Body

### *A. Cigarettes*

We literally consume a great number of products and encounter many more by direct physical contact. In the statistics of illness and death, perhaps the most quantitatively important products in the categories of products literally consumed or involving direct contact are tobacco products, principally cigarettes. We reviewed the numbers of deaths caused by cigarettes in Chapter Three.[1]

Congress has attacked the toll of cigarettes in at least three different major statutes, starting with efforts to convey information about the hazards of smoking and eventually progressing to some regulatory measures. The Cigarette Labeling and Advertising Act of 1965 made it illegal to sell cigarettes without the package warning "Caution: Cigarette Smoking May Be Hazardous to Your Health."[2] The 1969 legislation substituted the words "Is Dangerous" for the words "May Be Hazardous"[3] and broadly prohibited any "requirement or prohibition based on smoking and health" from being "imposed under State law with respect to the advertising or promotion of any cigarettes the packages of which are labeled in conformity" with the legislation.[4] An important regulatory provision banned cigarette advertising on radio and TV. [5]

These statutes propelled the Supreme Court into the thicket of the law of federal preemption, specifically with reference to the question of whether their terms barred state law tort actions for cigarette-caused illness. As noted above, a four-member plurality of the Court concluded that the 1965 law "did not pre-empt state law damages actions."[6] However, the plurality opinion sliced the statutory language of the 1969 law more thinly, saying that it preempted products liability claims for failure to warn, to the extent that the plaintiffs argued that the defendants' "post-1969 advertising or promotions should have included additional, or more clearly stated, warnings."[7] At the same time, Justice Stevens's opinion for the plurality said that the 1969 act did not bar suits based on intentional misstatements, and that therefore the plaintiffs could sue for "express warranty, intentional fraud and misrepresentation, or conspiracy,"[8] a view fully backed by three other members of the Court who thought that Congress had not intended to preempt any state law damages suits.[9]

An event of great quantitative importance was the conclusion in 1998 of a private agreement labeled the Master Settlement Agreement. The signatories were forty-six state attorneys general and the four major makers of cigarettes, which promised to pay $206 billion to the states over a twenty-five-year period in exchange for the states dropping lawsuits they had brought against the companies. As two authors summarized it, the payments represented "compensation for the additional cost that state Medicaid programs had allegedly incurred for treatment of Medicaid recipients with smoking-related diseases and as a penalty for deceptive trade practices" of the cigarette makers. Among other things, the agreement "dissolved the Tobacco Institute and other organizations promoting industry interests, prohibited advertising directed to youths, and provided for the release of industry documents that were previously inaccessible to the public."[10]

In 2009, Congress focused its regulatory guns to target sales to people under eighteen.[11] That statute set a federal minimum age of eighteen for sales of tobacco products, and, as the FDA summarized it, "limit[ed] [the] color and design of packaging and advertisements, including audio-visual advertisements" and banned "free samples of cigarettes and brand-name non-tobacco promotional items." The law also required larger type in warning labels and limited font colors to white and black, required warnings "to cover the top 50 percent of both the front and rear panels of the package," and set out nine specific warning messages that had to be "equally and randomly displayed and distributed in all areas of the United States," along with "color graphics showing the negative health consequences of smoking cigarettes."[12]

The majority of a divided panel of the DC Circuit concluded that nine images selected by the FDA violated the First Amendment. As an example of images that "could be misinterpreted by consumers," the court chose an image of a man smoking through a tracheotomy hole, which the majority said "might be misinterpreted as suggesting that such a procedure is a common consequence of smoking—a more logical interpretation than FDA's contention that it symbolizes 'the addictive nature of cigarettes,' which requires significant extrapolation on the part of the consumers." The majority added that "the graphic warnings are not 'purely' factual because—as FDA tacitly admits—they are primarily intended to evoke an emotional response, or, at most, shock the viewer into retaining the information in the text warning." Moreover, it said that the graphic warnings not only limited "the Companies' ability to advertise, but also . . . forc[ed] the Companies to bear the cost of disseminating an anti-smoking message." For good measure, the majority pointed out that "many of the images do not convey any warning information at all, much less make an 'accurate statement' about cigarettes." It said that "images of a woman crying, a small child, and the man wearing a T-shirt emblazoned with the words 'I QUIT' do not offer any information about the health effects of smoking." The majority concluded that the images could not "rationally be viewed as pure attempts to convey information to consumers" but rather that they were "unabashed attempts to evoke emotion (and perhaps embarrassment) and browbeat consumers into quitting." Its premise for material that would be constitutional apparently requires images that "impart purely factual, accurate, or uncontroversial information to consumers."[13]

A further dimension of the continued experiment that tobacco companies were conducting on the American people, without giving them full information about health hazards, appeared in the causation questions that arose from the combination of smoking and workplace exposure to substances with potential carcinogenic effects. A powerful judicial pronouncement on this question appeared in a California Supreme Court decision that awarded workers' compensation to a fireman who smoked, in a case in which his governmental employers argued that he should not get compensation, because he smoked.

There was testimony by the fireman's wife that "he had suffered terrible coughing spells, and that he had complained about the smoke that he had inhaled at . . . fires," and by another firefighter that "he had seen decedent affected by smoke many times and that he had observed him being carried out of a burning building in a semiconscious condition." A medical witness for the claimant testified that "smoke from burning tar or creosote 'may well' contain the same type of carcinogen found in cigarette smoke," and another medical witness said that "many of the carcinogens found in 'air pollution'" are "produced by almost any type of incomplete combustion of almost any product." Moreover, the court summarized testimony by the other firefighter as saying that "the fires which decedent fought involved creosote."

Ruling against the claimant, the workers' compensation appeals board concluded that there was not enough "evidence as to the toxicity of the smoke inhaled or as to the amount of decedent's exposure to smoke" and that the claimant "had not adduced a satisfactory and detailed showing of the manner in which smoke inhalation may cause lung cancer." Rejecting these arguments, the supreme court declared that although in the future it might "be possible to pinpoint with certainty the cause of each case of the disease," the legislature, in enacting the workers' compensation law, "did not contemplate years of" harm without compensation "pending such scientific certainty." It concluded that it was "bound to uphold a claim in which the proof of industrial causation is reasonably probable, although not certain or 'convincing' . . . even though the exact causal mechanism is unclear or even unknown."[14]

### *B. Asbestos*

*1. The plague.* Asbestos has produced an enormous reservoir of the illness caused by substances to which people are exposed in both the workplace and the broader consumer environment. Incidentally in the case of asbestos, both of those environments are places where the probability of illness is heightened by the smoking of cigarettes.

The first "data set" on the long-running human experiment with asbestos appears as early as the first century in reports of lung disease associated with asbestos exposure.[15] If one skips almost two millennia, companies increasingly began to discern uses for this "magic mineral"—thousands of industrial and commercial uses, many of them tied to the resistance of asbestos to fire and others linked to its ability to absorb and to filter.[16]

Along with those uses came medical evidence of the fact that asbestos caused a variety of diseases. Modern reports of those linkages emerged in the late nineteenth century, and by the 1920s there appeared in Great Britain a substantial literature on a particular disease: asbestosis. By 1935, a medical school professor in South Carolina had tied a case of cancer to asbestos.[17] By 1955, the distinguished British epidemiologist Richard Doll, using 113 autopsies of men exposed to asbestos for more than twenty years, found that they had a risk of lung cancer that was eleven times that "of men in the general population of England and Wales."[18]

The ubiquity of asbestos in both the workplace and the general environment is remarkable. At a Senate hearing in 2007, an NYU medical professor summarized a range of statistics in declaring that "23 million Americans have been occupationally exposed to asbestos in the last 50 years and are now at risk for health problems."[19] This paralleled a prediction in a remarkable study published in 1982 by William J. Nicholson, George Perkel, and Irving Selikoff, which became known as the "Nicholson study." These authors estimated that the population "potentially exposed to asbestos" from 1940 to 1979 that could be counted "at risk" was 27,500,000.[20] Paralleling that statistic was a finding that by 1960, "asbestos bodies" had been found in one quarter of five hundred autopsies of "ordinary urban dweller[s]," a number theorized to be due to various exposures in city life, including fragments from brake linings of vehicles.[21]

Let us imagine that mass tryouts of products on consumers are viewed as akin to clinical experimentation, requiring a kind of informed consent. In this hypothetical universe, with the amount of consumer information about hazards serving as a rough surrogate for choices freely made to confront risk, there often would be little in the way of choice for workers and consumers. Just illustrative is testimony of a worker at a medical college where there was asbestos in the air. He said that he and his coworkers did not know "what asbestos was; they simply called it dust."[22] Another example, especially pathetic because of its grounding in a recreational environment, features "the baseball diamonds and piles of vermiculite"—a mineral that was often contaminated with asbestos—that surrounded the "expanding plant" of the W. R. Grace Company in Libby, Montana. One resident, who said she "watched games there, my children played there," recalled that "the children who were too young to play baseball used to play beyond the outfield in the piles of vermiculite there." She said, "It was worse even than the ballfields. It was filled with asbestos dust."[23]

2. *Lawsuits.* As attorneys for sufferers from asbestos disease began digging into the industrial history of the fiber, they produced one of the legal sagas of the last century. Originating with a lawsuit filed in Texas in 1969[24] came an avalanche of litigation that continues still. Up to 2002, it was estimated that 730,000 suits had been filed for asbestos-caused illness,[25] and one estimate of litigation yet to be filed brought the total figure to as many as two million lawsuits by the middle of this century.[26] The impact of this wave of lawsuits has been profound. By 2004, seventy-three companies had been driven into bankruptcy by asbestos claims, with a study published in that year reporting, "Bankruptcy is more common today than in the past, with as many new petitions filed in the 2000s as were filed in the previous two decades combined."[27] One of the saddest statistics in this story was that claimants' net compensation of about $30 billion through 2002 was only "about 42 percent of total spending on asbestos litigation through that year."[28]

There was a significant increase in asbestos litigation—variously described as an "explos[ion]" and a "spike"—in the years bridging the turn of the century.[29] By 2002 two commentators wrote that "the asbestos litigation system nearly collapsed" with "the perfection of screening techniques and increasingly sophisticated forum shopping" by claimants' lawyers.[30]

3. *Proposed compensation legislation.* The results of this tide of lawsuits might be described as a legal experiment following what in retrospect was a disastrous mass-market experiment. The reverberations of asbestos litigation generated pressure on Congress to craft a solution to a problem that included elements of unfairness both to companies struggling with litigation and to workers who were undercompensated or not compensated at all. The principal proposed solution, first introduced in Congress in 2003, was the Fairness in Asbestos Injury Resolution (FAIR) Act, which has been summarized as "creat[ing] a privately financed national fund to compensate asbestos claimants and keep asbestos litigation out of the courts."[31] Supporters of the proposed legislation, drafted in various versions, grappled for more than three years with a cluster of different interests until the bills became doomed not only "by the vicissitudes of politics" but also by "substantive issues inherent in any effort to replace the tort system with an administrative compensation system."[32]

*4. Ongoing issues in litigation.* As efforts to fashion legislation that would attract congressional majorities ground on, plaintiffs' lawyers continued their search for solvent pockets that could plausibly be tied to asbestos-caused illness. One extension of this search was suits by people whose exposure to asbestos was relatively indirect but who could still produce evidence of devastating impacts of disease. The results in court of these types of cases have varied. A federal court of appeals, applying Oklahoma law, rejected a failure-to-warn claim for mesothelioma suffered by a woman who breathed in asbestos when she was washing the work clothes of her husband, who had worked with asbestos products as an insulator. Positing that the duty to warn "only extends to ordinary consumers and users of . . . products," the court said that it would be an "overextension" of state law to hold that the defendants "could reasonably foresee" that the plaintiffs' decedent would be exposed to the defendants' products "in the manner in which she was."[33] A direct contrast appears in a Maryland case in which the court applied a positive generalization of foreseeability to the case of a woman who had washed her stepfather's work clothes for ten years, and who testified that the "clothes were very dirty and covered in a whitish-gray dust." The Maryland Court of Special Appeals cited precedent for the idea that "the fact that the ultimate harm suffered was not foreseeable does not preclude liability." Drawing on expert testimony that "asbestos fibers do not biodegrade and could cause continuous exposure of asbestos," the court said that "a jury . . . could reasonably conclude" that the illness of one decedent was "foreseeable" and that the defendant "had a duty to warn of household exposure."[34]

Paralleling these "second-hand exposure" cases were so-called "low dose" cases in which, rather than describing workplace environments hazy with dust clouds, plaintiffs showed the flaking of asbestos from products—for example, dust containing asbestos generated by friction on brake pads when mechanics replaced worn pads. In one case in which multiple defendants argued against liability because the plaintiffs could identify one maker of such products but not others, the court sympathetically noted the plaintiffs' allegations that "the 'vast majority' of their exposure to brake dust came from used brake pads which were unidentifiable at the time because their trade names and trademarks had been worn off," and that "the abrasion of use destroyed the opportunity to identify the maker of the product." In a decision that permitted the plaintiffs to use a "market share" liability theory against the unidentified multiple defendants, the court said there was "a greater likelihood that plaintiffs were exposed to the products of any given manufacturer with roughly the same frequency that that manufacturer's brake pads occupied the market."[35] With bankruptcies piling up, commentators suggested that "the biggest threat to the asbestos litigation system has always been its own success." They posited that somewhere the pattern "should eventually reach a limit," although "no one knows where that limit is or when it will appear."[36]

By 2012, an article published by the litigation section of the American Bar Association reported that the pace of asbestos claims showed "no signs of slowing down," that diagnoses of mesothelioma "are at an all-time high," and that "some predict that the number will continue to grow well into the next decade."[37]

The sum of this remarkable, continuing saga was that the process of American law, recorded in judicial decisions and unsuccessful attempts at producing a legislative solution to the many injustices generated by asbestos-caused illness, was itself an experiment in progress. It involved the formulation of several ideas for solution—and some complex hypothesis testing.

*5. Causation riddles*. The problem of proving causation of illness by asbestos exposure poses difficult questions for the idea of the judicial system as a crucible for truth. The question of whether asbestos causes colon cancer illustrates the ferocity of the law/science controversy. A particular bone of disagreement was on the legal standard for what is known as the "relative risk factor," with the crucial question being how much extra risk a plaintiff must show to pin an illness on a product. In one case, the New Jersey appellate court explained the concept:

> The term "expected mortality" refers to the rate of mortality for the general public, unexposed to the suspected risk. The term "observed mortality" refers to the rate of mortality in the study group. By dividing the expected mortality into the observed mortality the investigator arrives at a "risk-ratio" or "relative risk." From that is derived the attributable risk, "representing the proportion of the disease that is statistically attributable to the factor. . . . The attributable risk, therefore, is a composite measure that takes into account both the relative risk of disease if exposed and the proportion in the population so exposed."[38]

The plaintiffs' witness in this case "chiefly relied" on an epidemiological study by the noted asbestos specialist Irving Selikoff that "reviewed the results of a study of the occupational history and exposures of 17,800 insulators located in the United States, principally in the northeast, and in Canada" and found "59 deaths from colon cancer in the study population of which 38 were 'expected.'" The article determined the "relative risk of the study group" to be 1.55, "reflecting an attributable risk of approximately 35%." The appellate court thought this ratio did not clear the necessary bar. Referring to prior decisions that "recognize[d] the requirement that an epidemiological study show a relative risk in excess of two in order to be statistically significant," the court said that "the strength of the association shown by such a risk ratio does not sufficiently demonstrate causation so as to validate the witness's opinion."[39]

The New Jersey Supreme Court disagreed, however. It noted that the defendant's attorneys had "acknowledged that under certain circumstances a study with a relative risk of less than 2.0 could support a finding of specific causation," giving as examples such circumstances as "individual clinical data, such as asbestos in or near the tumor or a documented history of extensive asbestos exposure." More generally, it declared that "a relative risk of 2.0 is not so much a password to a finding of causation as one piece of evidence, among others, for the court to consider in determining whether the expert has employed a sound methodology in reaching his or her conclusion." It noted that the plaintiff's expert had reviewed the scientific literature, "assumed that decedent was exposed to asbestos and that his exposure, in both intensity and duration, was comparable to that of the study populations described in the literature," and also "assumed that other known risk factors for colon cancer did not apply to decedent." The supreme court sent the case back for an assessment of the witness's conclusion "that decedent's exposure more likely than not had been the cause of his colon cancer." That assessment, the supreme court said, should "include an evaluation of the validity both of the studies on which he relied and of his assumption that the decedent's asbestos exposure was like that of the members of the study populations" as well as a judgment on whether "the relevant scientific community accepts the process by which [the witness] reasoned to" his conclusion on causation.[40]

A parallel set of contrasting opinions in federal courts eventuated in another holding for the plaintiff, whose husband, John Maiorana, had died from colon cancer after workplace exposure to materials that contained asbestos. The jury gave damages to the plaintiff, but the trial judge set aside that verdict. He hammered away at what he viewed as the statistical insignificance of the studies on which the plaintiff relied. He noted eight studies proffered by the plaintiff that "reveal an apparent increased risk in contracting colorectal cancer from exposure from cancer with SMRs [standardized mortality ratios] for colorectal cancer ranging from 1.14 to 1.47."[37] He observed that "while an SMR of less than 1.50 is statistically insignificant," the plaintiff's witness had "asserted that these studies, when taken together, reveal a pattern of causation which is statistically significant" and had said that "the fact that these studies consistently yielded colorectal cancer SMRs greater than 1.0 indicated . . . that there is a causal link between exposure [to] asbestos and colorectal cancer." However, the trial judge scorned this conclusion, saying that

> no matter how many studies yield a positive but statistically insignificant SMR for colorectal cancer, the results remain statistically insignificant. Just as adding a series of zeros together yields yet another zero as the product, adding a series of positive but statistically insignificant SMRs together does not produce a statistically significant pattern.[41]

Paralleling the appellate profile of the New Jersey case, the Second Circuit reversed the trial court on the causation issue and reinstated the plaintiff's jury verdict. It said that the trial judge had "erred in failing to draw all reasonable inferences in favor of plaintiff" and "in rendering independent assessments of the epidemiological evidence far beyond the role authorized by" the Supreme Court's major opinion on proof of scientific causation in *Daubert v. Merrell Dow Pharmaceuticals Co.*[42] In particular, it criticized the trial judge for "rejecting all epidemiological studies that yielded an SMR below the unexplained floor of 1.50" and for what it characterized as "the bold assertion that SMRs of less than 1.50 are statistically insignificant and cannot be relied upon by a jury to support a finding of causation." It also criticized the trial judge for "generally encroaching upon the factfinding role of the jury." Moreover, it found "conspicuously absent from the district court opinion" "any mention of federal government agency reports that were before the jury." It summarized those reports, from both OSHA and the EPA, as concluding, "upon their review of available epidemiological studies, that a strong causal link does exist between asbestos exposure and gastrointestinal cancer, including colon cancer."[43]

These two sets of opinions provide a cameo of the problems in measurement that attend various kinds of mass experiments. First comes the painful, slow accumulation of data, a process that may take many years. Then come arguments about interpretation of the data, including both the accuracy of the numbers and the setting of thresholds for significance.

### *C. Drugs and Devices*

*1. The studies.* Recent medical history and case law on drugs and devices provide important markers on mass experiments, featuring the process of laborious gathering of data followed by a halt to experiments. In a previous book, I discussed at some length the terminations of two studies on hormonal products used to combat postmenopausal symptoms. In 2002, investigators halted one study on an estrogen-progestin combination that involved thousands of women, explaining that "health risks exceeded health benefits over an average follow-up of 5.2 years." Those risks included breast cancer and "'evidence for some increase' in coronary heart disease, stroke, and pulmonary embolism."[44] Two years later, the National Institutes of Health lowered the curtain on a study, at least for women with hysterectomies who were on an estrogen-only product, advising them to "stop taking their study pills." The focus here was on the risk of stroke, with the events following the pattern described above of post-data controversy about policy. Dr. Barbara Alving, who had directed the Women's Health Initiative (WHI), which had launched the hormone trials, and who was acting director of the National Heart, Lung, and Blood Institute, described disagreement among members of the WHI Data and Safety Monitoring Board about "whether the pills should be continued, provided that a letter would be sent to the participants clearly informing them of" various risks, including the risk of stroke.[45]

*2. The defect question: "unreasonably dangerous"?.* Courts deciding products liability cases on drugs and medical devices have sought to establish principles for deciding these cases, which by their nature involve ongoing data collection while medical products are used by thousands and even millions of people. An important attempt to codify the law to limit liability appears in comment k to section 402A of the Restatement (Second) of Torts. That comment essentially immunizes medical products "which, in the present state of human knowledge, are quite incapable of being made safe for their intended and ordinary use." It says that such products, if "properly prepared, and accompanied by proper directions and warnings," are "not defective, nor . . . unreasonably dangerous."[46] The California Supreme Court basically adopted this test in a case focusing on the hormone product diethylstilbestrol, the subject of many lawsuits, which was taken by pregnant women to prevent miscarriage. The court premised that the "alleged defects in the drug . . . were neither known by defendants nor scientifically knowable at the time the drug was distributed." It expressed concern that "the likelihood of the producer's liability would increase with significant advances in scientific knowledge, discouraging the development of new and improved drugs to combat disease." Moreover, it said that "the additional expense of insuring against such liability—assuming insurance would be available—and of research programs to reveal possible dangers not detectable by available scientific methods could place the cost of medication beyond the reach of those who need it most."[47]

The Colorado Supreme Court employed comment k in a case about an oral contraceptive, Ortho-Novum 1/80, which was prescribed to the plaintiff to prevent breakthough bleeding, but the application of legal doctrine was somewhat complex. On its way to the decision, the court referred to testimony that "the increased risks of adverse reactions occasioned by the extra thirty milligrams of estrogen in Ortho-Novum 1/80 outweighed any benefits the product might produce" and said that "there was a sufficient factual basis for the court to have given an instruction on [the plaintiff's] theory that Ortho-Novum 1/80 was unreasonably dangerous, without regard to the availability of warnings because of a design defect."[48] However, ultimately the court reversed a judgment for the plaintiff and remanded the case for trial because the trial court had refused an instruction on comment k. Among the factors it mentioned favoring the defendant were that because Ortho-Novum 1/80 prevented breakthrough bleeding—the "specific problem" that the plaintiff "encountered on the lower dose" of a 50-milligram product—the benefits of the 80-milligram product "outweighed its risks." The court also mentioned "testimony that no other alternative could prevent break-through bleeding and maintain the same high degree of effectiveness against pregnancy" and that "the risk was unavoidable."[49]

A Utah decision provided especially strong support for the comment k idea in the tragic case of a woman who shot and killed the plaintiff's mother, allegedly as a result of intoxication induced by the defendant's anti-insomnia drug. The court premised that "despite inherent risks, *and in contrast to any other product,* society has determined that prescription medications provide a unique benefit and so should be available to physicians with appropriate warnings and guidance as to use." It declared, broadly, that it was "persuaded that all prescription drugs should be classified as unavoidably dangerous in design because of their unique nature and value, the elaborate regulatory system overseen by the FDA, the difficulties of relying on individual lawsuits as a forum in which to review a prescription drug's design," and various "public policy considerations."[50]

Although comment k has won the approval of many courts, it has not persuaded others. The Nevada Supreme Court delivered a stinging criticism of the comment in a case in which a vaccine allegedly caused severe results to a seventeen-month-old boy, Thomas Allison, including encephalitis followed by "blindness, deafness, mental retardation and spastic contractures." The court viewed "the whole idea behind strict liability" as "that the manufacturer, not the consumer, should bear the responsibility for injuries, even when the product is ostensibly properly prepared and marketed and when the plaintiff is not in a position to prove the origin of the defect." It saw "no public policy need for changing our law or for shifting from the drug manufacturers to the consumer/victim the responsibility for all of the 'unfortunate consequences' suffered by the Allisons of the world." It said that immunization of drug manufacturers from liability, if it were to be done, was for the legislature, and commented, "Considerable research and legislative committee activity would be necessary before an intelligent and informed judgment could be made as to whether we should leave 'unfortunate' victims of drug injury to their own resources and free drug manufacturers from tort liability, on the unsubstantiated pretext that such a drastic measure is necessary in order to encourage drug research and development."[51]

There has been disagreement among courts about whether comment k bars suits against makers of medical devices, as distinct from drugs. The Eighth Circuit said that it did not, in a case involving an intrauterine contraceptive device (IUD), the CU-7. Saying that "the better reasoned opinions support the view that the unavoidably unsafe exception should only apply upon a showing of exceptional social need," that court rejected the idea that comment k should broadly immunize prescription drugs. It declared that the policy behind the comment had "no greater relevance to prescription drug products than to other products having life-saving or life-bettering characteristics." As to IUDs, the court said that the maker of the CU-7 had "made no showing that

CU-7s, or IUDs in general, are exceptionally beneficial to society," noting the availability of "alternative methods of birth control." It viewed as an "important factor" the fact that "IUD manufacturers, through mass advertising and merchandising practices," had "generated a general sense of product quality, making it difficult for consumers to fully understand the risks involved with the use of an IUD." It also opined that "manufacturers were in a better position than the users of IUDs to identify potential risks" and said that "by identifying and quantifying these risks, manufacturers could better spread the costs of injuries caused by IUDs to all customers of such products."[52]

The Hawaii Supreme Court weighed in against an application of comment k to a pacemaker that had been on the market, in an opinion of particular interest because it essentially distinguished experimentation in the clinical stage from mass-market experimentation. The court said that "in light of the documented medical experience with" the device, it did not believe that it was "was sufficiently analogous to a new and experimental drug to warrant comment k exemption from strict products liability." It noted evidence that at the time the pacemaker sued upon was made and distributed, "there were many different types of pacemakers available on the market, all of which were designed to perform the same function" as the defendant's product. It "therefore conclude[d] that the device was not an unavoidably unsafe product within the meaning of comment k."[53]

A set of California appellate decisions took an opposite position. The product at issue in one of these cases, a decision often cited since, was an inflatable penile prosthesis, which caused the plaintiff to have an almost constant erection with attendant "persistent pain and emotional distress." The appellate court, drawing on the state supreme court's application of comment k to drugs, broadly declared that a "manufacturer is not strictly liable for injuries caused by an implanted prescription medical product which has been (1) properly made and (2) distributed with information regarding risks and dangers of which the manufacturer knew or should have known at the time." Noting that medical devices were "commonly crucial to the well-being of the patient," it explained, with a particular focus on the prosthesis in the case, that such products "serve the salutary purposes of restoring a degree of normalcy to the lives of those who suffer organic dysfunctions and an impaired quality of life." It referred to the policy considerations of "the public's interest in development, availability and affordability of medical devices" and the concern that "the harsher rule of strict liability may discourage manufacturers from researching and marketing new medical devices due to realistic fear of substantial adverse judgments, the high cost of strict liability insurance and the uncertainty that such insurance will even be available."[54] In the same year, another appellate court applied comment k to an IUD,[55] and two years later, the court that had ruled in the penile prosthesis case did the same with a group of coordinated cases involving breast implants, saying that "the entire category of medical implants available only by resort to the services of a physician are immune from design defect strict liability."[56]

The legal skirmishes over the applicability of comment k, both generally and as applied to particular products, present an interesting parallel to market experimentation with products. In the products liability litigations, relevant data pertain to the untoward effects of drugs and devices, and questions arise about the evidence—sometimes unavailable and sometimes contested—about the effects of decisions either way on the application of comment k.

A nice theoretical solution would focus on the availability of information to consumer patients. However, the theory begins to break down when one considers the realities of the sale of prescription drugs and devices. There are two levels of experimentation in these categories. The first is at the manufacturer level, where launches of new products are—even after clinical testing—by their nature experimental on the mass market. The other is at the trench level of prescription, which necessarily involves the "learned intermediary," the physician. At that point, one encounters a group of barriers to the communication of meaningful information to the patient. Many patients first become interested in particular prescription products from television advertisements, which extol the benefits of a product while at the same time rapidly running through a list of side effects, some of which may be frightening. Patients then seek prescriptions from physicians who probably span a spectrum of receipt of communications about the details of risk, and of understanding of those details. Finally, patients themselves lie on a range of sophistication and understanding with respect to the comparison of risks and benefits. All of these complex factors are in operation at the moment a patient takes a pill or enters an operating room for the implantation of a medical device.

## II. Engines of Progress in the Highway Environment

Roads and highways are a prime environment for experimentation with risk levels. Experiments occur each time a new-model vehicle appears on the market. Indeed, they continue as vehicle makers make design and production changes, sometimes subtle, as they acquire information on new models. At the micro level, each trip is a fresh experiment for the motorist, with many variables popping up from block to block and mile to mile. These include defects in the vehicle, the behavior of other drivers, and various problems in the roadway itself, of which a very simple example is the new pothole in the pavement.

*A. The Vehicle*

A focal point of argument about policy and law concerns the design of vehicles with respect to injuries to passengers after their vehicles collide with other things—often other vehicles, but also objects near the roadway, like trees and telephone poles. This is the problem that Ralph Nader, employing a phrase used by an Indiana highway patrolman, put into the lexicon as the "second collision." Up to the 1960s, there was little thought that vehicle manufacturers were responsible for—to use another term from the lexicon—the "crashworthiness" of their products. In the 1950s, Ford did mount an advertising campaign that focused on safety features in its automobiles. However, General Motors prevailed in intra-industry competition when it decided that such advertising would repel potential buyers of cars, an idea compressed into the phrase "safety doesn't sell."[57] The provision of seat belts was a central feature in the discussion. But, as Nader summarized it, after Ford backed away from its campaign in 1956, "industry seat belt policy entered a period where belts were offered as an extra-cost option but were not widely promoted," that omission perhaps accounting for the fact that "the manufacturers . . . seemed mystified because more car buyers did not demand this option."[58] Over the next decade, seat belts did become "standard equipment," to the point that by 1965, their "installed cost to the car buyer" had become "about one third of what they cost" five years before.[59] Yet the human costs of "second collisions," quantified in the billions, continued.

Then a pivotal document appeared—Nader's 1965 book *Unsafe At Any Speed,* which was subtitled *The Designed-In Dangers of the American Automobile.* Nader placed the responsibility for much of this "carnage" on the automakers. Speaking to the problem of consumer inability to prevent product injuries was his observation that the costs of preventable collision injuries "fall to users of vehicles, who are in no position to dictate safer automobile designs."[60] Just one set of examples of possible design improvement was his summary of a list of seven dashboard improvements compiled by a safety researcher named John Swearingen.[61]

The publication of this book proved a remarkable stimulus to legislative action. The next year, Congress changed the experimental neighborhood of traffic accidents with its passage of the National Traffic and Motor Vehicle Safety Act. That legislation created the first of a series of agencies—since 1970 the National Highway Traffic Safety Administration (NHTSA)—for the achievement of "motor vehicle safety." It defined that phrase to include the protection of the public "against unreasonable risk of accidents occurring as a result of the design, construction or performance of motor vehicles" and protection "against unreasonable risk of death or injury to persons in the event accidents do occur."[62] Over two generations, government regulations have toughened up cars to minimize deaths and injuries by strengthening the protection of vehicles against front-end collisions, side impacts, and rollovers.

Paralleling these regulations was the development of a veritable cottage industry of litigation, with injured vehicle passengers suing carmakers for alleged defects in design that render vehicles insufficiently crashworthy. A landmark in this history was the Eighth Circuit's 1968 decision in *Larsen v. General Motors Corporation.*[63] The case arose from severe injuries to a driver in a head-on collision when the steering mechanism of his car thrust into his head. As the court summarized it, the plaintiff alleged that "the rearward displacement of the steering shaft on the left frontal impact was much greater" on his car, a Corvair, "than it would be in other cars that were designed to protect against such a rearward displacement."

GM's main argument was essentially that there could be no claim for a lack of crashworthiness, and it had a major precedent to cite: the 1966 decision of the Seventh Circuit in *Evans v. General Motors Corporation.* The court there declared, "The intended purpose of an automobile does not include its participation in collisions with other objects, despite the manufacturer's ability to foresee the possibility that such collisions may occur."[64] The Eighth Circuit in *Larsen* took direct issue with this idea, in an opinion that has prevailed and gave rise to the crashworthiness industry for lawyers. It found the "intended use" idea "much too narrow and unrealistic." Acknowledging that "automobiles are not made for the purpose of colliding with each other," it said that "a frequent and inevitable contingency of normal automobile use will result in collisions and injury-producing impacts." It concluded that there was "no rational basis . . . for limiting recovery to situations where the defect in design or manufacture was the causative factor of the accident," because "the accident and the resulting injury, usually caused by the so-called 'second collision' of the passenger with the interior part of the automobile, all are foreseeable."[65]

The power of this idea is evident in a much later New York case in which the plaintiff's husband, driving while drunk, suffered fatal injuries when he drove his Volkswagen Jetta off an exit ramp in the early morning hours and hit a steel utility pole at thirty-five miles an hour. The New York Court of Appeals reversed a summary judgment for the carmaker, given expert testimony that "structural deficiencies in the manufacture of the vehicle" were responsible for the fatal injuries, which would have been "minimal" with better-designed safety features. Although the plaintiff widow did not argue against Volkswagen's contention that her husband's "intoxication was the cause of the vehicle's *collision* with the utility pole," it rigorously applied the crashworthiness doctrine against the manufacturer. Although it saved for the automaker the possibility that it might be found that intoxication was the "*sole* cause" of a motorist's injuries, it declared, "If Volkswagen did defectively design the Jetta as asserted by plaintiff's expert, it breached a duty to any driver of a Jetta involved in a crash regardless of the initial cause." It said that the duty the plaintiff sought "to impose on Volkswagen originates not from her husband's act, but from Volkswagen's obligation to design, manufacture and market a safe vehicle."[66]

Also pushing the boundaries of crashworthiness was a decision by an Oregon appellate court in a case in which a horse "suddenly appeared in front" of the plaintiff's Pinto. With no time for him to swerve, his vehicle hit the animal, throwing it up over the hood, with the result that the roof rail collapsed, instantly killing his wife. Although the court said that liability for design defects did "not extend to cases where the risk of injury from the product's failure is so remote that a reasonable manufacturer would not consider it in design decisions," it referred to evidence of the plaintiff "that collisions with large animals, including horses, are common and foreseeable." Rejecting the defendant's argument that "it was not foreseeable that such a collision would produce an impact on the roof concentrated at a particular point rather than being more evenly distributed," the court said, "The problem with that argument is that its converse is equally true: It was just as unpredictable that the impact from a collision would fall evenly on the entire roof rather than land with greater force on its weakest part." It concluded that the fact "that the horse landed with its full weight on the header did not make the accident any more a freak occurrence than if the weight had been distributed evenly." It noted that the design of the plaintiff's vehicle "was unusual" because of some weaknesses in the strength of the roof, mentioning expert testimony that "reinforcement of the roof was technically and economically feasible and would have prevented its deformation so that it would not come into contact with a passenger's head." It concluded that "the accident and the manner of injury were not unforeseeable, as a matter of law" and that there was "sufficient evidence of defective design to justify submission of the case to the jury."[67]

There are controversies about the level of proof that plaintiffs must present in crashworthiness cases. On one side is a Third Circuit case requiring plaintiffs to show "proof of what injuries, if any, would have resulted had [an] alternative, safer design been used" and also that "the plaintiff must offer some method of establishing the extent of enhanced injuries attributable to the defective design."[68] On the other side is a group of decisions that are significantly more liberal to plaintiffs. In one of these cases, the plaintiff sued both his driver and the maker of the car in which he was a passenger for paraplegia that resulted after his ejection from the vehicle after a rollover. The Eighth Circuit concluded that it was error for the trial court not "to rule that the paraplegic injury was indivisible as a matter of law and was therefore not capable of apportionment." The appellate court said that "the jury should have been instructed that if it found the defective design was a substantial factor in producing the paraplegia, the manufacturer would be liable as a joint and several tortfeasor with the driver of the car."[69]

These cases on crashworthiness are simply illustrations of a massive, ongoing highway experiment on vehicle design, involving thousands of personal tragedies annually, upon which is layered an ongoing legal experiment, in which courts argue about the best rules to apply to such cases.

### *B. Use of Cell Phones*

Intense political controversy, with philosophical content, has surrounded motorists' use of cell phones. An important study published in 1997 concluded that "using a cellular telephone was associated with a risk of having a motor vehicle collision that was about four times as high as that among the same drivers when they were not using their cellular telephones."[70] The authors derived their data from tracking the billing records of 699 drivers who "were involved in motor vehicle collisions resulting in substantial property damage but no personal injury." They found that "the relative risk of a collision associated with using a cellular telephone was consistent among subgroups with different characteristics," including age, sex, type of employment, and driving experience, as well as experience with cell phones.[71] They cautiously said that their data "indicates an association but not necessarily a causal relation," noting, for example, that "emotional stress may lead to both increased use of a cellular telephone and decreased driving ability." They also noted various limitations of the study, including the fact that it "did not include serious injuries" and that their data did "not indicate that drivers were at fault in the collisions."[72] They also noted the benefits of cell phone use in vehicles, pointing out, for instance, that in Canada there were a half million calls to 911 services from cell phones each year.[73]

More than a decade later, the National Safety Council (NSC) estimated that "at least 28% of all traffic crashes—or at least 1.6 million crashes each year—involve drivers using cell phones and texting." The NSC's figures attributed 1.4 million crashes to cell phones and another two hundred thousand to texting. The organization's estimates were founded on NHTSA statistics showing that "11% of all drivers at any one time are using cell phones," as well as research including the article mentioned above. The highest boundary of risk the organization found for texting went up as high as "a maximum of 1 million crashes."[74]

The nationwide experiment with cell phones was a particularly interesting one because it involved a large number of experimenters operating vehicles across the country every day, who were consensually exposing themselves to risk but also exposing many others to unconsented risks. This experiment was taking place in a special political environment. In that setting, although external victims were infuriated by their roles as subjects in a nationwide clinic, the experimenters—those who drove while conversing—were a potent political force who brought pressure against regulation.

## III. Engines of Progress in the Broad Environment

We have discussed experiments with products that are inhaled, ingested, or implanted and with products that create risks in the arena of streets and highways. A different set of challenges arise in the broader environment, literally in the air around us, the seas that surround us, and the earth under our feet. Collectively, these challenges arise from various kinds of pollution—substances that make it harder to breathe, that kill the fish in the oceans, and that in particles multiplied a millionfold create changes in the wider world of our climate.

Dramatizing a set of political and legal issues, and laden with human interest, is a case brought by the City of Kivalina and the Inupiat Eskimo village of Kivalina, the latter with a population of four hundred, focusing on the climate change that the plaintiffs said was threatening their homes. As the Ninth Circuit summarized the fragile geography of the area, "the City of Kivalina sits on the tip of a six-mile barrier reef on the northwest coast of Alaska, approximately seventy miles north of the Arctic Circle." The city, incorporated under Alaska law in 1969—ten years after Alaska became a state—had "long been home" to the Eskimo village, a "self-governing, federally recognized tribe" of which 97 percent were natives of Alaska. It alleged threats to its survival from "erosion resulting from wave action and sea storms for several decades." The village had depended on "the sea ice that forms on their coastline in the fall, winter, and spring each year to shield them from powerful coastal storms," but, as the court summarized it, "in recent years, the sea ice has formed later in the year, attached later than usual, broken up earlier than expected, and has been thinner and less extensive in nature."[75] As Janet Mitchell, the administrator of Kivalina, observed, the buildups of sea ice that had protected the area were not occurring, even in January. "We live in anxiety during high-winds seasons," she said.[76]

The gist of the villagers' claims was that erosion and "the possibility of future storms threaten buildings and critical infrastructure in the city with imminent devastation," creating a situation in which "if the village is not relocated, it may soon cease to exist."[77] The villagers' suit alleged that this situation was the result of "global warming," which they said had resulted "in part from emissions of large quantities of greenhouse gases" by twenty-two energy companies including Exxon Mobil, BP, Chevron, and Shell Oil. The plaintiffs described the causal chain of global warming as "occurring through the build-up of carbon dioxide and methane (commonly referred to as 'greenhouse gases') that trap atmospheric heat and thereby increase the temperature of the planet." The next events in this mournful climate script were the heating of the earth, with the result that "the oceans become less adept at removing carbon dioxide from the atmosphere," an "increase in surface temperature [that] also causes seawater to expand," and a rise in sea levels "due to elevated temperatures on Earth, which cause the melting of ice caps and glaciers."[78] The village sought compensation of up to $400 million to pay the cost of relocation.[79]

The legal issue centered on the role of the Clean Air Act and the power of the Environmental Protection Agency. Borrowing a metaphor from a precedent, the trial court declared that the plaintiffs "have not and cannot show that Defendants' conduct is the 'seed' of [their] injury."[80] It also opined that the plaintiffs' theory of causation was tenuous, commenting that it was "dependent on a series of events far removed in both space and time from Defendants' alleged discharge of greenhouse gases." As the court of appeals summarized it, the trial court decided that "Kivalina could not establish that it was within sufficient geographic proximity to the Energy Producers' alleged 'excessive' discharge of greenhouse cases to infer causation."[81] More technically, the trial court decided that a decision on a nuisance claim by the village would require a "determination of what would have been an acceptable limit on the level of greenhouse gases emitted by" the defendants "and *who* should bear the cost of global warming" and said that these were issues more "appropriately left for determination by the executive or legislative branch in the first instance."[82]

The Ninth Circuit court affirmed the trial court. Although it noted that there was some precedent for applying public nuisance law to "transboundary pollution suits,"[83] it found compelling a Supreme Court decision in a suit against four private power companies and the Tennessee Valley Authority on public nuisance claims "based on greenhouse gas emissions." In that case, the Supreme Court held that the Clean Air Act "and the EPA actions it authorizes displace any federal common law right to seek abatement of carbon-dioxide emissions from fossil-fuel fired power plants."[84] As the Ninth Circuit viewed the Court's rulings in the area, the result was that plaintiffs like the village could not bring "federal common law public nuisance actions seeking damages, as well as . . . actions seeking injunctive relief."[85] "The solution to Kivalina's dire circumstance," the Ninth Circuit said, "must rest in the hands of the legislative and executive branches of our government, not the federal common law."[86]

A reporter noted that not many years before, such suits would have been thought frivolous, but that "no one is laughing now." He noted that the big insurance firm Swiss Re had "compared the suits to those that led dozens of companies in asbestos industries to file for bankruptcy, and predicted that 'climate change-related liability will develop more quickly than asbestos-related claims.'" He also noted that a report by the American Justice Partnership, which he described as "a business-oriented group that is critical of the plaintiffs' bar," had said that a conspiracy claim in the Kivalina complaint had made the case "the most dangerous litigation in America."[87]

It was interesting that although success for Kivalina presumably would have had a substantial impact on corporate behavior, a lawyer for the Kivalina plaintiffs had insisted that his target was not to "affect public policy." Rather, said Matthew F. Pawa, he had filed the Kivalina suit and another suit in Connecticut "because I expect and want to win in court. I'm a litigator, and that's what I do." It was not clear whether such suits had a future, but Michael B. Gerrard, a Columbia law professor who was director of its Center for Climate Change Law, noted that after many failures, lawyers suing tobacco companies "kept on trying new theories" "and eventually won big."[88]

The gladiators in the legal Colosseum of climate change were pushing against one another in different legal venues: legislatures, administrative agencies—particularly the EPA—and the courts. The case of climate change thus required different approaches to the making of public policy, through public law but with private litigation as a bee buzzing around the argument that the question of how to regulate a vast experiment with the environment was entirely political and for that reason was beyond the effective, or proper, reach of courts. It may be noted that Carol Browner, President Obama's senior adviser for energy and climate change—who cited the Connecticut lawsuit as an indication that "courts are starting to take control of this issue"—had said that the setting of environmental standards was "best done through legislation."[89]

## Notes

1. See Chapter Three, text accompanying notes 84–85.
2. Pub. L. 89-92, § 4 (1965).
3. Pub. L. 91-222 § 4 (1970).
4. Ibid., § 5(b).
5. Ibid., § 6.
6. *Cipollone v. Liggett Group*, 505 U.S. 504, 520 (1992) (language of Justice Stevens). See Chapter 8, text accompanying notes 5–7.
7. Ibid., p. 524.
8. Ibid., p. 531.
9. See ibid., pp. 531–44 (Blackmun, J., concurring in part and dissenting in part).
10. Frank Sloan and Lindsey Chepke, "Litigation, Settlement and the Public Welfare: Lessons from the Master Settlement Agreement," 17 *Widener L. Rev.* 159, 159-61 (2011).
11. Family Smoking Prevention and Tobacco Control Act, Pub. L. 111-31 (2009).
12. FDA, "Overview of the Family Smoking Prevention and Tobacco Control Act: Consumer Fact Sheet," last updated Oct. 22, 2013, viewed on the Internet March 22, 2014.

13. *R. J. Reynolds Tobacco Co. v. FDA*, 696 F.3d 1205, 1216-17, 1221 (D.C. Cir. 2012).
14. *McAllister v. Workmen's Compensation Appeals Bd.*, 445 P.2d 313, 314-19 (Cal. 1968)
15. Paul Brodeur, "A Reporter at Large: The Magic Mineral," *New Yorker*, Oct. 12, 1968, pp. 117 and 120.
16. See ibid., pp. 117–18.
17. See ibid., p. 131.
18. Ibid., p. 132.
19. See "Asbestos: Murray Introduces Bill to Ban Asbestos in Move to Reduce Worker Deaths, Injuries," 37 *O.S.H. Rep.* (BNA) 203 (March 8, 2007).
20. William J. Nicholson, George Perkel, and Irving J. Selikoff, "Occupational Exposure to Asbestos: Population at Risk and Projected Morality—1980–2030," 3 *Am. J. Indus. Med.* 259 (1982).
21. See Brodeur, supra, p. 138, apparently referring to J. G. Thompson et al., "Asbestos As a Modern Urban Hazard," 37 *So. Afr. Med. J.* 77-81 (1963).
22. "Ness, Motley, Loadholt, Richardson, & Poole, Profiles"—Dr. William Blackard, pp. 4–6, attached at Exhibit 5 to *In re W. R. Grace & Co. Bankruptcy Litig.*, cited in "Expert Witness Report of Marshall S. Shapo, Sept. 25, 2007," p. 75, text with note 321.
23. Michael Bowker, *Fatal Deception: The Terrifying Story of How Asbestos Is Killing America* (Simon & Schuster 2003), p. 26.
24. The appellate court's affirmance of a verdict for that first plaintiff, Clarence Borel, appears in *Borel v. Fibreboard Paper Prods. Corp.*, 493 F.2d 1076 (5th Cir. 1973).
25. See Stephen J. Carroll et al., *Asbestos Litigation* (Rand MG-162-ICJ, 2005), p. 106.
26. See ibid.
27. Ibid., p. 109.
28. Ibid., p. 104.
29. See for example Patrick M. Hanlon and Anne Smetak, "Asbestos Changes," 62 *N.Y. Surv. Am. L.* 525, 534 (2006-2007) ("exploded"); Deposition of David B. Siegel in *In re W. R. Grace & Co. et al.* (May 23, 2007), pp. 266–69 ("spike" in filings of asbestos claims against Grace in 2000).
30. See Hanlon and Smetak, p. 547.
31. Ibid., p. 580.
32. Ibid., p. 583.
33. *Rohrbaugh v. Owens-Corning Fiberglas Corp.*, 965 F.2d 844, 846-47 (10th Cir. 1992).
34. *Anchor Packing Co. v. Grimshaw*, 692 A.2d 5, 34-35 (Md. Ct. App. 1997).
35. *Wheeler v. Raybestos-Manhattan* 11 Cal.Rptr.2d 109, 111-12 (App. Ct. 1992).
36. Hanlon and Smetak, supra, p. 605.
37. Lee Blanton Ziffer, "Bankruptcy Trusts and Asbestos Litigation," Am. Bar Ass'n, Section of Litigation—Products Liability (June 11, 2012), http://apps.americanbar.org/litigation/committees/products/articles/spring2012-bankruptcy-trusts-asbestos-litigation.html, viewed on the Internet May 2, 2013.
38. *Landrigan v. Celotex Corp.*, 579 A.2d 1268, 1271-72 (App. Div. 1990).
39. Ibid., p. 1272.

40. *Landrigan v. Celotex Corp.*, 605 A.2d 1079, 1087-88 (1992).
41. *In re Joint E. & S. Dist. Asbestos Litig.*, 827 F.Supp. 1014, 1041-42 (S.D.N.Y. 1993)
42. See *In re Joint E. & S. Dist. Asbestos Litig.*, 52 F.3d 1124, 1139 (2d Cir. 1995), referring to *Daubert*, 509 U.S. 579 (1993).
43. See ibid., pp. 1139 and 1134–35.
44. The detailed story appears in Marshall S. Shapo, *Experimenting With the Consumer*, chapters 5 and 6 (Prager, 2009). A summary of the stopping of the first study appears in the same book on pages 160–61.
45. Ibid., p. 170.
46. Restatement (Second) of Torts § 402A, cmt. k (1965).
47. See *Brown v. Superior Court*, 451 P.2d 470, 478-81 (Cal. 1988).
48. *Ortho Pharmaceutical Corp. v. Heath*, 722 P.2d 410, 414 (Colo.1986).
49. Ibid., pp. 415–16.
50. *Grundberg v. Upjohn Co.*, 813 P.2d 89, 95-96 (Utah 1991).
51. *Allison v. Merck and* Co., 878 P.2d 948, 954-56 (Nev. 1994).
52. *Hill v. Searle Labs*, 884 F.2d 1064, 1069-70 (8th Cir. 1989).
53. *Larsen v. Pacesetter Systems, Inc.*, 837 P.2d 1273, 1286 (Hawaii 1992).
54. *Hufft v. Horowitz*, 5 Cal.Rptr.2d 377, 383-84 (App. Ct. 1992).
55. *Plenger v. Alza Corp.*, 13 Cal. Rptr.2d 811, 818 (App. Ct. 1992).
56. *Artiglio v. Superior Court*, 27 Cal.Rptr.2d 589, 593 (App. Ct. 1994).
57. See Ralph Nader, *Unsafe at Any Speed* (Grossman Publishers, 1965), pp. 118–19.
58. Ibid., p. 119.
59. Ibid., p. 128.
60. See ibid., p. viii.
61. See ibid., p. 107.
62. Then 15 U.S.C.A. § 1391(1).
63. 391 F.2d 495 (8th Cir. 1968).
64. 359 F.2d 822, 825 (7th Cir. 1966).
65. Larsen, supra, 391 F.2d at 502.
66. *Alami v. Volkswagen of America, Inc.*, 766 N.E.2d 574, 577 & n.1 (N.Y. 2002).
67. *Green v. Denney*, 742 P.2d 639, 641-42 (Or. Ct. App. 1987), review denied, 305 Or. 21 (1988).
68. *Huddell v. Levin*, 537 F.2d 726, 737-38 (3d Cir. 1976).
69. *Mitchell v, Volkswagenwerk, A.G.*, 669 F.2d 1199, 1201-02 (8th Cir. 1982).
70. Donald A. Redelmeier and Robert J. Tibshirani, "Association Between Cellular Telephone Calls and Motor Vehicle Collisions," 336 *N. Eng. J. Med.* 453, 456 (1997).
71. See ibid., pp. 455–56 and Table 2.
72. Ibid., p.457.
73. See ibid.
74. Release, "National Safety Council Estimates That At Least 1.6 Million Crashes Each Year Involve Drivers Using Cell Phones and Texting," Jan. 12, 2010, http://www.democraticunderground.com/discuss/duboard.php?az=view_all&address=389x7454092 printed from the Internet May 30, 2013.
75. *Native Village of Kivalina v. ExxonMobil Corp.*, 696 F.3d 849, 853 (9th Cir. 2012).

76. John Schwartz, "Courts in Battlefields in Climate Fights," *New York Times*, Jan. 26, 2010.
77. Kivalina case, 696 F.3d at 853.
78. ibid., p. 854.
79. See Schwartz, supra.
80. 663 F. Supp. 863, 881 (N.D. Cal. 2009).
81. 696 F.3d at 854.
82. 663 F. Supp. 2d at 876-77.
83. 696 F.3d at 855.
84. *Amer. Elec. Power Co. v. Connecticut*, 131 S.Ct. 2527, 2537 (2011).
85. 696 F.3d at 858.
86. Ibid.
87. Schwartz, supra.
88. Ibid.
89. Ibid.

# 12

# Methods and Structures of Responses to Experimentation

## I. Remedies

There is a small menu of remedies for experimentation that is pushed too far or has gone awry. For private litigants, the principal remedy is money damages, a legal result that varies considerably in the exactness of how it measures injury and how fully it is realized in practice.

In cases of physical injury and, to an extent, psychological injury, the typical breakdown of injury costs for damages purposes in tort cases includes medical bills, lost income, and a set of injuries loosely termed "noneconomic loss." In the baldest cases of unregulated, unconsented experimentation like the Tuskegee experiments, it often is unlikely that the remedy will catch up with the injury, because of the lag time it takes to discover the culpable nature of the experimenter's conduct. It also will be difficult to calculate medical costs over a period of years. Moreover, as is the case with many kinds of noneconomic loss, it will be hard to put a price tag on both suffering and the claimant's sense of insult.

Since most tort cases are settled, there almost always is a discount of the "true" injury figure, with the claimant trading certainty of getting some money against the uncertainty about whether she will recover anything at all, and how much a recovery on trial will approximate the cost of her injury. One thing that is certain, unless the claimant represents herself, is that her lawyer will take a fee that will probably be at least one quarter of her award. These discounts and uncertainties apply whether the case is one of direct medical experimentation or one of the experiments that are daily conducted on large-scale populations by drug makers or the sellers of new automobiles or other consumer products.

*West, Texas*

A broad range of compensation realities spans different kinds of injuries. Illustrative are two disastrous events. One of these was the explosion of a fertilizer plant in the town of West, Texas, which took at least fourteen lives, injured as many as two hundred people, and severely damaged at least fifty homes, causing structural damage to ninety other buildings. A Waco policeman described "roughly a 50-unit apartment complex" in which "walls were ripped off [and] roofs were peeled back."[1] In the immediate wake of the explosion, lawyers for survivors sued the parent company of the West Fertilizer Company. At that point it was speculative as to how much the plaintiffs might recover. Some of the calculation problems related to the value of the lives of those who died (whoincluded several volunteer firefighters), property damage to those who lost homes and businesses, and intangible losses associated with the aftereffects of the fright caused by the explosion. As we shall explain later, there were parallel problems with the relative lack of regulation of such plants, a subject that itself was a matter of controversy.

*Oil Spills*

In mid-June 1989, fourteen oil companies announced a "quick-response" disaster plan for oil spills, with five "regional response centers" that would be "manned around the clock with dedicated, trained personnel." The major triggering event for this announcement was the spill of eleven million gallons of oil from the tanker *Exxon Valdez* into the waters of Prince William Sound in Alaska. A Mobil official who was a member of the industry task force declared, "You can promise nothing less than your best effort." However, a leading congressional advocate of environmental safety, Representative George Miller of California, countered that "Congress will not rely on the promises of the oil industry," declaring that "the capability of the industry to respond to major oil spills must be a matter of law, not promises."[2]

Two decades later, on April 20, 2010, the industry came a cropper with a massive spill of oil that occurred when the BP rig *Deepwater Horizon* exploded off the coast of Louisiana, an event that proved ruinous to many businesses of the Gulf Coast in an arc from Texas to the Florida Panhandle. The consequences included the deaths of eleven workers on the rig and many destructive impacts on individuals, including psychological suffering, as well as harm to commercial enterprises that extended well beyond the Gulf Coast. The occurrence led to the use of a veritable arsenal of legal remedies and raised issues about others. I will point out how the variety of the compensatory remedies alone illustrates the difficulty of trying to achieve a comprehensive solution to such a vast environmental problem. I will also discuss the use of civil fines and even the criminal process, as well as some of the failures to regulate the colossal experiment that is offshore drilling.

Less than two months after the spill, more than one hundred lawsuits had poured into the courts. The plaintiffs ranged from cleanup workers to fishermen and real estate developers. Members of Congress, already attuned to the need for information—and presumably to the possibilities of making headlines—were already in full cry in efforts to sift evidence of injuries laid to the spill. In a hearing of the House Energy and Commerce Subcommittee on Oversight and Investigations held in Louisiana, a chemist said that workers and fishermen had experienced "health impacts including headaches, nausea, respiratory impacts, irritation of eyes, nose, throat, and lungs, and asthma attacks."[3]

A report published a full year after the spill indicated that it was indeed a large experiment in a vast outdoor laboratory. The complex elements of this experiment presented a picture of uncertainties that paralleled the uncertainties typical of early stages of clinical experimentation with drugs and devices. The writers of the report, led by Bernard Goldstein, said that "the full magnitude of the environmental, economic, and human health effects of this major disaster remain unknown." The first paragraph of their article, in addition to employing the word "unknown," used the word "uncertainty" twice.[4] The spill provided what appeared to be an ideal research design, because it contained "all five elements of a complete exposure pathway": "sources of contaminants, environmental media, points of exposure, routes of exposure," and populations "working or living near the site of the spill and the affected shoreline."[5] Illustrating the complexity of possibly relevant data were such factors as job assignments of workers responding to the spill, their duration of exposure, and "the extent of worker training and the use of personal protective equipment." Referring to studies of other spills ranging from Spain to Scotland, the authors noted that there had been "few studies of long-term health consequences."[6] With particular respect to benzene exposure, the authors pointed out that "the half-life of benzene in the environment and in the human body is measured in days and it does not bioaccumulate" and concluded that "community exposures should be relatively minimal." They also noted that "many hundreds of air samples . . . showed that no samples had concentrations of benzene or other volatile organic hydrocarbons ascribable to the Gulf oil spill that were above health-based standards." However, the authors noted that "although the monitoring was extensive, no monitoring scheme could cover all potentially affected locales."[7]

In this situation of thin data, another possibly confounding factor was the relatively poor health of populations in the area of the spill—for example, Louisiana ranked from forty-fourth to forty-ninth on various scales including death from cancer and premature death.[8] Chemical exposures were not the only source of health hazards. One important problem was heat stress, "a major factor in the hot summer months in the Gulf," and one that was "compounded by the necessity of using personal protective equipment." The authors noted that "inexperienced volunteers are particularly prone to heatstroke and exhaustion" and that "workers with heat stress are at increased risk for acute injury."[9] A section of the report on mental health consequences revealed limitations in both the available data and the interpretation of that data. One complicating factor was mental health problems suffered from Hurricane Katrina, which predated the Gulf spill by five years.[10]

The complexity of the subject was evident in the authors' summary of two workshops held by the Institute of Medicine, which they said focused "on addressing uncertainties by characterizing contaminant mixtures in all environmental media, detecting exposure sources," and "focusing on vulnerable populations."[11] For the practical purposes of personal injury law, all of the factors the authors identified fed into the difficulty of pinpointing causation but also the difficulty of putting dollar values on injuries and illnesses that may still have been in the sinister process of development in mind and body.

The legal attack on the BP spill became a multi-ring circus. Thousands of lawsuits became consolidated into what has become a permanent fixture for many kinds of mass injury litigation: the Judicial Panel on Multidistrict Litigation. In July 2010 lawyers fought an early battle about where the trial should take place. Lawyers for oil companies favored Houston, but claimants' attorneys made arguments for several states around the Gulf and even for South Carolina. A California lawyer who had represented plaintiffs in the *Exxon Valdez* litigation warned against the delay that is an endemic factor in such litigation, saying that "many of her clients had died before getting their money from the company."[12] A month later the judicial panel announced that it would consolidate the cases in New Orleans before Judge Carl

J. Barbier, whom it called "an exceptional jurist," one who had heard a number of oil spill cases and, as one reporter put it, who had "survived defendants' efforts to have him removed over accusations of conflict of interest."[13] At the same time, the umbrella organization of the plaintiffs' bar, the American Association for Justice, certified a Gulf Coast Oil Spill Litigation Group that would enable lawyers to share information and exchange ideas about legal strategies. Over many years, plaintiffs' lawyers had established such groups for more than one hundred kinds of cases,[14] developing what was essentially a cluster of databases that ran parallel to collections of information by governmental, industry, and medical sources on the many experiments that are constantly run on the environment and on consumers.

Within two months of the spill, BP, insisting that it would pay "all legitimate claims," had paid $132 million to "to individuals and businesses . . . for loss of income or net profit."[15] Dwarfing that number in dollars was the company's agreement with President Obama to establish a $20 billion fund for various kinds of losses, primarily economic losses, suffered as a result of the spill. The wheelhorse for the fund was Kenneth Feinberg, a Washington lawyer with much experience in administering such funds, his most famous venture being his role as special master of the September 11th Victims Compensation Fund. Appointed two months after the spill began, Feinberg noted that a major problem would be establishing limits to the compensability of "indirect" effects of the spill.[16]

Indeed, the general problem of liability for economic loss apart from personal injury was one that had generated a complex body of case law, in tort law generally, and particularly in the law of products liability. There was a loose general rule that one could not recover under the general injury law called torts for economic loss, as distinguished from personal injury or damage to tangible physical property. A few weeks after the Gulf spill, I had put a series of hypothetical cases to my grandchild Gabrielle Shapo, who was then eight and likes "law problems." Playing the Socratic law teacher, I asked her whether BP should have to pay fishermen whose catch had disappeared after the spill, and she said that clearly they should. I pressed the inquiry: What about the restaurant on the shore that loses the fishermen's business? Of course, she replied. Well, what about the man who sells milk and eggs to the restaurant? "Yes," she said. And the dairy farmer who owns the cows that produce the milk? "Sure," she said. "Gabrielle," I said, "how long will this go on?" She replied with a little grin, "Until it ends."

Well, not quite, although there is some case law that favors at least the fishermen suing for tort recoveries in spill cases. There have been major decisions by two federal courts of appeal on this question, in cases decided a dozen years apart. A Ninth Circuit decision in 1974 focused on facts that previsioned the BP spill. As the court summarized it in a suit by commercial fishermen, oil that escaped at a Union Oil Company platform in the Santa Barbara Channel was "carried by natural forces of winds and tides to . . . the ocean's surface and towards and in some instances to the adjacent coast lines." For the court, the key to decision lay in Union Oil's ability to foresee damage from the spill to the plaintiffs' interests. Saying that "the dangers of pollution were and are known even by school children," it declared that "to assert that the defendants were unable to foresee that negligent conduct resulting in a substantial oil spill could diminish aquatic life and thus injure the plaintiffs is to suppose a degree of general ignorance of the effects of oil pollution that is not in accord with good sense." Limiting its decision to the plaintiffs before it, and acknowledging the "general rule" against tort recovery for economic loss, the court pointed out that the injury sued upon was "a pecuniary loss of a particular and special nature, limited to the class of commercial fishermen which [the plaintiffs] represent."[17]

A Fifth Circuit decision in 1986 emphasized the need for limits in affirming summary judgment for defendants in a case that arose from a collision of two ships in which containers went overboard, housing about twelve tons of pentachlorophenol (PCP), a chemical with many uses, including as a wood preservative and in herbicides. The Coast Guard closed the Mississippi River outlet where the collision occurred and suspended "fishing, shrimping and related activity" in the outlet and in four hundred square miles of "surrounding marsh and waterways." The court of appeals affirmed summary judgment for the shipowners against a group of plaintiffs that included "shipping interests suffering losses from delays or rerouting, marina and boat operators, wholesale and retail seafood enterprises not actually engaged in fishing, shrimping, crabbing or oystering in the area, seafood restaurants, tackle and bait shops, and recreational fishermen, oystermen, shrimpers and crabbers."[18] The appellate court did not address the trial court's statement that commercial fishermen, crabbers, shrimpers, and oystermen "were exercising their public right to make a commercial use of those waters" and that their "special interest" justified recovery for "specific pecuniary losses" they could prove.[19]

Justifying its grant of summary judgment against the plaintiffs who were not commercial fishermen, the majority of a divided Fifth Circuit employed the foreseeability rationale with a seagoing metaphor. It said, "Review of the foreseeable consequences of the collision demonstrates the wave upon wave of successive economic consequences and the managerial role plaintiffs would have us assume." Finding benefit in the fact that the general "economic loss" rule "is identifiable and will predict outcomes in advance," it focused on the ability of parties like the plaintiffs to secure "first party or loss insurance," noting that "for the same reasons that courts have imposed limits on the concept of foreseeability, liability insurance might not be readily obtainable for the types of losses asserted here" and asserting that "first party insurance is feasible for many of the economic losses claimed here." Specifically, it said, "Each businessman who might be affected by a disruption of river traffic or by a halt in fishing activities can protect against that eventuality at a relatively low cost since his own potential losses are finite and readily discernible."[20]

The policy lines were firmly drawn in the battle over tort recovery for spills. The plaintiffs would argue that the defendants' negligence was the cause in fact of the plaintiffs' injuries, an "externality" of the defendants' activities. The defendants would argue that to allow recovery to a broad range of claimants could be out of proportion to the culpability involved and would create impossible problems in drawing the line for determining the classes of claimants and the types of injuries that should be compensated.

In the background of the Gulf spill was the $75 million limitation in the Oil Pollution Act on payments beyond "removal costs"—cleanup costs—for oil spills,[21] although it excepted from this limit claims for "gross negligence or willful misconduct."[22] Although BP had created a fund that bypassed this limitation, members of Congress vigorously criticized the company. In a hearing a little more than a month after the spill began, Congressman Jerrold Nadler of New York reported on fishermen's reports of "bad headaches, hacking coughs, stuffy sinuses, sore throats, and other symptoms" and pointed out to a BP vice president that the company was "not offering people respirators." He expressed his fear that "what BP is doing now is going to get thousands and thousands and thousands of people sick, maybe dead."[23] Maxine Waters of California told the BP official that she was going "to follow up to make sure that" small fishermen and oystermen were compensated. She took a sideswipe at Transocean Ltd., which had leased the drilling rig and provided the crew to BP, saying, "Transocean, I am suspicious of you, too . . . You know you can't be trusted."[24] In a hearing two months later, Senator Lautenberg pointed out, "We've seen this kind of catastrophe before." Observing that "oil is still contaminating the soil" around the *Exxon Valdez* spill of 1989, he said that Exxon had "fought the communities, the families and the fishermen over every penny," "knock[ing] down claims from $5 billion to $500 million."[25] In a contemporaneous hearing, Senator Sessions of Alabama sought a middle ground. Noting that Alabama communities affected by the spill were "hurting," with "a seafood industry that is basically shut down," and that "hundreds of low-wage workers have lost their jobs," he also pointed out that "the offshore industry is responsible for nearly 200,000 jobs around the Gulf of Mexico and over $13 billion a year in non-tax revenues for the gulf coast producing States."[26]

As Feinberg undertook his difficult task of deciding on compensation, he ruminated on the problems of line-drawing in a Senate hearing, asking, "What do I do with a restaurant in Las Vegas who writes a claim and says, 'We have lost 30 percent of our business because here in Vegas we are the only restaurant that has that Gulf shrimp,' and now it is gone and people are not coming to that restaurant?" "Where the proximity is so far removed from the Gulf," he asked, "where do you draw the line?" That, he said in a July 2010 hearing, he was "trying to figure out now."[27]

The fund administered by Feinberg, the Gulf Coast Claims Facility (GCCF), drew the approbation of the *New York Times*, which editorialized that Feinberg's plan "seem[ed] magnanimous and fair," providing "swift, short-term relief for Gulf Coast residents, and a process for measuring—and appropriately compensating—long-term losses." The editorial also referred to "legal and political ambulance chasers" who were "jumping on Mr. Feinberg," with plaintiffs' lawyers complaining "that his approach would deprive victims of the settlements they could command in case-by-case litigation."[28] Feinberg himself referred to the uncertainty that would attend the process, saying that there might be overcompensation or undercompensation for claimants, and that "it's a very murky crystal ball." However, he emphasized, "What's important is that it is adequate to end the uncertainty and bring the matter to a close."[29]

On a television show, Feinberg captured the emotions of many Gulf residents when he said that one should "not underestimate the emotion, the anger, the frustration that people in the gulf convey to me"—"Why this accident? It wasn't my fault. I'm an innocent victim. Why wasn't this prevented? Why am I now suffering financially?"[30]

Lending a little extra urgency to the need to develop rational schemes of compensation, as well as for regulation of drilling, was a fire that occurred on an oil platform in the Gulf on September 2. There were no serious injuries to crewmembers, but the event drove thirteen of them overboard. Fortunately, an automatic shutoff system on the platform sealed off oil and gas wells before the fire started, and "Coast Guard officials said that no oil could be seen on the water near the platform, contradicting an earlier report."[31]

A week later, a somewhat contrite Feinberg was acknowledging to Louisiana residents that, as a press report summarized it, he had "underestimated the time it would take to sort through the tens of thousands of applications for emergency aid, many of them woefully undocumented." Although the facility presumably was designed to allow people to get compensation without attorneys, Feinberg said in a speech in Orlando that he was "increasingly of the view as I go forward with this program that the lawyers around this country can play a very valuable role" by helping people package their claims. Feinberg pointed out that, as of when he spoke in September, the company had paid $398 million in emergency claims.[32] A little later, Feinberg said that lawyers who were "worried that $60 billion won't be enough" "might be right"—"especially if every single restaurant and hotel in Florida can simply stand up and say, 'Before the spill. After the spill. Pay me the difference.'" A reporter pictured him as "shrug[ging] like a man trying to wrap his arms around a number that is simply too large to fathom."[33]

This seemed to illustrate that, following BP's experiment with the environment, a parallel experiment was taking place in the development of a remedial process. That process included controversy over whether courts should regulate the work of the GCCF. A Plaintiffs' Steering Committee (PSC) made up of lawyers independently representing claimants, along with several state attorneys general, were demanding that the court supervise "communications that BP, the GCCF, and Feinberg were making to potential claimants" and that the court either modify or invalidate the releases that claimants had signed with the facility.[34] One commentator observed that these efforts at judicial regulation encountered an "unusual coalition" of opponents—not only BP, Feinberg, and the GCCF, but a group of plaintiffs' law firms that were not members of the steering committee. One of those firms represented "thousands of individuals, almost none of whom were parties" in the multidistrict litigation—people "who had filed or were planning to file claims with the GCCF." Those firms "accused the PSC of viewing the GCCF as 'nothing more than an obstacle to more fees.'"[35] By December 2010, Feinberg had added a sweetener—one reporter called it something amounting to a "signing bonus"—for people who had "already received emergency payments and [did] not intend to ask for more money from the fund." Individuals who signed a final release would get $5,000 within fourteen days of signing the final release, and businesses would get $25,000. Previously, the reporter noted, Feinberg had said that claimants "could file for quarterly payments that, like the emergency payments," placed "no limitation on the right to sue BP later."[36]

Just one resident who complained about a process that did not seem to be working was a Mississippi businesswoman, Tina Copeland, who was described as "wrangl[ing] with claims administrators over proper documentation during dozens of phone calls and 10 six-hour in-person visits" to the GCCF.[37] The parallel remediation processes, with private lawyers pursuing business at the same time the facility was operating, created confusion for many residents. Two reporters detailed allegations that people were finding out that law firms had wrongly claimed that they had signed up for representation. Reportedly, Vietnamese Americans said that they had received letters from a San Antonio lawyer, written in Vietnamese, who addressed them as "Dear Client," told them to send their financial records to the firm, and said that they should not "sign anything with BP or anyone else" than the firm. The lawyer, a member of the steering committee, reportedly declared that he had "met with resistance from" the BP Fund "when he tried to file emergency claims for all of his clients" in August. People said to be familiar with the fund process countered that "nearly every submission was listed as a deckhand with identical earnings." In rebuttal, the San Antonio lawyer said he had sent Feinberg the "raw information he asked for" but that Feinberg "kept changing the rules."[38]

Capturing the experimental nature of the claims process was a remark by Martha Bergmark, the president of the Mississippi Center for Justice, a nonprofit law firm. She said that the process was "getting invented on the fly."[39]

Into this already tangled group of remedial possibilities came remarks by the MDL judge, Judge Barbier, who said that plaintiffs who brought claims under the general maritime law could "plausibly allege punitive damages." Given a provision in the Oil Pollution Act (OPA) that preserved "admiralty and maritime law, '[e]xcept as otherwise provided,'" he said that although "punitive damages are not available under OPA," he did "not read OPA's silence as meaning that punitive damages are precluded under general maritime law." He observed that "Congress knows how to proscribe punitive damages when it intends to," as it had done in another statute, and said that there was "nothing to indicate that allowing a claim for punitive damages in this context would frustrate the OPA liability scheme." He also noted that the exception for gross negligence—the relatively liberal standard for punitive damages in general maritime law—would not "circumvent OPA's limitation of liability" to $75 million.[40]

A notable aspect of this decision was that it allowed MDL plaintiffs the chance to pursue a remedy—punitive damages—that was not available if they went into the GCCF fund. A theoretical criticism of the application of punitive damages came from Paul Rubin, a scholar who applies economic analysis to legal issues. He wrote that from a policy standpoint, there was "no advantage" in applying punitive damages to the Gulf spill, because that remedy was "mainly appropriate in cases where an injurer might have been able to hide his culpability"—clearly not the situation with respect to this event.[41]

Yet another voice entered the chorus of claimants, this time in the form of lawsuits under the federal False Claims Act—a kind of "whistleblower" suit. This suit alleged that BP had acquired "billions of dollars in oil and gas revenue" by "falsely certifying" that it was "in compliance with various federal regulations" in its operations at a site poetically named Atlantis, located about 190 miles south of New Orleans, "in water depths ranging from approximately 4400 to 7200 feet," and "rated to produce 200,000 barrels of oil per day and 180,000,000 cubic feet of gas per day." The plaintiffs argued that the company's false certification "'ha[d] the potential to influence the government's decision' to approve BP's production at Atlantis." They sought both compensation in dollars and an injunction against BP's drilling until it brought itself into compliance with regulations. In denying BP's motion to dismiss, a Texas federal court emphasized that the plaintiffs were "not required to show with 'scientific certainty' that BP 'caused the precise harm suffered by the plaintiffs' in order to show that an injury is 'fairly traceable' to BP's actions" but only "a 'substantial likelihood' that defendant's conduct caused [or could cause] plaintiffs' harm." It declared that BP's "alleged noncompliance" with regulations "introduces incalculable levels of risk to the Gulf of Mexico environment."[42]

Beating in the near background of the compensation circus for the Gulf spill was a drumfire of criticism based on reports of the event and on BP's conduct at other times and places, as well as arguments for prospective regulatory remedies beyond after-the-fact compensation. One of the worst prior cases was a 2005 explosion in BP's refinery in Texas City, a town that had been the site of a major explosion disaster in 1947 that eventuated in an important Supreme Court decision favoring the United States. The 2005 explosion killed fifteen people at the refinery, the second largest in the United States, which daily refined 460,000 barrels of crude oil into gasoline. Especially damning was the fact that two months before the blast, a consulting firm had said in a report, "We have never seen a site where the notion 'I could die today' was so real." According to one summary of the event, workers had been on twelve-hour shifts at the facility for more than a month, and "no one noticed" that a "170-foot tower . . . being filled with liquid hydrocarbons" had been "filled too high." The United States Chemical Safety Board concluded that the explosion had been "caused by organizational and safety deficiencies at all level of BP."[43] BP paid a $50 million fine for failures in maintenance of the equipment at the Texas City facility. It also paid a total of $20 million in three fines for an oil spill at a pipeline in Prudhoe Bay, Alaska.[44]

An umbrella criticism of BP's conduct appeared in a report by the Center for Public Integrity, a nonprofit research organization. As summarized in a trade publication, the report asserted that two refineries owned by BP had accounted for "97 percent of all 'flagrant' violations found in the refining industry by federal government inspectors" in the three years leading up to 2010.[45]

Echoes of the "I could die today" statement mentioned above sounded in a survey of workers on the *Deepwater Horizon* rig commissioned by Transocean, the owner of the rig, which was written before the spill occurred. Some workers were said to "voice concerns about poor equipment reliability, 'which they believed was as a result of drilling priorities taking precedence over planned maintenance.'" A separate report to Transocean said that "many key components—including . . . blowout preventer rams and failsafe valves—had not been fully inspected since 2000," although guidelines required inspections "every three to five years." About half of the Transocean workers indicated they did not report on perceived risks because they feared reprisal.[46] A later set of reports to Transocean referred to "at least 36 pieces of equipment in ill repair on the Deepwater Horizon that 'may lead to loss of life, serious injury or environmental damage as a result of inadequate use and/or failure of equipment.'"[47] Underlining the existence of precautions that could prevent spill accidents, yet another Transocean report indicated that a spill had been prevented because safety equipment on a North Sea oil rig had "functioned properly" in an emergency—four months before the *Deepwater Horizon* spill— created by "human error."[48]

Some near-term reports on the effects of the spill generated controversy. A Louisiana state official said, "Reports of injuries and illnesses among workers hired by BP and its subcontractors are steadily increasing."[49] There was disagreement over the lack of respirators for cleanup workers. One fisherman said there was "nobody" using respirators, that "it's got to be dangerous stuff, because it's thick," and that workers were not asking for respirators, because "they need a job, they need the money." However, an OSHA spokesman asserted that "everything that OSHA has seen so far in terms of air sampling data indicates that there's nothing necessitating the use of respirators at this time."[50] OSHA introduced some complicating dimensions to the respirators issue when it provided data indicating low air-quality levels for a number of substances, including benzene, and an agency official said that wearing respirators all day increased strain on hearts and lungs. However, criticisms came from both Congress and independent consultants. Congressman James Oberstar, chair of the House Transportation and Infrastructure Committee, and Congressman Jerrald Nadler sent a letter to OSHA and the EPA that mentioned carcinogens in the oil "as reason for workers to have respiratory protection." And a consultant criticized the OSHA data, saying that it included "no information about . . . volatile organic compounds it measured," which could "include many different toxic chemicals." Specifically, the consultant noted that OSHA had not provided "any sampling data on . . . dispersants" sprayed on the water to break up the oil into droplets.[51] At the same time, a former OSHA inspector declared that BP's data "contain[ed] too many gaps to provide a full assessment" of injuries to cleanup workers. With reference to the particular hazard of benzene exposure, a scientist with the National Resources Defense Council expressed concern that "long-term exposures, even at low levels, can be very hazardous."[52]

These various shadings of opinion, some of them in outright opposition to one another, captured the same kind of argument that proceeds in various kinds of scientific experiments: Investigators collect some data and then pile more data on top, and throughout the process, others provide opinions on both the limitations of the data and the correct interpretation of it. The gusher in the Gulf thus provides a moving picture of an environmental experiment that produced a costly set of externalities, the dimensions of which were debated for many months after the event.

In August 2010, a report at a White House briefing was fairly sanguine. As one press story put it, the report claimed that "most" of the oil "that could have leaked into the gulf could be accounted for . . . much of it was effectively gone already, and . . . most of the remaining oil was in a highly diluted form." The report estimated that about 25 percent of the oil had "either evaporated from the hot ocean surface or dissolved in the water into individual molecules of hydrocarbon." However, a marine scientist, Dr. Samantha Joye, was among critics who expressed doubt that more than 10 or 15 percent of the oil had disappeared in that way. Dr. Joye, who had been researching the spill, was acid in her comment, "If an academic scientist put something like this out there, it would get torpedoed into a billion pieces." Some scientists found the report plausible. Jeffrey Short, who worked for an environmental advocacy group and had studied the *Exxon Valdez* spill, said that the report's estimates were "better than nothing, and probably not very far off."[53] However, one report, based on the company's data on personal monitoring samples, showed that exposures to a particular toxic chemical, 2-Butoxyethanol, were at ten parts per million, up to twice the amount allowed by recommendations of the National Institute for Occupational Safety and Health.[54] And as the "on-the-one-hand, on-the-other-hand" argument went on, another scientist for an environmental group, Stan Senner, was sarcastic: "The government says that the oil is almost gone. . . . Wow. What a sigh of relief. Let's move on." One report had some environmentalists, including Senner, asserting that "the ecological impact . . . remained unclear and probably wouldn't be tallied for years."[55]

A procession of investigations on cause and responsibility began as early as August 2010. A federal panel headed by a former district court judge, which heard seventy-five witnesses "from roustabouts to senior vice presidents," revealed the kinds of uncertainties typical of early clinical trials in medicine. One witness, a lawyer for a firm that provided equipment in the *Deepwater* well, said, "I don't think we've truly gotten to the root causes. . . . There are still more questions than answers."[56]

By November, a preliminary report by a panel of fifteen other experts reportedly "found no single cause of the disaster" but strongly criticized BP for a lack of "management discipline" and problems with "delegation of decision-making" on the *Deepwater* platform. The chair of the panel spoke of "concern that there was no proper consideration of the tradeoffs between costs and schedule and risk and safety."[57] Echoing these conclusions with respect to Transocean was a Coast Guard report that said the firm "had serious safety management system failures and a poor safety culture." Transocean responded that seven months before the spill, the Coast Guard had "certified the rig as being fully compliant with all applicable U.S. and international marine safety compliance standards."[58]

In the same month, an adviser to a presidential commission found some causative responsibility in "muddled lines of authority within BP and between BP and its contractors."[59] A week later, an interim report of the National Academy of Engineering and the National Research Council spoke of "the lack of a suitable approach for and anticipating the inherent risks, uncertainties, and dangers associated with deep water drilling operations."[60] By January the presidential panel's final report, a 380-page production summarized by a reporter as "scathing," criticized not only BP, Transocean, and Halliburton, which had provided cement services on the well, but the oil industry generally. It referred to "systemic" problems in the industry, which it accused of "failing to prepare adequate plans to respond to a major oil spill." Moreover, it found the government itself culpable for what was characterized as "decades of lax regulation."[61]

Pouring out of a veritable pipeline of criticism came more reports. In September 2011 a joint report of the Coast Guard and the Bureau of Ocean Energy Management, Regulation and Enforcement focused its criticisms on BP but also laid responsibility on Transocean and Halliburton. It "found no evidence that BP performed a formal risk assessment of critical operational decisions made in the days leading up to the blowout" and specified "BP's failure to fully assess the risks associated with a number of operational decisions leading up to the blowout." It also found contributing causes in what were summarized as "cost- or time-savings decisions made by BP 'without considering contingencies and mitigation.'" It referred generally to the company's "failure to ensure all risks associated with operations on the Deepwater Horizon were as low as reasonably practicable."[62]

By 2012, a preliminary report of the Chemical Safety and Hazard Investigation Board condemned BP, Transocean, and regulators for failure to effectively learn "critical lessons or implement[ ] safety performance indicators" since the 2005 BP explosion in Texas City. As a reporter summarized it, the Board said that the firms had "focused on personal safety such as slips, trips, falls, and dropped objects, and infrequent lagging indicators" and that "hazard assessments of major accident risks . . . relied on correct manual intervention by the rig crew to prevent a catastrophe," adding that "dependence on a human reaction alone during an emergency is not a reliable safety layer."[63]

Another entry on the Gulf oil scene occurred when a November 2012 explosion on a platform owned by Black Elk Energy, twenty miles southeast of Grand Isle, Louisiana, killed a worker and critically burned several others, although the spillage of oil was only twenty-five gallons from a ruptured pipe. [64] Ironically, the explosion occurred the day after BP had pleaded guilty to eleven charges of felony manslaughter in connection with the *Deepwater* explosion and paid a criminal fine of $525 million and also an associated group of $4 billion in fines in what Attorney General Holder called "the single largest total criminal resolution . . . in the history of the United States." It appeared that BP could be responsible for as much as another $21 billion in civil penalties if the government could prove that the company was grossly negligent. [65]

Just a month later, Judge Barbier of the federal court in Louisiana approved a settlement with BP by a seventeen-member plaintiffs' steering committee for economic and property damage claims by individuals and businesses.[66] With the exception of a Seafood Compensation Program, which featured a guaranteed $2.3 billion fund, there was "no cap on the amounts that may be paid under the Settlement Agreement."[67] Judge Barbier said that the "plaintiffs' pursuit of class certification . . . a superior method of resolving these types of class claims . . . demonstrates they do in fact have the best interests of the class at heart, and hence are adequately representing the class."[68] And he labeled the settlement agreement as "clearly fair, reasonable, and adequate to putative class members."[69] He pronounced himself "satisfied that the probability of plaintiffs' success on the merits and the range of possible recovery weigh strongly in favor of approving the Settlement Agreement."[70]

BP went on the attack. As two reporters summarized it, the company had a "drastic" "change in attitude." Its position, manifested in "full-page ads, interviews and a gusher of court filings," was that its "good intentions are being hijacked by greedy lawyers and underhanded claimants."[71]

But BP's appeal fell on deaf ears with a majority of the Fifth Circuit, which tartly declared that there was "nothing fundamentally unreasonable about what BP accepted but now wishes it had not."[72] The court said that a reading of the many documents before it indicated that "the

Settlement Agreement does not require a claimant to submit *evidence* that the claim arose as a result of the oil spill." Noting that "each claimant does attest . . . under penalty of perjury, that the claim was in fact due to the *Deepwater Horizon* disaster," it said that although the attestations on claims forms on "financial figures and other details" were "not as protective of BP's present concerns as might have been achievable," they were "the protections that were accepted by the parties and approved by the district court."[73] Feinberg expressed dismay at the atmosphere that had enveloped the process, saying that it "too easily leads to the conclusion that an alternative resolution doesn't work, and in an oil spill you're better off with an Exxon-Valdez, decades-of-litigation approach." That, he said, was "a public policy missed opportunity."[74]

In the fall of 2014, Judge Barbier unleashed on BP a heavy weapon of characterization of its conduct, concluding that the company's "conduct was reckless,"[75] along with findings that its co-defendants Transocean and Halliburton had been negligent. The recklessness finding enabled claimants to avoid the damage cap in federal legislation and raised the possibility that the firm could be fined as much as $18 billion. Judge Barbier declared that several decisions by the company had been "primarily driven by a desire to save time and money, rather than ensuring that the well was secure."[76] He followed up this opinion with a holding that BP could not recoup payments to claimants it had already made but that it considered too generous, saying that the numbers were fixed by the terms of the settlement "as it was interpreted by the claims administrator and the court at that time."[77]

Thus, more than two years of investigation, argument, and rumination—in court, in panels of experts, in Congress, and at the White House—had produced a welter of opinions on causation and responsibility for a single mishap that had killed several workers and caused billions in damages of various kinds. How much the damages were was uncertain, but criticisms poured forth about the government's criminal settlement, which the director of the energy program of Public Citizen called "pathetic" and a "weak tea" punishment that carried "zero deterrence."[78]

Shadowing all this activity in law and politics was the gigantic experiment that was continuing to take place off the shores of the United States and many other countries. One observer, Edward C. Chow, who had been an oil company executive and was a senior fellow of the Center for Strategic and International Studies, focused on the central problem: "Our ability to manage risk hasn't caught up with our ability to explore and produce in deep water." [79] Robert Bea, a Berkeley professor, captured the figurative as well as literal depths of the problem when he said, "The industry has entered a new domain of vastly increased complexity and increased risks."[80]

Even the largest clinical trial of a drug or medical device could not match this experiment for either complexity or risk. True, many other ongoing experiments—for example, those carried out by millions of drivers daily in the risky environment of the highway—were both complex and risky. Truly, there is an arsenal of remedies available to persons injured by large-scale experimentation. The most common are ordinary compensatory damages in tort cases, to which occasionally punitive damages are tacked on. Another set of civil remedies is that of injunctions that prohibit certain kinds of conduct. A bridge remedy, discussed in Chapter Eleven, is the one that was sought by the Kivalina plaintiffs—not damages directly awarded for culpable conduct but payment of costs for remediation of a dangerous condition—in this case, relocation payments. But with respect to vehicle-caused injury and death, society had a statistical grip on the degree of risk and had over the years agreed on a set of legal institutions that balanced risks. Here, major problems were the uncertainty of the amount and severity of injury that might lie ahead and the lag between calculation of future risk and before-the-fact remediation, with the problem of valuation for after-the-fact remedies always closely lurking.

### *A Fertilizer Explosion*

A thread that runs through many kinds of experimentation across the country, and one that generates controversy, concerns the lack of regulation of dangerous activities and products. We briefly introduced earlier a most recent example, literally a reverberating one: the case of the April 2013 explosion of the fertilizer plant in West, Texas, in which large quantities of ammonium nitrate and anhydrous ammonia were stored.

Ammonium nitrate had been the focus of attention in two prior disasters stretching across seven decades. An explosion of fertilizer containing that substance had leveled the port area of Texas City in 1947, killing more than five hundred people. And the substance was the core of the material used to blow up the Alfred Murrah Federal Building in Oklahoma City in 1995, with a loss of 168 lives and destruction that affected residents of that capital for many years. There had been 540,000 pounds of ammonium nitrate stored at the plant in West, Texas, as reported in a filing to the Environmental Protection Agency. But the EPA "had not inspected or fined the facility in the past five years."

Moreover, there were other agencies whose regulatory activities were at best lax, or to whom the necessary reports were not made. OSHA records indicated that it had been twenty-eight years since the agency had inspected the plant, an inspection that produced a $30 penalty for five "serious" violations, including ones involving "improper storage and handling of anhydrous ammonia and improper respiratory protection for workers." In 2011, the Pipeline and Hazardous Materials Safety Administration of the Department of Transportation found "violations involving anhydrous ammonia," and in 2012 that agency fined the company $10,000, "citing inadequate markings on the tanks and deficient transportation plans for the fertilizer," later settling the fine for $5,250, according to agency records.

At the state level of regulation, reportedly, "the facility was grandfathered in" because it had been built in 1962, and although it was supposed to have been reauthorized in 2004, that did not happen. The executive director of the Texas Commission on Environmental Quality said that it had "investigated complaints of an ammonia smell" that was "very bad" in 2006 but that this issue was "resolved with the granting of two air permits to the company by the end of that year."[81]

Perhaps most startling in the regulatory context was the fact that the amount of the ammonium nitrate stored the plant was, as one report summarized it, "1,350 times greater than the threshold amount required for reporting to the Department of Homeland Security for possible regulation under an anti-terrorism law." The company had not submitted "the necessary paperwork for the department to consider whether to oversee it."[82] It was not until a year later that the chair of the United States Chemical Safety Board, summarizing its preliminary findings on the explosion, said that it "was preventable" and "should never have occurred." The official, Rafael Noure-Eraso, said that the event resulted "from the failure of a company to take the necessary steps to avert" it and "from the inability of federal, state and local regulatory agencies to identify a serious hazard and correct it." As a reporter summarized it, he noted that a reason that "a local emergency planning committee did not adopt an emergency plan for the plant . . . was that E.P.A. regulations did not require" such a plan for "retail sales of fertilizer chemicals," an exemption he said "should be revoked."[83]

The tension about permissible levels of experimentation with hazardous substances was evident in remarks by Governor Rick Perry of

Texas within a month after the explosion. In the immediate aftermath of the event, he called it "a truly nightmare scenario," saying that because of town's population of 2,700, "this tragedy has most likely hit every family."[84] But three weeks later, the tone of tragedy had given way to a declaration by the governor that, as reporters summarized it, "more government intervention and increased spending on safety inspections would not have prevented" the occurrence. Perry declared that "through their elected officials," Texans "clearly send the message of their comfort with the amount of oversight." At least some residents of West shared this point of view. One, a retired lawyer who had two cousins die in the explosion, said, "There has been nobody saying anything about more regulations." With the state priding itself on its "free-market posture," as reporters characterized it, what went with that attitude was "the highest number of workplace fatalities—more than 400 annually—for much of the past decade." It also was reported that "fires and explosions" in chemical and industrial plants had "cost as much in property damage as those in all the other states combined for the five years ending in May 2012."[85] The state's efforts to recoup the costs of the explosion ran into a roadblock when the Federal Emergency Management Agency said that the state had not given evidence that it "lacked the fiscal revenues to address" $17 million in damages to public buildings; the state's "Rainy Day Fund" totaled $8 billion. A reporter noted that the site was "strewn with crushed vehicles and mashed storage tanks."[86]

## II. Tort Reform

Woven into the arguments over how the legal system affects experimentation throughout society are the controversies over what is generically called "tort reform." That phrase refers to a group of proposals aimed at reducing the costs of tort law that arise from court judgments and settlements of injury cases. The published commentary on the subject is enormous. Andrew Popper has written of "thousands of articles in law reviews, peer-reviewed journals and other publications," also noting that there have been "thousands of legislative proceedings resulting in bills" that would make changes in the tort liability system.[87] Interestingly, it appears that the phrase "tort reform" was originally used in a student article published in 1974, which used it in a favorable way to describe the expansion of tort liability.[88] But by usage over the last generation, the term "tort reform" refers collectively to measures that change the playing field of experimentation for those who sell dangerous products and engage in various forms of risky activity, with one of the special targets of such proposals being the effect of tort rules on health care providers.

Just a sampling of the many kinds of argument on the subject indicates its birth as an anti-tort vehicle in the 1980s. A small pamphlet published in 1985 by Robert Malott, chairman and CEO of FMC Corporation, then a prominent manufacturer of machinery, captures many of the arguments in favor of modifying tort law. He speaks of how "the concept of liability for product-related injuries has been relentlessly expanded by both state and federal courts" " since the early 1960s." He identifies several kinds of industries in which manufacturers stopped production of various kinds of goods and, in at least one case, shut down a plant—all effects he attributed to products liability law.[89]

One snare for data collection on risky experiments is the trap of anecdotal data. One of the most famous tort cases of the latter part of the twentieth century arose from the scalding of an elderly woman by a cup of hot coffee from a McDonald's restaurant, which led to a punitive damages award of $2.9 million. This case became a standard example for tort reform advocates. However, as the Illinois Supreme Court pointed out in a decision that declared unconstitutional several provisions of a state tort reform law, that verdict was reduced to $480,000, and the plaintiff had undergone "numerous skin graft operations for third degree burns." The court also noted, citing a scholar's report, that "McDonald's had prior knowledge of hundreds of similar scalding incidents."[90] Beyond the McDonald's case, which in part became famous because of facts that were left out in the telling, there were many "urban legends" told and retold by tort reform advocates that were nothing more than legend. One story probably made up out of the whole cloth asserted that a man had sued a mower manufacturer because he was hurt while trying to trim a hedge with the mower.

Further illustrative of the breadth of interest in the controversy was the convening of the National Symposium on Civil Justice Issues, with the topic "In Search of Proper Balance," in 1986. The program for the conference, which I attended, included more than six hundred people and described the participants as ranging from corporate executives to "leading consumer advocates" and "creative legal thinkers."[91] The next year, the Brookings Institution held a conference on civil liability, contributions to which were published in a book, *Liability: Perspectives and Policy*.[92]

Between 1984 and 1991, two long monographs covered many aspects of the debate over tort liability and related issues. The 1984 book, of which I was the principal author, was a report of the Special Committee on the Tort Liability System of the American Bar Association. It concluded that despite its shortcomings, "tort law has important values both functionally and symbolically," being in the process of a "continuing creation of a system of substantive justice, with all the complexity that term implies, for disputes caused by a multitude of injuries."[93] The other work, published in 1991, was a two-volume monograph by a consortium of five "reporters," all leading scholars, that "defend[ed] the basic tort model as a valuable aspect of our personal injury system" but insisted that "liability rules must be modified in a way that better respects the tort system's appropriate place in the broader personal injury universe: juries should not be permitted to react intuitively, without meaningful legal guidelines, to open-ended claims for pain and suffering or punitive damages." These authors also said "there should be a sharp reduction in "wasteful multiple litigation over questions that are common to all the individual suits arising out of mass tort episodes."[94] I criticized this project, while it was being developed, in an article that was dubious about what I characterized as the reporters' notion that one could "assign[ ] injury tasks to one 'system' or the other"—the "systems" including tort law, regulation, and contracts. I suggested that the defect in this approach was that it assumed the existence of a "tsar" who could allocate those tasks to different legal and social institutions.[95]

The administrations of two presidents Bush weighed in for tort reform. In 1992, the administration of George H. W. Bush put forth a proposal that, among other features, emphasized a "loser pays" rule, applicable to claims in federal district court involving state law, that would require losing parties to pay winning parties for lawyer fees as much as the losing party's attorney fees. It also encouraged the use of alternative dispute resolution. Vice President Quayle, publicizing the proposal to an audience that included members of the American Tort Reform Association, declared that "the American people know we are right." The American Bar Association gave support to only part of the plan.[96]

A decade later, the second President Bush presented a double-barreled argument for tort reform, which a reporter said he had made "a signature issue."[97] In a 2002 address in Birmingham, Alabama, the president targeted "junk and frivolous lawsuits" that he said were hurting the economy, expressing particular concern for the effects of tort litigation on "small business owners."[98] His 2003 State of the

Union message focused the tort spotlight on health care malpractice. Mentioning "the constant threat that physicians and hospitals will be unfairly sued," he urged Congress "to pass medical liability reform."[99]

The menu of tort reform proposals is extensive. Many of them focus on the business end of tort liability practice: damages. They include proposals to limit the amount of "noneconomic damages"—largely those representing the category of "pain and suffering"—that may be recovered in tort cases. They also include measures that would limit recoveries for punitive damages. Other tort reform proposals aim to shorten the time limits the law imposes on those who sue for personal injury, limits contained in statutes of limitations and statutes of repose. Still other suggestions would change substantive legal rules that govern sellers, providers of services, and others who create risk to third parties—including those who engage in activities that come under the heading of pollution of air and water. Some of those rules have to do with liability doctrines, including doctrines that permit the imposition of liability for conduct that is very dangerous but cannot be called negligent. Another set of proposals focuses on whether liability could be imposed on one of several parties contributing to an injury—usually the most solvent party—for the entire amount of the damages. Yet another question, which has generated much litigation and several Supreme Court decisions, is whether the existence of a federal or state regulatory system, created by legislation, should bar tort actions by those injured by a product or process covered by that system.

Arguments have flown back and forth on the effects of tort law and the effects of tort reform legislation. A study published in 1993 suggested that tort damages for noneconomic loss effectively imposed an "involuntary insurance" policy on consumers who would not, left to their own choices, buy insurance for that kind of harm.[100] Indeed, they said, "Awards for pain and suffering may be imposing a substantial deadweight cost on consumers."[101]

A flurry of studies presented a mix of data on the effects of tort reform on medical care. One paper, focusing on caps on noneconomic damages, found "robust evidence" in data from the Centers for Disease Control that such caps "simultaneously increase and decrease treatment intensity, with an overall net decrease." The authors did conclude that such caps "increase the probability" that physicians would perform bypass operations, "particularly when providers face patients whose medical conditions enables providers to choose between" a bypass and an angioplasty—an effect "most evident for insured patients, which is when health care providers have the strongest financial incentives" to do a bypass. They suggested that tort reform thus "may encourage riskier but more remunerative procedures." On the whole, they concluded that "based on mortality data, patient outcomes did not change greatly, and may have slightly improved, even though treatments changed." They opined, "This combination of results is most consistent with a decrease in defensive medicine following tort reform."[102]

Another group of researchers focused on the effects of legislative tort reform in Texas on the elderly. They found "a dramatic impact on claim rates and payouts per claim." This result was in line with their expectation, because a higher proportion of the damages of elderly patients are noneconomic. They commented, among other things, that "the correspondence between . . . simulated and actual results adds to the credibility to both, and suggests that plaintiffs' lawyers had limited ability to respond to the caps by adjusting case mix toward cases with higher economic damages."[103]

More globally, the distinguished Cornell scholar Theodore Eisenberg declared that "the most common theme of the empirical findings" on tort reform, "other than the effect of draconian caps, is the absence of robust evidence of effects." It is worth summarizing some of his generalizations on particular sets of data. One observation was that "little evidence exists that reform of punitive damages affected the ratio between punitive and compensatory damages. This is consistent with punitive damages not having been out of control and in need of reform." Focusing on health care, Eisenberg concluded that "evidence of the effect of tort reform in the medical malpractice field is mixed"—that "caps on non-economic damages have reduced costs, thereby likely decreasing pressure on hospitals to improve care," and that "consistent evidence of effects on physician behavior and physician supply has not emerged." Eisenberg commented, "Tort reform has rarely sought to address the well-established problem of widespread harm caused by poor quality care." Noting that "products liability plaintiffs have had decreasing success over time," he said, "While one cannot rule out specific statutory reforms as achieving more favorable results for defendants, the national scope of plaintiffs' declining success supports an explanation based on the social construction of knowledge by well-funded industry groups."[104]

When we consider the nation as a laboratory for risky activity, many questions arise about the collection and interpretation of data, with other questions arising about the assignment of responsibility. The stakes are high for businesses as well as those who may be at risk from their activities. And the uncertainties run in several directions. Both businesses and consumers may be uncertain about risks before they mature, sometimes literally explosively. Businesses express concern about uncertainty in the law: Will they be liable at all, and if they are, what will the remedies be? Finally, there is after-the-fact scientific uncertainty about whether a particular product or activity has caused a particular disease or cluster of diseases.

Intertwined with these issues are choices that must be made about the appropriate remedy for injury—indeed, whether any remedy is appropriate. Questions about the scope and propriety of particular remedies run through the debates about whether to modify tort law in ways that reduce the frequency of litigation and the amounts awarded to injured persons. In fact, some advocates of tort reform argue that the organized personal injury bar itself advocates a form of "tort reform" to expand liability, including the "deputizing of private lawyers to sue on behalf of the state," the efforts to expand the field of tort claims to the kinds of suits that can be said to be "implied" by statutes but that the statutes do not specifically authorize, and the passage of consumer protection statutes that provide more opportunity for private suits.[105] The battle lines continue to shift on tort reform, with one question that often arises being whether courts should declare that legislation aimed to cut down litigation goes beyond constitutional boundaries of due process and equal protection of the laws. Each shift in the battle lines has an impact on the methods, detailed in this chapter, that society has developed to deal with risky experiments—sometimes experiments on a national scale—that put members of the public at risk. The warfare on these issues itself constitutes an experiment in progress.

## Notes

1. See for example Fernanda Santos and Clifford Krauss, "Emerging From the Rubble in a Texas Town," *New York Times*, April 19, 2013; Ian Urbina et al., "After Plant Explosion, Texas Remains Wary of Regulation," *New York Times*, May 10, 2013, pp. A1 and A10; Alyssa Newcomb, "West Texas Fertilizer Plant Explosion: Some Residents Allowed to Return Home," *Good Morning America*, April 20, 2013, printed from the Internet.
2. Thomas W. Lippman, "Oil Industry Unveils Plan for Disaster-Response Teams," *Washington Post*, June 21, 1989, p. A2.
3. Suzanna Pagano and Greg Hellman, "Fishermen, Oil Spill Workers Most Exposed, Face Greater Risk of Adverse Health Effects," 40 *Occup. Safety & Health Rep.* (BNA) 481-82 (June 10, 2010).
4. Bernard Goldstein et al., "The Gulf Oil Spill," 364 *N. Eng. J. Med.* 1334, 1334 (2011).

5. Ibid., p. 1335.
6. Ibid., p. 1339.
7. Ibid., p. 1335.
8. See ibid., p. 1339.
9. Ibid., pp. 1339–40.
10. See ibid., pp. 1344–45.
11. See ibid., p. 1346.
12. See John Schwartz, "Lawyers, Far From Gulf, Skirmish on Spill Claims," *New York Times*, July 30, 2010, p. A13.
13. See ibid. and John Schwartz, "U.S. Judge in New Orleans Will Hear Gulf Spill Cases," *New York Times*, Aug. 11, 2010, p. A11.
14. See "New Oil Spill Litigation Group Certified," *Trial*, August 2010, p. 49.
15. Allison Torres Burtka, "Ripple Effect," *Trial*, August 2010, pp. 42 and 45.
16. See Jackie Calmes, "For Gulf Victims, Mediator With Deep Pockets and Broad Powers," *New York Times*, June 23, 2010, p. A17.
17. *Union Oil Co. v. Oppen*, 501 F.2d 558, 568-70 (9th Cir.1974).
18. *State of La. ex rel. Guste v. M/V TESTBANK*, 752 F.2d 1019, 1021 n.2 (5th Cir. 1985).
19. *State of La. ex rel. Guste v. M/V Testbank*, 524 F.Supp. 1170, 1174 (D. La. 1981).
20. 752 F.2d at 1029.
21. 33 U.S.C. §2704(a)(3).
22. Ibid., §2704(c)(1)(A).
23. Congressman Nadler in "Legal Liability Issues Surrounding the Gulf Coast Disaster," hearing before the House Judiciary Committee, 111 Cong. 2d Sess., Serial No. 111-130 (May 27, 2010), p. 140.
24. Congresswoman Waters, ibid., p. 159.
25. Senator Lautenberg in "The Gulf of Mexico Oil Spill: Ensuring a Financially Responsible Recovery, Part I & II," hearings before the Federal Financial Management, Government Information, Federal Services, and International Security Subcommittee of the Senate Committee on Homeland Security and Governmental Affairs Committee, 111th Cong. 2d Sess., (June 16 & July 22, 2010), p. 70 (hereafter, Financially Responsible Recovery).
26. Senator Sessions, in "The Risky Business of Big Oil: Have Recent Court Decisions and Liability Caps Encouraged Irresponsible Corporate Behavior?" hearing before the Senate Judiciary Committee, 111th Cong. 2d Sess., Serial No. J-111-96 (June 8, 2010), pp. 5–6.
27. Kenneth Feinberg in hearing, "Financially Responsible Recovery," supra note 25, p. 50.
28. Editorial, "Mr. Feinberg and the Gulf Settlement," *New York Times*, August 30, 2010, p. A16.
29. Kristin Choo, "The Price of Oil," *ABA Journal*, August 2010, pp. 34 and 40.
30. Michael Cooper, "Two Funds, Same Goal: Compensate," *New York Times*, Aug. 22, 2010, p. A14.
31. Campbell Robertson, "An Oil Rig Burns, Blanketing the Gulf With Angst," *New York Times*, Sept. 3, 2010, pp. A1 and A14.
32. See Campbell Robertson and John Schwartz, "Rethinking the Process for BP Spill Claims," *New York Times*, Sept. 16, 2010, pp. A14 and A16.

33. See David Segal, "Should the Money Go Where the Oil Didn't?" *New York Times*, Oct. 24, 2010, business section, pp. 1 and 6.
34. Colin McDowell, comment, "The Gulf Coast Claims Facility and the Deepwater Horizon Litigation: Judicial Regulation of Private Compensation Schemes," 64 *Stan. L. Rev*. 765, 773 (2012).
35. Ibid., pp. 773–74.
36. John Schwartz, "Administrator of BP Fund Offers Bonuses to Spill Victims Who Bypass Suits," *New York Times*, Dec. 13, 2010, p. A16.
37. Rachel M. Zahorsky, "Biloxi Blues," *ABA Journal*, Nov. 2012, pp. 44 and 47.
38. Campbell Robertson and John Schwartz, "Many Hit by Spill Are Now Caught in Claim Process," *New York Times*, April 19, 2011, p. 14.
39. John Schwartz, "Man With $20 Billion to Disburse Finds No Shortage of Claims of Critics, Cities," *New York Times*, April 19, 2011, p. 14.
40. "In re: Oil Spill by the Oil Rig 'Deepwater Horizon' in the Gulf of Mexico, on April 20, 2010," 808 F. Supp.2d 943, 962 (E.D. La. 2011).
41. Paul H. Rubin, "A Gulf Spill Tort Primer," *Wall Street Journal*, August 1, 2010.
42. *Abbott v. BP Exploration and Production Inc.*, 781 F. Supp. 2d 453, 457, 467, 471 (S.D. Tex. 2011).
43. Sarah Lyall et al., "In BP's Record, a History of Boldness and Blunders," *New York Times*, July 13, 2010, pp. A1 and A14.
44. See Ralph Lindeman, "Criminal Charges Said Likely in Gulf Spill: Corporate Penalties, Prison Terms Possible" *U.S. Law Week*, July 6, 2010, pp. 1019–1020.
45. Patricia Ware, "BP Refineries Said to Account for 97 Percent of 'Flagrant' Violations Found at Refineries," 40 *O.S.H. Rep*. 421 (May 20, 2010).
46. Ian Urbina, "Workers on Doomed Rig Voiced Concern on Safety," *New York Times*, July 22, 2010, pp. A1 and A16.
47. Ian Urbina, "Oil Rig's Owner Had Safety Issue At 3 Other Wells," *New York Times*, Aug. 5, 2010, pp. A1 and A16.
48. See Robbie Brown, "Another Rig's Close Call Altered Rules, Papers Say," *New York Times*, Aug. 17, 2010, p. A19.
49. Stephen Lee, "Louisiana State Officials Demand OSHA Study Emerging Threats to Oil Spill Workers," 40 *OSH Rep*. 480 (June 10, 2010).
50. Stephen Lee, "Oil Spill Cleanup Workers in Gulf of Mexico Being Denied Respirators, Eyewitnesses Say," 40 *OSH Rep*. 439, 440 (May 27, 2010).
51. See Greg Hellman and Patricia Ware, "OSHA, EPA Monitoring in Gulf Oil Spill Indicates Low Levels of Toxic Substances," 40 *OSH Rep*. 479 (June 10, 2010).
52. See Greg Hellman, "BP Data Show Potentially Dangerous Exposures for Gulf Cleanup Workers," 40 *Occup. Safety & Health Rep*. (BNA) 597 (July 15, 2010); Gina Solomon's Blog, "NRDC Switchboard," posted May 24, 2010,[IT'S RIGHT THERE] updated June 20, 2010.
53. Justin Gillis and Leslie Kaufman, "Oil Spill Calculations Stir Debate on Damage," *New York Times* Aug. 5, 2010, p. A16.
54. See Greg Hellman, "BP Data Shows Potentially Dangerous Exposures for Gulf Cleanup Workers," 40 *OSH Rep*. (BNA) 597 (July 5, 2010).
55. Leslie Eaton and Elizabeth Williamson, "Doubts Arise That Crude Is Subsiding," *Wall Street Journal*, Aug. 4, 2010.

56. Robbie Brown, "In Oil Inquiry, Panel Sees No Single Smoking Gun," *New York Times*, Aug. 28, 2010, p. A12.
57. See John M. Broder, "Spill Report Faults BP and Contractors," *New York Times*, Nov. 18, 2010.
58. John M. Broder, "Companies, Crews and Regulators Share Blame in Coast Guard Report on Oil Spill," *New York Times*, April 23, 2011, p. A9.
59. Alan Kovski, "Questionable Management of Rig Operations, Limited Expertise Cited in Gulf Spill Report," 40 *OSH Rep.* 980 (Nov. 25, 2010).
60. See ibid.
61. John M. Broder, "Tougher Rules Urged for Offshore Drilling," *New York Times*, Jan. 12, 2011, p. A12.
62. Quotations from report in Rodd Zolkos and Michael Bradford, "Risk Management Faulted in Probe of BP Disaster," *Business Insurance*, Sept 19, 2011, p. 4.
63. Susanna Pagano, "CSB Finds BP, Transocean Focused More on Injury Rates, Not Safety Precautions," 42 *OSH Rep.* 667 (July 26, 2012).
64. See Bruce Rolfsen, "Gulf of Mexico Oil Platform Investigation by BSEE, Coast Guard," 42 *OSH Rep.* (BNA) 1033 (Nov. 22, 2012).
65. Susanne Pagano, "BP Reaches $4.5 Billion Settlement With U.S. Government in Gulf Spill Case," 81 *U.S. Law Week* 728 (Nov. 20, 2012).
66. *In Re: Oil Spill by the Oil Rig "Deepwater Horizon" in the Gulf of Mexico, on April 20, 2010*, 910 F. Supp.2d 891 (E.D. La. 2012).
67. Ibid., p. 904.
68. Ibid., p. 920.
69. Ibid., p. 930.
70. Ibid., p. 934.
71. Campbell Robertson and John Schwartz, "How a Gulf Settlement that BP Once Hailed Became Its Target," *New York Times*, April 27, 2014, pp. A1 and A20.
72. *In re Deepwater Horizon*, 744 F.3d 370, 377 (5th Cir. 2014), petition for rehearing denied, 753 F.3d 516 (5th Cir. 2014).
73. Ibid., pp. 376–77.
74. Robertson and Schwartz, supra, p. A20.
75. See *In re Oil Spill By the Oil Rig "Deepwater Horizon" in the Gulf of Mexico, on April 20, 2010*, 21 F. Supp.3d 657, p. 743 (E.D. La.2014). See also ibid., pp. 746, 747, and 757 (E.D. La. 2010), for various other applications of the term to BP's conduct by Judge Barbier.
76. See ibid., p. 693. See also Campbell Robertson and Clifford Knauss, "BP May Be Fined Up to $18 Billion For Spill in Gulf," *New York Times*, Sept. 5, 2014, p. A1; Margaret Cronin Fisk et al., "BP Found Grossly Negligent in 2010 Spill: Fines May Rise for Oil Giant in Decision," 83 *U.S. L. Wk.* 364 (Sept. 9, 1914).
77. See John Schwartz, "Judge Denies BP's Request to Recoup Overpayments," *New York Times*, Sept. 25, 2014, p. A13.
78. Pagano, supra note 63, p. 729.
79. Jad Mouawad and Barry Meier, "Risk-Taking Rises to New Levels As Oil Rigs in Gulf Drill Deeper," *New York Times*, Aug. 30, 2010, p. A1.
80. Ibid., p. A10.
81. See Manny Fernandez and John Schwartz, "Plant Explosion Tears At the Heart of a Texas Town," *New York Times*, April 18, 2013; Fernando Santos

and Clifford Krauss, "Emerging from the Rubble in a Texas Town," *New York Times*, April 19, 2013; Robert Iafolla, "Texas Fertilizer Explosion Reveals Gaps in Regulations for Hazardous Chemicals," 43 *OSH Rep.* (BNA) 382-83 (April 25, 2013).

82. See Iafolla, supra.
83. See Manny Fernandez, "Lax Oversight Cited As Factor in Deadly Blast at Texas Plant," *New York Times*, April 23, 2014, pp. A11 and A15.
84. See Fernandez and Schwartz, "Plant Explosion Tears At the Heart of a Texas Town," supra.
85. See Ian Urbina et al., "After Plant Explosion, Texas Remains Wary of Regulation," *New York Times*, May 10, 2013, pp. A1 and A16.
86. See Manny Fernandez, "FEMA Denies Texas Request for Full Disaster Aid, Rankling Stricken Town," *New York Times*, June 23, 2013, p. A18.
87. Andrew F. Popper, *Materials on Tort Reform 11* (West, 2010), an excellent collection of arguments on various dimensions of the subject.
88. See Carl T. Bogus, "Introduction: Genuine Tort Reform," 13 *Roger Williams L. Rev.* 1, 1 (2008), referring to "Comment, Judicial Activism in Tort Reform: The Guest Statute Exemplar and a Proposal for Comparative Negligence," 21 *UCLA L. Rev.* 1566 (1974).
89. Robert A. Malott, "America's Liability Explosion: Can We Afford the Cost?" talk at Northwestern University Law School, Corporate Counsel Inst., Oct. 10, 1985. A contemporaneous press article on "new legal theories that would significantly expand liability for negligence" and that are "reverberating in judicial decisions and law review articles from California to New Zealand" is Nicholas Kristof, "Theories Expand Concept of Liability," *New York Times*, Oct. 14, 1986, p. 10.
90. *Best v. Taylor Mach. Works*, 689 N.E.2d 1057, 1068 n.1 (Ill. 1997), citing Michael Rustad, "Nationalizing Tort Law: The Republican Attack on Women, Blue Collar Workers and Consumers," 48 *Rutgers L. Rev.* 673, 720-21 (1996). Rustad reports that there were more than seven hundred prior complaints. See also Michael A. Rustad, "The Endless Campaign: How the Tort Reformers Successfully and Incessantly Market Their Groupthink to the Rest of Us," Suffolk University Law School research paper 20–32 (July 7, 2010), SSRN.com.
91. Program, National Symposium on Civil Justice, "In Search of Proper Balance," April 30–May 1, 1986, New York.
92. Robert E. Litan and Clifford Winston (eds.), *Liability: Perspectives and Policy* (Brookings, 1988).
93. American Bar Association, Special Committee on the Tort Liability System, "Towards a Jurisprudence of Injury: The Continuing Creation of a System of Substantive Justice in American Tort Law," pp. 14–12 (M. Shapo Rptr. 1984).
94. *II Enterprise Responsibility for Personal Injury* (American Law Institute, 1991), pp. 579–80.
95. Marshall S. Shapo, "Tort Reform: The Problem of the Missing Tsar," 19 *Hofstra L. Rev.* 185 (1990), referring to Richard Stewart, "Crisis in Tort Law? The Institutional Perspective," 54 *U. Chi. L. Rev.* 194 (1987).
96. See Mark A. Hofmann, "Administration Unveils Package of Tort Reforms," *Business Insurance*, Feb. 10, 1992, p. 1; Mitchell Locin and Amy D. Burke, "Quayle Offers Bill to Cut Lawsuits," *Chicago Tribune*, Feb. 5, 1992; Meg

Fletcher, "ABA Supports Part of Tort Reform Package," *Business Insurance*, Feb. 10, 1992, p. 4.
97. Adam Liptak, "Shot in the Arm for Tort Overhaul," *New York Times*, Nov. 17, 2002, sec. 3, pp. 1 and 10.
98. Steven Harras, "Bush Says 'Junk Lawsuits' Hurt Economy: Tort Reform Supporters and Opponents React," 30 *Prod. Safety & Liab. Rep.* (BNA) 653 (July 29, 2002).
99. George W. Bush, State of the Union address, 2003.
100. See John C. Calfee and Clifford Winston, *The Consumer Welfare Effects of Liability for Pain and Suffering: An Exploratory Analysis* (Brookings, 1993).
101. See ibid., p. 134.
102. Ronen Avraham and Max Schanzenbach, "The Impact of Tort Reform on Intensity of Treatment: Evidence From Heart Patients," 39 J. Health Econ. 273 (2015).
103. Myungho Paik et al., "How Do the Elderly Fare in Medical Malpractice Litigation, Before and After Tort Reform? Evidence from Texas," 14 *Am. L. & Econs. Rev.* 561, 595-96 (2012).
104. Theodore Eisenberg, "The Empirical Effects of Tort Reform," in *Research Handbook on the Economics of Torts* (Edward Elgar Pub. Ltd., 2013), pp. 513 and 543.
105. See for example "Defrocking Tort Reform: Stopping Personal Injury Lawyers from Repealing Existing Tort Reform and Expanding Rights to Sue in State Legislatures," white paper of the American Tort Reform Association (2008), reprinted in Popper, supra, note 87, pp. 167–78.

# 13

# Cultures of Risk and Experiment

Experimentation of all kinds, formal and informal—and indeed the daily process of living—involves risk. Formally, should I enter this closely supervised clinical research program that seeks cures for a life-threatening illness? Less formally, should I try this this spicy dish I have never eaten? Should I take the shorter highway or the longer expressway to work? Should I marry this person?

Our answers to questions like these have roots in our personalities and our experiences, and in the culture that surrounds us.

## I. Philosophical Perspectives[1]

Culture weaves threads that run in and out of our understanding of risk. An essay by George Foster, written in 1965, speaks of "a common cognitive orientation which is, in effect, an unverbalized, implicit expression" of the understanding of "the members of every society" "of the 'rules of the game' of living imposed upon them by their social, natural, and supernatural universes" and refers to the "unconscious acceptance" by people of "the 'rules of the game' implicit in their cognitive orientation."[2] In a 1990 essay, Aaron Wildavsky and Karl Dake identified several theories of risk perception: theories of "knowledge," "personality," "economic," "political," and cultural.[3] Finding "compelling" the conclusion that "*self-rated knowledge and perceptual accuracy have a minimal relationship with risk perception,*"[4] they declared that "*however conceptualized—whether as political ideology or cultural biases—worldviews best account for patterns of risk perception.*"[5] Parallel to these views, the metaphor of a complex psychology appears in the idea that personal choice emerges from cultural backgrounds. John Lawrence Hill, writing of the role of duress in law, summarizes work of Michael Moore on the proposition that people should be held responsible only "when they act from internalized values, goals and beliefs," "sources of motivation" that "have been incorporated or 'integrated' into the personality of the person over time, as the result of conscious choice."[6]

A separate set of questions concerns the reality of risk acceptance. Robin West criticizes a view, which she ascribes to Richard Posner, that "the presence of consent, without more, satisfies the requirements of an ideal of autonomy and on an implicit assumption that people consent to changes in their worlds in order to improve their well-being."[7] Professor West cites stories by Franz Kafka as "illustrat[ing] the simple truth" that "to say that the risk of a loss is consensually assumed is not to imply that the subsequent 'ownership' of a set of risks promotes either one's well-being or one's sense of autonomy."[8] She comments, "It is not true, as Posner blithely assumes, that all men calculate all the time. Sometimes we calculate. Other times, we simply obey, acquiesce, or submit."[9] I would comment that in many situations involving experimentation broadly defined, people often "acquiesce" or "submit."

We have been speaking here of the perception of risk by individuals. A broader view of the subject deals with risk estimates by governmental actors. An EPA official specializing in radiation programs premised that in practice, "social decisionmaking relies on subjective risk estimates," and that "despite the absence of an objective probability of reward and punishment, human behavior generally is based on subjective assessments of reward and punishment." From this, he concluded that "objective risk estimates provide a sounder basis for governmental decisionmaking."[10]

An important element in government regulation of risks is the degree of paternalism that it represents. There is a range of definitions of paternalism. In an often-cited work focused on criminal law, Joel Feinberg distinguishes "hard" and "soft" versions of paternalism. Hard paternalism justifies government intervention in personal choice through criminal legislation on the ground that "it is necessary to protect competent adults, against their will, from the harmful consequences even of their fully voluntary choices and undertakings."[11] By comparison, soft paternalism has been summarized as justifying intervention only when it "is necessary to determine whether the person being interfered with is acting voluntarily and knowledgeably."[12] One critic of the distinction, citing Feinberg's justification of a prohibition on dueling, has said that Feinberg has "all but admitted that his determinations of voluntariness are subjective."[13]

Viewing the term in a broad connotation, one author who notes its "pariah status" suggests that it may not "even [be] accurate to think of public health paternalism as directed to the individual at all but instead directed towards overall societal welfare," but he says that "paternalistic policies can be highly effective in preventing injuries and deaths in the population" generally. However, he opines that "it is at least worth considering whether" paternalism "is ever justified to regulate harms that are apparently self-imposed, but which are deeply socially embedded and pervasively harmful to the public"[14]—an observation in which the idea of a "risk culture" seems at least implicit.

From a different perspective, one group of authors proposes an approach that they term "asymmetric paternalism," a concept that "creates large benefits for those who make errors, while imposing little or no harm on those who are fully rational."[15] This idea takes into account the premise that "rationality and willpower are as bounded as many behavioral economists believe."[16] As one author summarize the concept of "bounded rationality," it refers to people's uses of "mental shortcuts and rules of thumb" that make up for the finite character of "human cognitive abilities." Existing alongside it are "bounded willpower"—the way people "take actions that they know to be in conflict with their own long-term interests," for which they can "take steps to mitigate its effects"—and "bounded self-interest." The latter category refers to the fact that "in many market and bargaining settings . . . people care about being treated fairly and want to treat others fairly if those others are behaving themselves fairly."[17]

The concepts discussed above bear on the question of when regulation of various kinds of experimentation is appropriate. A simple justification for regulation is that "people sometimes do mispredict their utility at the time of decision"—that they are "sometimes unable . . . to assess what [an] experience will actually be like." Yet clouding the case for regulation is the possibility that governmental decisions to control risky activities will over-respond to short-term collections of anecdotes about the "pollutant-of-the-month" and the "crisis-of-the-month."[18]

However, Richard Thaler and Cass Sunstein have stressed that sometimes it is necessary to employ some form of paternalism, emphasizing that "in some cases individuals make inferior choices, choices that they would change if they had complete information, unlimited cognitive abilities, and no lack of willpower."[19] Their abstract solution—an idea on which Sunstein has played several variations—is to "preserve freedom of choice" but to "authorize both private and public institutions to steer people in directions that will promote their welfare."[20]

The politics of regulation of large-scale experimentation are complex. One writer has said that "it may seem astonishing" that laws like statutes on auto safety and worker safety and anti-pollution legislation have been passed. He observes that it "requires the efforts of a skilled entrepreneur"—for example, Ralph Nader—"who can mobilize public sentiment" as "the vicarious representative of groups not directly part of the legislative process."[21]

## II. Empirics

There are many influences on people's inclination to take risks, including the varied set of risks associated with experiments in which they participate that they may not know are experiments. A body of evidence indicates that "risk taking seems to be influenced jointly by the situation and characteristics of the decision maker." There is a spectrum of particular situations, ranging from financial investing to "social choices" and to "health decisions" and gambling, in which it appears that "the same person often shows different degrees of risk taking."[22] It further appears that in several of these areas, "sensation seeking" is correlated with "greater risk taking." An interesting hypothesis is that "apparent differences in risk taking may be the result of differences in the perception of the riskiness of . . . choice options, and not of differences in attitudes toward (perceived) risk."[23] Thus, "groups known for high levels of sensation seeking (e.g., teenage boys) seem to take large risks because they perceive the levels of risk to be smaller than other groups, and not because they cherish (perceived) risk to a greater extent."[24] More generally, "person-centered characteristics," like age, gender, culture, and personality, "influence risk taking mostly by changing people's perception of the riskiness of decision alternatives, rather than by affecting their willingness to take on more or less risk."[25]

Another study concluded, not surprisingly, that "both general and specific risk taking have strong and clear personality underpinnings."[26] These researchers measured "risk propensity in terms of reported frequency of risk behaviors" in six "domains"—that is, "recreation, health, career, finance, safety and social."[27] Measuring "overall risk propensity" on an established "Five Factor" personality inventory," they found a "clear . . . pattern" that "combin[ed] high extraversion and openness," two of the five factors, with "low neuroticism, agreeableness, and conscientiousness"—the other three factors.[28] Cutting across these generalizations were three sets of risk takers, categories that were "not mutually exclusive." A "minority group" but one "of significant proportions" was people "for whom risks are intrinsically exciting," who "bear risk as a pleasure to be consumed." The authors reported a dichotomy between "goal achievers" and "risk avoiders," with the goal achievers being "people whose drive for success, popularity, prominence, or gain leads them to be prepared to bear major risk in order to get what they want." For these people, the "willingness to bear risk is a combination of emotional coolness, toughness, activity and a tendency to casualness about control and rules." Finally, there was a group of "people whose risk taking is quite specific to areas of endeavor and activity"—for example, people in finance.[29]

An important influence on people's views of risk is what has been called "affect"—the "rapid[ ]" and "automatic[ ]" response to a stimulus as contrasted with a more "systematic analysis" of a situation.[30] A primary root of research on "the role of affect in judgments of risk" is a 1983 article by Eric Johnson and Amos Tversky on experiments they conducted based on "brief accounts of tracing deaths of a single person from a specific cause"—for example, leukemia, a fire, and a homicide.[31] Their data "demonstrate[d] that mood induced by brief reports has a large and pervasive impact on estimates of the frequency of risks and other undesirable events." And indeed, they found "no connection between the information contained in a story and its impact on the estimated frequency of death"; the "overriding factor" was "not the story told but rather the mood it induces in the reader."[32]

"Affect" responses, according to the decision researcher Paul Slovic and his colleagues, derive from survival mechanisms that developed in human beings "long before there was probability theory, risk assessment and decision analysis," a time when "instinct and gut feeling" often kept people alive in dangerous environments.[33] The implications of various studies were that "people base their judgements of an activity or technology not only on what they think about it but also on how they feel about it." These feelings move people toward judgments on the risks and benefits of the activity or technology.[34] Thus, in a study of people's "quick, intuitive" reactions to mentions of "very small exposure[s]" to certain chemicals, the results were not what one might expect. Instead of judgments of risks that were "uniformly low and unvarying," "there was a strong correlation across chemicals between affect and judged risk" of the small exposures.[35]

An analogous terminology for expressing this kind of response appears in the concept of a "phenomenological state of mind," which "refers to how something 'feels' rather than its mere perception." A term for "feel" in this sense is "the qualia of the perception," with "qualia" "appear[ing] to be more akin to bodily sensations that arise from some primal internal process designed to alert decision makers to the quality of their thoughts, quite apart from the use of formal reasoning." A commonsense expression of this kind of decision making refers to the idea that a "decision must 'feel right' as well as 'look right.'"[36]

A particularly powerful linkage of this body of research to action appears in the case of beginning smokers. The research lines up with the problem of "misprediction" noted earlier: "most beginning smokers lack the experience to appreciate how their future selves will perceive the risks from smoking or how they will value the trade-off between health and the need to smoke." In announcing this conclusion, Paul Slovic and his colleagues commented, "This is a strong repudiation of the model of informed rational choice."[37] They declared that while generally the "affect heuristic" "works beautifully when our experience enables us to anticipate accurately how we will like the consequences of our decisions," "it fails miserably when the consequences turn out to be much different in character than we anticipated."[38] A troubling set of findings with particular respect to cigarettes is that "both smokers and nonsmokers lack basic knowledge about the nature and severity of illnesses associated with smoking," that "the public does not yet have the minimal information needed to make a decision about cigarette use," and that "we have not come close to conveying a full appreciation of the harms in store for many who begin to smoke."[39]

A specific factor closely associated with risk taking is adolescence, a time in which "sensation seeking" combines with egocentricity,[40] with one important "subscale" being "thrill and adventure seeking," which "concern the individuals' inclination to engage in novel and intense recreation such as water skiing or mountain climbing." Further confirmatory of intuition is a "disinhibition scale," which "concerns social drinking, enjoyment of loud and lively parties, and sexual attitudes."[41] Various biological factors, including levels of sex hormones, are related to sensation seeking.[42] Also associated with adolescent recklessness is "a failure of probability reasoning"; adolescents' perceptions of systems of "distributions or frequencies" of events "are skewed by their desire for sensation and by [a] personal fable that convinces them of their immunity from disaster."[43] The good news is that as people move into their late twenties and early thirties, recklessness declines—one explanation is that they have had to "suffer the consequences" of such behavior.[44]

A major element of risk is uncertainty, and it is uncertainty that perfuses many decisions people make about the experimentation they constantly confront and undertake in life. A poignant example is medical care, where "uncertainty exists about the magnitude or severity of possible benefits and risks" and also "about the strength of current evidence—for example, concerning a treatment or the quality of care offered by a hospital." Researchers have noted that "in processing information of uncertain accuracy or reliability, people tend to accept information fully or reject it completely, without adjusting for data quality." Other uncertainties that weigh on patient and consumer decisions pertain to "how to weigh risks and benefits in choices" and what the likelihood is of "different outcomes."[45]

Part of the problem in decision making—for professionals as well as laypersons—lies in the "shocking lack of statistical understanding of the outcomes of modern technologies, from standard screening tests for HIV infection to DNA evidence." Illustratively, "doctors with an average of 14 years of professional experience" gave widely varying assessments of a test to screen for colorectal cancer. Two authors have suggested that for laypeople, it sometimes may be better to present risk information in absolute terms, as contrasted with the more technical frame of presentation in terms of relative risk. In line with the "affect heuristic," they premise that "human beings have evolved into good intuitive statisticians and can gain insight, but only when information is presented simply and effectively."[46]

We now examine a few specific examples of risk taking that depend on the inclination to take risk in particular activities. An important subculture in the exposure of others to risk is the clinical trial in medicine, which compares results of medical interventions, including drugs, devices, and other therapeutic regimes. The problem in measuring the understanding of research subjects arises from the facts that populations used in the studies tend to be randomized between, for example, those receiving a drug under investigation and those getting a placebo—and investigators do not know which of these a particular patient is receiving. Patients often will not know something that is well known to researchers, which is that "research is always conducted in order to achieve scientific goals and contribute to generalizable knowledge."[47] This lack of knowledge contributes to the "therapeutic misconception"—that is, the situation "when individuals do not understand that the defining purpose of clinical research is to produce generalizable knowledge, regardless of whether the subjects enrolled in [a] trial may potentially benefit from" the trial.[48] Authors of a study on the therapeutic misconception have reported that in a workshop of experts, there was disagreement over whether a question on the purposes of a study instrument designed to measure the phenomenon should be worded "both to help patients enrolled in the study and patients in the future" or "only to help patients in the future."[49]

Other authors point out that "the core of the therapeutic misconception is subjects' failure to grasp that the risks they face from participating in research protocols are inherently different from those involved in receiving ordinary treatment," with the results that "subjects appear frequently to overestimate the likely benefits" of participation, "to be confused about the nature of randomized assignment," and "generally to conflate research with ordinary treatment."[50] From the responses of a group of potential subjects of clinical research studies, they concluded that "more than 85% of subjects" did not "referenc[e] any of the disadvantages that are inherent in the methodologies of clinical trials," with 45 percent reporting "*risks of the experimental treatment*" but not "risks or disadvantages associated with the research design itself." Moreover, they said that "no subject provided a comprehensive picture of the ways in which being in a clinical trial may interfere with treatment; most subjects reported only side effects of medications as a risk."[51]

Some of these differences may appear precious, but the important point is that in an important subculture of direct experimentation, the subjects do not have the most basic knowledge that is second nature to the experimenters.

A somewhat different set of opposite parallels appears in the context of nuclear plant radiation. Writing after the accident at the Fukushima Daiichi Nuclear Power Station, discussed in Chapter Two, Paul Slovic focused on "stigma associated with radiation contamination" as "a reality that cannot be ignored in risk management," noting that Japanese consumers were "avoid[ing] food and other products" from the Fukushima prefecture, even products that "show[ed] no contamination."[52] A particularly interesting observation was that "in every context except the use of nuclear weapons, public perception of radiation risk appears to differ from the majority of expert assessments." Slovic said that "in some cases, members of the public see far greater risks associated with radiation technology than do technical experts," while "in others, the public is much less concerned than the experts believe they should be."[53]

To this point we mostly have been discussing situations in which one person or group puts in the balance the lives and health of other persons and groups. We turn now to the case in which a potential victim of injury puts his or her own life at risk. An important set of subcultures involves participation in recreational activities that are variously known as "extreme sports"[54] and "high-risk" sports.

One writer, noting that "the term 'extreme sport' is 'increasingly amorphous,'" says that "it has been used to describe forms of motorcycle racing, bull riding, running, diving, surfing, and even pogo-stick-hopping."[55]

Many people would apply these labels to activities that literally get up in the world—on shorter trips by climbing rocks and on longer ones by climbing mountains. Surveys of rock climbers produce results that generally seem to accord with common sense. In one recent study of climbers in indoor and outdoor venues, the researchers focused on "self-efficacy," defined as a "belief in one's capabilities to organize and execute the courses of action required to produce given attainments."[56] They concluded, "Climbers may participate more frequently, take calculated additional risks, and attempt higher climbs when they feel confident in their abilities and are high in self-efficacy." These results, they opined, "reinforce the importance of self-efficacy when 'pushing the limits' and taking calculated risks."[57] The differences between this data and subjects' knowledge in clinical medical experimentation settings are dramatic. Rock climbers' knowledge includes both self-knowledge and extrinsic information about risks; the culture is that of informed risk takers who are potential victims of injury. Clinical subjects—also potential victims of injury—often possess very little knowledge, and the dominant culture is that of the experimenter.

The summit of vertical extreme sports, literally, is climbs on Mount Everest. Climbs on Everest on May 10, 1996, in which eight people died, provide a point of departure for one analyst of legal issues.[58] He points out that the physical and mental stresses of climbing Everest are far beyond those of, for example, riding horses and playing baseball—physically, "a weakened and limited state for all climbers," and mentally, "once above 8000 meters, a human's mental acuity drops to thirty percent of normal levels to the point where basic arithmetic is virtually impossible." In fact, "the combination of exhaustion and hypoxia often lead to hallucinations."[59]

Those who died and those who survived were mostly people with "previous climbing experience," and all had "paid substantial sums of money" for the attempt. They presumably also knew that just three years before, "the 'best' year on Everest, one hundred twenty-nine climbers summited and eight died." Capturing the cultural bonds of this band of experimenters is the observation that Everest climbers "are not only aware of the likelihood of death, but choose to confront it and, in fact, may be drawn by that very facet of the expedition."[60] A vivid illustration of a risk-assuming sensibility appears in a summary of the attitude of a professional motocross competitor, Travis Pastrana, who continued to compete despite the fact that by the time he was eighteen, "he had endured ten concussions, undergone twelve operations, and broken more than thirty bones." He said, "Every time I've gotten hurt . . . has been worth it."[61]

It is useful here to discuss in some detail a court case that graphically presents the problem of decisions to confront risks in narrowly defined subcultures. This Michigan case, especially interesting from both a legal and a human point of view, arose in a recreational setting that featured deep judicial probes into legal doctrine. It began when a thirty-year-old man dived off the edge of an aboveground swimming pool in the backyard of a neighbor's home. He had been in the pool at least two times before and, as one opinion of the Michigan Supreme Court said, "he was familiar with the shallow end of the pool and its three-foot depth" and "did not need depth markers to remind him of the water's depth." An experienced swimmer with "lifesaving certification which qualified him to become a lifeguard," he acknowledged that he did not slip or trip when he made the dive and that "he knew serious injury could result from diving into shallow water," although he said, "Just exactly what type of injury would result from it, I couldn't have said at the time." Diving into three and a half feet of water, he hit his head on the bottom, with the result that he became quadriplegic.[62] He sued the maker of the pool, contending that it had failed to warn him of the "dangerous conditions existing in the pool." The trial court gave summary judgment for the defendant, but the appellate court reversed, saying that it was not "convinced that the danger of serious injury from a dive is a risk of which the public is generally aware" and commenting sympathetically, "A simple act of pleasure on a hot summer's day, a dive into a pool, can result in a lifetime of heartache, frustration, pain and loss."[63]

A majority of the Michigan Supreme Court disagreed with the appellate court, both philosophically and legally. The majority said, "Since the dangers associated with diving into visibly shallow water in an above-ground pool are open and obvious to the reasonably prudent user, plaintiff in the instant case must, as a matter of law, be held to the knowledge and appreciation of the risk likely to be encountered in his headfirst dive." It concluded that "the defendant manufacturer owed no duty to warn the plaintiff on the facts of this case."[64] The linguistic nuances of legal doctrine in the case are evident in the fact that the majority used at least four separate ideas in the short paragraph just quoted: The concept of "open and obvious" danger, the idea of what is often called "assumption of risk" contained in the words "knowledge and appreciation of the risk," the "no duty to warn" argument, and the idea of contributory negligence embodied in the words "reasonably prudent user," a category that in some versions of defenses based on plaintiffs' conduct can be said to embrace "assumption of risk."

However, instead of holding for the defendant outright, a plurality of the supreme court sent the case back for a "determination of the threshold question whether the duty of reasonableness imposed on the defendant required warning."[65] That statement reflected the position of Justice Boyle, who, in a separate opinion joined by Justice Levin, said, "The fundamental problem in cases such as this is that we lack the information necessary to make an intelligent decision, even with regard to the obviousness of the dangers of diving." That, as he viewed it, included information about "such crucial questions as the efficacy of warnings against diving when they are provided, whether there is, in fact, any safe way to dive into shallow water, and what dangers are actually perceived by the users of above-ground pools."[66] In another, vigorous separate opinion, Justice Archer took on the "obviousness" argument directly. He asked, "Exactly *what* was obvious in this case? Injury in general? Danger in general?" He noted that the plaintiffs were arguing "that the specific risk of quadriplegia was not obvious."[67]

So divisive were the disagreements in the court that it granted a rehearing in the case, which featured something of a turnaround by Justice Boyle, who this time wrote for the majority in holding for the defendant. Drawing on a concept of "simple product" that the court had used in previous cases, he said that in a case involving an alleged failure to warn, "the obvious nature of the simple product's potential danger serves the core purpose of the claim, i.e., it functions as an inherent warning that the risk is present. . . . [I]f the risk is obvious from the characteristics of the product, the product itself telegraphs the precise warning that plaintiffs complain is lacking."[68]

On this rehearing Justice Levin argued for the plaintiffs, saying that the use of the term "'simple product' begs the question, since it assumes that all characteristics of a 'simple' product are universally known, and therefore such products cannot present a latent danger." He said,

"Under the majority's approach, a latent danger could never be found, and a warning never would be needed with a 'simple product' because the characteristics of such products are, *by definition*, 'universally known.'" He argued that the majority's "claim that there is nothing 'enigmatic' about such pools is not accurate," noting that "the plaintiffs presented evidence of properties inherent in a shallow aboveground pool that are indeed enigmatic and not observable upon casual inspection." He noted that "under the analytical framework adopted by the majority, if there is an obvious *general* danger associated with using a product, the manufacturer does not have an obligation to warn of any latent *specific* risk in using the product." But he countered, "The obligation to warn of a risk in using a product does not . . . depend on whether the risk is 'general' or 'specific,'" saying, "The essential question respecting an obligation to warn is whether the risk complained of is obvious." He declared that failure-to-warn cases pivoting on "'patent,' 'latent,' 'general,' and 'specific' characteristics of product-related dangers" "share a common thread: whether there is an obligation to warn depends on the latency of the *specific* risk, not the general risk." "If there is a specific latent risk," he said, "there is an obligation to warn, even if there is a more general obvious risk."[69]

This set of arguments, carried on over three separate printed reports of the case—one by the appellate court and two by the state supreme court, in its initial decision and again on rehearing—indicates the complex nature of personal decisions in even backyard risk cultures.

We now turn back to the case where an experimenter puts the lives of others in the balance. Here some instructive case law turns on the meaning of the term "misuse" in products liability cases, where the nature of choice and its link to specificity of knowledge is important.

In a very sad case, fourteen-year-old Michael Harless and a friend decided to inhale the product called Pam, which is used to keep food from sticking to pots and pans. The method they used, which apparently they had learned just two days before from out-of-town friends, was to "tak[e] the core of a roll of toilet paper," "stuff tissue paper into the middle of the core," and then take a deep breath of Pam sprayed into the core, "producing a tingling sensation." Michael, who had been told by his brother not to inhale Pam, died from inhaling the freon propellant in the product.

An issue that threaded through the case concerned the manufacturer's argument that Michael had misused the product. The jury found for the manufacturer but the Fifth Circuit reversed. What the appellate court called "the only relevant warning on the can" was the words "Avoid direct inhalation of concentrated vapors. Keep out of reach of children." The court noted "uncontroverted evidence" that the defendant "had notice of 45 deaths allegedly occurring from the misuse of Pam during the four years preceding Michael's death." Three months before Michael died, the defendant had sent a new warning to the printer that referred to the possibility that death could occur from inhaling Pam, but it did not recall the cans with the old labels, one of which was the one Michael used. The defendant presented expert testimony that "in essence" said "that it did not matter what type of warnings were placed on the label by the manufacturer"—that "teenagers were not going to read them or obey them if they did read them." The experts also "testified that labels warning of possible death may cause greater misuse of the product." In the end, however, the appellate court concluded that a jury instruction on the adequacy of the label warning was "confusing and internally inconsistent." Quoting a state law precedent on the idea that manufacturers had a duty to give "a fair and adequate notice of the possible consequences of use or misuse" of a product, the court said that "it was proper for the jury to determine if appellee had fulfilled its duty to warn 'with a degree of intensity that would cause a reasonable man to exercise for his own safety the caution commensurate with the potential danger.'"

Key to the court's decision on this living room experiment by a teenager was the fact that the principal designer of the experiment, the maker of Pam, had knowledge about a hazard from a use of the product even though it had not designed it for that use, information on which it did not act. That information concerned what evidently was an established practice in a youthful subculture.

An interesting contrast appears in a Louisiana state case in which, however, there was a specific warning about the possibility that inhaling propellants in a product could be "harmful or fatal." The product in this case was an airbrush propellant in a handheld canister. The user, like Michael Harless literally a sensation seeker, inhaled the content of the can while he was driving "for the purpose of 'getting high.'" The plaintiffs were the survivors of a completely innocent third person, who was hit by the driver using the propellant and who died three years later from the severe injuries she suffered. The driver and his passenger died at the scene. The plaintiffs alleged that the maker of the product knew of a "secondary market" for it that "had developed among young people who intentionally inhaled the product for the purpose of experiencing an intoxicating-like effect." They claimed that the company knew of thirty prior incidents involving inhalation of the product, and that it could have used an additive, oil of mustard, that would deter attempts at inhalation. Indeed, they gave evidence that the defendant had added oil of mustard to glues it manufactured before the accident in question.

The plaintiffs argued that the product had a design defect that was "unreasonably dangerous." Disagreeing, the court relied on a definition in the state products liability statute on design defects that focused on whether a user "was engaged in a 'reasonably anticipated use' of [a] product." It noted that the statute defined "reasonably anticipated use" as "a use or handling of a product that the product's manufacturer should reasonably expect of an ordinary person in the same or similar circumstances," pointing out that this definition was "narrower in scope" than the one used in decisions that had preceded the statute. Saying that "the standard for determining a reasonably anticipated use is an objective one," measured only by "those uses it should reasonably expect of an ordinary consumer," the court said flatly that the "intentional inhalation" of the product "contrary to the warnings on the product" was, as "a matter of law," not "a reasonably anticipated use of that product by an ordinary person" and held that it was proper to give summary judgment for the manufacturer.[70]

We can now begin to identify polar positions on risk cultures. The strongest written version of risk assumption is the written disclaimer executed by a person potentially subject to injury. Many decisions enforce such disclaimers, but other cases refuse to do so, often because of imbalances in power between the parties and sometimes because the disclaimers are not clear and conspicuous. Clear written warnings may serve to immunize from suit parties who provide those warnings. Paralleling those often fact-oriented defenses to injury suits is the anti-paternalism argument. Beyond that is a philosophically resigned position that may be summed up as viewing fate as the cause of certain injuries, with the conclusion that no one was personally responsible.

Quite as odds with those positions is the idea that in many cases where one creates a risk to others, it is difficult to say that an injury victim has assumed a risk, because it is often not possible to have meaningful knowledge about the risk. This view applies to risks hidden inside risks, as might be said to be the case with therapeutic misconceptions.

Bundled into all of these competing views and positions are many factors. Among them are individual differences in personality, including inclinations toward sensation seeking. Another set of factors is affective responses rooted in millennia of survival techniques. Also in the mix are mood differences induced by frightening stories of injuries or illness caused by specific kinds of hazards.

All of these things, rooted in diverse cultures of risk, are dynamically in play in the daily experiments we conduct on ourselves and on others. These factors are relevant to both the legal and the philosophical judgments we make about injuries that occur from those experiments.

## III. Wringing Out Utility

When people experiment on others, there are a number of tensions associated with their attempts to wring out the last drop of utility from their activities. Wringing-out episodes that have generated public controversy have roots in diverse assumptions that are part of very different cultures, including the cultures of businesses, scientists, and ordinary consumers.

Entrepreneurs often face decisions about whether to squeeze out the last dollar of profit while giving up a marginal fraction of safety. A familiar story in products liability cases, which may be generalized from the case of Michael Harless and Pam summarized above, is the situation where a manufacturer continues to sell a product when it knows of a hazard. A rending example is a case in which a four-year-old girl, Lee Ann Gryc, was horribly burned when her pajamas ignited as she reached over a stove to shut off a timer. There was substantial evidence that for many years before this 1969 accident there were products that "were capable of being applied to lightweight cotton flannelette"—the material of Lee Ann's pajamas—that would "significantly increase" the flame retardant characteristics of the fabric and would last for fifty washings. However, experts for the defendant said that "there were no durable flame retardant chemicals which could be applied to the fabric without severely reducing its tensile and tear strength, its soft feel, increasing its weight and cost, and adversely affecting the color of the fabric." There was also evidence that "there were no mills producing flame retarded flannelette for public consumption in any volume in 1967," but experts for the plaintiffs said that "the flame retardant chemicals and the process for applying them could have been made commercially available as early as 1962–1966, if only the textile mills had so desired."

There was also evidence that the maker of Lee Ann's pajamas "and other garment manufacturers were uniquely aware of" the "highly flammable characteristics of untreated cotton flannelette." Additionally, there was proof that the defendant knew of the "invalidity" of a test its fabric had passed and that "unreasonably dangerous fabrics passed the test." Moreover, the defendant "knew that persons were suffering severe burn injuries when [its] flannelette ignited" and it had faced half a dozen lawsuits on the flammability of the fabric. Perhaps most damaging was a memorandum, entitled "Flammability Liability," from a top official of the company. Written thirteen years before Lee Ann's burns, the memo said, "We are always sitting on somewhat of a powder keg as regards our flannelette being so inflammable." Another document, a letter written in 1968 by an official of the defendant, "explained that satisfactory runs were made with flame-retarded flannelette using various chemicals, but that [the defendant] was not going to use these products until federal law so required because of the cost factor."[71]

An enraged Minnesota Supreme Court affirmed a judgment for the plaintiffs that included an award of $1,000,000 in punitive damages, noting that the defendant "was aware of the danger and the means for reducing this danger" but had "continued to market this product even though there were economically feasible measures which could have been taken to reduce this danger to a fairly acceptable level."[72] Given the court's references to the intra-company memoranda, the decision amounted to a condemnation of the defendant's corporate culture.

At least ideally, scientists engage in a quite different process of "wringing out" in their investigations. What they prize is the last piece of available knowledge on the object of their inquiry. To be sure, there are dark chapters in which utility takes precedence. One example noted earlier is the Tuskegee Syphilis Study. More classically scientific were the efforts of DNA researchers on their own to define containment levels for their experiments and the continuing research on the effects of mammograms. Often as scientists go about their work, they must make judgments on the effects of their experiments on their subjects. A dramatic example mentioned in Chapter Eleven comes from two studies on postmenopausal estrogens that were discontinued, one after the other, after accumulating data showed adverse side effects. Although it may seem to laypersons that scientists work in mysterious ways, their processes are well established: fashion hypotheses, collect data, move to new hypotheses, and continue collecting data. Often after several collections of data, they come out in different territory than they would have first predicted. The search for the last piece of useful knowledge defines their professional lives; it is a personal challenge in addition to their bread and butter. When laymen experiment on themselves and on others, they engage in a similar, if less formalized, process, although they might not consciously recognize it.

One other group that seeks to wring out something from risky situations is regulation-minded people, of whom the principal public faces are consumer advocates and environmentalists. What they seek is the last achievable margin of safety. In the common law area, some commentary and judicial decisions speak of "maximum protection" for consumers. This general language appears in a comment to section 402A of the Restatement (Second) of Torts.[73] Just one judicial iteration of the idea appears in a declaration by the Delaware Supreme Court in a case involving a rental truck. Rationalizing the imposition of strict liability on the lessor of the truck, the court says, "The present-day magnitude of the motor vehicle rental business, and the trade practices which have developed therein, require maximum protection for the victims of defective rentals."[74] Somewhat more moderate language, tempered by balancing terms like "unreasonable" but still pushing in the direction of consumer safety, appears in many federal statutes. The Federal Hazardous Substances Act, for example, defines "hazardous substance" in terms that speak of substances that "may cause substantial personal injury or substantial illness during or as a proximate result of any customary or reasonably foreseeable handing or use, including reasonably foreseeable ingestion by children."[75] The Consumer Product Safety Act, declaring in its preface that Congress had found "an unacceptable number of consumer products which present unreasonable risks of injury,"[76] created an agency that could issue "consumer product safety standards" that were "reasonably necessary to prevent or reduce an unreasonable risk of injury."[77] In the arena of the workplace, the "general duty clause" of the Occupational Safety and Health Act requires employers to furnish "employment and a place of employment which are free from recognized hazards that are causing or likely to cause death or serious physical harm to . . . employees."[78] The unqualified word "free" in that provision is the strongest term in this group of statutes, but each of these laws, and many others, represents a push forward in the efforts to control vast experiments on the public. Another strong set of provisions appears in the Clean Air Act's provisions that require "major" pollution sources to use "the maximum degree of reduction in emissions of . . . hazardous air pollutants," reductions that "shall not be less stringent than the emission control that is achieved in practice by the best controlled similar source."[79]

Purely illustrative of the thrust by environmental advocates in many areas is a statement in a Web publication of the National Resources

Defense Council that refers to the use of the so-called conditional registration process for pesticides. Employing as an example the conditional registration of the nanotechnology product nanosilver in textiles, including clothing and bedsheets, the NRDC writer notes that the EPA had "found that of approximately 16,000 pesticides currently on the market, more than two-thirds were conditionally registered," and that the agency had "no system to track whether the data and studies it asked a company to provide for full registration have ever appeared." She also pointed out that there was no way "for the public to access any of the records on these pesticides." She noted that the EPA had said that "most of the conditionally registered pesticides were . . . 'me-too' products, which are substantially similar to ones already on the market." However, she summarized the view of critics that the process was "not adequate" and their insistence "that the agency immediately cancel all the pesticide registrations that have overdue studies"—the number of which was not clear. She quoted a staff attorney for NRDC as saying that the conditional registration process "should only be used in very rare circumstances."[80]

An empirical problem embedded in all the pushing and hauling on statutory language and degrees of enforcement lies in the attempt to measure the effects of regulation on innovation—in consumer products, the broad environment and the workplace. It often will be difficult, if not impossible, to know what useful products or activities have been throttled by regulation.

This is just one of the uncertainties that arise from the clashes, both direct and indirect, among risk cultures—entrepreneurial, scientific, and consumer—that bear on experimentation, clashes that are part of a process that seeks to reduce uncertainty of our knowledge about the world. Moreover, as we shall explain in the concluding chapter, a fascinating aspect of the subject of this book is the way that legal experiments have impacts on experiments by businesses and scientists.

## Notes

1. I am grateful to several students for their research in materials discussed in this section. These include Leighton Leib, Jonathan Shaub, Kelly Hollingsworth, James Larry, and Jody Platt.
2. George M. Foster, "Peasant Society and the Image of Limited Good," 67 *American Anthropologist* 293, 293-94 (1965).
3. Aaron Wildavsky and Karl Dake, "Theories of Risk Perception: Who Fears What and Why," 119(4) *Daedalus* 41, 42-43 (1990).
4. Ibid., p. 49.

5. Ibid., p. 56.
6. John Lawrence Hill, "A Utilitarian Theory of Duress," 84 *Iowa L. Rev.* 275, 291 (1999), citing Moore, "Causation and the Excuses," 73 *Cal. L. Rev.* 1091 (1985).
7. See Robin West, "Authority, Autonomy, and Choice: The Role of Consent in the Moral and Political Visions of Franz Kafka and Richard Posner," 99 *Harv. L. Rev.* 384, 386 (1985).
8. Ibid., p. 411.
9. Ibid., p. 425.
10. William D. Rowe, "Governmental Regulation of Societal Risks," 45 *Geo. Wash. L. Rev.* 944, 958 (1976-77).
11. Joel Feinberg, *The Moral Limits of the Criminal Law: Harm to Self* (Oxford Univ. Press, 1986), p.12.
12. See for example the "Paternalism" entry in the *Stanford Encyclopedia of Philosophy*, first published Nov 6, 2002; substantive revision June 1, 2010, consulted on the Internet, May 14, 2014.
13. Thaddeus Mason Pope, "Is Public Health Paternalism Really Never Justified? A Response to Joel Feinberg," 30 *Okla. City L. Rev.* 121, 164 (2005), criticizing Joel Feinberg, *Harmless Wrongdoing: The Moral Limits of the Criminal Law* (Oxford 1988).
14. Lawrence O. Gostin, "General Justifications for Public Health Regulation," 121 *Public Health* 829, 832-33 (2007).
15. See Colin Camerer et al., "Regulation for Conservatives: Behavioral Economics and the Case for 'Asymmetrical Paternalism,'" 151 *U. Pa. L. Rev.* 1211, 1212 (2003).
16. Ibid., p. 1222.
17. See Christine Jolls et al., "A Behavioral Approach to Law and Economics," 50 *Stan. L. Rev.* 1471, 1477-79 (1998).
18. See ibid., pp. 1518 and 1542–43.
19. "Libertarian Paternalism," 93 *Am. Econ. Rev.* 175, at 175 (2003).
20. Ibid., p. 179.
21. See James Q. Wilson (ed.), *The Politics of Regulation* (Basic Books, 1980), p. 370.
22. Elke U. Weber, "Personality and Risk Taking," in N. J. Smelser and P. B. Galtes (eds.), *International Encyclopedia of the Social and Behavioral Sciences* (N.J. Smelser & P.B. Galtes eds. 2001), p. 11274. The study authors' conclusions are also summarized in Elke U. Weber et al., "A Domain-Specific Risk-Attitude Scale: Measuring Risk Perceptions and Risk Behaviors," 15 *J. Behav. Dec. Making* 263, 283 (2002).
23. Ibid., p. 11275.
24. Ibid., p. 11276.
25. Ibid.
26. Nigel Nicholson et al., "Personality and Domain-Specific Risk Taking," 8 *J. Risk Research* 157, 171 (2005).
27. Ibid., p. 157 (abstract).
28. See ibid.
29. Ibid., p. 171.
30. See Paul Slovic et al., "Risk As Analysis and Risk As Feelings," in *The Feeling of Risk: New Perspectives on Risk Perception* 21–22 (Earthscan 2010) (reprinted from 2004 Risk Analysis (2), at 311 (2004).

31. Eric J. Johnson and Amos Tversky, "Affect, Generalization, and the Perception of Risk," 45 *J. Personality & Social Psych.* 20, 21-22 (1983).
32. See ibid., pp. 26–29.
33. Slovic et al., supra note 30, p. 23.
34. See ibid., p. 26. A specific application of this perceptual phenomenon in the area of prescription drugs appears in Paul Slovic et al., "Risk Perception of Prescription Drugs: Results of a National Survey," in Slovic et al., supra note 30, pp. 261 and 281–82.
35. See ibid., p. 28.
36. Robert A. Olsen, "Variance and Beta As Perceived Risk: Questionable Science," 1 *Qualitative Research in Markets* No. 2, 97, at 101 (2009).
37. Slovic et al., supra note 30, p. 34.
38. Ibid., p. 36.
39. See Neil D. Weinstein et al., "Public Understanding of the Illnesses Caused by Cigarette Smoking," 6 Nicotine and Tobacco Research No. 2, p . 349, at 355 (2004).
40. See, generally, Jeffrey Arnett, "Reckless Behavior in Adolescents: A Developmental Perspective," 12 *Developmental Review* 339 (1992).
41. See ibid., p. 344.
42. See ibid., pp. 345–47.
43. See ibid., p. 350.
44. Ibid., p. 366.
45. See Ellen Peters et al., "Numeracy Skill and the Communication, Comprehension and Use of Risk-Benefit Information," in Slovic et al., supra note 31, p. 347.
46. See Gerd Gigerenzer and Adrian Edwards, "Simple Tools for Understanding Risks: From Innumeracy to Insight," 327 *Br. Med. J.* 741, 741, 744 (2003).
47. Gail E. Henderson et al., "Clinical Trials and Medical Care: Defining the Therapeutic Misconception," 4 *PLOS Medicine* 1735, 1736 (2007).
48. Ibid., p. 1736, Box 1.
49. Ibid., p. 1737.
50. Charles W. Lidz et al., "Therapeutic Misconception and the Appreciation of Risks in Clinical Trials," 58 *Soc. Sci. & Med.* 1689, 1691 (2004).
51. See ibid., pp. 1694–95. A recent suggestion for at least improving the treatment results of such trials suggests the use of "adaptive trials"—"randomized clinical trials that allow for adaptation in the study design while the study is being conducted." See for example Rieke van der Graff et al., "Adaptive Trials in Clinical Research: Scientific and Ethical Issues to Consider,: 307 *JAMA* 2379 (2012).
52. Paul Slovic, "The Perception Gap: Radiation and Risk," 68(3) *Bull. Atomic Scientists* 67, 71 (2012).
53. Ibid., p. 73.
54. See for example David Horton, "Extreme Sports and Assumption of Risk: A Blueprint," 38 *U.S. F.L. Rev.* 599 (2004); David J. Llewellyn et al., "Self-Efficacy, Risk Taking and Performance in Rock Climbing," 45 *Personality & Individual Differences* 75 (2008).
55. Horton, supra, p. 652.
56. Llewellyn, supra, p. 75, quoting A. Bandura, *Self-Efficacy: The Exercise of Control* (Freeman, 1997), p. 3.

57. Ibid., p. 80.
58. See Dylan P. Kletter, "Negligence in the (Thin) Air: Understanding the Legal Relationship Between Outfitters and Participants in High-Risk Expeditions Through Analysis of the 1996 Mount Everest Tragedy," 40 *Conn. L. Rev.* 769 (2008) (using the terms "high-risk" and "extreme" on p. 773 ).
59. Ibid., pp. 779–80.
60. Ibid., pp. 782–84.
61. Horton, supra, note 54, p. 600.
62. *Glittenberg v. Doughboy Recreational Industries, Inc.*, 462 N.W.2d 348 (Mich. 1990).
63. *Glittenburg v. Wilcenski*, 435 N.W.2d 480, 482 (Mich. Ct. App. 1989).
64. 462 N.W.2d at 359 (Mich. 1990).
65. 462 N.W.2d at 359-60.
66. Ibid., p. 361 (separate opinion of Boyle, J.).
67. Ibid., p. 363 (separate opinion of Archer, J.).
68. *Glittenberg v. Doughboy Recreational Indus., Inc.*, 491 S.W.2d 208, 216 (Mich. 1992) (on rehearing).
69. Ibid., pp. 226–27 (Levin, J., dissenting).
70. *Butz v. Lynch*, 762 So. 2d 1214, 1216-19 (La. Ct. App. 2000), writ denied, 774 So.2d 980 (La. 2000).
71. *Gryc v. Dayton-Hudson Corp.*, 297 N.W. 2d 727, 731, 734, 740.
72. Ibid., p. 741.
73. See Restatement (Second) of Torts § 402A cmt. c (1965). ("the consumer of such products is entitled to a maximum of protection at the hands of someone, and the proper persons to afford it are those who market the products").
74. *Martin v. Ryder Truck Rental, Inc.* 353 A.2d 581, 587 (Del. 1976).
75. 15 U.S.C.A. §1251(f)(1)(a).
76. 15 U.S.C.A. § 2051(a)(1).
77. 15 U.S.C.A. § 2056(a).
78. 29 U.S.C.A. § 654 (a)(1).
79. See 42 U.S.C.A. §7412(a)(1),(6), (d)(2),(3).
80. Laura Fraser, "EPA Lets Pesticides on the Market Untested," NRDC On Earth Online Cover Story, March 27, 2013, http://archive.onearth.org/articles/2013/03/epa-allows-pesticides-on-the-market-without-first-testing-for-safety (consulted on the Internet May 15, 2014).

# 14

# Approaches to Risky Experimentation

There are many different approaches that society, and law representing society, can take to deal with the kinds of experiments in which its members engage that put others, and sometimes themselves, at risk.

## I. The Technological Approach

The *technological approach* defines people's needs, wants, and desires as problems to be solved from a technical point of view, with the solutions achieved by combinations of software and hardware. This approach relies significantly on the collection of information about people's preferences and behaviors. For that purpose, businesses monitor a great variety of products and activities, sometimes through diverse kinds of hardware with screens of various sizes. Among the goods that are monitored are many products that are ingested—those that would conventionally be labeled as foods and as medicines. Bridging those categories are things the appearance of which are beverage-type foods but that arc into the purpose of changing "the structure or . . . function of the body," words that the food and drug statutes apply to products that are classified as drugs or devices.[1] Here we find goods like energy drinks. In the next lane of competitors for the consumer dollar are medical products, sometimes technically available only by prescription, that satisfy what some may view as "lifestyle" choices. These include products that counteract erectile dysfunction and their commercial cousins, the "Low-T" drugs.

Many kinds of software reflect preferences drawn from numerous sources of data—for example, sales figures for particular models of a seller's products and those of competitors, and consumer surveys. The range is broad: from dishwashers and refrigerators to trucks, automobiles, and truck-like automobiles. As information from many sources accumulates about consumer and preferences, designers of products make changes in their blueprints, and sellers modify their promotional messages. The base of this activity is technological, beginning with the initial design and including additions to and subtractions from the features of products and production processes. Manufacturers add stronger metallic parts to their goods. New locking mechanisms appear, with the purpose of making products stronger under the pressure of what becomes known about everyday use. Among the subtractions will be reductions in sugar or salt content in foods and food-like products—as indeed there may be additions of both. A constantly changing technology fuels experimentation that is ongoing. A symbolic phrase in the jargon is the "technological fix." In some cases where the fix is not made, it can be costly to both consumers and producers.

## II. The Economic Approach

The *economic approach* bites at the margins of the technological approach and sometimes dominates it. Policymakers and judges refer to several formulas that come under this general heading. One that has been much in vogue is cost-benefit analysis. The idea, applicable both to minimizing injuries and illnesses and to providing remedies for them, is that in the experiments that take place every day with safety, one compares the quantifiable costs with their benefits. The difficulty often lies in quantification, especially when a firm is deciding whether to do an experiment, whether it is with a novel drug, a new model airplane, or an industrial chemical. On the benefits side, a company will have projections about sales and profits, which roughly serve as surrogates for social benefits from a product or activity—although even these are subject to the vagaries of consumer desires and wants. As to costs, however, because of the unpredictability of adverse effects—unforeseen illnesses associated with a drug or the unexpected failure of complex electronics on an aircraft—it is hard and may even be impossible to assign probabilities in advance of experimentation on the market. This difficulty includes prediction of the nature of a defect or side effect and also the amount of damage it will cause.

After an experiment begins, it will be more practical to measure benefits, taking into account "consumer surplus"—essentially a measurement, based on price, of what consumers will pay for goods. However, when the focus is on specific injuries or illnesses, a different set of obstacles arises for calculating costs. These problems arise in the realm of regulation aimed at minimizing types of harms in the future that have occurred in the past. Different federal agencies have placed vastly different valuations on human life in deciding on regulatory schemes. These have ranged from approximately $6.1 million for the Department of Transportation (increased from an original calculation of $3.5 million) to $9.1 million for the Environmental Protection Agency.[2] And the Occupational Safety and Health Administration alone has used calculations per statistical life that are as little as $100,000 for one type of regulation and as much as $98,000,000 for another.[3]

In the law governing civil suits for harm that already have occurred—tort law—estimates of the costs of injuries to individuals are also arrayed along a broad spectrum of dollars. Poignantly illustrative are judicial decisions on the amount of damages that should be given for the pain and suffering that has grown out of the vast, tragic national experiment with asbestos, which has gone on for decades. One desolating case in point focused on a $12 million award for the pain and suffering of John Consorti, a pipe insulation worker who died an agonizing death from mesothelioma, a disease that in most cases is associated with exposure to asbestos fibers. In concluding that the highest award that would be reasonable under state law would be $3.5 million, a federal appeals court reviewed decisions in several cases by a state court judge who had handled all New York state asbestos litigation. That judge, Helen Freedman, had reduced at least fifteen awards for pain and suffering in mesothelioma death cases, including reductions to $3 million of two awards of $5 million made to plaintiffs whose decedents had suffered for periods comparable to Consorti's thirty-two months of agony.[4]

One other illustration of the challenges in calculating costs as tort damages comes from a smaller-scale experiment: the use of computer keyboards that cause repetitive stress injuries. An example is an opinion that considered the cases of three keyboard users.[5] The respected district judge Jack Weinstein delved into statistical analysis to determine whether the awards he was reviewing—a jury had valued the pain and suffering of one of the plaintiffs, Patricia Geressy, at $3,490,000—had been "material deviation[s] from the "mean settlement[s] or verdict[s]" in prior tort cases involving pain and suffering from injuries of various kinds. Providing an appendix running for a dozen pages with a tabular chart of comparable cases,[6] he said that if he had not granted a new trial in Ms. Geressey's case on the basis of new evidence, he would have insisted on a ceiling of $2,000,000, noting that this figure itself was "subject to reconsideration at a new hearing aided by statisticians."[7] In saying that "the court is well advised to rely on sophisticated statistical experts," he remarked that "the entire enterprise is expected to provide only a rough approximation, close to an intelligent and well-informed guess."[8] This one case, drawn from a multitude of opinions reviewing tort damages, is simply representative of the problems of determining what costs are for purposes of damage calculations in civil litigation.

Quite as difficult are the conceptual problems in determining what a loss is. An example, laden with pathos, is a case in which injuries in an accident, attributed to a federal employee's negligent driving, rendered the plaintiff, William Flannery, permanently semi-comatose. Among other items of damages was an award by the trial court, against the government, of $1,300,000 for "loss of the ability to enjoy life." Answering a certified question from a federal appellate court, the West Virginia Supreme Court noted a lack of "theoretical cohesion" in the law governing damages for personal injury. However, although it recognized that a semi-comatose plaintiff was by definition "not aware of his loss of life's enjoyment," it concluded that he was entitled to recover for that loss "as a measure of the permanency of his injuries." It said it did not think that a plaintiff's "subjective knowledge of the extent of his loss should be controlling," analogizing it, for example, to the case of a child blinded by "excessive amounts of oxygen in the incubator" who "would be unaware of what full vision meant."[9] The complexity of legal concepts that bore on the topic was evident when the federal appeals court gave a technical interpretation of the law governing suits against the government, which prohibits punitive damages. The federal court decided that the award for loss of enjoyment of life was effectively punitive in nature, as contrasted with compensatory. It reasoned that that part of the award could not provide Flannery with "any consolation or ease any burden resting on him."[10]

Articulating a more direct challenge to separate awards for loss of enjoyment of life, along with recognition of the subtlety of the subject, was a decision of the New York Court of Appeals. In a case in which oxygen deprivation from anesthesia caused the plaintiff to become permanently comatose, the court concluded that "cognitive awareness is a prerequisite to recovery for loss of enjoyment of life." Although declaring that it would not "require the fact finder to sort out varying degrees of cognition and determine at what level a particular deprivation can be fully appreciated," it said that "with respect to pain and suffering," it approved the trial court's charge that "there must be 'some level of awareness' in order for plaintiff to recover." Beyond that, the court refused to approve "separate awards for pain and suffering and loss of enjoyment of life."[11]

An important facet of the economic approach to social control of experimentation is information. What do members of the public know about the risks to which they are subjected from various kinds of broad-scale experiments? The availability of information about risk is an element in litigation involving the most everyday kinds of products. One case presenting that issue focused on a product no more complicated than a one-half-inch manila rope. The plaintiff, Vernon Todd, used rope made by the defendant to climb sixty feet up an eighty-foot tree. After his first descent as he rappelled down, the rope broke when he started to kick out, and he fell thirty or thirty-five feet, suffering multiple injuries. A witness for Todd, testifying on what he viewed as the inadequacy of the defendant's warnings about the hazards of the rope, said that "the presence of knots in the rope" would substantially diminish its breaking strength, which would result in a break in the rope if a tree-worker used it. He also said that the defendant knew that "tree-workers commonly knot their ropes" and had "chose[n] to communicate the effect of knots in obscure charts." Moreover, he asserted that the defendant's "warnings that dynamic loading could place 'two, three or even more times the normal load involved [on the rope]' seriously underestimated the effect upon the rope that rappelling presented." He concluded that the "net effect" of the defendant's warnings did not "even begin to impress upon the reader a sense of the possible harm that could occur with the ordinary usage of [the defendant's] manila rope." This testimony supported a judgment for Todd.[12]

In the tree rope case, the threads of availability of information and adequacy of warning run together. In many other cases, courts have been fairly severe in describing the requirements of adequacy as they relate to consumer knowledge. Only illustrative is a case involving a rear-end collision with a Ford Explorer driven by the plaintiff, Jeanne Moore, who was six feet tall and weighed around three hundred pounds. The force of the collision caused the driver's seat to collapse backward, fracturing a vertebra and causing the plaintiff to become quadriplegic. She sued on the basis that the defendant, Ford, had not warned that front seats on the vehicle could collapse in a rear impact. She "testified that she paid attention to weight warnings when she purchased products because of her size and because her husband and son were both tall and heavy" and said that "she routinely read warnings, instructions and manuals if they involved something in which she was interested." She also asserted that she "would not have bought the Explorer had she known that the seats were not designed for people of her size." In this example of the experiments that take place every day with safety, the Missouri Supreme Court reversed a judgment for Ford on the basis that there was evidence that would support a jury verdict for the plaintiff on failure to warn under theories of strict liability and negligence. The court carefully limited the scope of its holding to a case where "the evidence shows that Ford knew its design meant that its seats were more likely to collapse backward in rear-end collisions when used by persons of more than normal weight, subjecting them to the risk of serious injuries such as those sustained by Ms. Moore." It said that "a jury could find that" the company "had a duty to warn the consumer of that increased risk so the consumer could make an informed choice whether to use the seats despite that danger."[13] Such cases highlight the legal dimensions of the information element of an economic approach to experimentation. Whether the question is focused on the duty to warn in civil litigation or on what information a regulator should require manufacturers of chemicals or mechanical products to provide to workers or consumers, the idea of people choosing combinations of risk and benefits in a free market includes the premise that they will be adequately informed about risks.

We note that a major obstacle for economic analysis often lies in the breadth of estimates of even gross statistics. A much-cited set of statistics comes from a study of medical injuries published in 2000 by the Institute of Medicine. The authors calculated that the number of deaths arising from "preventable" errors in the process of medical care fall in a range between 44,000 and 98,000 fatalities.[14] Where intensive study of injuries in a massive activity produces that broad a range, it suggests caution in reliance on such estimates in doing cost-benefit or risk-utility calculations for purposes of economic analysis of experimentation. More broadly, it suggests that although these approaches can be useful in making policy judgments and legal decisions, their utility is limited.

## III. An Attitudinal Approach

Those who make judgments about the proper boundaries for experimentation, both in controlled settings and in the wider world, must take into account the way people think about risk. These ways of thinking have deep roots in personal attitudes conditioned by backgrounds that include upbringing, personal experience, and ideological conviction. Those who conduct experiments, both scientists and businesspersons, will tend to have attitudes that strongly favor experimentation and tend to minimize risk—especially when they are not subjects of experiments themselves.

Personal experiences with activities—as medical patients, as consumers of products ranging from automobiles to foods to drugs—are likely to exert powerful influences on the decision about whether to try something new. On the other side of risk creation, there is testimony from entrepreneurs that legal judgments imposing liability on products or activities like their own will tend to make them more cautious about innovation.

Ideology also enters the picture. Many people tend to favor an experimental approach to life, including the risks of life. This view, which emphasizes keeping the way open for products and activities that hold promise for the production of new kinds of goods, tangible and intangible, becomes part of their political outlook. Others, who tend to be risk-averse in the way they live, favor relatively tight controls on the ability to take chances with other people's safety. For them—just as for those who prefer a broad range of opportunities for exposure to risk of others as well as themselves—these attitudes may result in a commitment with almost religious overtones.

People who build businesses that involve risk creation are inclined to the idea of "climb every mountain," even if others get hurt in the process. Their attitudes parallel those of some scientists who may shade or even conceal risks and uncertainties when they seek to persuade patients to become subjects of clinical research. For them, the long-run benefits from testing hypotheses about experimental treatments are worth the potential risk to the people who will become their data points. In an outdoor arena, the recent, continuing environmental experiment with fracking has brought stories of landowners whose properties border fracking zones, and residents of communities that draw on compromised water supplies, who did not know until later about their status, effectively, as experimental subjects.

## IV. The Behavioral Approach

Attitudes to risk taking blur into another set of approaches, which center on how people actually behave when they confront situations that are experimental for them. In some cases, the experiment is entirely new to the people who may be at risk: they may be the first research subjects to try out a new drug, or even the first drivers of a new-model car. In other cases, the experiment consists of an ongoing tryout with some form of risk. This may be taking a marketed drug for a long period of time, or it may be continuing to work on an industrial machine, the hazards of which are in some way evident, but without knowledge of the data on accidents with that type of machine.

A case involving a very dangerous everyday product used recreationally, cigarettes, presents the sad example of a man who kept experimenting with his own body by continuing to smoke, to the point where both legs were amputated from cigarette-caused illness. This man, David Burton, began smoking in 1950 when he quit high school and smoked for forty-three years because "he enjoyed the taste." When a doctor advised him in 1993 that he should "stop smoking or his legs were going to rot off," he did not immediately stop. But after the amputation of both legs below the knee in the next several months, and after a doctor told him that "if it took your legs, it will take your arms," he finally did stop.

After a prolonged litigation, a federal appellate court upheld a jury verdict for Burton on a failure-to-warn theory that included a claim based on addiction. Although the court noted that the applicable Kansas law did not require Burton "to testify that he would have behaved differently had he been properly warned," it noted that he "did testify that he quit smoking after being warned by his doctors that he would lose his arms if he continued to smoke, and further that he would not have begun smoking in 1950 if he had been shown 'this' at that time." Interpreting "the term 'this' to refer to Burton's injuries—his addiction, PVD [peripheral vascular disease], and resultant loss of his legs," the court rejected the manufacturer's argument that "no matter what warning was issued to Burton, he would have continued to smoke Camel cigarettes, become addicted, and develop[ed] PVD." It also rejected the defendant's contention that the evidence showed "that no warning would have altered Burton's use of cigarettes, thereby challenging the jury's determination on causation." Referring to general warnings about the dangers of smoking that existed before 1969, the court said crisply that such "general warnings . . . do not necessarily have the same impact as a frank warning that smoking may cause the loss of a limb." Saying that the consequences Burton suffered was "stark," the court concluded that "because . . . the proof points [in] more than one direction on the issue of causation," the jury's verdict for Burton must stand.[15]

Issues of this sort, which run through the case law on injuries and illnesses caused by products, raise the question of when a person's conduct that has a part in his or her injuries is voluntary. In a book focusing on criminal law, Joel Feinberg said, "We must remember the distinction between agreements *in* unequal circumstances and agreements *from* (caused by) unequal circumstances." He noted that "Aristotle distinguished . . . between choices in ignorance (but such that they would not change even if there were knowledge) and choices 'by reason of ignorance.'" He said, "If we count the former as deficient in voluntariness, it is only because we do not know for sure whether the ignorance plays a determining role and we wish to be *sure* that the actor's choice is voluntary, not because we think it cannot be voluntary even in ignorance."[16]

Cases involving machines and machine components show the complex relationship between particularity of knowledge and voluntary choice to confront danger. An interesting contrast appears in two cases involving large machines.

In an Alaska case, a loader operator died when his machine apparently rolled over on an embankment, flipping 180 degrees, and crushed him. His widow sued Caterpillar, the maker of the loader, for failure to equip it with a rollover protective shield (ROPS). Working its way through a tangle of state precedents having to do with plaintiffs' fault, the Alaska Supreme Court effectively approved a jury instruction that required the defendant to show that the decedent "had an actual awareness of the alleged design defect"—that is, "an awareness of the absence of a roll bar or rollover protective structure." This language was threaded into the court's conclusion that "when the design defect is the lack of a safety device, the jury may be instructed that the plaintiff may be comparatively negligent in the knowing use of a defective product only if he voluntarily and unreasonably encounters the known risk."[17]

A comparison appears in a Pennsylvania case involving a bulldozer that was being used to remove topsoil, a job that could not be done with the combined use of a dump truck and a loader. The operator, who died from his injuries, was, with his brother, a co-owner of a construction firm that had bought the bulldozer and had declined to purchase an optional ROPS for it, although they owned another bulldozer that had such a device. Referring to language parallel to that of the Alaska court in the loader case, the Pennsylvania appellate court recited the rule that a plaintiff cannot recover in a products liability case "if he or she knows of the specific defect eventually causing his injury and voluntarily proceeds to use the product with knowledge of the danger caused by the defect." But here, the facts of the accident led the court to a conclusion favoring the defendants. The court noted that "the decedent operated the ROPS-less [machine] in a slow, deliberate and systematic fashion on a steeply sloped topsoil mound for more than one-half hour before the fatal accident occurred, thereby raising the logical inference that he knew what he was doing was very dangerous." Pointing out that the decedent had "long experience with operating heavy construction machinery," it concluded that "the jury could infer that the decedent was subjectively aware of the defective nature of the ROPS-less [machine] and appreciated the danger of using this defective bulldozer on a steeply sloped surface, so that the jury could conclude that the decedent assumed the risk of his fatal injuries."[18]

Although there are clearly circumstances where a plaintiff can be said to choose even a fatal risk, it should be noted that a manufacturer cannot in effect set up a product user for injury. An example is a case in which the plaintiff, John Beacham, a mine employee, was serving as the helper of the operator of a roof bolter made by the defendant. So that the operator could extend the bolter to the ceiling of the mine, Beacham had to stand on wooden crib blocks on an uneven mine floor. As he tried to steady or reposition a steel mat, he slipped or lost his balance and "instinctively reached out and grabbed the canopy support arm" of the machine. The operator simultaneously "was lowering the drill boom and the canopy," and Beacham's hand got caught in a pinch point, severing four fingers. In a legal environment in which a worker could be denied recovery because he had engaged in an "unreasonable use," but not for simple "contributory negligence," the court concluded that Beacham's "instinctive" grab for the support arm did not bar his suit. Saying that for an "unreasonable use" defense to prevail, "the user must consciously decide to use the product despite his awareness of the defect," the court noted evidence that "Beacham and other helpers at times had no choice but to stand close to the bolter and its pinch points in the performance of their duties." It said that for Beacham's "conduct to be voluntary and unreasonable," he "would have to decide to place himself in a position where the pinch points could cause him harm."[19] The effect of the decision is that product designers must take into account the possibility that the circumstances of use in a workplace may require quick reactions that create peril to a user who has not deliberately chosen to confront a particular risk. Beacham's case may be seen as one in which the machine designer was conducting a running experiment with the use of roof bolters in which it had not advised workers of the painful results of a slip in slippery conditions.

The behavioral arena where information in the raw is particularly crucial is medicine. Many routine doctors' visits yield data points for what in effect are ongoing experiments on disease processes, but a sharp edge of the topic of how people behave exists with direct clinical experimentation. A North Carolina court set down guidelines for what patients must be told about avowed experimental procedures. The case involved the use on Michael Estrada, a gunshot victim, of a procedure, "still relatively new," called "percutaneous steel coil embolization." This procedure involved the insertion of a small steel coil into an artery in an attempt to relieve what was termed a "false aneurysm" probably caused by the bullet wound. Estrada signed a consent form, but the operation was not a success, with the result ultimately that the capillaries in the wounded leg stopped functioning, and his lower leg had to be amputated. Setting out the stark proposition that "reasonable standards of informed consent to an experimental procedure require disclosure to the patient that the procedure is experimental,"[20] the court emphasized that the plaintiff "could only understand *what the surgeons told him.*" It concluded from his deposition that the defendants "informed Estrada only of the risks inherent in the standard surgical procedure and the chance that the embolization might not work." It commented that "the various depositions of . . . hospital personnel reflect at best a vague knowledge of the risks of embolization in this sort of case" and that "this knowledge" appeared to be "traceable exclusively to a single medical article and to the ill-defined experience of one of the radiologists, apparently including only one prior operation, with little to suggest he communicated it to the surgeons."[21]

The ethics of informed consent, and the law pertinent to it, have been a subject of controversy for half a century, with the first formal recognition by courts of a doctrine with this name coming in the early 1970s.[22] An important aspect of the problem lay in the inability of many research subjects to "distinguish research from therapy." One author, giving as an example a study for the treatment of chronic ulcers, said that "until the moment when he told [a patient] 'thank you very much' and 'the experiment is over,' there was little in our interactions that could have allowed her to understand clearly the difference between being the subject of a research experiment versus a patient getting therapy."[23]

By the late seventies, scientists were expressing concern about possible over-richness of disclosures of risk. A 1979 commentary referred to studies indicating that "to a variable but often scarifying degree, explicit suggestion of possible adverse effects causes subjects to experience those effects"—indeed, that on occasion, stress produced by such disclosures "might prove fatal." These authors said that although "a statement to the subject describing the procedure and the general level of risk is reasonable," "detailed information should be reserved for those who request it"—a standard difficult to apply in situations where subjects do not have a basis in personal knowledge to decide whether they desire the detailed information. They declared that "when a specific risk is disclosed, it should be discussed in the context of placebo effects in general, why they occur, and how to guard against them." Reflecting the antipathy of researchers to very full disclosures, they said that "a move in this direction may ensure that a subject will not be at greater risk from self-appointed guardians than from the experiment itself."[24] Thirty years later, another writer noted that in genetics research, "every potential subject . . . should be considered vulnerable," in the sense of having "compromised capacity for informed consent."[25] He gave as examples the provision of DNA information that resulted in a subject's fiancée breaking off an engagement, or an "award of custody to [an] estranged and son-to-be-divorced spouse."[26]

The year 1979 had also brought an article by Marvin Zelen proposing "a new design for clinical trials" that touched off further discussion. Zelen suggested that patients be "allocated into two groups by a random or chance allocation," with the first group receiving "standard treatment" and the members of the other group being "asked if they will accept the experimental therapy," with the option of getting standard treatment if they declined.[27] One commentator, noting that it was "clear that knowledge could advance more rapidly if there were fewer regulations," opined that "even if a clear majority" of patients "favored a policy of randomization without consent, the thorny problem of the minority who desired full information would remain." He quoted Charles Fried on the idea that "the essence of rights" lies in the way they provide "constraints on the pursuit of social goods."[28] Another writer, expressing his belief that federal regulations "would not require that [the] control group be given the opportunity to receive [a] new drug," said that those patients "could, nevertheless, refuse to allow examination of their records and comparison of their course of treatment with that of the experimental group." He said that "if they asked questions about alternative treatments, it would be proper and necessary to tell them of the randomization," with the "degree of disclosure" being "up to the investigators." The researchers, he said, "must not be untruthful"; "they must not actively deceive patients or fail to correct a false impression."[29]

A most dramatic example of the linkage between information and consumer behavior is an experiment mentioned earlier[30] that wound up in a lawsuit: the case of the first use of a totally mechanical heart on a human being. We noted that a famous Texas surgeon, Dr. Denton Cooley, employed the device on Haskell Karp, a Skokie, Illinois man whose heart was failing. After Karp originally rejected Cooley's suggestion that he have a heart transplant, Cooley came forward with a proposal to use the mechanical heart as a bridge to transplantation of a donor heart. A suit against Cooley followed Haskell Karp's death sixty-four hours after the implantation and thirty-two hours after transplantation of a donor heart. Mrs. Karp, in her testimony about her conversation with Cooley after she read the consent form, asserted that Cooley had not revealed any differences of his device from those that previously were "ordinarily used for open heart surgery."

> However, Dr. Cooley testified that he had told Haskell Karp that this device had not been used in human beings; that it had been used in the laboratory; that we had been able to sustain the circulation in calves and that it had not been used in human beings. . . . I told him that we had been successful in keeping an animal alive for more than forty hours with the device, but that this was a calf. It was a 300-pound animal in which the demands on the pump were far greater than would be in the human body, and that I was reasonably confident that this device would sustain his life until we could get a heart transplant. But no guarantees were made at all.

The court noted that there was "no question" that Mr. Karp signed the consent form, that this "was against the backdrop of at least two conversations with Dr. Cooley, at which Mrs. Karp was not present," and that "Mr. Karp was presented and signed the consent document." It noted that the form was "consistent with Dr. Cooley's testimony of what he told Mr. Karp" and indicated that under state law, Mrs. Karp's consent was not necessary in the circumstances of the case.[31]

There was a highly charged side drama involving Dr. Cooley's great rival, Michael DeBakey, also a Texas surgeon, but the appellate court thought it was not an error for the trial court to exclude testimony by Dr. DeBakey. It noted that his "testimony would have shown at most that, in his opinion, the pump tested under his supervision was not ready for use in humans and that he would not have recommended its use." The court further observed that Dr. DeBakey "may have demonstrated that . . . animals tested with a prosthetic device at Baylor died of renal failure, but he refused to state that the prosthetic heart used in those experiments was the reasonable medical probable cause of the renal failure."[32]

Important to the court's decision affirming a judgment for Dr. Cooley was its declaration that what was "missing from the evidence presented [was] the requisite expert testimony as to what risks under these circumstances a physician should disclose." It said there was no evidence "to show a lack of Karp's informed consent or of breach of Dr. Cooley's duty to adequately apprise Karp of the nature and risks of the operation," which would warrant submission of an informed consent issue to the jury.[33]

The issues of human reality embedded in such dramas, often masked by legal technicalities, concern how people really behave in pressurized circumstances like those in Haskell Karp's hospital room. What can we assume about what people learn, or "know," concerning what they are told by physicians about the risks and benefits of procedures or courses of therapy? One study concluded that when patients were asked to describe major medical procedures within a day of signing consent forms, "only 60 percent of all patients correctly described what the treatment would involve, 59 percent could describe the essential purpose of the treatment," and "only 55 percent were able to list even a single major risk or complication."[34] A roster of questions arises about the lack of basic information on the part of patients. How much is their judgment about comparative risks and benefits affected by lack of education and sophistication? How much is due to an understandable denial of bad news? How many patients simply take the position, whether they express it or not, that the doctor knows best, with the result being that they shut off details about their treatment? All of these questions relate to how information about risks and benefits of various activities influences the choices that lead to behavior. I simply raise them, without suggesting how they would be answered in particular cases like that of Haskell Karp.

A recent document from the Department of Health and Human Services has sought to make more precise the "regulatory framework for protecting human subjects." A summary of this document on "comparative effectiveness research" (CER) describes it as enhancing the "enmeshment of research and standard clinical care." Accenting the complexity of the communication deemed desirable to research subjects in randomized clinical trials is a list of no fewer than "nine different types of potential risk." These range from "risks associated with the standard of care" and risks, as well as benefits, of different interventions to "risk due to masking of 'standard' interventions" and "risks due to acknowledgement of uncertainty." The authors of the summary say, "An analysis of the overall risks and benefits of such studies—by IRBs or federal oversight committees—must take into account each of these domains separately and then integrate them into an assessment of the risks and benefit of the study as a whole." Yet the very care taken in preparing this list makes one wonder how realistic is the authors' premise about the potential for patients' understanding, in what the authors themselves call the "balancing act" necessary to "the communication of information on these various forms of risks and benefits."[35]

## V. A Moral Approach

A distinctive perspective on how society should respond to experimentation emphasizes morality. This approach does not necessarily conflict with evidence on how people behave, and sometimes it may be in line with their attitudes, including their attitudes toward risk. Although sometimes at odds with risk-benefit and risk-utility analysis, the results it yields may, on other occasions, coincide with an economic approach.

The key to a moral approach, which distinguishes it from the other approaches analyzed above, is that it is normative. It does not focus on efficiency, nor does it focus on the facts of people's attitudes or their behavior. It deals in conceptions of right and wrong. Often its touchstone is the admittedly elastic idea of fairness. In the broad realm of experimentation, the practical definition of fairness often depends on the power relationship between the experimenter and the subject. In many cases, the experimenter has access to knowledge about risk that the subject does not possess. Various circumstances, including but not limited to that imbalance of information, may effectively put the subject in the power of the experimenter. One way to describe this relationship is to ask whether a party has access to decision making—has the power to decide. Sometimes the subject has some access, which may be manifested by her signature on a consent form or on a contract for the purchase of a product with a clear disclaimer of liability. In many cases, however, the question verges on an empirical boundary: How meaningful is a consent or manifestation of an intention to assume a risk?

Overhanging these considerations is the question of what society owes to the subjects of experiments. This topic subdivides into prevention and compensation. Government regulation takes on a substantial part of the prevention burden. For early-stage medical experiments, institutional review boards (IRBs) at medical centers make preliminary judgments about whether the potential risks of experimental products are justified by their hoped-for benefits. Another level of protection, based on the assumption that patients can understand information presented to them about risk, lies in regulations requiring that investigators inform patients about the main details of experiments. Illustrative is the language of the FDA's regulations in the special case of the "Treatment IND," a process governing drug experiments with patients who have—in the current language—"serious diseases or conditions, when there is no comparable or satisfactory alternative drug or therapy to diagnose, monitor or treat the patient's disease or condition."[36] For such patients, the FDA has required that investigators provide "information in lay language that truthfully explains the possible benefits and potential risks" of an investigational drug.[37]

In some cases, even carefully designed regulatory systems do not prevent what turn out to be unacceptable levels of injury from experimental products and activities. This may happen because the database for initial investigations is too small or the investigational period too compressed in time. On occasion, undesirable side effects and defects unpredictable at the design stage of products do not manifest themselves until a product is used by many thousands—even millions—of people over time.

When injuries do occur from broad-scale experiments—injuries that could not be prevented by regulation—the question turns to what, if anything, is owed to those who are hurt. The obvious remedy is monetary compensation, paid by the experimenter, which quantifies at least the dollar value of injuries. There is a substantial body of commentary on the rationales that support a requirement that parties who cause injuries should pay compensation to those who are injured. A principal theory, which traces back to Aristotle, is that of "corrective justice." One author has said that "corrective or rectificatory justice is concerned with wrongful gains and losses"—a remedy that rectifies "distortions which arise from unjust enrichments or wrongful losses."[38] He notes that when the injurer is at fault, there are two different cases that may justify compensation based on corrective justice: where the injurer both causes loss to the other and also gets a gain, and the case where "an individual secures a wrongful gain through his fault, though his gain is not the result of another's loss."[39] We might puzzle over how this classification system applies to various kinds of experimentation. In the particular case of medical experiments, we may ask whether, when there is undoubtedly a loss to an injured subject, we can say that the experimenter has received a gain. A commonsense use of that term in this area would be to say that there is a gain to the experimenter when doing the research enhances her chances of getting research grants, even if she has not been directly paid for conducting the experiment.

A principal proponent of corrective justice theory, Ernest Weinrib, has emphasized that the theory focuses only on two parties: the injurer and the injured person. It is in this sense "non-instrumental," because it does not draw on social policies that may be furthered by the imposition of civil liability, but rather it is limited to "an immediate normative connection between what the defendant has done and what the plaintiff has suffered."[40] A parallel idea, which has been advanced to rationalize civil liability on both fault and non-fault grounds, emphasizes that "a victim has a right to recover for injuries caused by a risk greater in degree and different in order from those created by the victim and imposed on the defendant—in short, for injuries resulting from non-reciprocal risks."[41]

There also exists a quite different set of rationales that support broadly based compensation for those injured by experiments, either in controlled clinical settings or on the mass market. One way to classify these rationales focuses on the idea of social justice, an approach that may not require a showing of fault on the part of the injurer. One theory is that since innovation produced by experimentation tends to benefit society at large, society should pay the victims of experiments—surely experiments that produce an unacceptably inefficient number of losses but perhaps even those that cause losses that are dwarfed by the gains of the experiment. Writing in 1972, the great French scholar of accident law Andre Tunc said that the "moral law" "does not demand the liability of someone who has unfortunately been involved in an accident by reason of one of those errors that we all make more or less continually." At the same time, he argued that "moral law" does not "allow the victim of an accident to be abandoned to his misfortune"—that "human brotherhood will not permit it." In such cases, Tunc wrote, "since the fate of the victim cannot be entrusted to Good Samaritans, society itself must play the role of the Good Samaritan and take care of the injured: this is the task of public health authorities and social security." In default of adequate compensation through social security or private insurance, he said, society should establish a "general fund for injuries and diseases, coupled with a continued effort to increase the amount of compensation it can pay or at least the enforcement by statute of non-fault insurance for patently dangerous activities."[42]

In the current economic times, the success of proposals for expansions of governmental compensation for victims of injuries inflicted without fault seems highly unlikely. One should note, however, another rationale that supports the argument that those who engage in risky activity, even without fault, should pay those injured by it. This is the rationale of risk-spreading, which, generally speaking, requires payment on the basis that those who ultimately benefit from risky activity should pay a small premium to fund compensation for those who are hurt by it. This rationale provides a backup justification for the tort compensation paid by faulty injurers. But it also has been used, on occasion, to justify the imposition of a strict form of liability. A principal example is the case of manufacturing defects in products, where one statement of the justification for strict liability has been on the "fairness grounds" that "it arguably causes the financial burden of accidents to be borne by those who benefit directly from [a] product and do not suffer harm."[43] This rationale has the advantage of locating financial responsibility for injuries most closely in those who engage in risky activity rather than throwing it onto society with its overburdened fiscs.

At its simplest, the moral approach to remediation for injuries caused by various kinds of experimentation that involve the safety of others has roots in the bible and religious commentary. In Leviticus, the Lord declares, "Love your neighbor as yourself."[44] And Hillel said, "What is hateful to you, do not to your neighbor: this is the whole Torah; the rest is mere commentary."[45] These famous declarations suggest a foundation for a moral approach to experimentation. They capture an idea, an ideal, of human decency.

## VI. The Media Approach

Media of various kinds surround us, pelting us with reports, sometimes backed by facts, about the consequences of experimentation throughout society. What knits these reports together is that they are snapshots and anecdotes; they are not formal studies on identified experiments, including benefits derived and rates of injuries. Sometimes they may summarize scientific studies, but they remain snapshots and anecdotes. Yet they contain elements of the approaches we have described above. With their popularized summaries of the results of advancing technologies, they influence attitudes about the benefits and risks of experimentation and its tangible products. They thus affect how people behave when they decide on courses of conduct—about accepting many kinds of medical advice, about whether to buy particular vehicles, about whether to allow drilling on neighboring land.

Experimenters in both formal and informal settings do seek facts, or react to what appear to be facts. On a parallel track, consumers respond to media presentations that often purport to have factual content. We thus must take seriously the role of media in constructing what for consumers is their factual universe. Sometimes the anecdote overwhelms science's best guess at what the "facts" are. Many studies have shown that under the influence of media stories, consumers both underestimate and overestimate what data show to be the best calculations of the danger of various technologies. Just one example of how people get risk statistics wrong is the fact that after the attacks of September 11, 1.4 million people chose to drive to destinations to which they ordinarily would have flown. Their aversion to the risk of flying reportedly cost about one thousand extra fatalities in traffic accidents.[46]

Another example stems from perceptions of the risks of nuclear power. For a time, there was a belief in the nuclear industry, unsupported by empirical studies, "that the public cared much more about multiple deaths from large accidents than about equivalent numbers of casualties resulting from a series of small accidents." However, studies conducted later "suggested that what bothers people about catastrophic accidents is the perception that a technology capable of producing such accidents cannot be very well understood or controlled."[47] Even well-trained scientists sometimes fail in making statistical estimates. Two examples are misestimations by "senior scientists of the rest mass of the electron" and "subjective estimates by civil engineers of the height at which a test embankment would fail."[48] Whether media influences were at work in these particular misestimations or not, two behavioral researchers note that there is evidence, "anecdotal" itself—of "the limits to expert judgment . . . in many cases where fail-safe systems have gone seriously awry or where confidently advanced theories have been proved wrong." One illustration is how "DDT came into widespread and uncontrolled use before the scientific community had seriously considered the possibility of side effects."[49] Another, involving a classic example of the employment of significant numbers of patients as subjects for nationwide experiments involving drugs, was the use of the hormone DES to prevent miscarriages,[50] a use that resulted in many cases of vaginal cancer in daughters of the women to whom the drug was given.

## VII. The Scientific Approach

By comparison with those who devise technologies to meet consumer wants and desires, the main goal of scientists is to acquire information about the impact of technologies in various stages of experimentation. The lines between science and technology do often blur. But scientists begin with a search for what they and their peers are willing to call truth, provisional as it may be. Ideally, the quest is for facts for their own sake. This is indeed a quest that for many scientists has a moral urgency. They may even justify experimentation on human beings with a statement of "ethical principles" that include "social beneficence requiring the systematic collection of data that are critical for determining the safety and efficacy of new drugs"[51]—a statement that itself illustrates the blurriness of the boundaries between a relatively pure kind of science and marketplace applications.

Scientists' search for truth often has ideological and economic overtones at many levels of social choice, including those embodied in the law. It is a search that affects, and is affected by, the standards that legislatures and courts fashion to determine the boundaries of permissible experimentation and to define the remedies for injuries caused by experiments.

## VII. The Legal Approach

To round out this group of approaches to experimentation, we briefly summarize the features of how the legal system, defined broadly, approaches risk—a topic on which we elaborate in the next chapter and in the conclusion. A major component of the law that bears on experimentation is legislation. Statutes in dozens of areas of human activity set standards, typically expressed in fairly abstract language, about what kinds of risks may be taken. These standards range from a reference to workplace conditions that "could reasonably be expected to cause death or serious physical harm immediately or before the imminence of such danger can be eliminated" through specified enforcement procedures (the Occupational Safety and Health Act)[52] to standards that are "reasonably necessary to prevent or reduce an unreasonable risk of injury associated with" a product[53] (the Consumer Product Safety Act), and they include language like "not generally recognized, among experts . . . as safe and effective"[54] (defining "new drug" under the Food, Drug and Cosmetic Act).

In civil litigation, judicial approaches to the issue of liability for injuries resulting from diverse kinds of experiments draw on a plastic set of doctrines. These include doctrines that define the broad concept of negligence and those that define the concept of "defect" in cases involving product injuries.

## Notes

1. See 21 U.S.C.A. §321(g)(1) ("drug"); 21 U.S.C.A. § 321(h)(3) ("device").
2. See for example Binyamin Applebaum, "As U.S. Agencies Put More Value on a Life, Businesses Fret," *New York Times*, Feb. 16, 2011.
3. See Cass Sunstein, "Is OSHA Unconstitutional?" 94 *Va. L. Rev*. 1407, 1440-43 (2008), with three pages of tables of cost valuations per life for several agencies.
4. *Consorti v. Armstrong World Indus., Inc.*, 72 F.3d 1003, 1014 (2d Cir. 1995).
5. *Geressy v. Digital Equip. Corp.*, 980 F. Supp. 640 (E.D. N.Y. 1997).
6. See ibid., pp. 664–76.
7. Ibid., p. 662.
8. Ibid., p. 658.
9. *Flannery v. United States*, 297 S.E.2d 433, 435, 438-39 (W.Va. 1982).
10. *Flannery v. United Sates*, 718 F.2d 108, 111 (4th Cir. 1983).
11. See *McDonald v. Garber*, 536 N.E.2d 372, 375-77 (N.Y. 1989).
12. *Columbian Rope Co. v. Todd*, 631 N.E.2d 941, 946 (Mich. Ct. App. 1994).
13. See *Moore v. Ford Motor Co.*, 332 S.W.3d 749, 754-56, 757-61 & n.6, 764-65 (Mo. 2011).
14. Linda Kohn et al. (eds.), *To Err Is Human: Building a Safer Health Care System* (Institute of Medicine, National Academies Press, 2000), p. 26.
15. *Burton v. R.J. Reynolds Tobacco Co.*, 397 F.3d 906, 918-19 (10th Cir. 2005).
16. Joel Feinberg, *Harm to Self* (Oxford University Press, 1986), p. 116.
17. See *Caterpillar Tractor Co. v. Beck*, 593 P.2d 871, 888-92, including 888 at n.54.
18. *Kupetz v. Deere & Co.*, 644 A.2d 1213, 1220-22 (Pa. Super.), appeal denied, 653 A.2d 1232 (Pa. 1994) (table).
19. *Beacham v. Lee-Norse*, 714 F.2d 1010, 1014-15 (10th Cir. 1983).
20. *Estrada v. Jaques*, 321 S.E.2d 240, 255 (N.C. Ct. App. 1984).
21. Ibid., p. 252–53.
22. See for example *Canterbury v. Spence*, 464 F.2d 772 (D.C. Cir. 1972).
23. Frederick Fennell, *Everyday Practice of Science* (Oxford University Press, 2009), p. 136.
24. Elizabeth F. Loftus and James F. Fries, "Informed Consent May Be Hazardous to Health," 204 *Science* 644 (1979).
25. See Fennell, supra note 23, pp. 154–55.
26. See ibid., p. 144.
27. Marvin Zelen, "A New Design for Randomized Clinical Trials," 300 *N. Eng. J. Med.* 1272 (1979) (abstract).
28. Norman Fost, "Consent as a Barrier to Research," 300 *N. Eng. J. Med.* 1272, 1272-73 (1970).
29. William J. Curran, "Reasonableness and Randomization in Clinical Trials: Fundamental Law and Governmental Regulation," 300 *N. Eng. J. Med.* 1273, 1275 (1979).
30. See Chapter One, text accompanying notes 43–47.

31. *Karp v. Cooley*, 493 F.2d 408, 413-14, 421.
32. Ibid., p. 425.
33. Ibid., p. 421.
34. Barrie R. Cassileth et al., "Informed Consent: Why Are Its Goals Imperfectly Realized?" 302 *N. Eng. J. Med.* 896, 897 (1980).
35. See Chris Feudtner et al., "Risks (and Benefits) in Comparative Effectiveness Research Trials," 369 *N. Eng. J. Med.* 892 (2013). A lengthy, related report is Eric Schneider, et al., "Evaluation, Dissemination and Adoption of Comparative Effectiveness Research Findings, When Findings Challenge Current Practices," http://158.74.49.3/healthreports/2013/CERRdissemmation/rpt_RANDFmal.cfm.
36. 21 CFR §312.300 (consulted online June 4, 2014).
37. 52 Fed. Reg. 19466, 19469 (1987). The current statute on "expanded access to unapproved therapies and diagnostics" is 21 U.S.C.A. §360bbb.
38. See Jules L. Coleman, "Moral Theories of Torts: Their Scope and Limits: Part II," 2 *Law & Philos.* 5, 6 (1983).
39. Ibid., p. 9.
40. Ernest Weinrib, "Causation and Wrongdoing," 63 *Chi.-Kent L. Rev.* 407, 409 (1987).
41. George Fletcher, "Fairness and Utility in Tort Theory," 85 *Harv. L. Rev.* 537, 542 (1972).
42. Andre Tunc, "Tort Law and the Moral Law," 30 *Cambridge L.J.* 247, 255-56 (1972).
43. See Restatement (Third) of Torts: Products Liability, § 2, cmt. a, at 41.
44. Leviticus 19:18.
45. Shab. 31a.
46. See for example Maia Szalavitz, "10 Ways We Get the Odds Wrong," *Psychology Today*, Jan. 1, 2008, https://www.psychologytoday.com/articles/200712/10-ways-we-get-the-odds-wrong, last consulted July 4,2015.
47. Baruch Fischhoff and Jon F. Merz, "The Inconvenient Public: Behavioral Research Approaches to Reducing Product Liability Risks," in Janet Hunziker and Trevor Jones (eds.), *Products Liability and Innovation* (1994), pp. 159 and 168.
48. See text and charts, ibid., pp. 169–70.
49. Ibid., p. 170.
50. See ibid.
51. A position summarized in Ellen C. Cooper, "Changes in Normal Drug Approval Process in Response to the AIDS Crisis," 45 *F.D.C. L.J.* 329, 338 (1990).
52. 29 U.S.CA. § 662(a).
53. 15 U.S.C.A. § 2056.
54. 21 U.S.C.A. § 321(p).

# 15

# Principles for Decision

Many kinds of experimentation surround and infect our lives, from the early stages of testing on unproved drugs to purchases of consumer goods both large and small, and including our labors in workplaces that may include exposure to toxic chemicals and dangerous machinery. These experiences extend to routine work and leisure in and around the home, where we also encounter various kinds of chemicals as well as products powered by electronic innards and by gases that occasionally may ignite flammable objects or vapors. This book has emphasized the deadly nature of cigarettes over several generations, but just as this book was finished, concern was rising over the risks of electronic cigarettes. In 2015, the European Union announced that beginning in 2016, it would ban advertising for those products, would require graphic warnings about their risks to health, and would limit the amount of nicotine in the products to twenty milligrams. The FDA was considering the issuance of regulations for e-cigarettes.[1]

By an order of magnitude more frightening were some of nature's continuing experiments with human health, of which the most troubling was the rise of Ebola in West Africa. Not only did the death toll increase into several thousands, but also there were potential effects on businesses ranging from airlines to mining and energy.[2]

Society has a stake in all these experiments, many of which it directly promotes and often encourages because of the benefits of the innovations they bring. That stake extends to the costs, some of which are physically palpable and others less tangible, of the injuries that sometimes occur from many kinds of experiments. Always in the picture is the question of when society should encourage or place limits on experimentation.

The question of when governments should provide funds or other means of encouragement for experimental projects has come to the fore recently. A recent, politically controversial example is Solyndra, a company that made solar panels. This firm, which had a substantial investment from a billionaire Democratic fundraiser, received a $535 million loan of federal stimulus money in 2009, only to declare bankruptcy in 2011.[3] Another, contemporaneous example is the case of A123, a company that made electric batteries for cars. It filed for bankruptcy in 2012 after having received $130 million of a $249 million stimulus grant.[4] These episodes are double-level experiments, in which a test of the market for environmentally friendly products lies on top of political experiments in government support for advanced technologies. Although the desirability of government promotion of experimental ventures is worth extended separate treatment, our quest here is to identify principles that should guide lawmakers and agency officials in decisions on whether to limit experimentation, and for judges asked to award compensation to those injured by experiments.

An initial practical consideration, which is clear from the many cases we have discussed in the preceding chapters, is that decision makers must recognize the constantly experimental features of life. We have noted that these include even intimate personal decisions that law ordinarily does not touch.

Decision makers must consider the importance of information, including information about uncertainty, about the potential consequences—both positive and negative—of experimentation. Recognizing, as Anthony Giddens has said, that an important characteristic of modern society is "the transition from external risk to *manufactured* risk,"[5] they must ask how available information about risk is and to whom, and they should seek to assure that information about potential hazards is as accessible as it can be to those who may be at risk.

Folded into the element of information are considerations of choice and the power to choose. In many cases, the power of choice concerning exposure to risk lies in the risk creator, and parties who may be injured are in vulnerable positions. An aspect of that vulnerability is the fact that even after injuries occur, often information about risk—and about causation of harm—is difficult, or may even be practically impossible, to gather. We must consider, in this regard, that stonewalling is one pattern of behavior on the part of risk creators that is observable in many current controversies. There are various motivations behind refusals to disgorge information about risk and refusals to stop various activities. Sometimes the basis for stonewalling is sincere belief that the product or activity does not create unreasonable risk. On other occasions it is a desire to squeeze out the last dollar of sales before a company must stop them.

Further minimizing the possibility of meaningful choice are lack of sophistication and lack of capacity to understand risk on the part of those exposed to it. To be sure, this is an element of how we live our lives generally. We are always taking chances on risks in areas where government does not—cannot—go. Yet it is worth noting that often there are constraints on choice for those exposed to risk for which there are no reciprocal constraints on those who create it. A difficult case is the one where the risk creator genuinely has no inkling beforehand of the dangers his activity or product presents to others. The best a regulator can do to minimize such dangers is to fashion rules that require intensive inquiry into potential risks. We discuss below how the problem presents itself to judges.

This reference to the conscientious risk creator who is ignorant of risk requires us to think about the concept of responsibility and how ideas of fault figure into that concept. The idea of fault has many moral and legal dimensions. The moralisms of fault are part of the working vocabulary of even young children. The idea of fault incorporates an objective standard that is descriptive of basic rules of society: under those rules, a judgment of fault is a statement that a person whose actions have been shown to have caused harm to another should have behaved otherwise.

A little classic of tort law that involves a child as a defendant appears in the transcript of a trial of a boy who was five years and nine months old at the time of the injury at issue and was eight at the time of the trial. The boy, Brian Dailey, was accused of having pulled a chair out from under an elderly woman, Ruth Garratt, with the result that she suffered a broken hip. The plaintiff's lawyer puts an aggressive question to the young defendant: "You did feel responsible for Ruth's falling, didn't you?" The boy answers, "Yes." His lawyer objects "to the form of the question." The trial judge tries to help out. He asks the young defendant, "What do you mean when you say you think that you felt responsible? What does that mean to you?" The boy replies, "I just felt responsible." As the colloquy continues, the judge asks, "Well, do you mean that you felt badly, because this lady was hurt?" "Yes," the boy replies. The judge persists: "Is that what you mean by responsible?" "Yes," the boy says. The judge presents an alternative meaning: "Or do you think that you felt that you caused her to be hurt? Which do you mean? Do you think felt bad, because she was hurt, or do you feel that you were the one that caused it?" The child replies, "I felt badly that she was hurt." The judge tries to nail it down: "That's what you mean, when you say that you felt responsible?"[6]

This case, which generated two decisions by the Washington Supreme Court, turned on a technical definition of the tort of battery, which the court defined to mean knowledge "to a substantial certainty" that a "harmful or offensive contact or an apprehension thereof" will result.[7] In the first trial of the case, the trial judge had found that the young defendant "did not have any wilful or unlawful purpose" in doing what he did and that "he did not have any intent to injure the plaintiff."[8] On a later appeal of the case, however, after the trial court had found for Ms. Garratt, the supreme court referred to the trial judge's finding that the arthritic plaintiff "had begun the slow process of being seated when the defendant quickly removed the chair and seated himself upon it, and that he knew, with substantial certainty, at that time that she would attempt to sit in the place where the chair had been." This, the supreme court said, was "sufficient to charge the defendant with intent to commit a battery," and it affirmed the judgment for the plaintiff.[9]

The result in this particular case, a case celebrated only among tort teachers, is not as important as the way that it indicates how legal and moral judgments sometimes become intermingled in injury cases. Courts have tended to be fairly rigorous in imposing objective standards on defendants, even those who may be incapable of living up to the norms of society generally. In a famous nineteenth-century case, an English court applied such a standard to a man who may have been of subnormal intelligence, and was experimenting with, among other things, the safety of a neighbor. This defendant stubbornly rejected the neighbor's complaint that he was maintaining a "dangerous" "condition" on his property that led to a destructive fire. The court concluded that the defendant's conduct must be measured by a standard of "ordinary prudence," rather than one tailored to his limited capacities.[10] Oliver Wendell Holmes Jr. remarked that for such a defendant, "no doubt his congenital defects will be allowed for in the courts of heaven, but his slips are no less troublesome to his neighbors than if they sprang from guilty neglect" and that therefore he would be properly required "to come up to their standard."[11]

There are many nuances in the concept of fault that involve moral responsibility. Certainly fault, conventionally defined as a departure from ordinary standards of research and investigation of potential risks, is a basis for imposing liability on experimenters. A more difficult question is whether to impose liability without fault on risk creators. There are bodies of law that assign liability for injuries caused by dangerous conduct even in the absence of fault. These cases have included harm inflicted by "abnormally dangerous activities"[12] and from "unreasonably dangerous" products.[13] Here we encounter questions, bordering on traditional concepts of fault, about what could have been known or predicted about risk if research had been done on existing sources of risk and prudent extrapolations made on the basis of analogy—and about what risks were truly unknowable before a litigated injury occurred. Moral considerations are infused in cases decided under strict liability theories and under negligence law as well.

Commenting on a case in which negligent conduct by the defendant's employees led to a strange chain of events that caused the destruction of ship by an explosion and subsequent fire,[14] a great scholar referred to "a deep sense of early common law morality that one who hurts another should compensate him."[15]

In the case of truly unknowable risks, the question for courts requires policy judgment. The problem is one of competing fairnesses: is it more unfair to require a sincerely unknowing creator of risk to pay an injured person or to tell the injury victim, typically not the prime mover in experimental risk creation, that certain types of injury are the price we pay for living in an experimental society? One solution is that compensation for injuries in such cases should be provided by a fund, derived, for example, from taxes on risky activities—or in the extreme, from the general revenues. Again, however, we encounter the problem of straitened public finances, which puts the ball in the court of . . . the courts, which ordinarily are not supposed to redistribute wealth in ways usually thought of as legislative.

The courts' menu of theories for product-caused injuries ranges from doctrines that require highly culpable conduct—fraud, intentional exposure of others to risk, and reckless conduct—to negligence and strict liability. A subtle argument for imposing strict liability appears in a New Jersey decision, rendered in a case of asbestos-caused illness, that is an outlier in the case law. In this case, *Beshada v. Johns-Manville Corp.*,[16] the court, in concluding that strict liability could be imposed for failure to warn of dangers of asbestos that by hypothesis were "undiscoverable at the time of manufacture," emphasized that "in strict liability cases, culpability is irrelevant." It said that because a product was "unsafe because of the state of technology does not change the fact that it was unsafe." It noted the defendants' argument that it was "unreasonable to impose a duty on them to warn of the unknowable" but responded, "By imposing strict liability, we are not requiring defendants to have done something that is impossible." It referred to "a major concern of strict liability" as that "the distributor of the product should compensate its victims for the misfortune that it inflicted on them." The court justified its decision on various policy grounds. Among other rationales, it said that "spreading the costs of injuries among all those who produce, distribute and purchase manufactured products is far preferable to imposing it on the innocent victims who suffer illnesses and disability from defective products." Moreover, it found "highly questionable" the assumption that "it is possible to define what constitutes 'undiscoverable' knowledge and that it will be reasonably possible to determine what knowledge was technologically discoverable at a given time," and it referred to the costs that would mount up in the effort to determine that issue. Beyond that, the court referred to the difficulties of determining whether manufacturers had adequately invested in safety.[17]

Although the *Beshada* decision goes further than other case law on strict liability for failure to warn, because of the products involved, it provides a particularly powerful statement of the case for a broad rationale for imposing liability on experimenters when injury victims are entirely innocent of knowledge about hazards. It is especially symbolic because of its genesis in one of the most destructive experiments ever conducted on a mass scale: that of the use of asbestos in the workplace and its presence in the general environment. There is something of an irony in the case, because although the court's decision focused on the alleged unknowability of the dangers of asbestos, there clearly was increasing knowledge in the industry of those hazards during the years that the *Beshada* plaintiffs were exposed to asbestos products—from 1930 to 1981.[18]

A special problem in assessing experiments on large numbers of people is the case in which a product or activity affects only a few persons adversely. One might describe this as the "allergy" problem, but many other labels have been attached to it: "hypersensitivity," "idiosyncrasy," "abreaction." A defendants' lawyer specializing in product liability cases has rejected the argument that such reactions are due to defects in products, saying, rather, that such responses are due "to a defect in the person."[19] Whatever one's view of this clever characterization, the initial problem is one for policy makers. They must decide whether to allow such a product on the market at all, what warnings should be required for it if it is sold—and whether persons injured by such a product should be compensated apart from compensation awarded in civil suits.

The tort doctrines applicable specifically to certain categories of products include efforts to define the functional characteristics of those products as they bear on injuries. One such theory, specifically pertinent to a set of products that are much discussed in this book—medical products—is that of the "unavoidably unsafe" product. A central statement of this idea appeared in comment k to section 402A of the Restatement (Second) of Torts. The drafters of the comment applied it to products like drugs and vaccines, "which, in the present state of human knowledge, are quite incapable of being made safe for their intended and ordinary use." The drafters said that if such products were "properly prepared and marketed" and had "proper warning[s]," sellers should "not be held to strict liability."[20]

The California Supreme Court summarized its reasons for adopting comment k in a case involving the hormone DES by emphasizing "the public interest in the development, availability, and reasonable price of drugs."[21] The court acknowledged that a drug "might be made safer if it was withheld from the market until scientific skill and knowledge advanced to the point at which additional dangerous side effects would be revealed." However, it said that "in most cases such a delay in marketing new drugs—added to the delay required to obtain approval for release of the product from the Food and Drug Administration—would not serve the public welfare." It asserted that "if drug manufacturers were subject to strict liability, they might be reluctant to undertake research programs to develop some pharmaceuticals that would prove beneficial or to distribute others that are available to be marketed, because of the fear of large adverse monetary judgments." Moreover, it declared that "the additional expense of insuring against such liability—assuming insurance would be available—and of research programs to reveal possible dangers not detectable by available scientific methods could place the cost of medication beyond the reach of those who need it most."[22]

The comment has not escaped criticism. The Nevada Supreme Court attacked its premises in a vaccine case. It rhetorically posed the question of "whether an exception should be made in a case in which a drug manufacturer injures a consumer with a drug that it knows is dangerous, but not *too* ('unreasonably') dangerous." Putting the question another way, the court asked, "Should a drug manufacturer be allowed to profit with impunity from the distribution of a drug that it knows is capable of resulting in physical injury, so long as the drug can somehow be certified as not being *unreasonably* dangerous?"

It declared that "a drug manufacturer should, under the strict liability jurisprudence of this state, be held liable in tort even when the drug is 'properly prepared and marketed' (that is to say, *non-negligently*) and even when the known danger inherent in the drug may be what the comment calls 'reasonable.'"[23]

In an area of continuing experimentation on mass markets, that of motor vehicles, the courts have developed the "crashworthiness doctrine," which provides grounds for suit against vehicle manufacturers for failure to provide sufficient protection to vehicle occupants against injuries suffered in so-called second collisions. Just one example of how courts have applied this doctrine in favor of plaintiffs is a case in which a driver, seriously injured in a collision with another car, sued General Motors (GM) for injuries he ascribed to the inadequacy of his seat belt and the tendency of the hood of his car to "buckle and contact the windshield." The Tenth Circuit rejected GM's argument that plaintiffs had to show that the defective restraint system had enhanced their injuries, saying that the plaintiffs "were not required to establish enhancement in order to prove causation."[24]

Illustrative of the controversy in the area is a Third Circuit decision, a staple in the defenses offered by auto manufacturers in crashworthiness cases. The court there insisted that "the plaintiff must offer proof of what injuries, if any, would have resulted had the alternative, safer design been used" and that "the plaintiff must offer some method of establishing the extent of enhanced injuries attributable to the defective design."[25] It applied this idea in rejecting a suit for fatal injuries suffered in a rear-end collision that occurred when the car of the plaintiff's decedent was stopped because he had run out of gas. It said that "without proof to establish what injuries would have resulted from a non-defective head restraint, the plaintiff could not and did not establish what injuries resulted from the alleged defect in the head restraint" and thus that "the jury could not have properly have assessed responsibility against G.M. for the death."[26]

These cases in the area of medical products and automobile design are just illustrative of the variety of doctrines, ranging across the spectrum of culpability, that courts apply in civil suits to the many experiments that occur every day with widely marketed products. It should be noted that there are several different flavors in the concept of negligence, which is a mainstay of the litigation that deals with the diverse injuries that occur from experimentation, both formal and informal. As I have indicated, the usual standard for sorting out negligence claims is that of ordinary prudence. Some courts have drawn on quantitatively oriented standards like cost-benefit analysis and risk-utility analysis. Both these and standards cast in more legal language require decision makers to balance various individual and social interests from an efficiency point of view. Balancing is also an element of negligence tests that focus on elements of decision making that are not centered on efficiency. For example, Kenneth Simons has written that the "decisionmaker properly considers morally relevant features of the situation other than aggregate welfare," including "intentions, motives, rights, consent, social role of responsibility, justifiable expectations or reliance of others, and reciprocity and distribution of risk."[27] And Richard Wright has fashioned a reciprocity-oriented concept of "interactive justice," which "requires that others who interact with you in ways that may affect your person or property do so in a way that is consistent with your right to equal negative freedom." He says that one should be able to expose others to risk only if to allow that conduct "by everyone in similar circumstances will increase everyone's equal freedom, rather than increasing some persons' external freedom at the expense of others' external freedom."[28]

Taken together, the cases and commentaries I have reviewed on negligence and strict liability provide a fair amount of running room for courts to decide on whether to impose liability for experiment-caused injuries.

Regulators also draw on a variety of standards in deciding on the breadth of permission for risky activities and constraints on those activities. We briefly reviewed a few of these standards in prior chapters.[29] We provide here some other examples to further illustrate those kinds of statutory standards. The Flammable Fabrics Act requires regulations to be based on findings that they are "needed to adequately protect the public against unreasonable risk of the occurrence of fire leading to death, injury, or significant property damage" and that they are "reasonable, technologically practicable, and appropriate."[30] The Poison Prevention Packaging Act, which determines how difficult it is for you to open your aspirin bottle when you have a headache, allows the Consumer Product Safety Commission to establish "standards for the special packaging of any household substance if it finds" that hazards to children require such packaging to protect them "from serious personal injury or serious illness resulting from handling, using, or ingesting such substance" and the special packaging is "technically feasible, practicable, and appropriate for" a substance."[31] The Federal

Insecticide, Fungicide, and Rodenticide Act (FIFRA) defines its key terms "protect health and the environment" and "protection of health and the environment" to mean "protection against any unreasonable adverse effects on the environment."[32] Standards of varying specificity apply to federal meat inspection,[33] mine safety,[34] and transportation of hazardous materials.[35] The highly specific Federal Hazardous Substances Act defines several categories of substances according to the specific kinds of risks they present—for example, it defines "highly toxic" in terms of the effects produced on "half or more than half of a group of ten or more laboratory white rats each weighing between two hundred and three hundred grams."[36] But the more typical kind of standard is an abstract one, using terms like "reasonable" and "feasible" or "imminent danger." These kinds of standards provide room for interpretation by agencies and, ultimately, courts. Their generality may generate frustration among entrepreneurs whose businesses, requiring innovation, often entail risk.

* * *

We offer here some basic guidelines for various levels of decision makers with regard to potential injury problems associated with experimental activities and products:

- For businesspersons, the communication to the public of information about potential risks, as well as benefits, of their activities and products, in clear, understandable language
- For regulators deciding whether and how to regulate, and judges deciding on questions of liability in civil cases, communication to businesses of rules and guidelines in understandable language, providing signals that are as clear as possible about room for, or constraints on, experimentation
- The need to acquire data about what people know and understand about experimental risks, and also about their beliefs regarding those risks
- The acquisition of data on how people behave with respect to particular kinds of risk
- The acquisition of data on the effects of market constraints on experimentation, including the existence and availability of public information about risk
- Consideration of the degree of meaningful choice available to people who may be injured by risky activities and products
- The practicability, and desirability, of decision makers sending signals to the public about the moral correctness, or lack of correctness, of choices about risk

- Consideration of fairness to both businesses and consumers in the allocation of risk burdens
- Consideration of *perceptions* of fairness to businesses and consumers
- Recognition of the pervasiveness of experimentation in all areas of life.

## Notes

1. See David Jolly, "Europe Putting E-Cigarettes Under Strict Regulations," *New York Times*, Feb. 27, 2014, p. B1.
2. See Bill Kenealy and Rodd Zolkos, "Ebola Pandemic Breaks Supply Chains," *Business Insurance*, Aug. 8, 2014, p. 23.
3. See Joe Stephens and Carol Leonnig, "Solyndra Solar Company Fails after Getting Controversial Federal Loan Guarantees," *Washington Post*, Aug. 31, 2011.
4. See Carol D. Leonnig, "Battery Firm Backed By Federal Stimulus Money Files For Bankruptcy," *Washington Post*, Oct. 16, 2012.
5. Anthony Gliddens, "Risk and Responsibility," 62 *Modern L. Rev*. 1,4 (1999).
6. From transcript, in the possession of the author, of the Washington state case of *Garratt v. Dailey*.
7. See *Garratt v. Dailey*, 279 P.2d 1091, 1093-94 (Wash. 1955), referring to test of Restatement of Torts § 13, cmt a. (1934).
8. See ibid., p. 1092.
9. *Garratt v. Dailey*, 304 P.2d 681, 682 (Wash. 1956).
10. *Vaughan v. Menlove*, 3 Bing., N.C. 468, 132 Eng. Rep. 490 (C.P. 1837).
11. O. W. Holmes, Jr., *The Common Law* (Little Brown, 1881), p. 108.
12. See Restatement (Second) of Torts § 520 (1976); Restatement (Third) of Torts § 20 (2010).
13. See Restatement (Second) of Torts § 402A (1965).
14. *In re Polemis* (1921) 3 K.B. 560 (C.A.).
15. Leon Green, "Foreseeability in Negligence Law," 61 *Colum. L. Rev*. 1401, 1412 (1961).
16. 447 A.2d 539 (N.J. 1984).
17. See ibid., pp. 546–49.
18. See ibid., pp. 542–43.
19. Warren Freedman, "A Hatband and a Tube of Lipstick: The New Jersey Minority Rule on Allergic Reactions," 43 *U. Det. L.J.* 355, 355 (1966). For a summary of the law of products liability on the topic, see Shapo on the Law of Products Liability § 8.06[F] (2013).
20. Restatement (Second) of Torts §402A cmt. k (1965).
21. *Brown v. Superior Court*, 751 P.2d 470, 477 (Cal. 1988).
22. Ibid., p. 479.
23. *Allison v. Merck & Co.*, 878 P.2d 948, 954 (Nev. 1994).
24. *Hinds v. General Motors Corp.*, 988 F.2d 1039, 1044-45 (10th Cir. 1993).
25. *Huddell v. Levin*, 537 F.2d 726, 737-38 (3d Cir. 1978).
26. Ibid., p. 738.
27. Kenneth Simons, "The Hand Formula in the Draft Restatement (Third) of Torts: Encompassing Fairness as Well as Efficiency Values," 54 *Vand. L. Rev*. 901, 919 (2001).
28. Richard Wright, "Justice and Reasonable Care in Negligence Law," 47 *Am. J. Jurisprudence* 143, 166 (2002).

29. See for example Chapter 11, text with note 62; Chapter 14, text with notes 52–54.
30. 15 U.S.C. §1593(b).
31. 15 U.S.C.A. §1472(a).
32. 7 U.S.C.A. §136(x).
33. 21 U.S.C.A. § 601(m) (defining products as "adulterated" when they consist "of any filthy, putrid, or decomposed substance" or are "for any other reason unsound, unhealthful, unwholesome, or otherwise unfit for human food").
34. 30 U.S.C.A. § 802(j) (defining "imminent danger" to mean "the existence of any condition or practice in a coal or other mine which could reasonably be expected to cause death or serious physical harm before such condition or practice can be abated").
35. 49 U.S.C.A. § 5102(5) (defining "imminent hazard" to mean "the existence of a condition relating to hazardous material that presents a substantial likelihood that death, serious illness, severe personal injury, or a substantial endangerment to health, property, or the environment may occur before the reasonable foreseeable completion date of a formal proceeding begun to lessen the risk of that death, illness, injury, or endangerment").
36. 15 U.S.C.A. § 1261(h)(1).

# Conclusion

## Experimenting With the Law

We have reviewed many activities in which experimentation is part of our lives, analyzing various ways in which society deals with experiments of diverse kinds. All of these methods connect to the legal system viewed broadly, and they include legislatively based safety regulation and judge-made law in injury litigation. We focus in this conclusion on aspects of the law that exist in plain sight but may not be obvious to people who view the law as a fairly static entity. What we learn is that the legal system itself is an experiment, an ongoing process of forming and testing hypotheses about public policies and the resolution of disputes, in which the goal is to find solutions that are at least provisionally optimal, or at least sensible, for society as a whole.

## Characteristics of Experimentation

A 1979 editorial in the *Washington Post*, initially focusing on the release of deadly gases from a train derailment that forced the evacuation of a quarter of a million Canadians from their homes, wondered why there were "yawns over chemical accidents" that contrasted with "instant headlines about even the hint of a nuclear danger." It observed that "commercial nuclear power has been around" for a "substantially longer" time than "people have recognized the relationship between chemicals and cancer." Referring to a phenomenon we have noted—that "society... reacts differently to risks that a mathematician would say were equally grave"—the editorial said, "A central theme of the 1980s will be coping with the discrepancy between the technical capacity to generate, detect and measure risks, and our much more rudimentary social abilities to control, accommodate and manage them."[1] This problem is as much "a central theme" of our existence today as it was a third of a century ago.

Scientific and technological experimentation takes many forms. One of the most successful enterprises of this kind was fostered by the environment at Bell Labs, where Mervin Kelly—ultimately chairman of the board of the firm—put together an "institute of creative technology" that "housed thinkers and doers under one roof." The Bell Labs transistor project, for example, mixed "physicists, metallurgists and electrical engineers" and included "specialists in theory, experimentation and manufacturing." A key to the idea was "not only freedom but time"—"lots of time—years to pursue what" the Bell Labs workers "felt was essential." The things this produced included the transistor, the silicon solar cell, the first patent for a laser, the first communications satellites, and the first fiber-optic cable systems.[2] This was an ideal environment for technological progress, but Jacques Ellul, writing in 1964, expressed forebodings about how technology "forcibly imposes" "social plasticity and a clear technical consciousness" on "every area of the world," "dissociat[ing] the sociological forms, destroy[ing] the moral framework, desacraliz[ing] men and things, explod[ing] social and religious taboos, and reduc[ing] the body social to a collection of individuals."[3]

There are other important dimensions of the kinds of experimentation that bring innovation. Recent commentary on the commercial success of Apple, including its business model, noted that the company's public relations firm "embraced" the idea of "consumer engineering"—"the science of finding customers"—which "involves the making of customers when the findings are slim."[4] Paralleling this view was the criticism of Lewis Mumford, who declared, "For most Americans, progress means accepting what is new because it is new, and discarding what is old because it is old."[5] Evgeny Mozorov observed that

> those who attack Apple as a quasireligion are more correct than they know: the company does function on the assumption that its designers, and Steve Jobs above all, are qualitatively different from the rest of us. The cult of the designer is the foundation of Apple's secular religion. And there is a way for the rest of us to participate in the truth upon which the design is based, and to rise to the human level of the designers themselves: it is to buy an iPhone or an iPod.[6]

There was, as a biographer of Steve Jobs remarked, a substantial element of risk—" "bet-the-company' risks"—in Apple's rise: As a reporter summarized it, "At its core, innovation is a risk."[7] But this is business risk. Another consequence of innovation is physical risk to consumers and bystanders: the experimentalist is a gambler with other people's safety.

An innovator who is quite conscious of his role as an experimenter—and indeed of the magnitude of experiments in the age of the Web—is

Christian Rudder, who oversees the research of OKCupid, described as "an irreverent online-dating site reportedly used by millions." In a blog post headlined "We Experiment On Human Beings," he told members, as a reporter summarized it, that the site had itself "manipulated information seen by some users." The post said, "Guess what, everybody. . . . [I]f you use the Internet, you're the subject of hundreds of experiments at any given time, on every site."[8]

### Levels of Experimentation in Politics and Law

The broad range of experimentation in realms related to the law begins with politics in the raw. Franklin Roosevelt was an avowed experimenter, trying out idea after idea to find ways to lift the nation from the Depression. Arthur M. Schlesinger Jr. captured the essence of FDR's approach to problem solving for the nation in many ways: "the temperamental expression of a restless, curious, and untidy personality"[9]; the "emergency agency" as "an essential instrument in the Rooseveltian technique of administrative improvisation"[10]; "a time of crisis" that "placed a premium on initiative and innovation"[11]; "he wanted an inventive government rather than an orderly government"[12]; "the first experiments in structural coordination failed"[13]; "the fluidity of change in society" "was Roosevelt's delight"[14]; "the New Deal . . . had built-in mechanisms of feedback, readjustment, and self-correction"[15]; "Could the pragmatic experiment possibly work?"[16] By contrast, one might view less adventurous chief executives as nonexperimenters, who effectively provide the placebo in social experiments that extend over decades.

Congress, and the safety agencies it creates, engage constantly in experimentation. Just one example, briefly summarized in Chapter 14, is the progression of regulations put forth by the FDA that allowed the approval of so-called treatment INDs, which, as a practical matter, were born of intense political activity by persons with AIDS. In the late 1980s and early 1990s, the agency, with parallel documents issued by the Public Health Service, promulgated a series of rules that made investigational drugs more available for "serious or life-threatening" illnesses.[17] Congress followed in 1997 with a law that established a "fast track" for new drugs under treatment INDs.[18]

The Supreme Court initiated a far-reaching judicial experiment in social policy in *Brown v. Board of Education* in 1954, in which it declared that racially segregated schools were "inherently unequal."[19] The radiations of that opinion extend to the present day. Among the questions it has raised are the effects on the learning experiences, and the psyches, of African American students who attend segregated schools. At least with respect to higher education, there is some conflicting data as to the relative advantages and disadvantages of attendance at historically black colleges and universities (HBCUs).[20]

One of the most far-reaching experiments in national life in the last few years came to light with the beginnings in 2008 of the financial crisis that came to be called the Great Recession. Bankers playing with "other people's money"—a phrase of Brandeis—engaged in conduct that threatened both the national economy and global economies. I remarked in a book published early in 2009 that "the dysfunctions of systems involving intangible financial instruments, and resulting panics, pose challenges that make our efforts to control man-made biological risks appear relatively rational."[21] A study published in 2011 was summarized as "compar[ing] big banks such as Lehman Brothers with what epidemiologists call 'superspreaders'—infected people or organisms which endanger entire networks through their web of connections."[22]

### A Disastrous Example of Risky Experiments in the Wider World

In the Texas City disaster case,[23] briefly mentioned in Chapter Twelve, Justice Jackson presciently pinpointed key elements of the experimental mode of product development. In that case, the explosion of ammonium nitrate on ships in the harbor of Texas City killed 560 people, injured 3,000, and caused immense property damage. The trial judge held for the plaintiffs in their suit against the government, which was going to ship the fertilizer for relief of war-torn European countries. He referred to both "early experiments" and "experiments, events and incidents" "after the manufacture and/or the shipping, distribution, and handling of Fertilizer had begun," of which the government "knew, or . . . could have known by the use of the diligence of a reasonably prudent person." These occurrences, he said, would at least have put the government on inquiry that the fertilizer that exploded "was an inherently dangerous and hazardous material, a dangerous explosive, and a fire hazard."[24] Indeed, the majority itself—although it denied recovery—had noted that "reported instances of heating or bag damage were investigated and experiments, to the extent deemed necessary, were carried on."[25]

Justice Jackson's masterful summary of the case referred—and this in 1953—to "a day of synthetic living, when to an ever-increasing extent our population is dependent upon mass producers for its food and drink, its cures and complexions, its apparel and gadgets." He declared, "These no longer are natural or simple products but complex ones whose composition and qualities are often secret." "Such a dependent society," he said, "must exact greater care than in more simple days and must require from manufacturers or producers increased integrity and caution as the only protection of its safety and well-being." He gave specific examples: "purchasers cannot try out drugs to determine whether they kill or cure," and "consumers cannot test the youngster's cowboy suit or the wife's sweater to see if they are apt to burst into fatal flames."[26]

Now he fixed on a central concept of this book, which I italicize in this quotation:

> Carriers, by land or by sea, cannot *experiment* with the combustibility of goods in transit. Where *experiment* or research is necessary to determine the presence or the degree of danger, the product must not be tried out on the public, nor must the public be expected to possess the facilities or the technical knowledge to learn for itself of inherent but latent dangers. The claim that a hazard was not foreseen is not available to one who did not use foresight appropriate to his enterprise.[27]

The risks in the disaster, Justice Jackson emphasized, were "completely controlled or controllable by" the government and "far beyond the knowledge or control of the victims; they were not only incapable of contributing to it but could not even take shelter or flight from it."[28]

These themes—of the power of experimenters to control risk, and of the ignorance and helplessness of victims—replicate themselves in many environments discussed here. They run through cases involving chemicals that seep into drinking water, toxic materials used in workplaces, and prescription drugs that cause side effects that were unknown to patients when they took them.

## Implications of Biotechnology "Beyond Therapy"

There are broader implications in the marketing of products that may have social impacts far beyond individual physical harm to consumers. The President's Council on Bioethics ventures a broad analysis of the uses of biotechnology "beyond therapy," contrasting that concept with the "common understanding" of "therapy" as "the use of biotechnical power to treat individuals with known diseases, disabilities, or impairments, in an attempt to restore them to a normal state of health and fitness."[29] As the authors summarize it, "new technological possibilities for going 'beyond therapy'" include "using techniques of genetic screening and selection" to improve the "native endowments" of children or using "drugs that might make them more accomplished, attentive, or docile" and using "genetic or pharmacologist enhancement" to achieve "superior performance"—for example, in athletics. They also mention employing new "genetic interventions to increase the strength and vigor of muscles" or eventually "to retard the general processes of biological senescence" and mention "using pharmacologic agents that dull painful memories or brighten mood."[30]

The philosophical position of the authors is evident in their discussion of "direct-to-consumer advertising of pharmaceutical and other companies—for mood-brighteners, fatigue lesseners, youth preservatives and behavior modifiers" as "a harbinger of things to come." They speak, forebodingly, of these products as "providing quick solutions for short-term problems or prompt fulfillment of easily satisfied desires," and of a state of the world in which "the character of human longing could be altered, with large aspiration for long-term flourishing giving way before the immediate gratification of smaller desires."[31]

## Continued Experiments with the Law's Methods of Encountering and Controlling Risk

We have reviewed the basic approaches society employs in encountering and attempting to control experimental risk. A principal one is direct regulation by agencies created by the legislature. Each safety statute, from those regulating the marketing of cigarettes and the design of automobiles to those that require prescription drugs and devices to jump scientific hurdles and those that mandate certain labels on pesticides, is an experiment in progress. Statutory language, once set in legislative concrete, will change only infrequently, but often the fashioning and administration of rules promulgated under statutes may vary under political influences.

A less direct method of control of experimental risks, but one powerful enough that it often generates complaints from businesses, is through court-administered private law—basically tort suits. Here judicial experimentation is a fact of litigation life. It has been so in the law of medical malpractice. Beginning in the 1960s, courts loosened the requirements for proof, including proof by circumstantial evidence, in medical cases.[32] In a notable set of cases starting in the early 1970s, courts invented the doctrine of "informed consent" for medical malpractice suits.[33]

A most remarkable development in tort law has occurred during the last half century in the law of products liability. The 1960s saw the expansion of the theoretical basis for suits on injuries ascribed to products with the creation of the doctrine of strict liability for products. This development, which owed much to the publication of section 402A of the Restatement (Second) of Torts in 1965, continued through the 1970s. The explosion of products liability law began to slow down after that, and a counterrevolution began to take place. A primary document in that history was the publication in 1998 of the Restatement of Products Liability, which placed significant restrictions on the definition of product defects, especially design defects.

Counterrevolutions also occurred in state legislatures in the fields of both medical malpractice and products liability. State "tort reform" statutes tightened the substantive rules for proof of medical malpractice and imposed limits on the amounts of damages that patient claimants could receive for "noneconomic losses" like pain and suffering. Tort reform legislation in some jurisdictions also cut back on theories available to plaintiffs in products cases.

Even when there were legislative modifications of tort liability, however, experimentation with tort law continued. With varying success, plaintiffs attacked tort reform statutes on the grounds that they were unconstitutional—claiming, for example, that some of those laws denied equal protection to claimants.

We note the doomsday character of some arguments that are thrown back and forth in battles over whether there should be more, or less, control of risky experiments by law. On the one hand are arguments that the clusters of risks imposed on people by various kinds of chemicals insidiously threaten the health of millions. A truly global form of this argument, focusing on greenhouse gas emissions, emphasizes threats to the planet itself in the form of climate change. On the other side are arguments that legal constraints imposed on businesses by regulation, and financial burdens imposed by liability judgments, are seriously damaging the firms' ability to service consumer needs and choking economic growth. In the background of these volleys are disputes about the level of experimentation by the law for controlling risk.

A related problem for policy makers is when to react to a problem, as if it signals the cries of the canary in the coalmine, used to detect the presence of deadly gases. In the initial stages of evidence on possible hazards, there will be questions as to whether the canary is accurately flagging a particular risk, and how serious that risk is. Attending this problem is a lack of the resources for investigation. As early reports tumble out about injuries that may be ascribable to experiments, both innovators and government regulators must make decisions about whether to collect data on potential hazards—a process that often is expensive.

## Playmakers for Society

Constantly, appeals to judges and legislators present choices concerning responses to experimental risk. These choices are often difficult because there are weighty social interests on both sides, or on several sides. Legislators and judges faced with these controversies become playmakers for the benefit of society, all believing that their decisions will be to its long-range benefit. In analyzing this playmaker role, I begin with a model of a general decision maker on issues of regulation of risky experimentation and liability for injuries it causes. This person would be an imaginative and all-powerful overseer of research on experimental innovation and risk, who would formulate predictions about risk in conditions of uncertainty and would conceive and administer programs for controlling risk and set guidelines for the compensation of injured persons.

## Premises and Rationales for Decision Making

The experimentation decision maker would have to take into account several things. He or she would focus on the information about risk that is available to those who create it and to those who may be affected by it. Another set of considerations would be the incentives created by his or her decisions. These would include incentives for those who engage in risky experimental behavior; for example, health care providers and product manufacturers. They also would include incentives that the rules would provide for the personal behavior of those subject to risk.

The decision maker would have to identify his or her premises about the rationality of actors, including how people form beliefs about risk and how accurately those beliefs correspond with reality. A philosopher has said, with respect to the "confident and straightforward moral convictions" people hold, that "when they are asked about what makes those beliefs true they flounder, grasp at straws, or give up the claim to truth."[34] This remark, which focuses on ideas, applies directly to people's views about the "facts" concerning risk. It identifies traps that lie in the path of those who seek rational decisions on behalf of society for control of experimental risk. A related set of traps lies in the relatively constrained ability of ordinary people to decipher and interpret data about risk. Paralleling those pitfalls are problems arising from understandable inclinations to deny that risk exists—and, in another dimension of the risk-calculation spectrum, a kind of terror that is beyond rational, arithmetical comparisons of risk.

A pertinent question in the assessment of experimentation focuses on reliance on experts. Experts provide the basic fuel for innovation and indeed for the judgment of the risks and benefits of innovation. Yet both democratic theory and human nature establish boundaries on that reliance, some of which pertain to our trust in experts. Ordinary people judging the opinions of experts will want to know about their financial stakes, and their reputational stakes, in experiments. Bound up with the reputational stakes of experts is their love for their craft and their desire to do good for others. Beyond these considerations is the fact that experts so often disagree on what the basic facts are. Two scientists evinced a seemly humility in describing "the most precise measurement" of the radius of the proton in "two complementary experiments." When they started this "exercise," they wrote, they "suspected that our results would help add levels of precision to the known size of the proton." But, they said, "We were wrong"—"our measurements of the proton's radius differ by a huge gulf." That difference, they said, was "more than five times the uncertainty in either measurement, implying that the probability that this is all due to chance is less than one in a million."[35] Their striving-oriented conclusion was that resolving "the radius puzzle" "just might be the thread we have to pull to unravel the next chapter in the book of nature." They summed up a driving ambition that animates all experimenters: "Pull we will."[36]

We note in this regard that among the various roles that scientists play is that of debaters. At many junctures of experiments involving risk, we find fierce exercises in advocacy. These are fueled not only by sincere belief but also by incentives to defend professional reputations.

Finally, the experimentation decision maker must consider how the abstract concept of fairness applies to specific activities, taking into account the much-quoted aphorism of Justice Potter Stewart that "fairness is what justice really is." As we have indicated, the concept of fairness has many guises in diverse applications. It may refer to the individual relationship of risk creators and those injured by experimental risk. It has a different set of foundations in the distribution of wealth among groups subject to risk, and it may be applied as a basis for spreading losses among those who benefit from risky activities. The decision maker must determine how much weight to give to any of these concepts of fairness and should identify the one on which he relies.

We point out, in this connection, that the menu of alternatives for controlling experimental risk includes simple regulations that require certain types of product design that may have salutary, indirect effects by forcing choices on people. Ezekiel Emanuel has pointed out that a simple matter of product packaging may have a significant influence on a dreadful kind of injury: suicide. He cites a British study that concludes that requiring blister packs for the active ingredient in Tylenol reduced suicide deaths from overdoses of the drug, other accidental deaths from medication poisoning, and liver transplants made necessary by Tylenol poisoning.[37] It is much easier to swallow dozens of pills from a vial than it is to force open the same number of pills from a blister pack.

## Lawgivers and Lawmakers As Experimenters

Both legislators and judges are experimenters, sometimes in bursts of intellectual energy and sometimes at glacial paces spread over years. American courts simultaneously operate laboratories of law all over the country. Brandeis felicitously coined the metaphor of states as laboratories of "social and economic experiments."[38] The principal task of courts is to resolve specific disputes. But inevitably they refer difficult decisions to considerations of policy. More or less consciously, they seek to persuade readers of their decisions that they have sought a mixture—a fair mixture—of justice and efficiency, with efficiency defined in both economic and social terms.

Controversies about the allocation of experimental risk tend to bubble up first in individual disputes. When they replicate themselves in large numbers, those disputes become grist for the mill of legislation, which, as we have noted, is itself experimental. Congress becomes the center of argument on problems that become recognized as having national dimensions. When it enacts statutes, it nationalizes society's response to those problems—in the workplace, in the air, in polluted streams, on the doctor's prescription pad. The application of statutes by safety agencies reflects the tugs and pulls of politics. Attitudinal changes in the population about acceptable risks—including statistical levels of risk and fears of particular kinds of risk—will bear on the administration of laws focused on improving safety. That is part of the process of legal experiments enacted for control of market experiments. In seeking to minimize victimization by experiment, we must face the need to prioritize among risks, thus taking a chance on many things.

I note that a particularly powerful push for regulation occurs when an influential public figure—or a family member of such a person—suffers a serious injury from a product or activity. A good recent example is the Virginia Graeme Baker Pool and Spa Safety Act.[39] The inciting accident was the drowning in a residential pool of the granddaughter of James Baker, the former secretary of state and a powerful Republican politician.[40] The legislative findings include the fact that "in 2004, 761 children aged 14 and under died as a result of unintentional drowning."[41] The statute requires every pool or spa drain made in the United States to "conform to the entrapment protection standards" of the standard-setting organizations ASME and ANSI.[42] Data and emotion can thus combine to generate regulation of products whose presence on the national landscape constitutes a continuing experiment with young lives.

The idea that decision making about risk is best done by individuals acting on their own, without government interference, is very attractive. Yet, as Benjamin Friedman has pointed out, citing examples ranging from Social Security, Medicare, and Medicaid to bank deposit insurance, crop insurance, and flood insurance, "government has been central to the way Americans have shared life's risks" since the 1930s.[43]

## Choice

All innovation arises from experiments, large and small, planned and unplanned. The unplanned discovery may have great positive influence on public health: just one example is Alexander Fleming's stumble onto penicillin—at that time, just a mold in a petri dish. An important set of issues involves the question of how many aspects of an experiment, controlled or uncontrolled, should be explained to its subjects. Initially we can refer to a model of informed consent in discrete settings—explanations of the risks and benefits of treatment, by doctors in their offices or by institutional review boards that shape proposals for early-stage experimental use of medical products.

This model can take us only so far as experiments move into broader settings: the release of drugs into the general market, businesses' use of toxic chemicals that may find their way into the wells of neighbors, decisions on whether to recall automobiles as information develops about safety problems. Still, the basic elements of the issues are the same: How much information about experimental risk is available, and how clearly, if at all, is it communicated to those potentially at risk? What are the power relationships between the parties, with respect to control of risk? How broadly are the benefits of risky activity likely to be spread, and how do they compare with the injuries and illnesses that may be suffered?

When we confront problems as complex as those analyzed here, we often do not have the luxury of a single simple solution. But although we may fix on elements of the problem one by one—information, power and morality, economic balancing—one thing that stands out clearly is choice, including the ability to choose.

One should point out, in this connection, that some market-fueled experiments may advantage one group of consumers at the expense of another. An example comes from the field of vehicle design. In certain cases, vehicles that are relatively more crashworthy will advantage their drivers—for example, protecting them in rollovers. But in others, a more solidly built vehicle, especially a bigger one, will be more likely to injure people in a lighter, less crashworthy vehicle in a collision.

I observe that although this work largely focuses on risk, we must always recognize the great benefits that come from experimentation. An outstanding example, embodying a simple suggestion for self-medication, is the possibility that aspirin might turn out to be effective as an inhibitor of breast cancer and indeed beneficial to longevity generally. One group of researchers concluded in a paper originally published in 2012 that "aspirin use after a breast cancer diagnosis was associated with a decreased risk of distant recurrence, breast cancer death, and death from any cause."[44] This finding simply illustrates the point that because of the potential benefits from experimentation, we cannot reflexively back off from it because of apprehension about potential risks. Yet we do not have to accept a full-blown precautionary principle to know that it is always useful to have a voice whispering in the background to be cautious about the prospect of experimentally caused danger. That could be the voice of an institutionalized Cassandra, utilizing formal-process safeguards. At least it must be in the ear of all who do experiments that may impinge on the health and safety of others.

## Really Hard Choices and Simple Realities

This book addresses difficult problems that arise from the many continuing sagas of our experimental society. I select just one case, which symbolizes the really hard choices that confront us in dealing with experimental risk. This is the case of asbestos, a substance used in its various forms for almost two millennia that has been responsible for hundreds of thousands of cases of illness over a span of almost three generations and that is likely to produce many thousands more cases of agonizing disease over a period that reaches beyond the next decade. The extreme difficulty of the case stems from many sources. These include the magnitude of the number of illnesses and their severity, the costs associated with them that have driven dozens of firms into bankruptcy, and the competitions among many—including sufferers, bankruptcy trustees, and lawyers—who hold economic as well as emotional stakes in the problem. We noted in Chapter 11 that these competitions in the clinches of economics and politics have presented insuperable hurdles to efforts to fashion an administrative compensation system. The result has been the continuance of tort litigation that drains more than 60 percent of available dollars from what theoretically are funds available for relief of victims. As we pointed out, the case of asbestos has been one of complex hypothesis testing in the search for a solution to a problem that arose from a vast national experiment on millions of workers and others who have been affected by the tiny fibers of the several substances that are called asbestos.

In considering the case of asbestos, and also that of cigarettes, we may pose a thought experiment in the context of the justifiable anxiety about the prospect of terrorist attacks on the nation. If we feared that such attacks would have the cost in human life and suffering caused by those products, would we not consider fashioning a color alert scheme about the risks of attacks that went beyond the orange of "high" and even the red of "severe"?

The social experiment in dealing with asbestos-caused illness struggles along. In a day in which technology has vaulted far beyond anything that the Henry Adams who repaired to Mont St. Michel and Chartres could have imagined, it accentuates a reality for our time. That reality has historical roots that reach back to eras when the first human beings and their primitive ancestors used stones and parts of bones to construct simple tools for self-defense, hunting, and agriculture. When those forbears discovered that they could move loads by putting them on rounded bases rather than dragging them outright, they were responding to the same drives that pushed the Wright Brothers, Thomas Edison, and Samuel F. B. Morse—and Albert Einstein, an overwhelming genius of a theoretician who, on the side, patented a refrigerator with Leo Szilard. What threads together this list of prehistoric ancestors and modern geniuses is the pervasiveness of the experimental spirit. Often it works out well; sometimes it does injury. But it is always with us, and it threads its way even among the various means of social control we call law.

## Notes

1. Editorial, "Everyday Risks," *Washington Post*, Nov. 26, 1979, p. A22.
2. See Jon Gertner, "True Innovation," *New York Times*, Feb. 26, 2012.
3. Jacques Ellul, *The Technological Society* (Alfred A. Knopf, 1964), p. 126.
4. See Evgeny Morozov, "Form and Fortune: Reviewing Walter Isaacson, Steve Jobs," *New Republic*, March 15, 2012, pp. 18 and 22.
5. Ibid., p. 27, quoting Mumford.
6. Ibid., pp. 22–23.
7. See Matt Dunning, "Steve Jobs' Biographer to Discuss Innovation As a Risk," quoting biographer Walter Isaacson, *Business Insurance*, April 2, 2012, p. 12.
8. See Natasha Singer, "OKCupid's Unblushing Analyst of Attraction," *New York Times*, Sept. 7, 2014, p. B3.
9. Arthur M. Schlesinger Jr., *The Coming of the New Deal* (Cambridge: Riverside Press, 1958), p. 528. See also ibid., p. 523, referring to an "approach to cross-check the official system and keep it alert as well as to assure himself the balanced and various product without which he could not comfortably reach decisions."
10. Ibid., p. 534.
11. Ibid., p. 536.
12. Ibid., p. 544.
13. Ibid., p. 549.
14. Arthur M. Schlesinger Jr., *The Politics of Upheaval* (Cambridge: Riverside Press, 1960), p. 649 (fluidity phrase Tugwell's).
15. Ibid., p. 654.
16. Ibid., p. 655.
17. The history is summarized in Marshall S. Shapo, *Experimenting With the Consumer* (Prager, 2009), pp. 34–45. An updating citation with modified language appears supra, Chapter 14, text accompanying note 36.
18. See Shapo, supra, pp. 45–46. The current "fast track" statute is 21 U.S.C.A. § 356.
19. *Brown v. Board of Education*, 347 U.S. 483, 495 (1954).
20. *Compare, for example,* Roland G. Fryer Jr. and Michael Greenstone, "The Changing Consequences of Attending Historically Black Colleges and Universities," *Applied Economics*, Vol. 2, No. 1 (2010), p. 116 (although "HBCUs may have provided unique educational services for blacks in the 1970s," "by the 1990s, this advantage seemed to have disappeared on many dimensions and, by some measures, HBCU attendance appears to retard black progress") *with* Gregory Price et al., "The Relative Returns from a Historically Black College/University: Propensity Score Matching Estimates from the National Survey of Black Americans," 38 *Rev. Black Polit. Econ.* 103 (2011) ("on average, graduation from an HBCU affords its graduates superior long-run labor market outcomes relative to graduating from a non-HBCU"; "consistent with a theory in which colleges/universities aim to inculcate a high self-image among its graduates, our results . . . suggest that HBCUs confer upon their graduates relatively superior psychological outcomes which indirectly enhance earnings").
21. Shapo, *Experimenting With the Consumer*, supra note 17, postscript following page 227.

22. "Too Contagious to Fail," *Scientific American*, April 2011, p. 22, summarizing an article by Robert M. May and Andrew G. Haldane.
23. *Dalehite v. United States*, 346 U.S. 15 (1954).
24. See ibid., pp. 45–46 (appendix, summarizing trial court's opinion).
25. Ibid., p. 38.
26. Ibid., p. 51 (Jackson, J., dissenting).
27. Ibid., pp. 51–52.
28. Ibid., p. 48.
29. President's Council on Bioethics, *Beyond Therapy: Biotechnology and the Pursuit of Happiness* (2003), p. 13.
30. Ibid., pp. 21–22.
31. Ibid., pp. 304–05.
32. See for example *Clark v. Gibbons*, 426 P.2d 525, 535 (Cal. 1967).
33. See for example *Canterbury v. Spence*, 464 F.2d 772 (D.C. Cir. 1972).
34. Thomas Nagel, "The Facts Fetish," *New Republic*, Nov. 22, 2010, p. 30.
35. Jan C. Bernauer and Randolf Pohl, "The Proton Radius Problem," 310 *Sci. Am.*, 32, at 34 (Feb. 2014).
36. Ibid., p. 39.
37. Ezekiel Emanuel, "A Simple Way to Reduce Suicides," *New York Times*, June 3, 2013, p. A7, citing a study by Oxford researchers.
38. *New State Ice Co. v. Liebmann*, 285 U.S. 262, 311 (1932) (Brandeis, J., dissenting).
39. 15 U.S.C. §§ 8001 ff (2014 version).
40. See "Senate Commerce Committee Reports Out Swimming Pool, Spa Safety Bill," 35 *Prod. Safety & Liab. Rep.* 685 (July 23, 2007).
41. 15 U.S.C. § 8001(3).
42. 15 U.S.C. § 8003(b). The act, passed during the administration of George W. Bush, provides for states to meet "minimum State law requirements" that, among other things, mandate not only anti-entrapment standards but also "the enclosure of all outdoor residential pools and spas by barriers to entry that will effectively prevent small children from gaining unsupervised and unfettered access to the pool or spa" (ibid., § 8005[a]). It also sets up a program for federal grants to states for the purpose of implementing and enforcing pool standards and educating sellers and pool owners about the standards (ibid., §8006).
43. Benjamin Freedman, "How Americans Face Risk," *New Republic*, Aug. 5, 2013, pp. 50 and 53.
44. See Michelle Holmes et al., "Aspirin Intake and Survival After Breast Cancer," 28 *J. Clin. Oncology* 1467, 1471 (2010).

# Postscript

### Fracking and Vaping

Experimentation with life and health continues unabated. It is as if a superchief of social experiments, a person of unlimited curiosity, undertook to investigate the effects of all kinds of products and activities in order simply to satisfy her curiosity.

I mention here very recent evidence on just two of these experiments: one involving the environment at large, and the other a set of products designed for inhalation by individuals.

Chapter 2 presented some details of the controversy over hydrofracking, a process for extracting oil and gas that brings both benefits and risks. Among other things, we noted that a 2014 study had suggested that 2,547 small earthquakes in Oklahoma might be associated with fracking activities in the state. As this book was in its final stages in 2015, with the 2014 total of Oklahoma quakes having reached 5,417, a researcher for the federal Earthquake Science Center declared that "as long as you keep injecting wastewater along that fault zone, you're going to continue to have earthquakes," and a Republican state representative from a central Oklahoma town referred to fracking as "a dangerous game of Russian roulette."[1] In April 2015, the state created a website with map of earthquake locations,[2] and the state geological survey opined, as a reporter summarized it, that it was "'very likely' that wastewater wells are causing the majority of the state's earthquakes." That same week, in what was described as the "first comprehensive assessment" of the subject, the United States Geological Survey identified sixteen regions in eight states where fracking was associated with quakes. The chief author of that report, Mark Petersen, said that where "Oklahoma used to experience one or two earthquakes per year of magnitude 3 or greater . . . now they're experiencing one or two a day."[3]

A very different experiment was going on in a much more limited physical environment. This was the use of e-cigarettes, one of several nicotine delivery devices meant to help cut down on smoking. In Chapter 3, we examined the death-dealing effects of cigarettes. Now, it has been estimated that twenty million Americans have started to use e-cigarettes and vaporizer products that deliver nicotine but not the tar that the combustion of cigarettes deposits in the systems of smokers. Just one example of the market explosion of these products is the increase in so-called vape shops in Oklahoma City from fifteen to two hundred in the two years leading up to 2015.[4] Nationally, it was reported that in 2014, 17 percent of twelfth-graders had used an e-cigarette in the last month, with 13.6 percent having smoked a traditional cigarette. For tenth-graders, the figures were 16 percent for e-cigarettes, as compared with 7 percent for cigarettes. And 8.7 percent of eighth-graders used e-cigarettes, as compared with 4 percent who smoked regular cigarettes.[5]

Researchers found that there was evidence that "some vaporizing systems exposed users to heavy metals" and that vaporizing liquids at high temperatures "could expose users to high levels of formaldehyde, a known carcinogen." A Johns Hopkins investigator found, as summarized in one report, that "the lungs of mice exposed to e-cig vapor" showed "evidence they were less capable of fighting infection" and contained "free radicals, the same dangerous chemicals found in tobacco smoke." A side battle was being fought between the big tobacco companies and vape shops. Whereas e-cigarettes enclosed their nicotine, vape shops offered "open systems, so customers can pour e-liquids into open vaporizers." The big companies were trying to outlaw the "open systems."[6]

A major concern—a thread that weaves through this book—was the lack of concrete knowledge about the effects of this large experiment. Mitch Zeller, director of the FDA's Center for Tobacco Products, said, "We can't even tell you what the compounds are in the vapor."[7] A medical journal article coauthored by a Georgetown University pulmonologist concisely summarized key elements of the problem, saying, "Currently lacking and urgently needed are product standards for device safety, nicotine content, additives, and chemical compounds."[8] Dr. John Spangler, who directs a smoking cessation clinic at Wake Forest Baptist Medical Center in North Carolina told a reporter that although "it is true that electronic cigarettes are safer than regular cigarettes," "there are some effects in the lung of the vapors which mimic the same kind of changes that go along with asthma." That, he said, "happens within

5 minutes of using an electronic cigarette. We don't know how long that will last or whether it will lead to permanent lung damage."[9]

Of particular concern was the risk that children using e-cigarettes would become addicted to nicotine. Zeller of the FDA declared, "Kids should not be initiating even an e-cigarette that contains no burning tobacco leaves because of the effect that nicotine can have on the developing brain."[10]

Finally, I note that as this book was in the press, an echo pertaining to many kinds of consumer products sounded in a commentary by Linda Birnbaum, the head of the national toxicology program of the Department of Health and Human Services, and Philippe Grandjean, discussing a group of chemicals called poly- and perfluoroalkyl acids (PFASs). These chemicals, which previously had been removed from such products as Teflon pans, were now being used in thousands of products—"as surfactants and as water and oil repellents, in a variety of consumer products such as cosmetics, food packaging, furnishings, and clothing."[11] Paralleling publication of this article was a statement signed by two hundred scientists from many disciplines urging restrictions on the use of PFASs.[12]

The essay by Birnbaum and Grandjean provides just one illustration of the scientific complexity often involved in large-scale experiments on the population. There are two kinds of PFASs: "long-chain" and "short chain." There had been "extensive research" on the long-chain group showing that these chemicals are "highly persistent, bioaccumulative, and toxic"—essentially poisons in the systems of people who ingested them—and they were "being phased out in many countries."

While there was general agreement on the danger of long-chain PFASs, there was controversy about the hazards of the short-chain products. On the one hand, Birnbaum and Grandjean summarized the 2014 Madrid Statement on Poly- and Perfluoroalkyl Substances as "document[ing] the scientific consensus about the extreme environmental persistence, bioaccumulation, and potential toxicity of the overall class of PFASs."[13]

However, there was disagreement from the FluoroCouncil, described as "represent[ing] the world's leading fluorotechnology companies." In an article published the same time as that of Birnbaum and Grandjean, Jessica Bowman, writing for the council, further exhibited the complexity of the classifications of this group of chemicals. She detailed the usefulness of fluoropolymers, used by "chemical and pharmaceutical manufacturers . . . in linings for pipes, valves, and tanks," and the employment of those substances in "aircraft, trucks, buses, and cars" that "utilize high-reliability, durable, lightweight tubing and hoses made from fluoropolymers that reduce overall weight and prevent evaporation of fuel vapors, reducing greenhouse gas emissions and increasing fuel efficiency." She also said that these substances "exhibit unique dielectric properties that enable high-speed data transfer for wireless communications in smart phones and other devices." She noted also that a class of substances called fluorotelomer-based polymers "provide protective surface finishes for textiles such as surgical gowns and drapes that shield against fluid-borne pathogens, protecting patients and health care workers." Those products are also used in "uniforms to protect chemical workers, military personnel, and firefighters" and in firefighting foams. Bowman concluded that a "robust set of published data as well as data submitted to regulatory authorities" "support the conclusion that the short-chain PFASs studied to date are not expected to harm human health or the environment." She said, "Although the structures of short-chain PFASs may be similar to their long-chain equivalents, data show the short-chain chemistry in general is very different from the long-chain chemistry," pointing out that "short-chain substances are eliminated more rapidly from the body and are less toxic than long-chain substances."[14]

By contrast, Birnbaum and Grandjean voiced the familiar theme of the need for more research—on "the potential for adverse health effects from exposure to the short-chain PFASs, especially regarding low-dose endocrine disruption and immunotoxicity," and they asked "whether these chemicals [should] continue to be used in consumer products in the meantime, given their persistence in the environment." Observing that the question of whether consumers were "willing to give up certain product functionalities, such as stain resistance, to protect themselves against potential health risks," they commented, "These conundrums cannot be resolved by science alone but need to be considered in an open discussion informed by the scientific evidence."[15]

A crucial theme runs through the large environment of fracking, the mini-environments of e-cigarettes and vape shops, and a wide range of consumer products in which fluorotechnology is embedded. The theme is that of large-scale experiments on consumers who have not known—or do not presently know—of the hazards of these experiments. If one views consumer choice as the principal goal, these ventures raise the question of how much room we are willing to provide the scientific curiosity of the hypothetical experimenter with which we began this postscript.

## Notes

1. Richard J. Oppel Jr. and Michael Wines, "Industry Blamed as Earthquakes Jolt Oklahoma," *New York Times*, April 4, 2015, pp. A1 and A13.
2. http://earthquakes.ok.gov/what-we-know/earthquake-map, last consulted July 6. 2015...<
3. Richard Perez-Pena, "U.S. Maps Where Human Acts Lead to Thousands of Quakes," *New York Times*, April 24, 2015, pp. A1 and A17.
4. *PBS NewsHour*, "Does Vaping Save Smokers or Create New Nicotine Addicts?" May 6, 2015.
5. See Sabrina Tavernese, "E-Cigarettes Top Smoking Among Youths," *New York Times*, Dec. 17, 2014, p. A21.
6. The bulk of the material cited in this is paragraph is quoted or summarized by the *PBS NewsHour* special correspondent John Larson in the segment cited in note 4 above.
7. Maggie Fox, "What's So Bad About E-Cigarettes?" *NBC News*, April 25, 2014.
8. Nathan K. Cobb and David G. Abrams, "The FDA, E-Cigarettes, and the Demise of Combusted Tobacco," 371 *N. Eng. J. Med.* 1649 (Oct. 16, 2014). Matthews Myers, president of the Campaign for Tobacco-Free Kids, declared, "The notion that people who have no chemical training, no safety training are mixing concoctions in the back room or their bathtub and giving it to the consumer means we're doing a human guinea pig experiment on literally millions of Americans without any knowledge of what the consequences are" (*PBS NewsHour*, supra note 4).
9. *NBC News* broadcast, supra note 7.
10. Ibid.
11. Linda S. Birnbaum and Philippe Grandjean, "Alternatives to PFASs: Perspectives on the Science," 123 *Environ. Health Perspectives* 1289/ehp,1509944 (May 2015).
12. Eric Lipton and Rachel Abrams, "Commonly Used Chemicals Come Under New Scrutiny," *New York Times*, May 1, 2015, business section, pp. 1 and 6.
13. Birnbaum and Grandjean, supra note 11.
14. Jessica S. Bowman, "Fluorotechnology Is Critical to Modern Life: The FluoroCouncil Counterpoint to the Madrid Statement," 123 *Environ. Health Perspectives* 1289/ehp.1509910.
15. Birnbaum and Grandjean, supra.

# Index

For Product Safety Concerns and Information please contact our EU representative GPSR@taylorandfrancis.com Taylor & Francis Verlag GmbH, Kaufingerstraße 24, 80331 München, Germany

**Batch number: 10725979**

Printed by Printforce, the Netherlands